FARMINGDALE PUBLIC LIBRARY
116
FARMINGDALE, N.Y. 11735

grzimek's
Student Animal Life Resource
• • • •

grzimek's
Student Animal Life Resource

••••

Fishes

Catherine Judge Allen, MA, ELS

Madeline S. Harris, project editor
Neil Schlager and Jayne Weisblatt, editors

THOMSON
GALE

Detroit • New York • San Francisco • San Diego • New Haven, Conn. • Waterville, Maine • London • Munich

THOMSON GALE

Grzimek's Student Animal Life Resource: Fishes
Catherine Judge Allen, MA, ELS

Project Editor
Madeline S. Harris

Editorial
Melissa Hill, Heather Price

Indexing Services
Synapse, the Knowledge Link Corporation

Rights and Acquisitions
Sheila Spencer, Mari Masalin-Cooper

Imaging and Multimedia
Randy Bassett, Michael Logusz, Dan Newell, Chris O'Bryan, Robyn Young

Product Design
Tracey Rowens, Jennifer Wahi

Composition
Evi Seoud, Mary Beth Trimper

Manufacturing
Wendy Blurton, Dorothy Maki

© 2005 Thomson Gale, a part of the Thomson Corporation.

Thomson and Star Logo are trademarks and Gale and UXL are registered trademarks used herein under license.

For more information, contact
Thomson Gale
27500 Drake Rd.
Farmington Hills, MI 48331-3535
Or you can visit our Internet site at http://www.gale.com

ALL RIGHTS RESERVED
No part of this work covered by the copyright hereon may be reproduced or used in any form or by any means—graphic, electronic, or mechanical, including photocopying, recording, taping, Web distribution, or information storage retrieval systems—without the written permission of the publisher.

For permission to use material from this product, submit your request via Web at http://www.gale-edit.com/permissions, or you may download our Permissions Request form and submit your request by fax or mail to:

Permissions
Thomson Gale
27500 Drake Rd.
Farmington Hills, MI 48331-3535
Permissions Hotline:
248-699-8006 or 800-877-4253, ext. 8006
Fax: 248-699-8074 or 800-762-4058

While every effort has been made to ensure the reliability of the information presented in this publication, Thomson Gale does not guarantee the accuracy of the data contained herein. Thomson Gale accepts no payment for listing; and inclusion in the publication of any organization, agency, institution, publication, service, or individual does not imply endorsement of the editors or publisher. Errors brought to the attention of the publisher and verified to the satisfaction of the publisher will be corrected in future editions.

LIBRARY OF CONGRESS CATALOGING-IN-PUBLICATION DATA

Allen, Catherine Judge.
  Grzimek's student animal life resource. Fishes / Catherine Judge Allen ; edited by Neil
Schlager and Jayne Weisblatt.
      p. cm.
  Includes bibliographical references and index.
  ISBN 0-7876-9242-5 (hardcover : alk. paper)
  1. Fishes—Juvenile literature. I. Schlager, Neil, 1966- II. Weisblatt, Jayne. III. Grzimek, Bernhard. IV. Title.
  QL617.2.A55 2005
  597—dc22   2005000037

ISBN 0-7876-9402-9 (21-vol set), ISBN 0-7876-9242-5

This title is also available as an e-book
Contact your Thomson Gale sales representative for ordering information.

Printed in Canada
10 9 8 7 6 5 4 3 2 1

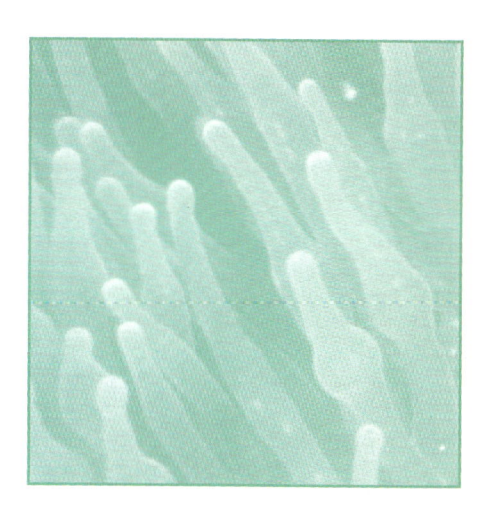

Contents

FISHES

Readers Guide ix
Pronunciation Guide for Scientific Names xi
Words to Know xvii
Getting to Know Fishes xxi

Hagfishes 1

Lampreys 5

Chimaeras, sharks, skates, and rays 9

Coelacanths and lungfishes 21

Bichirs 28

Sturgeons and paddlefishes 32

Gars 37

Bowfins 41

Bony tongues and relatives 46

Ladyfishes and tarpons 50

Bonefishes and relatives 55

Eels and morays 60

Swallowers and gulpers 68

Herrings 73

Milkfish and relatives 79

Minnows, carps, and relatives 84

Characins 92

Catfishes 101

South American knifefishes and electric eels 109

Pikes and mudminnows 116

Smelts, galaxiids, and relatives 121

Salmons 127

Dragonfishes and relatives 136

Lizardfishes and relatives 142

Lanternfishes 148

Opahs and relatives 153

Beardfishes 158

Troutperches and relatives 162

Cusk-eels and relatives 167

Grenadiers, hakes, cods, and relatives 173

Toadfishes 181

Anglerfishes 187

Mullets 194

Rainbowfishes and silversides 198

Needlefishes and relatives 202

Killifishes and live-bearers 210

Whalefishes and relatives 219

Roughies, flashlightfishes, and squirrelfishes 223

Dories 229

Sticklebacks, seahorses, and relatives 233

Swamp and spiny eels 242

Gurnards, flatheads, scorpionfishes, and relatives . .247

Perches, basses, and relatives 256
   Perches, darters, and relatives 259
   Cichlids, surfperches, and relatives 272
   Eelpouts and relatives 281
   Southern cod-icefishes 288
   Weeverfishes and relatives .292
   Blennies 299
   Ragfish 305
   Clingfishes and singleslits 308
   Dragonets and relatives 313
   Gobies 317
   Surgeonfishes and relatives 326
   Barracudas, tunas, marlins, and relatives 334
   Butterfishes and relatives 343
   Labyrinth fishes 347
   Snakeheads 353

Flatfishes 357

Pufferfishes, triggerfishes, and relatives 366

Species List by Biome xxxi
Species List by Geographic Range xxxiii
Index xlix

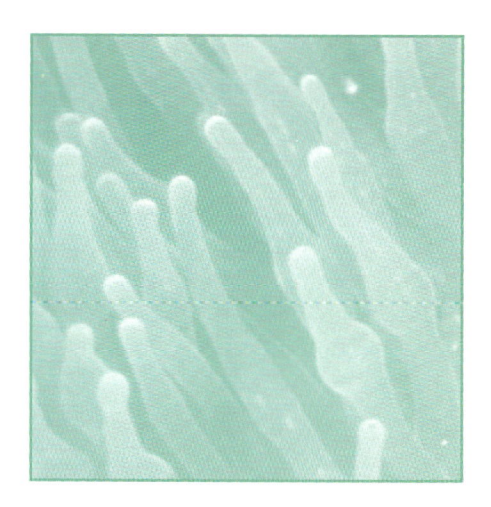

Reader's Guide

Grzimek's Student Animal Life Resource: Fishes offers readers comprehensive and easy-to-use information on Earth's fishes. Entries are arranged by taxonomy, the science through which living things are classified into related groups. Each entry includes sections on physical characteristics; geographic range; habitat; diet; behavior and reproduction; fishes and people; and conservation status. All entries are followed by one or more species accounts with the same information as well as a range map and photo or illustration for each species. Entries conclude with a list of books, periodicals, and Web sites that may be used for further research.

ADDITIONAL FEATURES

Grzimek's Student Animal Life Resource: Fishes includes a pronunciation guide for scientific names, a glossary, an overview of fishes, a list of species in the volume by biome, a list of species by geographic range, and an index. The volume has 225 full-color maps, photos, and illustrations to enliven the text, and sidebars provide additional facts and related information.

NOTE

Grzimek's Student Animal Life Resource: Fishes has standardized information in the Conservation Status section. The IUCN Red List provides the world's most comprehensive inventory of the global conservation status of plants and animals. Using a set of criteria to evaluate extinction risk, the IUCN recognizes the following categories: Extinct, Extinct in the Wild, Critically Endangered, Endangered, Vulnerable, Conservation Dependent, Near Threatened, Least Concern, and Data Deficient. These terms are defined where they are used in the text, but for a complete explanation of each category, visit the IUCN web page at http://www.iucn.org/themes/ssc/redlists/RLcats2001booklet.html.

ACKNOWLEDGEMENTS

Gale would like to thank several individuals for their assistance with this volume. Catherine Judge Allen wrote the entire text. At Schlager Group Inc., Neil Schlager and Jayne Weisblatt coordinated the writing and editing of the set, while Marcia Merryman Means and Leah Tieger also provided valuable assistance.

Special thanks are also due for the invaluable comments and suggestions provided by the *Grzimek's Student Animal Life Resource: Fishes* advisors:

- Mary Alice Anderson, Media Specialist, Winona Middle School, Winona, Minnesota
- Thane Johnson, Librarian, Oklahoma City Zoo, Oklahoma City, Oklahoma
- Debra Kachel, Media Specialist, Ephrata Senior High School, Ephrata, Pennsylvania
- Nina Levine, Media Specialist, Blue Mountain Middle School, Courtlandt Manor, New York
- Ruth Mormon, Media Specialist, The Meadows School, Las Vegas, Nevada

COMMENTS AND SUGGESTIONS

We welcome your comments on *Grzimek's Student Animal Life Resource: Fishes* and suggestions for future editions of this work. Please write: Editors, *Grzimek's Student Animal Life Resource: Fishes*, U•X•L, 27500 Drake Rd., Farmington Hills, Michigan 48331-3535; call toll free: 1-800-877-4253; fax: 248-699-8097; or send e-mail via www.gale.com.

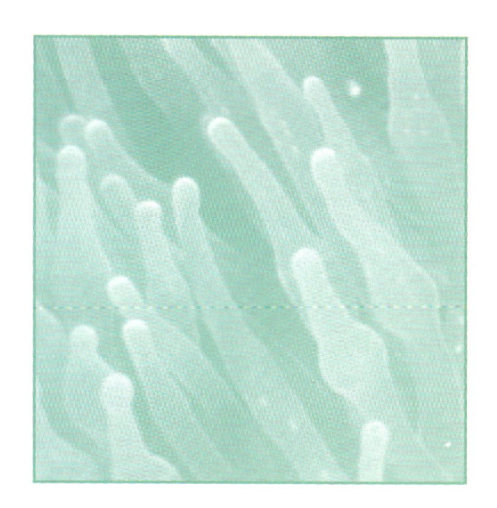

Pronunciation Guide for Scientific Names

Acanthuroidei uh-KAN-thuh-ROY-dee-EYE
Acanthurus lineatus uh-KAN-thuh-ruhs LIH-nee-ah-tuhs
Acipenseriformes AS-uh-pen-SER-uh-FOR-meez
Albula vulpes ALB-yuh-luh VUL-peez
Albuliformes ALB-yuh-luh-FOR-meez
Alepisaurus ferox ay-LEP-uh-SOR-uhs FAIR-awks
Amia calva uh-MEE-uh KAL-vuh
Amiiformes uh-MY-uh-FOR-meez
Ammodytes americanus AM-uh-DY-deez uh-MAIR-uh-KAN-uhs
Anabantoidei AN-uh-BAN-toy-dee-EYE
Anabas testudineus AN-uh-buhs TEST-yoo-DIH-nee-uhs
Anableps anableps AN-uh-BLEPS AN-uh-BLEPS
Anchoa mitchilli AN-koh-uh MITCH-uh-ly
Anguilla rostrata ang-GWIL-uh RAH-struh-duh
Anguilliformes ang-GWIL-uh-FOR-meez
Annarrichthys ocellatus AN-ner-RIK-theez os-uh-LAH-tuhs
Anomalops katoptron uh-NOM-uh-LOPS kuh-TOP-truhn
Aphredoderus sayanus AF-ruh-DOD-uh-ruhs say-AN-uhs
Arothon hispidus AR-uh-thon HIH-spuh-duhs
Astroscopus guttatus AS-troh-SKAH-puhs guh-TAH-tuhs
Atheriniformes ATH-uh-RIN-uh-FOR-meez
Atigonia rubescens AD-uh-GAH-nee-uh ROO-buh-sinz
Aulopiformes all-OP-uh-FOR-meez
Austrolebias nigripinnis AH-stroh-LEE-bee-uhs nih-GRIP-ih-nis
Balistoides conspicillum BAH-luh-STOY-deez kon-SPIS-uh-lum
Bathypterois qaudrifilis buh-THIP-tuh-roy kwah-DRIF-uh-lis

Batrachoidiformes BAT-truh-KOY-duh-FOR-meez
Beloniformes BEL-uh-nuh-FOR-meez
Benthosema pterotum ben-THOS-uh-muh tair-AH-dum
Beryciformes BY-ris-uh-FOR-meez
Betta splendens BED-uh SPLEN-dunz
Blennioidei BLEH-nee-OY-dee-EYE
Bothus lunatus BAH-thuhs LOO-nah-tuhs
Botia macracanthus boh-TEE-uh MAK-ruh-KAN-thuhs
Callionymoidei kuh-LON-ee-MOY-dee-EYE
Campostoma anomalum KAM-puh-STOH-muh uh-NOM-uh-lum
Canthigaster solandri KAN-thih-GUH-ster SOH-lan-dry
Carapus bermudensis KAR-uh-puhs BER-myoo-DEN-sis
Carcharodon carcharias kar-KAR-uh-don kar-KAR-ee-uhs
Cephalaspidomorphi SEF-uh-lah-SPIH-duh-mor-fee
Chaca chaca KAH-suh KAH-suh
Channa striata KON-nuh STRY-ah-tuh
Channoidei kan-NOY-dee-EYE
Chanos chanos KAH-nohs KAH-nohs
Characiformes kuh-RAS-uh-FOR-meez
Chauliodus sloani koh-LEE-uh-duhs SLOH-ny
Cheilopogon pinnatibarbatus californicus ky-LOP-uh-gon pih-NAT-uh-BAR-buh-tuhs kal-uh-FORN-uh-kuhs
Chondrichthyes kon-DRIK-thee-EEZ
Clupeiformes KLOO-pee-uh-FOR-meez
Coryphaena hippurus KOR-uh-FEE-nuh hih-PER-uhs
Cypriniformes sy-PRIN-uh-FOR-meez
Cyprinodontiformes sy-PRIN-uh-DON-tuh-FOR-meez
Dactyloptena orientalis DAK-tuh-LOP-tuh-nuh or-ee-EN-tuh-lis
Eigenmannia lineata EYE-gun-muh-NEE-uh lin-EE-ah-tuh
Electrophorus electricus uh-LEK-TROF-uh-ruhs uh-LEK-truh-cuhs
Elopiformes uh-LOP-ih-FOR-meez
Enneapterygius mirabilis EN-ee-OP-tuh-RIH-jee-uhs- MER-ah-buh-lis
Epinephelus striatus EP-uh-NEF-uh-luhs stry-AH-tuhs
Esociformes uh-SOS-uh-FOR-meez
Esox masquinongy EE-sawks mas-KWIH-nun-jee
Gadiformes GAD-uh-FOR-meez

Gadus morhua GAD-uhs mor-HOO-uh
Galeocerdo cuvier GAL-ee-oh-SAIR-duh koo-VEE-air
Gasteropelecus sternicla GAS-ter-RAH-puh-LEE-suhs STER-nik-luh
Gasterosteiformes GAS-ter-RAH-stee-uh-FOR-meez
Gasterosteus aculeatus GAS-ter-RAH-stee-uhs ak-kyoo-LEE-ah-tuhs
Gobiesocodei goh-BY-uh-SOS-uh-dee-EYE
Gobioidei GOH-bee-OY-dee-EYE
Gonorynchiformes GON-uh-RIN-kuh-FOR-meez
Gymnothorax funebris JIM-nuh-THOR-aks FYOO-neh-bruhs
Gymnotiformes jim-NOD-uh-FOR-meez
Hipppocampus erectus HIP-uh-KAM-puhs EE-rek-tuhs
Hippoglossus stenolepsis HIP-uh-GLOS-uhs STEN-uh-LEP-sis
Histrio histrio HIS-tree-oh HIS-tree-oh
Huso Huso HYOO-soh HYOO-soh
Hydrocynus goliath hy-DRAH-sih-nuhs guh-LY-uth
Hydrolagus colliei hy-DRALL-uh-guhs kuh-LEE-eye
Hypopthalmichthys molitrix hy-POP-thal-MIK-theez MOL-uh-triks
Icosteoidei EYE-kah-STEE-uh-dee-EYE
Icosteus aenigmaticus eye-KAH-stee-uhs ee-nig-MAH-tuh-cuhs
Ictalurus punctatus IK-tuh-LOOR-uhs PUNK-tah-tuhs
Labroidei LAB-roy-DEE-eye
Labroides dimidiatus LAB-roy-DEEZ dih-MID-ee-AH-tuhs
Lampridiformes lam-PRID-uh-FOR-meez
Latimeria chalumnae LAD-uh-MAIR-ee-uh kuh-LUM-nee
Lepidosiren paradoxa LEP-uh-dah-SUH-rin PAIR-uh-DOK-suh
Lepisosteiformes LEP-uh-SOS-tee-uh-FOR-meez
Lepisosteus oculatus LEP-uh-SOS-tee-uhs ah-KYOO-lah-tuhs
Leuresthes tenuis LOOR-es-teez teh-NYOO-is
Lophiiformes LAH-fee-uh-FOR-meez
Lophius americanus LAH-fee-uhs uh-MAIR-uh-KAN-uhs
Macquaria ambigua muh-KWAR-ee-uh am-BIG-yoo-uh
Makaira nigricans muh-KY-ruh nih-GRIH-sunz
Malacosteus niger MAL-uh-KOS-tee-uhs NY-jer
Manta birostris MAN-tuh BY-ros-truhs
Megalops atlanticus MEG-uh-lops at-LAN-tuh-kuhs

Meiacanthus grammistes MAY-uh-KAN-thus GRAM-uh-steez
Melanogrammus aeglefinus MEL-uh-NAH-gruh-muhs ee-gluh-FIN-uhs
Micropterus salmoides my-KROP-tuh-ruhs sal-MOY-deez
Mirapinna esau muh-ROP-uh-nuh EE-sou
Mugil cephalus MYOO-jil SEF-uh-luhs
Mugiliformes myoo-JIL-uh-FOR-meez
Myctophiformes mik-TOF-uh-FOR-meez
Myripristis jacobus mir-ih-PRIS-tuhs juh-KOH-buhs
Myxine glutinosa MIK-suh-nee gloo-tuh-NOH-suh
Myxini MIK-suh-ny
Nemateleotris magnifica NEM-uh-TEL-ee-OH-truhs mag-NIH-fuh-kuh
Notothenioidei NOH-duh-thuh-NOY-dee-EYE
Oncorhynchus tshawytscha ON-koh-RIN-kuhs chuh-WIH-chuh
Ophidiiformes OFF-uh-DEE-uh-FOR-meez
Ophiodon elongatus off-FEE-oh-don ee-lon-GAH-tuhs
Opsanus tau op-SAH-nuhs TOU
Osmeriformes oz-MER-uh-FOR-meez
Osteoglossiformes OS-tee-oh-GLOS-uh-FOR-meez
Oxyeleotris marmorata AWK-see-uh-LEE-oh-truhs mar-MOH-rah-tuh
Pantodon buchholzi PAN-tuh-don byoo-KOHL-zy
Paradiplogrammus bairdi PAIR-uh-dip-LOG-ruh-muhs BAIR-dy
Peprilus triacanthus PEP-rih-luhs TRY-uh-KAN-thuhs
Perciformes PER-suh-FOR-meez
Percoidei per-KOY-dee-EYE
Percopsiformes per-KOP-suh-FOR-meez
Periopthalmus barbarus PAIR-ee-op-THAL-muhs BAR-buh-ruhs
Petromyzon marinus PEH-troh-MY-zun muh-REE-nuhs
Phycodurus eques fy-KOH-der-uhs EK-weez
Plecoglossus altivelis PLEH-koh-GLOS-uhs al-TIV-uh-lis
Pleuronectiformes PLER-oh-NEK-tuh-FOR-meez
Polymixia nobilis PALL-ee-MIK-see-uh NOH-buh-luhs
Polymixiiformes PALL-ee-MIK-see-uh-FOR-meez
Polypteriformes PALL-up-TER-uh-FOR-meez
Polypterus ornatipinnis PALL-up-TER-uhs OR-nuh-TIP-ih-nihs
Pterois volitans TAIR-oy VALL-uh-tunz

Pterophyllum scalare TAIR-oh-FY-lum skuh-LAR-ee
Pygocentrus nattereri PY-goh-SEN-truhs nad-uh-RAIR-eye
Raja eglanteria RAH-juh eg-LON-tuh-REE-uh
Regalecus glesne ruh-GAL-uh-kuhs GLEZ-nee
Retropinna semoni ruh-TROP-ih-nuh SEH-muh-ny
Saccopharyngiformes SAK-oh-fuh-RIN-juh-FOR-meez
Saccopharynx ampullaceus SAK-oh-FAR-inks amp-yoo-LAY-see-uhs
Salmo salar SAL-moh SUH-lar
Salmoniformes sal-MON-uh-FOR-meez
Salvelinus fontinalis sal-vuh-LIN-uhs fon-tih-NALL-lis
Sarcopterygii sar-KOP-tuh-RIJ-ee-EYE
Scarus iseri SKAR-uhs EYE-suh-ry
Scombroidei skam-BROY-dee-EYE
Scorpaeniformes skor-PEEN-uh-FOR-meez
Siluriformes sih-LOOR-uh-FOR-meez
Solea solea soh-LEE-uh soh-LEE-uh
Sphyraena barracuda sfer-EE-nuh BAIR-uh-KOO-duh
Stephanoberyciformes stuh-FON-uh-BAIR-ris-uh-FOR-meez
Stomiiformes STOH-mee-uh-FOR-meez
Stromateoidei STROH-muh-tee-OY-dee-EYE
Strongylura exilis stron-juh-LOOR-uh ek-SIH-luhs
Strophidon sathete STROF-uh-don SATH-uh-dee
Synbranchiformes sin-BRAN-kuh-FOR-meez
Synbranchus marmoratus sin-BRAN-kuhs MAR-muh-RAH-tuhs
Tetraodontiformes TEH-truh-oh-DON-tuh-FOR-meez
Thunnus thynus THUH-nuhs THY-nuhs
Tomicodon humeralis toh-MIK-uh-don HYOO-muh-RAL-is
Toxotes jaculatrix TAWK-suh-teez juh-KYOO-luh-triks
Trachinoidei TRAK-uh-NOY-dee-EYE
Trematomus bernacchii treh-muh-TOH-muhs ber-NOTCH-ee-EYE
Vandellia cirrhosa van-duh-LEE-uh ser-OH-suh
Xiphophorus hellerii ZIF-uh-FOR-uhs huh-LOOR-ee-EYE
Zanclus cornutus ZAN-kluhs kor-NUH-tuhs
Zebrasoma flavescens ZEE-bruh-SOH-muh fluh-VES-unz
Zeiformes ZEE-uh-FOR-meez
Zoarces americanus zoh-AR-seez uh-MAIR-uh-KAN-uhs
Zoarcoidei zoh-ar-KOY-dee-EYE

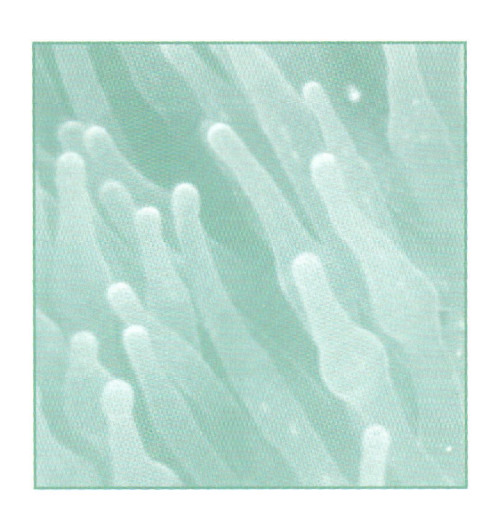

Words to Know

A
Adipose fin: Small fleshy rayless fin located behind the dorsal fin and in front of the caudal fin.
Algae: Tiny plantlike growths that live in water and have no true roots, stems, or leaves.
Amphibian: An animal that spends part of its life in water and part on land and has an internal skeleton, such as frogs and salamanders.
Anal fin: The unpaired fin that runs along the bottom of the body on the belly toward the rear.
Aquatic: Living in water.

B
Barbels: Long, thin feelers used for the senses of taste, touch, and smell, depending on the animal.
Buoyant: Capable of floating.

C
Canal: A tube-shaped passage or channel.
Cartilage: Tough, bendable tissue that forms part or all of the skeleton, depending on the animal.
Caudal fin: The fin at the end of the body; also called the tail fin; generates much of the thrust in swimming.
Caviar: Salted, unfertilized sturgeon eggs, eaten as a delicacy.
Clutch: A group of eggs.
Contract: Make smaller by drawing together; shrink.

Critically Endangered: Facing an extremely high risk of extinction in the wild.
Crustacean: An animal that lives in water and has a soft, segmented body covered by a hard shell, such as hermit crabs and shrimps.

D
Digestive tract: Part of the body that changes food into energy.
Dorsal fin: The unpaired fin that runs along the top of the body along the center and toward the back.

E
Eggs: The reproductive cells that are made by female animals and that are fertilized by the sperm, or reproductive cells, of male animals.
Endangered: Facing a very high risk of extinction in the wild.
Estivation: A period of inactivity during dry spells or during the summer.
Estuary: The wide part at the lower end of a river, where the river meets the sea.
Extinct: No longer living.
Extinct in the Wild: Known only to survive in cultivation, in captivity, or as a naturalized population well outside the past range.

F
Fan: To move water over eggs or newly hatched young animals to clean them and give them oxygen.
Fertilization: The joining of egg and sperm to start development.
Forage: To search for food.
Fossils: The remains, or parts, of animals that lived long ago, usually found set into rock or earth.

G
Genital: An external reproductive organ.
Gestation: Development of young inside a female animal.
Gill rakers: Comblike structures that sift plankton from water.
Gills: Organs for obtaining oxygen from water.

I

Incisors: Front cutting and chewing teeth in mammals.

Ingest: Swallow or take in as food.

Invertebrate: An animal that lacks a backbone, such as an insect, spider, or earthworm.

L

Larva: The early, or young, form of an animal, which must go through metamorphosis, or certain changes in form, before becoming an adult.

Lateral line: A series of pores and tiny tubes along each side of the body, used for sensing vibrations.

Least Concern: Does not qualify for a threatened category.

M

Metamorphosis: The changes in form that some animals make to become adults, such as tadpole to frog.

Microscopic: Too small to be seen with the eye.

Migrate: To move from one area or climate to another to breed or feed.

Mollusk: An animal with a soft, unsegmented body usually covered by a shell, such as a snail or a clam.

Mottled: Spotted with varying colors.

N

Navigation: Act of setting a course for ship or aircraft.

Near Threatened: Likely to qualify for a threatened category in the near future.

Nocturnal: Active at night.

Nomadic: Moving from place to place without a fixed home.

O

Obstacles: Things that block the way.

Opportunistic: Taking advantage of what is available.

Ovary: Organ that produces eggs.

P

Parasite: An animal or plant that lives on another animal or plant without helping it and often harming it.

Pectoral fins: The front pair of fins, corresponding to the front legs of four-footed animals; used to turn and maneuver while swimming.

Pelvic fins: The rear pair of fins, corresponding to the rear legs of four-footed animals.

Plankton: Microscopic plants and animals that drift in bodies of water.

Predator: An animal that hunts and kills other animals for food.

Prey: An animal that is hunted and caught for food.

R

Ray: One of the series of supporting rods inside a fin.

S

Scales: Flat, rigid plates that act as part of a body covering.

Scavenger: Animal that feeds on dead or dying animals.

Snout: Nose area.

Solitary: Alone.

Spawn: To produce or release eggs.

Species: A group of animals that share many traits and can mate and produce young with one another.

Sperm: The reproductive cells that are made by male animals and that fertilize the eggs of female animals.

Stagnant: Still and stale.

Subtropical: Referring to a climate with an average annual temperature 55°F to 68°F (13°C to 20°C).

Swim bladder: An internal sac that fishes use to control their position in the water; also called the gas bladder.

T

Taper: To grow narrower toward one end.

Transparent: See-through, clear.

Trawler: Fishing boat that drags nets to make a catch.

Tropical: Referring to a climate with an average annual temperature more than 68°F (20°C).

V

Vertebrae: The bones that make up the spinal column.

Vertebrate: An animal that has a backbone.

Vulnerable: Facing a high risk of extinction in the wild.

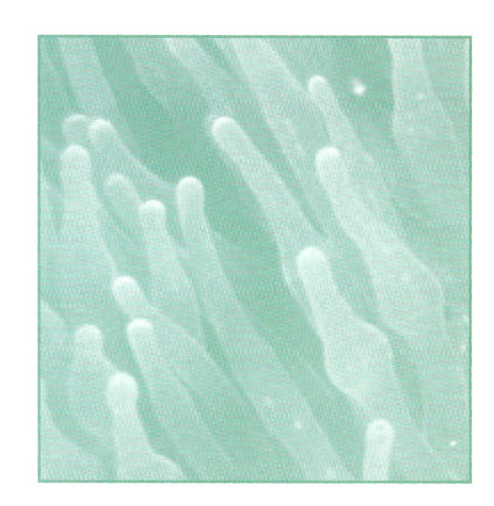

Getting to Know Fishes

PHYSICAL CHARACTERISTICS

Fossil records show that fishes have been in existence for 438 million years. They were the first vertebrates (VER-teh-brehts), or animal with a backbone. A fish is a cold-blooded vertebrate that lives primarily in water and has a skull, gills, and fins. Cold-blooded means the animal's internal temperature changes with its surroundings.

There are two types of vertebrates: those with jaws and those without jaws. The only jawless vertebrates are fishes: lampreys (LAM-prees) and hagfishes. Among the many vertebrates with jaws, two types are fishes. One type has a skeleton made of cartilage (KAR-teh-lej), a tough but bendable tissue. The other type, 95 percent of fishes, has a skeleton made of bone.

Fossil records show that fishes have been in existence for 438 million years. (Jonathan Blair/Corbis. Reproduced by permission.)

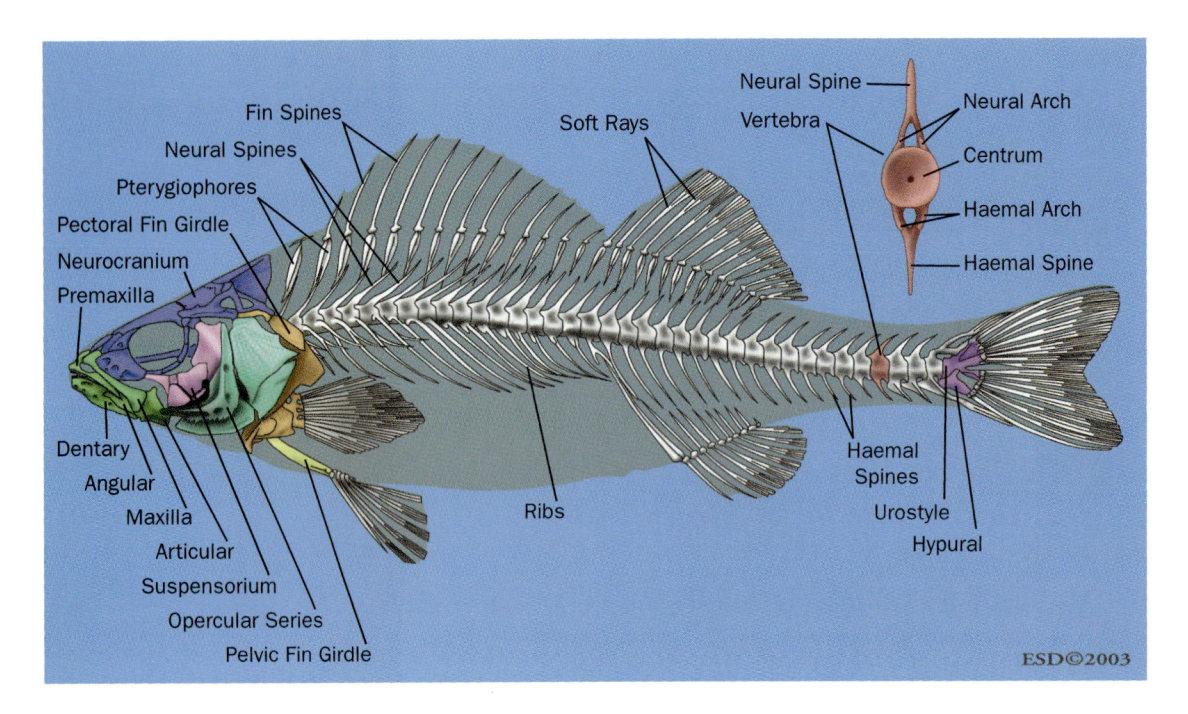

Side view of the skeleton of a yellow perch. Ninety-five percent of fishes have a skeleton made of bone. (Illustration by Emily Damstra. Reproduced by permission.)

Fishes vary in length from about one-eighth inch (a few millimeters) to more than 59 feet (18 meters). Fishes can be ribbon shaped like eels, pointed at the ends like salmons, flat from top to bottom like stingrays, or flat from side to side like flounders.

Most fins consist of spines or rays connected by a thin film. Some fins do not contain rays. Fishes have two sets of paired fins, several fins on the body midline, and a tail fin.

Scales protect the skin and deeper tissues from the environment. In some fishes, scales are bony plates that form armor over the surface of the body but do not overlap. Most fishes, however, have thinner, lighter scales that do overlap. The exposed edge of overlapping scales can be smooth or rough. Some fishes do not have scales at all.

The lateral (LAT-uhr-uhl) line runs along each side of a fish's body from head to tail. This line is a series of pores and tiny tubes that sense low vibrations, or sound waves, that cannot be heard. This structure helps fishes avoid obstacles, or things that block the way, and predators, or animals that kill and eat other animals, and find food. The lateral line canals can be seen in most fishes, and in many species are open grooves.

Fishes are unique in that they can move their upper jaw and their lower jaw, a feature that helps them eat large foods. The teeth of many fish predators are triangular and sawlike for cutting through prey, or the animals hunted and caught for food. Predators that swallow prey whole have long backward-pointing teeth that grasp the prey and prevent it from struggling out of the mouth. Many fishes have teeth adapted for biting and crushing hard material, such as shells and coral.

Gills are the organs that fishes use to breathe in water. The gills are behind the head on both sides of the body. Water flows through the mouth, over the gills, and back to the outside. While water flows over the tiny threads that make up the gills, oxygen in it passes into the blood. Some fishes gulp air at the

Different fishes have developed diifferent shaped fins: a. Sea robin; b. Catfish; c. Dogfish; d. Mosquitofish; e. Anglerfish; f. Lumpfish. (Illustration by Marguette Dongvillo. Reproduced by permission.)

Getting to Know Fishes | xxiii

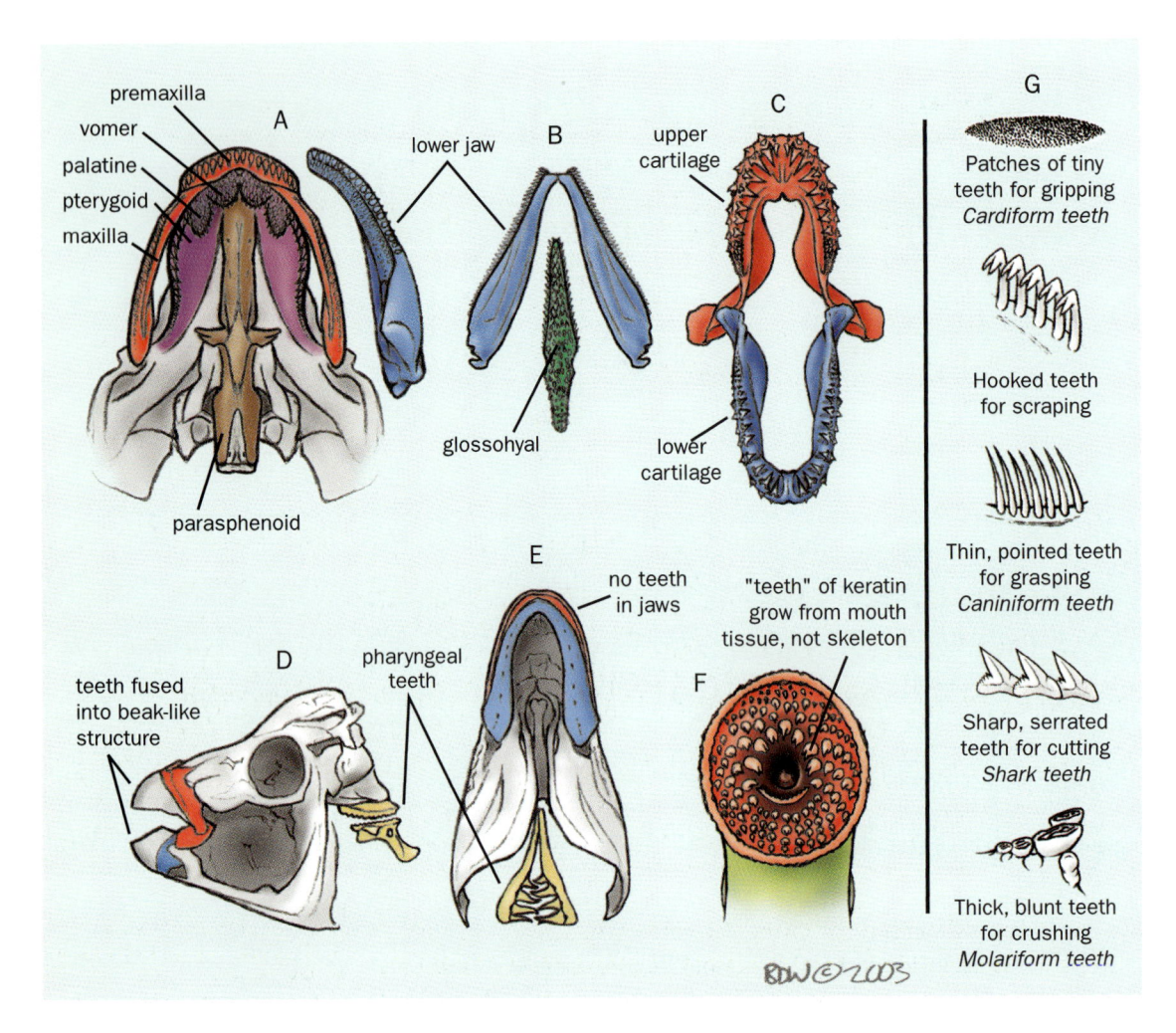

Tooth morphology and tooth-bearing structures typical of fishes: A. Bowfin; B. Mooneye; C. Sand shark; D. Parrotfish; E. Pike minnow; F. Sea lamprey; G. Tooth form and functions. (Illustration by Bruce Worden. Reproduced by permission.)

surface of the water and store it in lunglike organs. Other fishes use the swim bladder for breathing.

The swim bladder is a sac of gases in the body that helps a fish hold its position in the water. The fish rises as gas moves from the bloodstream into the swim bladder and moves down as gas leaves the swim bladder. Some fishes do not have a swim bladder. In these fishes oil in the liver keeps the fish steady. This system works because oil is lighter than water.

GEOGRAPHIC RANGE

Freshwater in lakes and rivers makes up less than 0.01 percent of the total amount of water on Earth, yet 42 percent of all fish species live there. The other 58 percent live in the oceans that make up 97 percent of Earth's water. (The other 2.99 percent of water is in ice, the ground, and the atmosphere.) Most ocean fishes live in the tropical and temperate zones, that is, in water 50°F (10°C) or warmer.

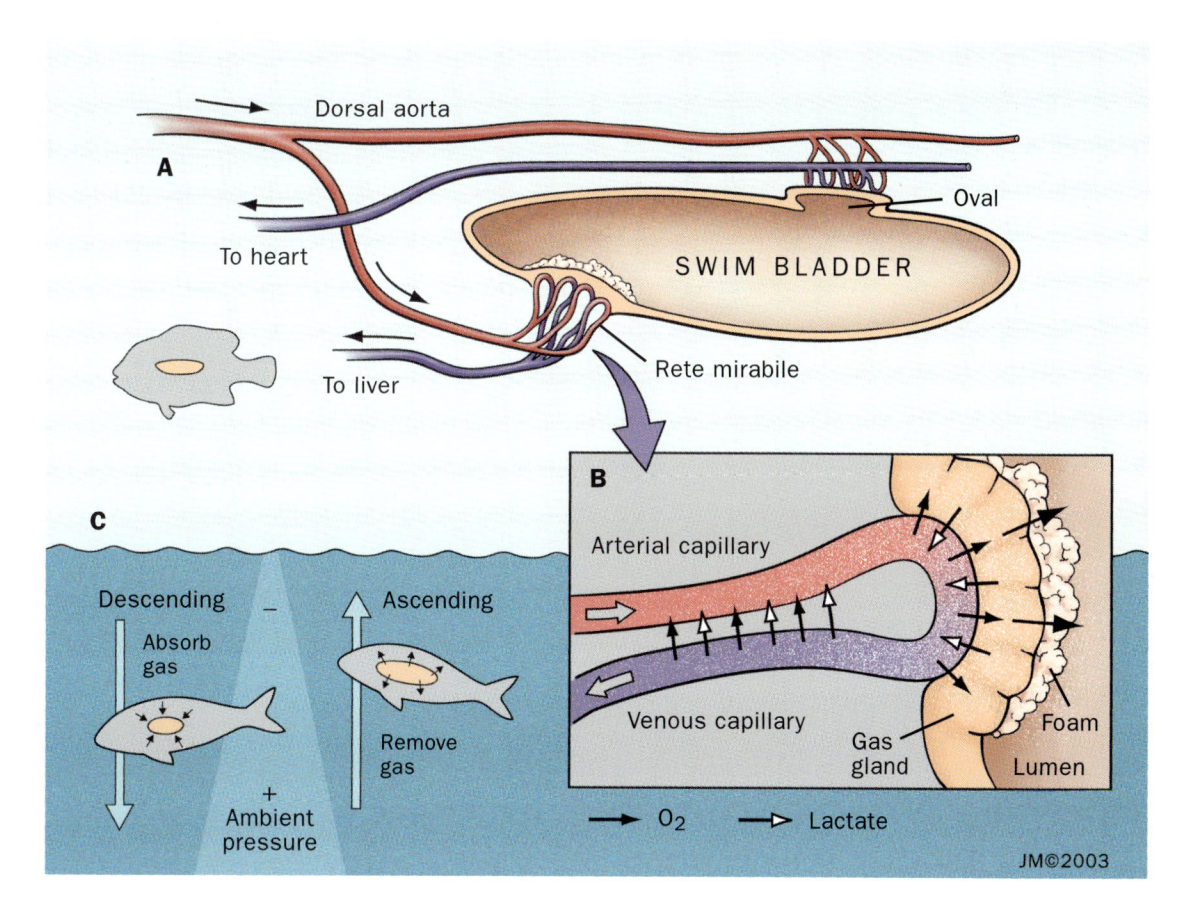

HABITAT

Most freshwater fishes live in streams, rivers, and lakes. Other freshwater habitats are wetlands such as marshes and swamps. Saltwater fishes live in oceans and seas near the shore, in coral reefs, on the deep ocean floor, and in open water.

DIET

Many fishes eat plankton, or microscopic (MAI-kro-SKA-pihk) plants and animals drifting in the water. The plankton is too small to be seen with the eye. Some fishes pluck the plankton particles from the water. Others take in plankton with the

The swim bladder is a sac of gases in the body that helps a fish hold its position in the water. The fish rises as gas moves from the bloodstream into the swim bladder and moves down as gas leaves the swim bladder. (Illustration by Jacqueline Mahannah. Reproduced by permission.)

Fishes eat many different things, from microscopic plankton to sea birds, reptiles, and mammals. Here a wolf eel makes a meal of a sea urchin. (Brandon D. Cole/Corbis. Reproduced by permission.)

water that flows over their gills. Comblike structures called gill rakers strain out the plankton before it gets to the gills and divert it to the digestive tract where it is changed into food energy. Some fishes eat bottom-dwelling algae (AL-jee), which are tiny plantlike growths that live in water but have no true roots, stems, or leaves; grasses, or even seeds and fruits from plants on the shore or river bank. Other fishes feed on invertebrates, or animals without a backbone, such as insects, spiders, or earthworms, and on other fishes. Invertebrate prey may be bottom dwelling, such as clams, or be in open water, such as squids. Fish eaters actively hunt, chase, herd, grasp, stun, club, shock, ambush, bite, or engulf other fishes. Large fishes may feed on floating sea birds, reptiles, and mammals in addition to fishes. Scavengers (SKAV-ihn-jerz) feed on dead or dying animals.

BEHAVIOR AND REPRODUCTION

Fishes swim by contracting or drawing together muscles at the bases of their fins to move the fins and by contracting their body muscles in a wave from head to tail to move the backbone. Fishes use chemical signals for navigation. For example, salmons use this sense to set a course and direction to find the stream in which they were born and to which they will return to reproduce and die. Some fishes, especially sharks, can sense barely detectable electrical currents discharged by prey. Electric signals are received in pit organs on the surface of the body.

Some fishes form shoals or schools for protection from predators, finding food, migration (MY-gray-shun), and reproduction. Shoals are unorganized, often temporary groups. They may consist of different species with a changing membership and may break up and form again quickly. Schools are organized groups that form permanently or temporarily. They usually are made up of only one species.

NOT FISHES

The "shellfish" found in restaurants and fish markets is not fish at all but crustaceans (krus-TAY-shuns), such as crabs, and bivalve mollusks (MAH-lusks), such as clams. Bivalve mollusks are invertebrates with a one-part body, a muscular foot but no legs, and a shell made of calcium carbonate. Crustaceans are invertebrates with jointed legs, a shell made of chitin, and a body that has several parts.

Salmons use chemical signals to return to the stream in which they were born. (Ralph A. Clevenger/Corbis. Reproduced by permission.)

Fishes reproduce by spawning, that is, producing or releasing eggs that are then fertilized (FUR-teh-lyezd), or united with the male's sperm, outside the female's body; by laying eggs that have been fertilized inside the female's body; or by giving birth to fully developed young that have grown inside the female after the eggs have been fertilized inside her.

Some fishes emerge from the egg as larvae (LAR-vee) and must undergo many changes before becoming adults. During this phase the larvae eat plankton and are plankton. The larval

Getting to Know Fishes

Some fishes care for their eggs and offspring. Here a male lumpfish is guarding its eggs. (Andrew J. Martinez/Photo Researchers, Inc. Reproduced by permission.)

stage ends when the skeleton, organ systems, skin color, arrangement of scales, and fins become fully developed, and the young fishes look like adults. The transition can take minutes to years.

Some fishes care for their eggs and offspring by behaviors such as nest building before spawning; mouth brooding, or keeping the eggs in a parent's mouth until hatching; nest guarding; and fanning, or using the fins to move water over eggs or hatchlings to clean them and give them oxygen.

FISHES AND PEOPLE

Fishes have been important in human life since ancient times. Fish themes appear in mythology, religion, literature, and art. Fishes are important to humans for food, employment, and income. Many people enjoy the sport of fishing and the hobby of keeping fishes in aquariums.

CONSERVATION

Fish populations are threatened by habitat alteration, such as by dam building, water pollution, overfishing, and introduction of competing species. Many people are trying to pro-

Shark fins, hanging to dry on a fishing vessel, are used for such delicacies as shark's fin soup. Federal regulators are trying to determine the impact of fishing on shark populations. (AP/Wide World Photos. Reproduced by permission.)

tect habitats and develop regulations to reduce overfishing and pollution.

FOR MORE INFORMATION

Books:

Cushing, Colbert E., and J. David Allan. *Streams: Their Ecology and Life.* San Diego: Academic Press, 2001.

Niesen, Thomas M. *The Marine Biology Coloring Book.* 2nd ed. New York: HarperResource, 2000.

Ricciuti, Edward R. *Fish.* Woodbridge, CT: Blackbirch, 1993.

Web sites:

"FisFAQ." Northeast Fisheries Science Center. http://www.nefsc.noaa.gov/faq (accessed on September 23, 2004).

"Fish." Science Fair Projects Encyclopedia. http://www.all-science-fair-projects.com/science_fair_projects_encyclopedia/Fish (accessed on September 20, 2004).

HAGFISHES
Myxini

Class: Myxini
Number of families: 1 family

class CHAPTER

PHYSICAL CHARACTERISTICS

Hagfishes look like eels and are about 18–30 inches (46–76 centimeters) long. The skeleton is made up of cartilage (KAR-teh-lej), or tough, bendable tissue, rather than bone. Hagfishes have no fins or scales—flat, rigid plates that act as body covering. They do not have jaws but have two raspy, or rough, biting plates. The mouth is an oval slit surrounded by four barbels (BAR-buhls), which are long, thin feelers used for finding food. The single nostril is surrounded by another set of barbels. The eyes are two dents on the top of the head that are covered by skin, and the fishes probably cannot see with them. Hagfishes have six to ten pairs of gills, or breathing organs, which may open directly to the outside or join to form one gill opening. The color of hagfishes ranges from reddish brown to grayish pink. Hagfishes have about 100 to 150 slime glands along the sides of their bodies.

GEOGRAPHIC RANGE

Hagfishes live in the Atlantic, Pacific, Indian, Arctic, and Antarctic Oceans and in the Bering, Mediterranean, and Caribbean Seas.

HABITAT

Most hagfishes live at the bottom of the ocean. Atlantic hagfishes live on soft, muddy bottoms, where they form burrows. Pacific hagfishes live on surfaces ranging from soft, muddy bottoms to boulders and sand, where they coil up and nestle among rocks.

phylum
● **class**
subclass
order
monotypic order
suborder
family

DIET

Hagfishes eat dead and dying fish, small worms, and crustaceans (krus-TAY-shuns), which are animals that live in water and have a soft, segmented body covered by a hard shell, such as hermit crabs and shrimps. Using its biting plate, a hagfish pierces the food animal and bores into it, eating the soft insides and leaving only the bones and skin or shell.

BEHAVIOR AND REPRODUCTION

Hagfishes live in large groups on the ocean floor. They defend themselves by producing slime. Their reproductive patterns are unknown. Fertilization (FUR-teh-lih-zay-shun), or the joining of sperm and eggs to begin development, is probably external, or outside the body. Male reproductive cells are called sperm and female's are called eggs. The fishes release eggs and sperm into the water, and eggs that come into contact with sperm are fertilized. Each clutch, or group of eggs, contains twenty to thirty yolky eggs that are 0.8–1 inch (2–2.5 centimeters) long. The eggs are enclosed in a tough shell with threads at each end, which anchor the eggs in the mud.

HAGFISHES AND PEOPLE

Hagfishes help the environment by cleaning the ocean floor. They also are caught for meat and their skins. People who buy leather goods made out of "eel skin" are actually buying products made with hagfish skin.

CONSERVATION STATUS

Hagfishes are not threatened with extinction.

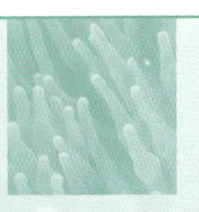

SLIME AND KNOTS

Hagfishes make slime in glands along the sides of their bodies. When attacked or handled, the fish forms a small amount of slime, which expands to a gallon or so when it comes in contact with the surrounding water. The hagfish then slips away. The hagfish rids itself of the slime by tying itself in a knot and scraping itself clean by moving the knot down its body.

Atlantic hagfish (*Myxine glutinosa*)

ATLANTIC HAGFISH
Myxine glutinosa

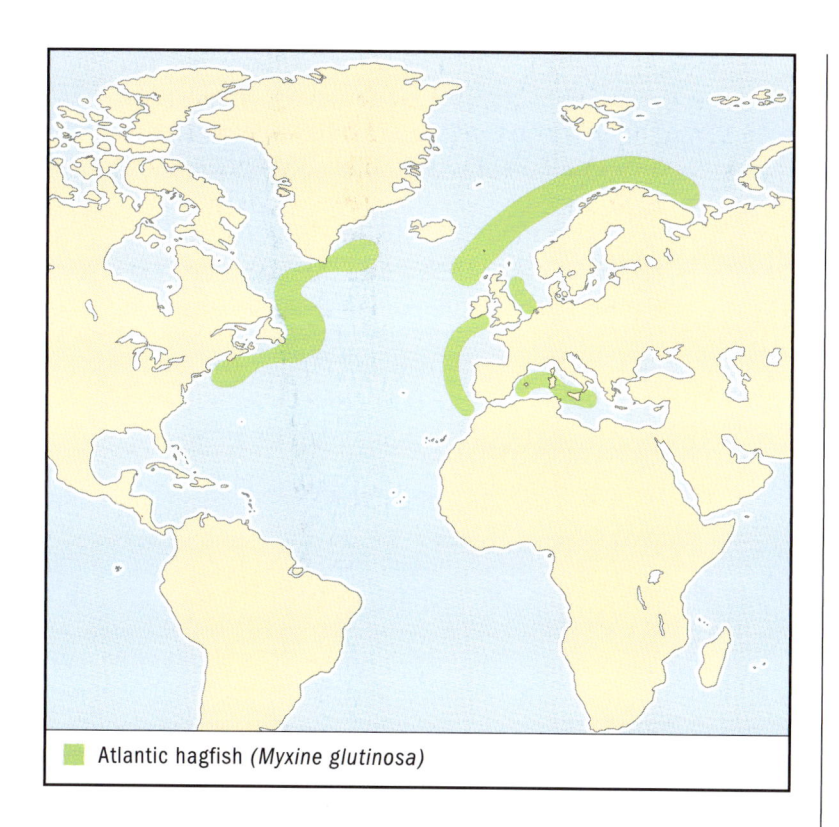

SPECIES ACCOUNT

Physical characteristics: Atlantic hagfishes are 18–31 inches (45–78 centimeters) long and grayish or reddish brown tubes. They are jawless and have four barbels around the mouth. The nose also is surrounded by four barbels. The eyespots are on top of the head and are covered with thick skin. Atlantic hagfishes have a single pair of gill openings. There are slime glands along the sides of the body.

Geographic range: Atlantic hagfishes are found on both sides of the North Atlantic Ocean, in the Arctic Ocean, and in the seas of Europe, except for the eastern Mediterranean Sea and the Black Sea.

Habitat: Atlantic hagfishes live in deep waters of 328–984 feet (100–300 meters) on soft, muddy bottoms, in which they form burrows.

Using its biting plate, a hagfish pierces its food and bores into it, eating the soft insides and leaving only the bones and skin or shell. (Illustration by Jacqueline Mahannah. Reproduced by permission.)

Diet: Atlantic hagfishes feed on dead and dying fishes; crustaceans, such as hermit crabs and shrimps; and other small invertebrates (in-VER-teh-brehts), that is, animals that lack backbones.

Behavior and reproduction: Atlantic hagfishes use slime to protect themselves from predators (PREH-duh-ters), or animals that hunt them for food. Atlantic hagfishes may make both eggs and sperm for part of their life cycle, reproducing as either male or female at other times. Females produce twenty to thirty eggs.

Atlantic hagfishes and people: The skin of Atlantic hagfishes is processed into leather goods and sold as "eel" skin.

Conservation status: Atlantic hagfishes are not threatened or endangered. ∎

FOR MORE INFORMATION

Books:

Gilbert, Carter Rowell, and James D. Williams. *National Audubon Society Field Guide to Fishes: North America.* New York: Knopf, 2002.

Schultz, Ken. *Ken Schultz's Field Guide to Saltwater Fish.* New York: Wiley, 2004.

Web sites:

Bigelow, Henry B., and William C. Schroeder. "Hagfish." *Fishes of the Gulf of Maine.* http://www.gma.org/fogm/Myxine_glutinosa.htm (accessed on August 28, 2004).

"Hagfish." OceanLink. http://oceanlink.island.net/oinfo/hagfish/hagfish.html (accessed on August 26, 2004).

"The Lowly Hag." *Safari Splash.* http://7thfloormedia.com/projects/safari/newsletter/wednesday/hagfish.html (accessed on August 26, 2004).

> **LAMPREYS**
> **Cephalaspidomorphi**
>
> **Class:** Cephalaspidomorphi
> **Number of families:** 3 families

class
CHAPTER

PHYSICAL CHARACTERISTICS

Lampreys (LAM-prees) are scaleless, eel-like fishes that have skeletons of cartilage (KAR-teh-lej) instead of bone. Lampreys do not have jaws, so they cannot close their mouths. The mouth and tongue are covered with many small, sharp teeth. Adult lampreys are 8–47 inches (20–120 centimeters) long. Lamprey larvae (LAR-vee) look like worms. Larvae are the early form of an animal that must go through metamorphosis (meh-tuh-MOR-pho-sus), or a change in form, before becoming an adult.

GEOGRAPHIC RANGE

Lampreys live in coastal waters on both sides of the North Atlantic Ocean; the western part of the Mediterranean Sea; the western, southern, and eastern coasts of Australia; New Zealand; Tasmania; both coasts of South America; and the Great Lakes of North America.

HABITAT

Lamprey larvae bury themselves in the sand or mud of rivers. In the early phase of their lives, lampreys live in open water in oceans or lakes. They return to freshwater streams to spawn, or produce and release eggs.

DIET

Lamprey larvae feed on plankton, or microscopic plants and animals drifting in bodies of water, and algae (AL-jee), tiny plantlike growths that live in water. Lampreys attach themselves

phylum
- **class**
subclass
order
monotypic order
suborder
family

to other fishes and suck out their blood and muscle. Lampreys do not feed during the spawning phase of their lives.

BEHAVIOR AND REPRODUCTION

After three to seven years in a freshwater stream, lamprey larvae metamorphose (meh-tuh-MOR-phoz), becoming freely swimming and leaving the stream for the open water of a sea or lake. For one to two years, lampreys live as parasites (PAIR-uh-sites), which are animals or plants that live on other animals or plants without helping them and often harming them. They then return to freshwater streams to spawn, which they do only once and then die.

LAMPREYS AND PEOPLE

In some areas governments are trying to maintain or increase lamprey populations, because lampreys, which are food for other fishes and for birds, help fishermen. In some regions, however, lampreys are a problem, because during the parasitic phase they harm other fishes.

CONSERVATION STATUS

Lampreys are not threatened or endangered.

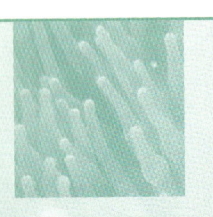

GREAT LAKES INVADED

The damage to fishing in the Great Lakes caused by the invasion of the sea lamprey resulted in one of the largest efforts to control a predator (PREH-duh-ter), an animal that hunts another animal for food, ever attempted. The lampreys are believed to have invaded the Great Lakes beginning with the opening of the Erie Canal, which connects the Hudson River and Lake Erie, in 1819 and the Welland Canal, which connects Lake Ontario and Lake Erie, in 1829. The lampreys traveled from the Atlantic Ocean up the Hudson and Saint Lawrence Rivers and through the canals into the lakes. By the 1930s sea lampreys had established themselves in all the Great Lakes. To help solve the sea lamprey problem, the Great Lakes Fishery Commission was established in 1955 by a treaty between Canada and the United States.

Sea lamprey (Petromyzon marinus)

SEA LAMPREY
Petromyzon marinus

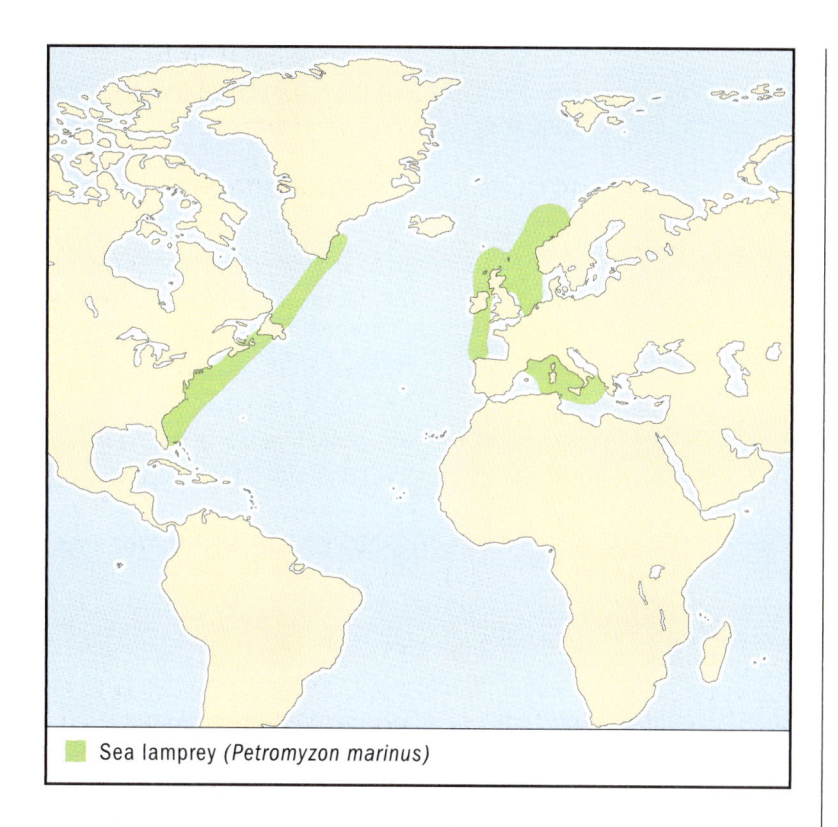

SPECIES ACCOUNT

Physical characteristics: Sea lampreys are about 47 inches (120 centimeters) long. The body is grayish brown on top and mottled, or spotted, yellowish brown along the sides.

Geographic range: Sea lampreys live on both sides of the North Atlantic Ocean, in the western Mediterranean Sea, and in the Great Lakes of North America.

Habitat: Sea lamprey larvae live in muddy or sandy freshwater streams. Mature sea lampreys live in open sea or lake water but return to freshwater streams to spawn.

Diet: Sea lamprey larvae feed on plankton and algae. During the early phase of their lives, they live as parasites, attaching to other fishes and sucking out blood and muscle. Sea lampreys do not feed after traveling upstream to spawn.

Mature sea lampreys live in open sea or lake water but return to freshwater streams to spawn. (Illustration by Emily Damstra. Reproduced by permission.)

Behavior and reproduction: Eggs and sperm, or male reproductive cells, develop in sea lampreys during the parasitic (pair-uh-SIT-ik) phase. The lampreys then return to freshwater streams to spawn. The female releases approximately 200,000 eggs, which are fertilized (FUR-teh-lyzed) by sperm released by the male. The adults die soon after spawning.

Sea lampreys and people: In some areas sea lampreys are considered helpful to the environment, and governments are trying to maintain or increase their populations. In the Great Lakes region, however, sea lampreys are ruining fishing, so authorities there are working to control them.

Conservation status: Sea lampreys are not threatened or endangered. ■

FOR MORE INFORMATION

Books:

Berra, Tim M. *Freshwater Fish Distribution.* San Diego, CA: Academic Press, 2001.

Gilbert, Carter Rowell, and James D. Williams. *National Audubon Society Field Guide to Fishes: North America.* New York: Knopf, 2002.

Ricciuti, Edward R. *Fish.* Woodbridge, CT: Blackbirch, 1993.

Schultz, Ken. *Ken Schultz's Field Guide to Freshwater Fish.* New York: Wiley, 2004.

Schultz, Ken. *Ken Schultz's Field Guide to Saltwater Fish.* New York: Wiley, 2004.

Web sites:

Fetterolf, Carlos. "Sea Lamprey in the Great Lakes." http://biology.usgs.gov/s+t/SNT/noframe/gl129.htm (accessed on August 27, 2004).

CHIMAERAS, SHARKS, SKATES AND RAYS
Chondrichthyes

Class: Chondrichthyes
Number of families: 57 families

class
CHAPTER

PHYSICAL CHARACTERISTICS

Chimaeras (kye-MIHR-uhs), sharks, and skates and rays are the class of fishes whose skeleton is made of cartilage (KAR-teh-lej), a tough but flexible supporting tissue. Chimaeras have large heads and long bodies that taper to a whiplike tail. The skin is smooth and rubbery and has no scales. Sharks and skates and rays have gills that open to the outside, have no swim bladder, and have a sandpaper-like skin covering rather than scales. Sharks range in size from tiny to huge. Skates and rays are flat from top to bottom and have massive pectoral (PECK-ter-uhl) fins and long, sometimes whiplike tails.

GEOGRAPHIC RANGE

Chimaeras, sharks, and skates and rays live all over the world except in the Antarctic region.

HABITAT

Chimaeras usually live on muddy bottoms near the shore. Sharks live in coastal waters on the bottom or out at sea in open water or at the bottom. Skates and rays live on the bottom in saltwater or freshwater or move back and forth between the two.

DIET

Chimaeras eat bottom-dwelling animals such as crabs, clams, and fishes. Some sharks are fierce predators (PREH-duh-terz) that hunt and eat every sort of sea animal. Others simply strain plankton, the microscopic (MY-kro-SKA-pihk), invisible to the

phylum
• class
subclass
order
monotypic order
suborder
family

Big Fish, Tiny Diet
The whale shark is the largest fish in the world at a length of 59 feet (18 meters) and eats the smallest food, plankton.

Man-eater?
More people have been killed by domestic livestock, such as pigs, than by sharks.

eye, plants and animals that drift in bodies of water. Most skates and rays eat bottom-dwelling shelled animals and bony fishes.

BEHAVIOR AND REPRODUCTION

All chimaeras, sharks, and skates and rays reproduce by internal fertilization (FUR-teh-lih-zay-shun), meaning egg and sperm unite inside the female. Some species lay fertilized (FUR-teh-lyezd) eggs, and the young develop outside the mother. In other species the young develop inside the mother, hatch within the mother, and are born freely swimming. Chimaeras, sharks, and skates and rays engage in parental care before laying eggs or giving birth to pups.

CHIMAERAS, SHARKS, SKATES, RAYS, AND PEOPLE

A few species of chimaeras are fished commercially for food. Sharks are used for their meat, oil, and hides, which are used for leather. Skates and rays are eaten in some areas, and the skin sometimes is used for leather.

CONSERVATION STATUS

The World Conservation Union (IUCN) lists eight species of sharks and skates and rays as Critically Endangered, seventeen as Endangered, thirty-two as Vulnerable, sixty-four as Lower Risk/Near Threatened, and one as Lower Risk/Conservation Dependent. Critically Endangered means facing an extremely high risk of extinction in the wild in the near future. Endangered means facing a very high risk of extinction in the wild in the near future. Vulnerable means facing a high risk of extinction in the wild. Near Threatened means at risk of becoming threatened with extinction in the future. Conservation Dependent means that if the conservation program were to end, the animal would be placed in one of the threatened categories.

Spotted ratfish *(Hydrolagus colliei)*

SPOTTED RATFISH
Hydrolagus colliei

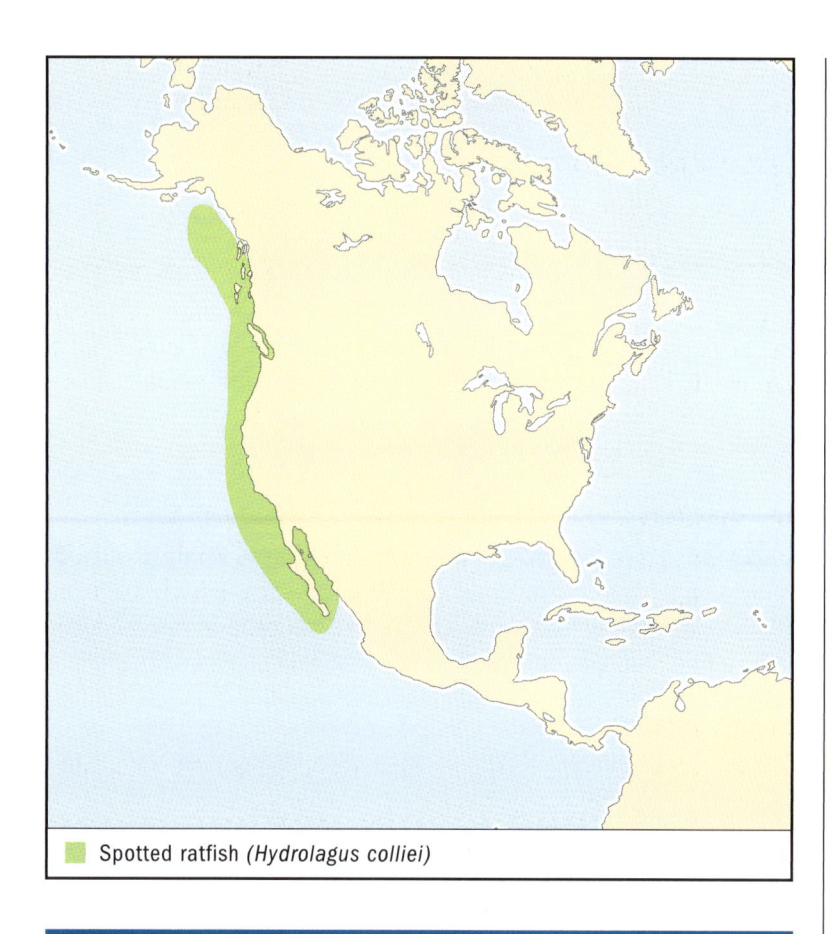

SPECIES ACCOUNTS

Physical characteristics: Spotted ratfish have a bluntly pointed snout. The body is reddish to dark brown with silvery-blue and gold highlights. There are many small white spots on the head and along the sides and back. They are called ratfish because their teeth look like rodent incisors (ihn-SY-zrz), the sharp front teeth of a rat.

Geographic range: Spotted ratfish live in the Pacific Ocean from southeastern Alaska to northern Mexico.

Habitat: Spotted ratfish live near muddy, sandy, or rocky bottoms.

Chimaeras, Sharks, Skates and Rays

In the past, spotted ratfish were caught for their liver oil. (Brandon D. Cole/Corbis. Reproduced by permission.)

Diet: Spotted ratfish eat bottom-dwelling invertebrates (in-VER-teh-brehts), which are animals with no backbones such as earthworms or insects, and other fishes.

Behavior and reproduction: Spotted ratfish migrate or move from deeper to shallower waters. They tend to gather in groups based on age and sex. The eggs are fertilized (FUR-teh-lyezd) inside the female by sperm from the male. Two egg capsules are laid every seven to ten days for months.

Conservation status: Spotted ratfish are not threatened nor endangered.

Spotted ratfish and people: At one time spotted ratfish were fished for their liver oil. ∎

Tiger shark (Galeocerdo cuvier)

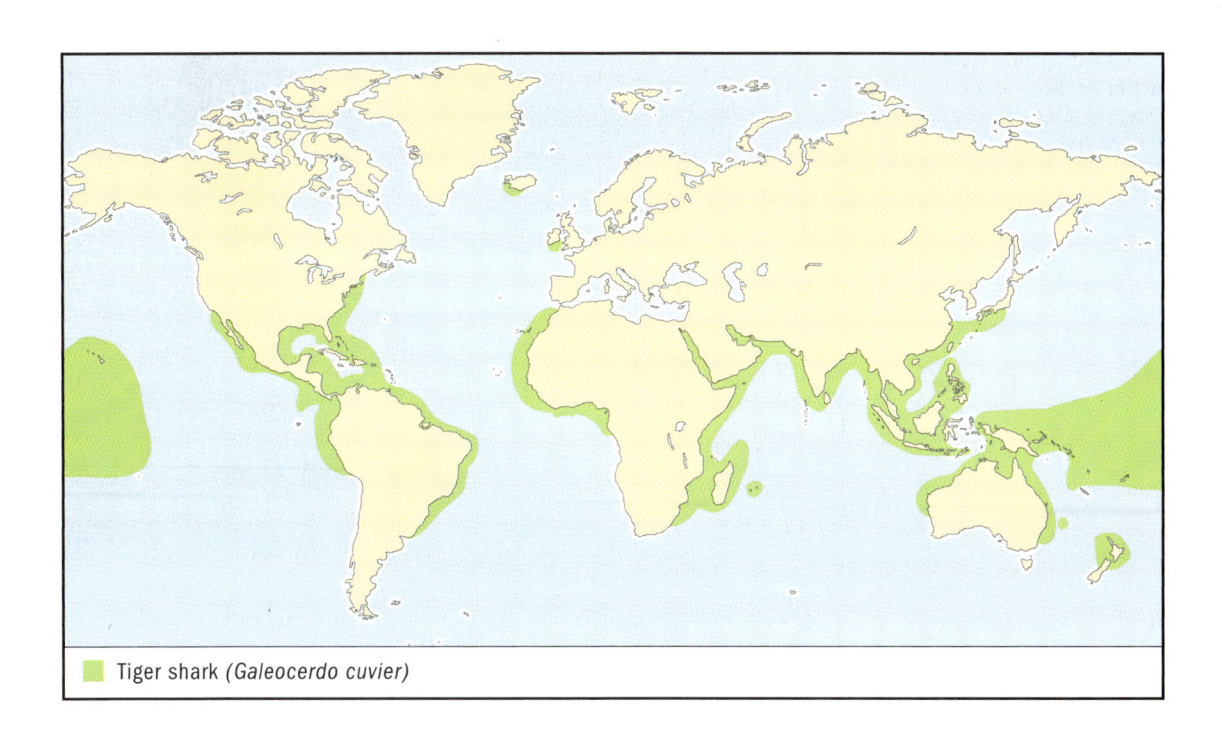

TIGER SHARK
Galeocerdo cuvier

Physical characteristics: Tiger sharks have a short, rounded snout and large first dorsal fins and tail fins. Young tiger sharks have dark vertical stripes over a gray background. Large females reach a length of 20 feet (6 meters). The teeth curve backward.

Geographic range: Tiger sharks live all over the world.

Habitat: Tiger sharks live mainly near the shore in muddy waters, where rivers meet the sea, near piers, in coral reefs, and in shallow lagoons. Tiger sharks may be found in open water offshore but are not truly oceanic sharks.

Diet: Tiger sharks eat whatever is available and are efficient predators. They have been known to ingest (ihn-JEHST) or swallow inedible objects, such as an amazing variety of trash. Prey varies from large fishes, reptiles, mammals, and birds to squid and shrimp.

Tiger sharks live mainly near the shore in muddy waters, where rivers meet the sea, near piers, in coral reefs, and in shallow lagoons. (Illustration by Barbara Duperron. Reproduced by permission.)

Behavior and reproduction: Tiger sharks are mostly nocturnal (nahk-TER-nuhl), or active at night, and strong-swimming. They usually swim alone. These sharks appear sluggish because they cruise at slow speeds near the surface. Young tiger sharks develop inside the female. The female gives birth to ten to eighty-two young that are 20 to 30 inches (51 to 76 centimeters) long.

Conservation status: Tiger sharks are not threatened nor endangered.

Tiger sharks and people: In many places tiger sharks are considered dangerous. Tiger sharks are fished for their meat, hide, and liver and for sport. They do not survive in aquariums.

White shark (Carcharodon carcharias)

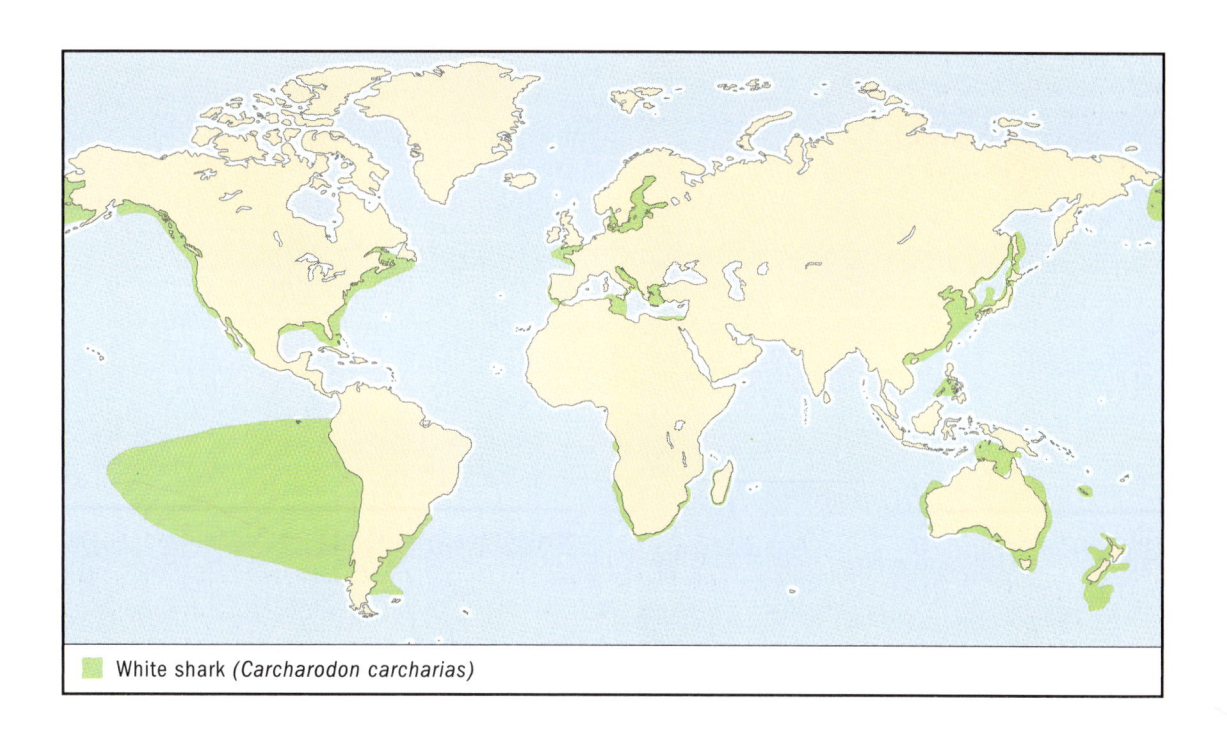

WHITE SHARK
Carcharodon carcharias

Physical characteristics: The average length of white sharks is 18 feet (5.5 meters). White sharks are white on the belly and gray-to-bluish on the back and sides. The first dorsal fin is much larger than the second, and the tail fin is large and crescent shaped. The pectoral fins have black tips. White sharks have a cone-shaped snout, large black eyes, and large triangular teeth with sawlike edges.

Geographic range: White sharks live worldwide but are most common off the coasts of California, Australia, and South Africa.

Habitat: White sharks cruise through relatively shallow waters near the surface or close to the bottom. They can travel long distances in open water.

Diet: White sharks feed on bony fishes, other sharks, sea turtles, seals, whale carcasses, and even sea birds resting on the surface.

Chimaeras, Sharks, Skates and Rays

Behavior and reproduction: White sharks are solitary (SA-le-TER-ee) and nomadic (no-MAE-dihk). They move from place to place alone without settling on a fixed home. They are capable of great bursts of speed and can leap completely out of the water. The young develop inside the female. The young measure 4 to 5 feet (1.2 to 1.5 meters) at birth and can weigh as much as 55 pounds (25 kilograms).

White sharks and people: People pay a great deal of money to watch white sharks from the protection of a submerged cage.

Conservation status: The IUCN lists white sharks as Vulnerable, which means they are facing a high risk of extinction in the wild. ■

Great white sharks are capable of great bursts of speed and can leap completely out of the water. (CORBIS. Reproduced by permission.)

Atlantic manta (*Manta birostris*)

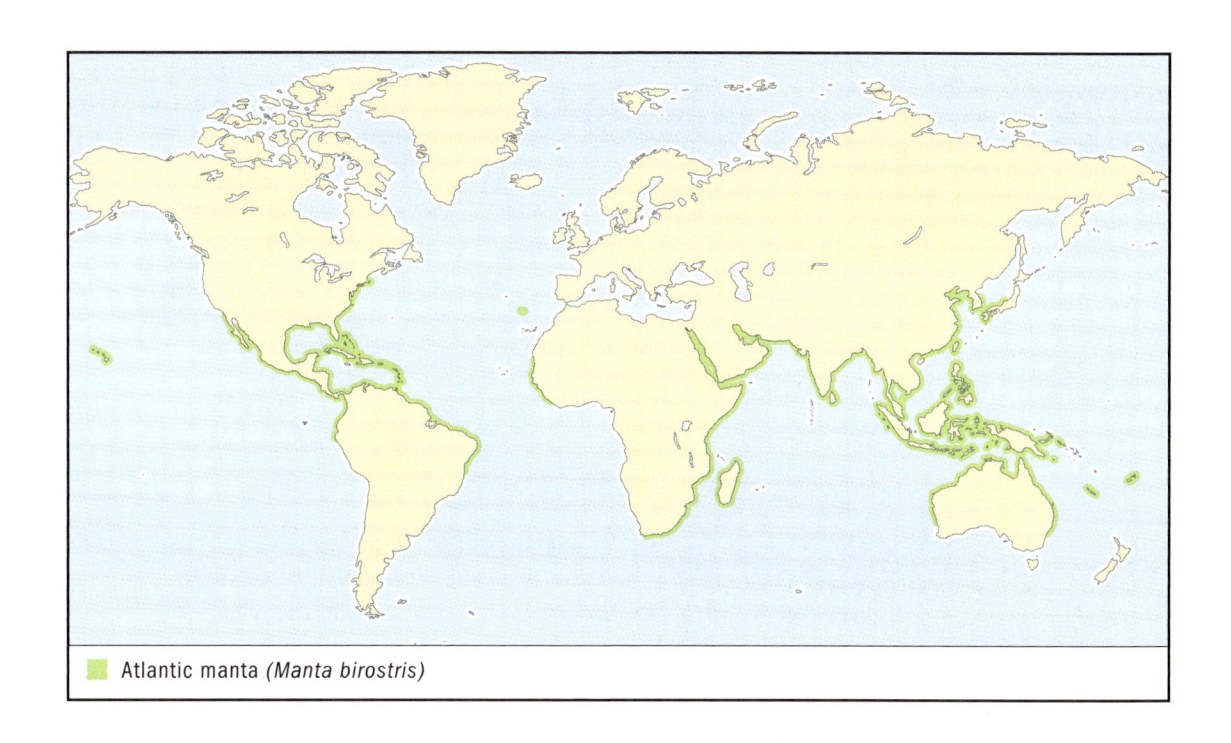

ATLANTIC MANTA
Manta birostris

Physical characteristics: The head, pectoral fin, and trunk of Atlantic mantas are flattened and join to form a disk that is much broader than it is long and has slightly curved outer corners. Adults have an average disk width of 22 feet (6.7 meters). Atlantic mantas have a short, whiplike tail. Atlantic mantas are brown to olive-green on the back and white to whitish on the belly.

Geographic range: Atlantic mantas live all over the world.

Habitat: Atlantic mantas live in open coastal waters.

Diet: Atlantic mantas eat animal plankton and freely swimming crustaceans (krus-TAY-shuns), such as shrimp.

Behavior and reproduction: Atlantic mantas perform somersaults while feeding. They sometimes leap partially or completely out of the water. They enter shallow reef areas to be cleaned of parasites by small

Chimaeras, Sharks, Skates and Rays

Atlantic mantas sometimes perform somersaults while feeding. They can leap partially or completely out of the water. (Illustration by Gillian Harris. Reproduced by permission.)

bony fishes. After internal fertilization of the eggs, the young develop inside the female. The litter size is unknown. Atlanta mantas are 4 feet (1.2 meters) wide at birth.

Conservation status: Atlantic mantas are not threatened nor endangered.

Atlantic mantas and people: Atlantic mantas are eaten in some parts of the world. Scuba expeditions are conducted to observe manta rays at their feeding sites. ■

Clearnose skate (Raja eglanteria)

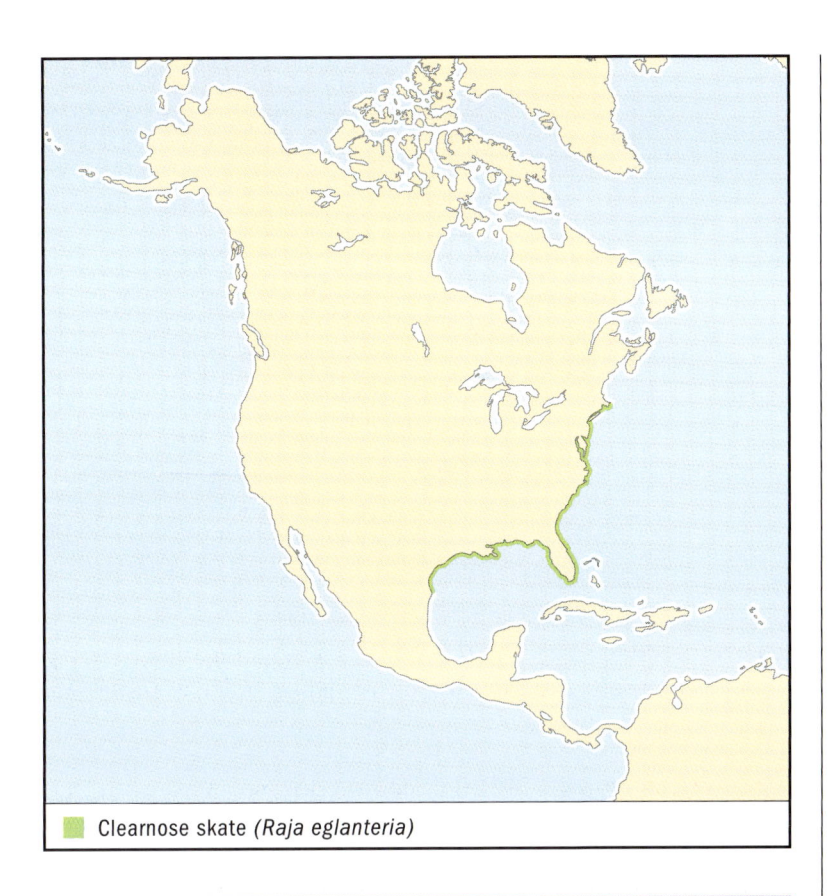

CLEARNOSE SKATE
Raja eglanteria

Physical characteristics: Clearnose skates reach a total length of 31 inches (79 centimeters). The head, pectoral fins, and trunk are flattened and join to form a broad disk. The tail makes up about one-half of the total length of the skate. The sides of the snout are not clear but are cloudy, like frosted glass. A row of thorns runs down the back. Clearnose skates are brown to gray on the back and whitish to yellowish on the belly. There are dark and light spots and dark bars on the back.

Geographic range: Clearnose skates live in the western part of the North Atlantic Ocean from Massachusetts to the northern Gulf of Mexico.

Clearnose skates live in the western part of the North Atlantic Ocean from Massachusetts to the northern Gulf of Mexico. (Illustration by Gillian Harris. Reproduced by permission.)

Habitat: Clearnose skates live on soft bottoms near the shore.

Diet: Clearnose skates eat worms, shrimps, crabs, and bony fishes.

Behavior and reproduction: In the northern part of their range, clearnose skates migrate (MY-grayt) north and near shore in the spring and south and offshore in the fall. After internal fertilization, the female lays eggs, and the young hatch from egg capsules after several months. At birth clearnose skates are about 5 inches (12.5 to 14.4 centimeters) long.

Conservation status: Clearnose skates are not threatened nor endangered.

Clearnose skates and people: Clearnose skates have been used in cancer research.

FOR MORE INFORMATION

Books:

Allen, Thomas B. *The Shark Almanac.* New York: Lyons, 1999.

Perrine, D. *Sharks and Rays of the World.* Stillwater, MN: Voyager Press, 1999.

Pope, Joyce. *1001 Facts about Sharks.* New York: DK, 2002.

Web sites:

"Ask a Scientist Answers to Chondrichthyes Questions." OceanLink. http://oceanlink.island.net/ask/chondrichthyes.html#anchor120253 (accessed on September 20, 2004).

"Chondrichthyes." Science Fair Projects Encyclopedia. http://www.all-science-fair-projects.com/science_fair_projects_encyclopedia/Chondrichthyes (accessed on September 20, 2004).

> **COELACANTHS AND LUNGFISHES**
> **Sarcopterygii**
>
> **Class:** Sarcopterygii
> **Number of families:** 4 families
>
> class CHAPTER

PHYSICAL CHARACTERISTICS

Coelacanths (SEE-lah-kanths) and lungfishes have rounded, fleshy fins. They are closely related to four-footed land vertebrates (VER-teh-brehts), or animals with a backbone.

GEOGRAPHIC RANGE

Coelacanths live on both sides of the Indian Ocean. Lungfishes live in South America, Africa, and Australia.

HABITAT

Coelacanths live in caves deep in the ocean. Lungfishes live in slow-moving rivers, swamps, lakes, floodplains, and ponds.

DIET

Coelacanths are opportunistic (ah-per-too-NIS-tik) bottom feeders, meaning that they take advantage of whatever is available at the bottom of their water habitat. Lungfishes are predators (PREH-duh-ters), or animals that hunt and kill other animals for food.

BEHAVIOR AND REPRODUCTION

Coelacanths give birth to live young. Lungfishes reproduce by external fertilization (FUR-teh-lih-zay-shun), meaning that eggs, or female reproductive cells, and sperm, or male reproductive cells, unite outside the female's body.

sidebar:
phylum
● class
subclass
order
monotypic order
suborder
family

COELOCANTHS, LUNGFISHES, AND PEOPLE

Coelacanths are valued mainly for research. Lungfishes are common in aquariums.

CONSERVATION STATUS

The World Conservation Union (IUCN) lists one species of coelacanths as Critically Endangered, meaning that it faces an extremely high risk of extinction in the wild in the near future. Lungfishes are not threatened or endangered.

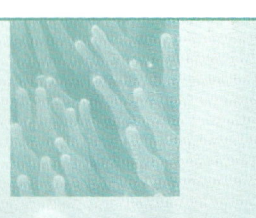

AMAZING DISCOVERY

The December 1938 find of a living coelacanth caused disbelief and created one of the greatest biological sensations of the twentieth century. Finding a living coelacanth, so similar to the fossil (FAH-suhl) specimens left in rocks more than seventy-five million years ago, was as inconceivable as meeting a living dinosaur. The living coelacanths are often celebrated as the most unusual case and important example of animal evolution.

Coelacanth (*Latimeria chalumnae*)

COELACANTH
Latimeria chalumnae

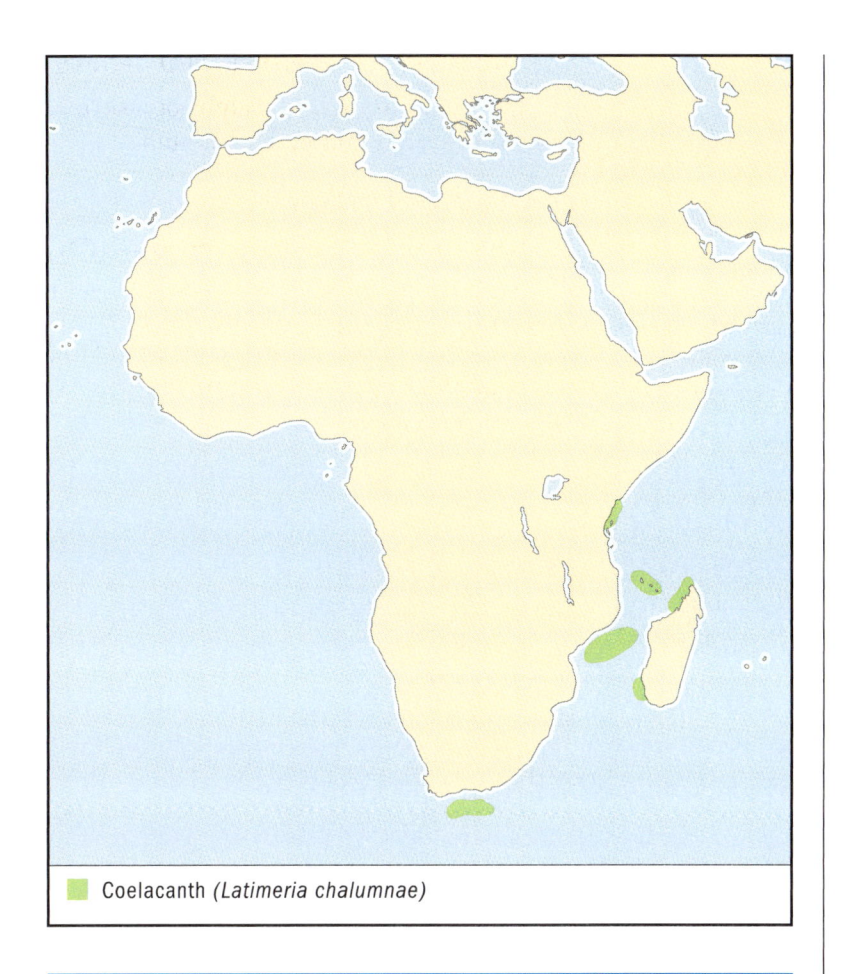

SPECIES ACCOUNTS

Physical characteristics: Coelacanths have fleshy fins. Instead of being made up of individual bones, or vertebrae (ver-teh-BREE), the backbone is a stiff tube. Coelacanths are bluish gray with white markings. They weigh 110–198 pounds (50–90 kilograms). Female coelacanths can be as long as 6 feet (1.9 meters) and males as long as 5 feet (1.50 meters).

Geographic range: Coelacanths live on both sides of the Indian Ocean.

Coelacanths eat whatever they find as they drift in the current. (©Peter Scoones/Photo Researchers, Inc. Reproduced by permission.)

Habitat: Coelacanths live in caves in tropical oceans below 328 feet (100 meters), in steep, sloping areas. At night they move up the slope to feed.

Diet: Coelacanths eat whatever they find as they drift in the current. Because they can lift the upper jaw as well as move the lower jaw, coelacanths can open their mouths quite far to suck prey from crevices.

Behavior and reproduction: While swimming, coelacanths move their pectoral (PECK-ter-uhl) and pelvic fins the way most four-footed animals move their legs. The pectoral fins are the front pair, and the pelvic fins are the rear pair. Coelacanths give birth to live young, but scientists do not know how they what sort of mating takes place. The gestation (je-STAY-shun) period, or time the young develops inside the female, is about thirteen months. Scientists believe females become mature for the first time when they are more than twenty years old.

Coelacanths and people: Coelacanths are valued for the information they can provide about evolution.

Conservation status: The World Conservation Union (IUCN) lists one species of coelacanth as Critically Endangered, meaning that it faces an extremely high risk of extinction in the wild in the near future. ∎

South American lungfish (Lepidosiren paradoxa)

SOUTH AMERICAN LUNGFISH
Lepidosiren paradoxa

Physical characteristics: Lungfishes have eel-like bodies and long, thin pectoral and pelvic fins. The skeleton is mostly cartilage (KAR-teh-lej). These fishes have two lungs and small gills, or organs for obtaining oxygen from water. South American lungfishes can grow to a length of 4 feet (1.25 meters). They are dark brown or gray and have dark and light spots on the top and sides.

Geographic range: South American lungfishes live in the Amazon River basin and in French Guiana.

South American lungfish have lungs and small gills. (©Tom McHugh/Photo Researchers, Inc. Reproduced by permission.)

Habitat: These lungfishes live in swamps, slow-moving rivers, floodplains, and pools.

Diet: South American lungfishes eat insects; insect larvae (LAR-vee), or insects in the early stage of growth; other invertebrates (in-VER-teh-brehts), or animals without a backbone; fishes; and algae (AL-gee), which are tiny, plantlike growths that live in water. They do not feed during estivation (es-tuh-VAY-shun), or the period of in activity during dry spells.

Behavior and reproduction: South American lungfishes swim by slow, wavy movement or by "crawling" on their pectoral and pelvic fins. Because their gill surfaces are not large enough to meet their oxygen needs, lungfishes drown if they stay underwater. For estivation, they dig burrows by biting the soil and expelling, or forcing, mud through their gill openings. They then breathe the oxygen in the hole. Spawning usually occurs during the wet season. Fertilization is external. Males guard and fan, or use their fins to move water over, newly hatched young to clean them and give them oxygen.

South American lungfishes and people: South American lungfishes usually are not eaten. They often are displayed in aquariums.

Conservation status: South American lungfishes are not threatened or endangered. ■

FOR MORE INFORMATION

Books:

Berra, Tim M. *Freshwater Fish Distribution.* San Diego, CA: Academic Press, 2001.

Weinberg, Samantha. *A Fish Caught in Time: The Search for the Coelacanth.* New York: HarperCollins, 2000.

Web sites:

"The Fish out of Time." http://www.dinofish.com (accessed on August 28, 2004).

BICHIRS
Polypteriformes

Class: Actinopterygii
Order: Polypteriformes
Number of families: 1 family

order
CHAPTER

phylum
class
subclass
● order
monotypic order
suborder
family

PHYSICAL CHARACTERISTICS

Bichirs (bi-CHURS) have a slender body that is 16–47 inches (40–120 centimeters) long. The dorsal (DOOR-suhl) fin, the one that runs along the top, is divided into a series of small spiny fins, called finlets. Bichirs have a tubular pair of nostrils that extends in front of the mouth, and they have many small, sharp teeth. These fishes have a dense covering of shiny, diamond-shaped scales arranged in diagonals. On the inside, bichirs have paired swim bladders that function as air-breathing organs. This feature is unusual, because fishes usually use the swim bladder to control their position in the water. The right swim bladder is larger than the left one. Bichirs are olive brown to dark brown on the top and sides and over the head but are creamy white on the bottom. Some have dark or clear spots and blotches and irregular stripes, but others are a solid color. The heads of most bichirs are spotted.

GEOGRAPHIC RANGE

Bichirs live in western and central tropical Africa. Some live in the Nile River. Bichirs do not live in rivers that drain into the Indian Ocean.

HABITAT

Bichirs live in fast-moving and slow-moving rivers, floodplains, swamps, lakes, and pools. Because they are able to breathe air, bichirs can live in stagnant, or still, stale water.

DIET

Bichirs feed mainly on invertebrates (in-VER-teh-brehts), or animals that lack a backbone. They eat insect larvae (LAR-vee), that is, insects in the early stage of development; snails; earthworms; and freshwater crustaceans (krus-TAY-shuns), or animals that live in water and have a soft, segmented body covered by a hard shell. They also eat fishes and amphibians (am-FIB-ee-uns), animals that live part of their lives on land and part in water. Bichirs are primarily nocturnal (nahk-TER-nuhl) predators (PREH-duh-ters), meaning that they are active at night and hunt and kill other animals for their food.

BEHAVIOR AND REPRODUCTION

Not much is known about bichirs. They are reported to "walk" over land for small distances to feed on insects, because they are able to absorb oxygen directly from the air for at least a few hours. In aquariums the behavior of bichirs varies from remaining motionless on the bottom for short periods to swimming about vigorously. Their pectoral (PECK-ter-uhl) fins, or front pair, function as paddles.

Male bichirs use their anal (AY-nuhl) and caudal (KAW-duhl) fins to surround a female's genital (JEN-ih-tuhl), or reproductive, opening, making a pouch that receives the eggs from the female. The anal fin is the one that runs along the bottom of the body, and the caudal fin is the one at the end of the body. Fertilization (FUR-teh-lih-zay-shun), the joining of egg and sperm to start development, occurs in the pouch made with the fins. The male releases the eggs by shaking his anal fin, and the eggs quickly attach to plants. Bichirs do not care for their eggs or their young.

BICHIRS AND PEOPLE

Bichirs are used in the ornamental fish business. Large bichirs are used for food in West Africa.

CONSERVATION STATUS

Bichirs are not threatened or endangered.

Bichir (*Polypterus ornatipinnis*)

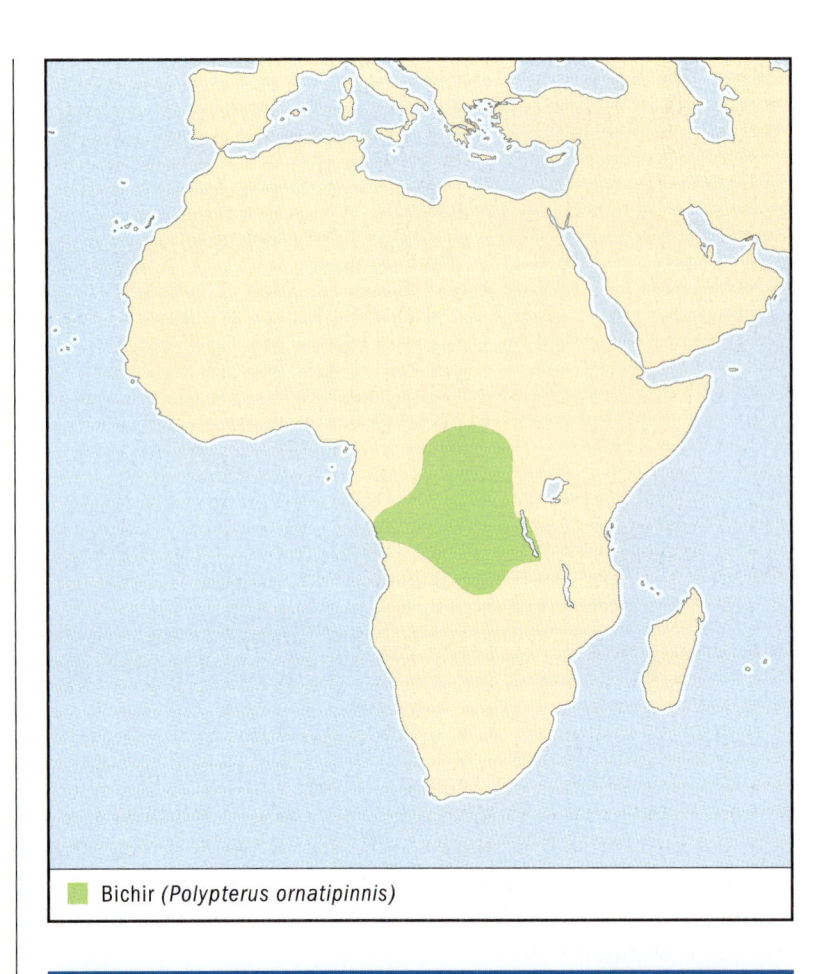

SPECIES ACCOUNT

BICHIR
Polypterus ornatipinnis

Physical characteristics: The maximum length of bichirs is 24 inches (60 centimeters). The body is protected by an armor of large, diamond-shaped bony scales. These fishes are long and thin and have nine or ten small dorsal finlets. The pelvic fins are near the tail. Bichirs have a white belly with dark spots on the head, sides, and top and have parallel bands on the fins.

Geographic range: Bichirs live in central and eastern Africa in the Congo Basin and Lake Tanganyika.

Habitat: Bichirs live in lakes, rivers, floodplains, and swamps, including waters with low oxygen content.

Bichirs are reported to "walk" over land for small distances to feed on insects. They are able to absorb oxygen directly from the air for at least a few hours. (Phillip Colla-V&W/Bruce Coleman Inc. Reproduced by permission.)

Diet: Bichirs feed mostly at night and seek prey such as other fishes, frogs, insects, and crustaceans.

Behavior and reproduction: Bichirs often sit motionless on the bottom, resting on their pectoral fins so that the head and front of the body are slightly elevated. They gulp air from the surface in stagnant water. During courtship, bichirs make energetic twisting, turning, and darting movements. The male surrounds the female's genital opening with his anal and caudal fins, fertilizes the eggs, and then scatters them by thrashing his tail.

Bichirs and people: Bichirs are a food fish and are captured for the aquarium business.

Conservation status: Bichirs are not threatened or endangered. ■

FOR MORE INFORMATION

Books:

Berra, Tim M. *Freshwater Fish Distribution.* San Diego, CA: Academic Press, 2001.

Ricciuti, Edward R. *Fish.* Woodbridge, CT: Blackbirch, 1993.

Web sites:

Caldas, Eduardo Pereira. "Bichir (*Polypterus ornatipinnis*)." WhoZoo. http://www.whozoo.org/Anlife99/eduardo/Bichir4.htm (accessed on August 29, 2004).

STURGEONS AND PADDLEFISHES
Acipenseriformes

Class: Actinopterygii
Order: Acipenseriformes
Number of families: 2 families

order
CHAPTER

PHYSICAL CHARACTERISTICS

Sturgeons (STUHR-jens) and paddlefishes are some of the largest freshwater fishes, ranging from 2.5 feet (0.8 meters) to about 28 feet (8.5 meters) in length. They have no scales and no lateral (LAT-uhr-uhl) line, or series of pores and tiny tubes along each side of the body used for sensing vibrations (vie-BRAY-shuns). Sturgeons and paddlefishes are dark on top but light or white on the bottom. Sturgeons are gray, brown, dark blue, olive green, or nearly black. Paddlefishes are bluish gray, brown, or black on top. The skeletons of sturgeons and paddlefishes are mostly cartilage (KAR-teh-lej), or tough, bendable support tissue. The only bones are the skull, the jaws, and the bones that support the pectoral (PECK-ter-uhl) fins, the front pair. These fishes have long snouts with barbels (BAR-buhls), or long, thin feelers used for the senses of taste, touch, and smell.

GEOGRAPHIC RANGE

Sturgeons and paddlefishes live in the Northern Hemisphere in North America, Europe, and Asia.

HABITAT

Sturgeons and paddlefishes live in seas, rivers, and lakes. Some spend a large portion of their lives at sea but enter coastal rivers to spawn. Others live only in freshwater rivers and lakes. Sturgeons live on sand, gravel, or rock bottoms.

DIET

Sturgeons find food by swimming close to the bottom and dragging their barbels along it. They eat slow-moving insects; worms; crustaceans (krus-TAY-shuns), or animals with a soft, segmented body covered by a hard shell; and mollusks (MAH-lusks), or animals with a soft, unsegmented body usually covered by a shell. They also sometimes feed on other fishes. Paddlefishes feed by swimming through the water with their mouths open and filtering water through comblike structures called gill rakers. The gills are the organs used to get oxygen from water. Paddlefishes eat mainly crustaceans and insect larvae (LAR-vee), or insects in an early developmental stage, in plankton, or microscopic plants and animals drifting in water. They occasionally eat larger invertebrates (in-VER-teh-brehts), or animals without backbones, and other fishes.

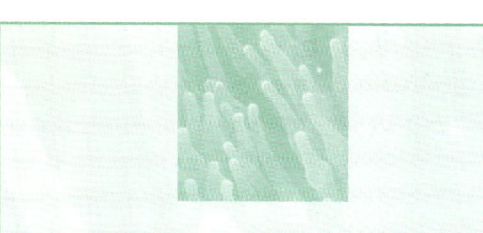

CAVIAR

Sturgeons have been valued for their caviar, the unfertilized eggs of the female, since the times of the ancient Persian, Greek, and Roman empires. The Chinese began trading caviar during the tenth century. Caviar became popular as a luxury food in Europe during the seventeenth and eighteenth centuries. In the early nineteenth century the United States was the largest producer of caviar. Caviar from beluga sturgeons is considered the best, and these sturgeons have become an endangered species because of the great demand for them.

BEHAVIOR AND REPRODUCTION

Sturgeons are active mainly during the day. All sturgeons spawn, or produce and release eggs, in freshwater, so those that live in the sea travel to freshwater during the spring and summer months. Before spawning, sturgeons roll near the bottom and leap out of the water. Female sturgeons produce several million eggs, which are deposited over shallow, rocky areas for fertilization (FUR-teh-lih-zay-shun), the joining of egg and sperm, or male reproductive cells, to start development. Paddlefishes swim constantly, both day and night, and travel upstream in the spring to spawn. Male and female paddlefishes broadcast eggs and sperm over the gravel bottom while swimming in groups. Sturgeons and paddlefishes do not tend their young.

STURGEONS, PADDLEFISHES, AND PEOPLE

Sturgeons are valued for caviar (KA-vee-ahr), which is salted, unfertilized eggs eaten as a delicacy. The smoked meat of sturgeons also is highly valued.

CONSERVATION STATUS

The World Conservation Union (IUCN) lists six species of sturgeons as Critically Endangered, or facing extremely high risk of extinction in the wild; eleven species as Endangered, or facing very high risk of extinction in the wild; and eight species as Vulnerable, or facing high risk of extinction in the wild. The U.S. Fish and Wildlife Service lists the Alabama, pallid, shortnose, and white sturgeons as Endangered, meaning that they are in danger of extinction throughout all or most of their range, and the gulf sturgeon as Threatened, or likely to become endangered in the near future.

Beluga sturgeon (*Huso huso*)

BELUGA STURGEON
Huso huso

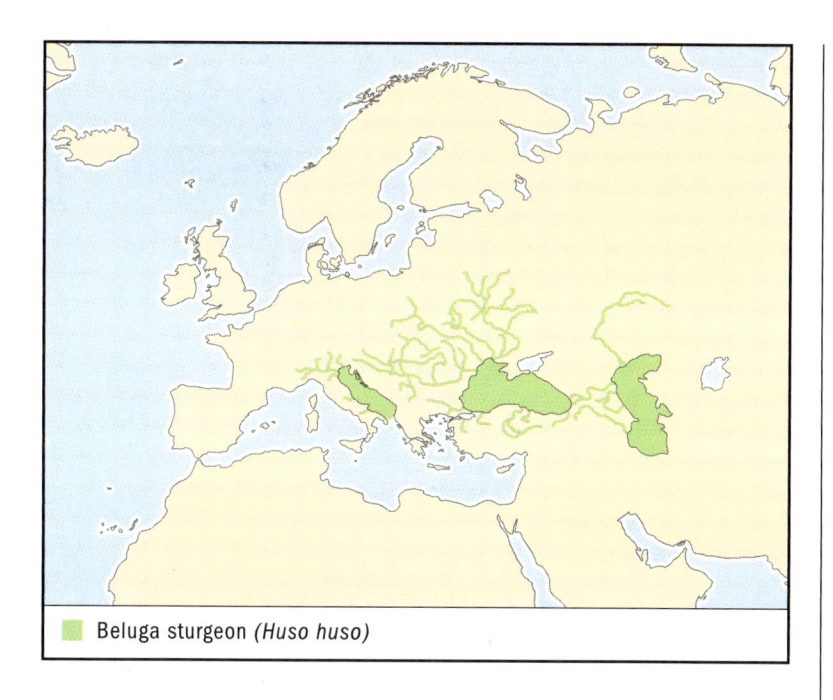

SPECIES ACCOUNT

Physical characteristics: The beluga is the largest sturgeon. It can be as long as 28 feet (8.5 meters) and can weigh 2,866 pounds (1,300 kilograms), although such large ones are rare. The body is gray or dark green with lighter sides and a white belly.

Geographic range: Beluga sturgeons live in the Black, Caspian, and Adriatic Seas in Europe and Asia and in most of their tributaries.

Habitat: Beluga sturgeons live near the shores of seas and in large channels of rivers.

Diet: Young beluga sturgeons eat invertebrates, such as mollusks, worms, and crustaceans. Adults eat other fishes.

Behavior and reproduction: Adult beluga sturgeons live at sea for most of the year but travel up large rivers to spawn in late spring. The young travel back to the sea immediately after hatching. Beluga sturgeons mature slowly and live as long as 150 years. Females may

The beluga is the largest sturgeon. It can be as long as 28 feet (8.5 meters) and can weigh 2,866 pounds (1,300 kilograms). (Illustration by Emily Damstra. Reproduced by permission.)

produce more than seven million eggs, but reproduction occurs only once every five to seven years. Beluga sturgeons spawn by scattering eggs and sperm in the water over the rocky bottom.

Beluga sturgeons and people: Beluga sturgeons are valued as a source of caviar.

Conservation status: The IUCN lists beluga sturgeons as Endangered. They may be extinct in the Adriatic Sea. ■

FOR MORE INFORMATION

Books:

Berra, Tim M. *Freshwater Fish Distribution.* San Diego, CA: Academic Press, 2001.

Gilbert, Carter Rowell, and James D. Williams. *National Audubon Society Field Guide to Fishes: North America.* New York: Knopf, 2002.

Ricciuti, Edward R. *Fish.* Woodbridge, CT: Blackbirch, 1993.

Schultz, Ken. *Ken Schultz's Field Guide to Freshwater Fish.* New York: Wiley, 2004.

Schultz, Ken. *Ken Schultz's Field Guide to Saltwater Fish.* New York: Wiley, 2004.

order CHAPTER

GARS
Lepisosteiformes

Class: Actinopterygii
Order: Lepisosteiformes
Number of families: 1 family

PHYSICAL CHARACTERISTICS

Gars have a long snout, or bill, and a long, armored body.

GEOGRAPHIC RANGE

Gars live in the freshwaters of eastern North America, as far west as Montana in the United States; as far north as Montana and southern Quebec, Canada; and as far south as Central America and Cuba.

HABITAT

Gars are primarily freshwater fishes, although some have been known to swim into saltwater areas near the ocean shore, such as the salt marshes of Louisiana. Gars can live in aquatic (uh-KWA-tik), or watery, environments of low oxygen content because they use their swim bladder, an internal sac usually used to control position in the water, to breathe air.

DIET

Gars eat mainly other fishes, but they also eat frogs and invertebrates (in-VER-teh-brehts), which are animals without backbones, such as crabs and crayfishes. They also sometimes eat garbage dumped into the water. Now and then they even eat other gars. Gars use their long, toothy jaws to grasp swimming prey with quick movements of their heads. Large alligator gars at times feed on water birds.

BEHAVIOR AND REPRODUCTION

Gars are sluggish but make extremely quick movements for short periods of time. They often lie motionless near the surface

phylum
class
subclass
● order
monotypic order
suborder
family

until prey swims within reach. Then, with a quick sideways thrust of its sharply toothed bill, the fish stabs the food animal and swallows it.

Gars spawn, or produce and release eggs, in freshwater, usually in the springtime. Fertilization (FUR-teh-lih-zay-shun), or the joining of egg and sperm, which are male reproductive cells, is external, or outside the body. Large numbers of gars come together on sandbanks for spawning and leave quickly afterward. Gars do not take care of their eggs or their young. The eggs are black and stick to rocks or plants. After hatching, the larvae (LAR-vee), or the young form of the fish, have suckers that help them stick to objects, even in moving water. The eggs are highly poisonous.

GARS AND PEOPLE

Gars are often thought of as a nuisance fish that harms game fishes, and they often break up the nets of commercial fishermen. The meat of gars is extremely bony and not generally used for food. The eggs of gars are poisonous. The bony scales of gars have been used for jewelry, arrowheads, and ornaments. Alligator gars are popular sport fishes in the southern United States and have been used in "fishing rodeos" and other tournaments. Florida gars have an attractive color pattern that makes them popular aquarium fishes.

CONSERVATION STATUS

Gars are not threatened or endangered. The gars that are thought of as harmful to game and commercial fishing receive little sympathy.

Spotted gar (Lepisosteus oculatus)

SPOTTED GAR
Lepisosteus oculatus

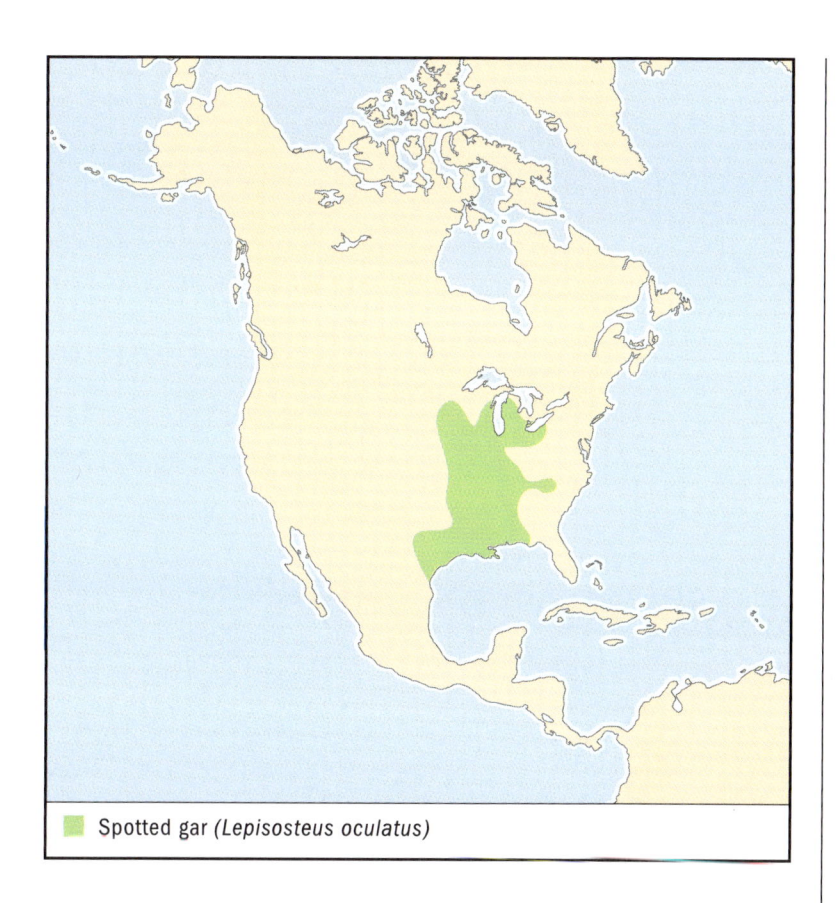

SPECIES ACCOUNT

Physical characteristics: Spotted gars can be as long as 44 inches (112 centimeters). They have many dark spots on the body, head, and fins. Adults have a series of small bony plates on the bottom. Females have been reported to have longer snouts than males.

Geographic range: Spotted gars live in North America from the southern shores of the Great Lakes in the north to the northern shores of the Gulf of Mexico and from northern Mexico to northwestern Florida.

Habitat: Spotted gars live in quiet, clear waters with much plant life. Some live in salty water along the Gulf of Mexico.

Diet: Spotted gars feed mainly on fishes but also may eat crabs and crayfishes.

Spotted gars can be as long as 44 inches (112 centimeters). (Garold W. Sneegas. Reproduced by permission.)

Behavior and reproduction: Spotted gars swim slowly unless they are hunting for prey. They spawn in shallow freshwater. The newly hatched larvae have an adhesive pad on the head that allows them to adhere, or stick, to the bottom or objects on the bottom.

Spotted gars and people: People fish for spotted gars and collect them for aquariums.

Conservation status: Spotted gars are not threatened or endangered. ∎

FOR MORE INFORMATION

Books:

Berra, Tim M. *Freshwater Fish Distribution.* San Diego, CA: Academic Press, 2001.

Gilbert, Carter Rowell, and James D. Williams. *National Audubon Society Field Guide to Fishes: North America.* New York: Knopf, 2002.

Ricciuti, Edward R. *Fish.* Woodbridge, CT: Blackbirch, 1993.

Schultz, Ken. *Ken Schultz's Field Guide to Freshwater Fish.* New York: Wiley, 2004.

Web sites:

Moore, Abby. "Spotted Gar." WhoZoo. http://www.whozoo.org/Intro2001/abbymoor/AEM_spottedgar.htm (accessed on August 30, 2004).

> **BOWFINS**
> **Amiiformes**
>
> **Class:** Actinopterygii
> **Order:** Amiiformes
> **Number of families:** 1 family

order
CHAPTER

phylum
class
subclass
● order
monotypic order
suborder
family

PHYSICAL CHARACTERISTICS

Bowfins have a long, curved dorsal (DOOR-suhl) fin, the one that runs along the top of the body. These fishes are called living fossils (FAH-suhls) because they have existed in the same form for more than one hundred million years. The skeleton is made up of both bone and cartilage (KAR-teh-lej), or tough, bendable supporting tissue. The tail fin is short and rounded. Bowfins have a large bony plate between their lower jawbones, and bony plates cover the skull.

GEOGRAPHIC RANGE

Bowfins live only in eastern North America.

HABITAT

Bowfins live in freshwater in lakes and slow-moving rivers that have a large amount of plant life.

DIET

Bowfins are predators (PREH-duh-ters) with huge appetites. Predators are animals that hunt and kill other animals for food.

BEHAVIOR AND REPRODUCTION

Bowfins are very strong. They can stand high temperatures and breathe air at the surface if necessary. They spawn, or release eggs, the female reproductive cells, in the springtime.

BOWFINS AND PEOPLE

Bowfins are not used for food or sport.

CONSERVATION STATUS

Bowfins are not threatened or endangered.

Bowfin (Amia calva)

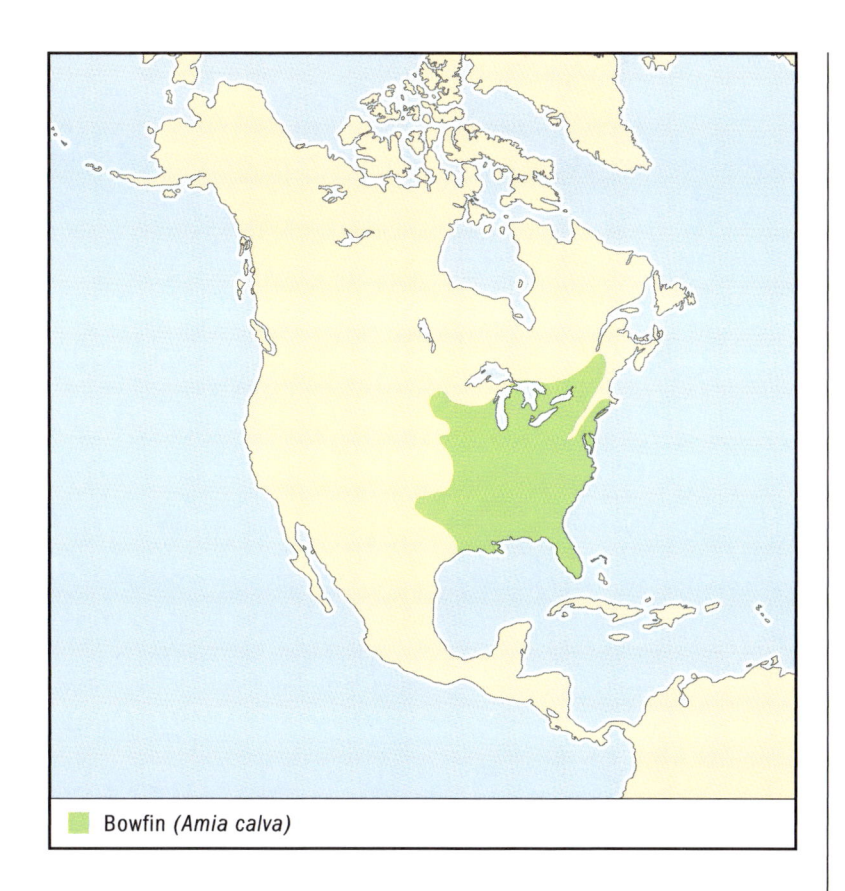

BOWFIN
Amia calva

SPECIES ACCOUNT

Physical characteristics: The long, curved dorsal fin of a bowfin has forty-two to fifty-three rays, or supporting rods, inside. Bowfins reach a length of about 35 inches (89 centimeters) but are usually shorter. The world-record bowfin weighed almost 22 pounds (10 kilograms), but the usual weight is 2 to 5 pounds (0.9 to 2.5 kilograms). Males are smaller than females. The long, thick body of bowfins is dark olive green on top, lighter on the sides, and cream to greenish yellow on the bottom. The tails of males have a dark spot rimmed in orange. Females also have a dark spot, but it is not rimmed in orange. Other names for bowfins are blackfish, cottonfish, cypress trout, freshwater dogfish, grindle, grinnell, marshfish, mudfish, scaled ling, and speckled cat.

Because they can breathe surface air, bowfins can live in water too polluted and stagnant for other fishes. (Illustration by Brian Cressman. Reproduced by permission.)

Geographic range: Bowfins live only in eastern North America. Their range includes the Saint Lawrence River system, which extends from the eastern part of the United States and Canada to the Great Lakes, and the Mississippi River system, which extends from Minnesota to Texas and Florida.

Habitat: Bowfins live in swampy, sluggish water in warm lakes and rivers that have a great deal of plant life. Because they can breathe surface air, bowfins can live in water too polluted and stagnant, or still and stale, for other fishes.

Diet: Bowfins are greedy predators. Young bowfins feed on small animals such as insect adults and larvae (LAR-vee), or insects at a young stage of life before becoming adults, and plankton, or microscopic plants and animals drifting in the water. Once bowfins grow to a length more than about 4 inches (10 centimeters), they eat other fishes. Adults also eat crayfish, shrimp, insect adults and larvae, frogs, and plants. Bowfins are sluggish and clumsy and stalk prey, or animals used for food, by scent as much as by sight. Bowfins capture their prey with sudden gulps of water.

Behavior and reproduction: Bowfins have gills, special organs for obtaining oxygen from water, but they also use their swim bladder, or an internal sac usually used for controlling position in the water, for breathing surface air. Male bowfins move into shallow waters of lakes and rivers to prepare a round nest hidden by plants or under a log. Once a female, and sometimes more than one, is attracted into the nest, she lays as many as sixty-four thousand eggs in four or five batches. The male then fertilizes (FUR-teh-lye-sez) the eggs, or deposits sperm, which unites with the eggs to begin development. The young hatch in eight to ten days and use a sticky organ on the tip of the snout, or nose area, to attach themselves to plants or other objects on the bottom. After seven to nine days, the young form a tight, sphere-shaped school that is guarded by the male for several weeks. After the school breaks up, bowfins move back into deep water.

Bowfins and people: Bowfins are often considered pest fishes because they compete for food with sport fishes. People seeking other fishes sometimes catch bowfins, but they usually let them go because bowfin does not taste good. Bowfins are important predators in some regions, because they control populations of unwanted fishes and keep populations of game fishes from becoming too large, which would stunt the growth of the individual fishes.

Conservation status: Bowfins are not threatened or endangered.

FOR MORE INFORMATION

Books:

Gilbert, Carter Rowell, and James D. Williams. *National Audubon Society Field Guide to Fishes: North America.* New York: Knopf, 2002.

Ricciuti, Edward R. *Fish.* Woodbridge, CT: Blackbirch, 1993.

Schultz, Ken. *Ken Schultz's Field Guide to Freshwater Fish.* New York: Wiley, 2004.

Web sites:

Paulson, Nicole, and Jay T. Hatch. "Bowfin *Amia calva* (Linnaeus, 1766)." Minnesota Department of Natural Resources' MinnAqua Aquatic Program. http://www.gen.umn.edu/research/fish/fishes/bowfin.html (accessed on September 2, 2004).

BONY TONGUES AND RELATIVES
Osteoglossiformes

Class: Actinopterygii
Order: Osteoglossiformes
Number of families: 6 families

order
CHAPTER

phylum
class
subclass
● order
monotypic order
suborder
family

PHYSICAL CHARACTERISTICS

Bony tongues are called that because most of their teeth are on the tongue and the roof of the mouth. They are odd-looking fishes. The head structure varies according to the way the different types of bony tongues feed. The tail fins of bony tongues have fewer rays, or supporting rods, than the tails of other fishes. Some bony tongues have long heads, and some have trunklike snouts, or nose areas. Bony tongues are 1.6 inches to 5 feet (4 centimeters to 1.5 meters) long.

GEOGRAPHIC RANGE

Bony tongues and their relatives live in tropical Africa; India, Indonesia, Malaysia, Thailand, Laos, Cambodia, and Vietnam; South America; New Guinea and Australia; and North America.

HABITAT

Many bony tongues and their relatives live near the surface of slow-moving rivers and lakes or ones that are stagnant, or still and stale. Some live at all depths in large rivers and lakes. Others prefer habitats with dense, or thick, plant life. Some bony tongues live in muddy water, sometimes in swift currents.

DIET

Bony tongues and their relatives eat plankton, that is, microscopic plants and animals drifting in the water; insect adults and larvae (LAR-vee), or young insects in the early stage of growth before becoming adults; crustaceans (krus-TAY-shuns), or shelled animals with jointed legs, such as shrimp; earthworms; snails; and other fish. Some even eat frogs and mice. Some bony tongues feed at the water surface, at middle depths, and others are bottom feeders. The bony tongues with long snouts find their prey in holes and crevices (KREH-vuh-suhz).

BEHAVIOR AND REPRODUCTION

Some bony tongues and their relatives are nocturnal (nahk-TER-nuhl), often hiding during the day in dense plant cover or under other kinds of cover and coming out to hunt in the evening. Others are active during the day, spending most of their time patrolling very close to the surface. During the summer, when the water surface becomes very hot, the fishes stay in deeper, cooler areas.

Most bony tongues and their relatives breed during the rainy season, usually the spring. The size of the eggs, or female reproductive cells, ranges from 0.07 inches (1.8 millimeters) to 0.6 inches (16 millimeters). Eggs number between a few hundred and more than one thousand, depending on the species, or type of fish. Some bony tongues spawn, or produce and release eggs, every few days, and others spawn once every several weeks. Some bony tongues are mouth brooders: the female or the male, depending on the species, takes the fertilized (FUR-teh-lyzed) eggs, the ones that have joined with sperm, or male reproductive cells, and have begun development, into its mouth and keeps them there until they hatch. In some species the males and, in others, the females guard and fan the nest, that is, use their fins to move water over the eggs to keep them clean and give them oxygen.

BONY TONGUES AND THEIR RELATIVES AND PEOPLE

Most bony tongues and their relatives, particularly the larger species, are important food fishes. Bony tongues are used in public and home aquariums.

CONSERVATION STATUS

The World Conservation Union (IUCN) lists one species of bony tongue, the Asian arowana or dragon fish, as Endangered, meaning that it faces very high risk of extinction in the wild.

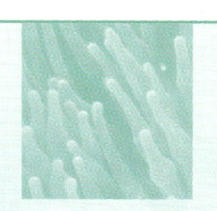

THE VARIETY OF BONY TONGUES

There are many species of bony tongues. Only one of them, the mooneye, lives in North America. The arapaima, which lives in the Amazon region of South America, is one of the largest freshwater fishes, weighing as much as 441 pounds (200 kilograms) and reaching a length of 15 feet (4.5 meters). The elephantfish is weakly electric. Other bony tongues are the arowana, the clown knifefish, and the elephantnose fish.

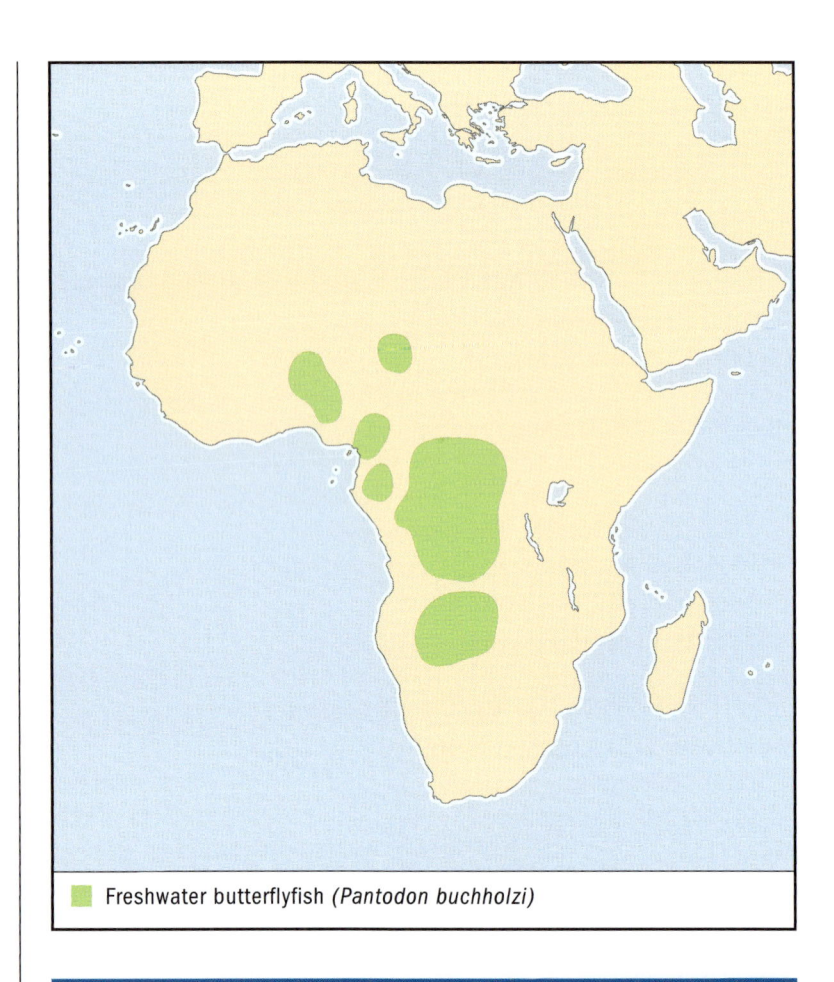

Freshwater butterflyfish (*Pantodon buchholzi*)

SPECIES ACCOUNT

FRESHWATER BUTTERFLYFISH
Pantodon buchholzi

Physical characteristics: Freshwater butterflyfishes (also called butterflyfishes) are called that because their large pectoral (PECK-ter-uhl) fins, the front set of paired fins, look like the wings of a butterfly. The pelvic fins, the rear set of paired fins, have long rays that are not covered with skin. The fanlike tail fin is quite large. Freshwater butterflyfishes reach a length of 3.9 inches (10 centimeters). The upper part of the body is olive green, and the bottom is silvery yellow with touches of red. Freshwater butterflyfishes are not related to the butterflyfishes that live in coral reefs.

Geographic range: Freshwater butterflyfishes live in central Africa.

Habitat: Freshwater butterflyfishes live near the surface in stagnant water.

Diet: Freshwater butterflyfishes eat crustaceans, insects, and small fishes.

Behavior and reproduction: Freshwater butterflyfishes can jump out of the water. They do this for feeding or to escape predators (PREH-duh-ters). They have been seen gliding 13 to 16 feet (4 to 5 meters), but scientists want more proof of this behavior, because they do not believe the muscles that support the pectoral fins are large enough for lengthy flight. These fishes can use the swim bladder, an internal sac that fishes use to control their position in the water, to breathe air.

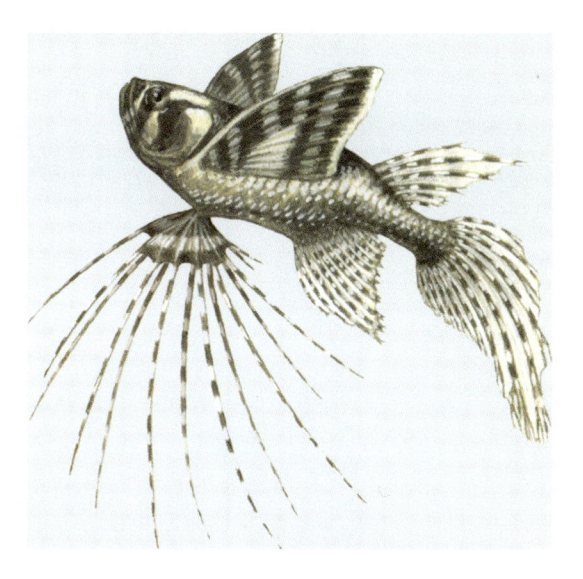

Freshwater butterflyfishes have a long spawning season. Each night they lay between eighty and two hundred buoyant eggs, or eggs that can float on the water. The embryos hatch after thirty-six hours. These fishes grow quickly, reaching their adult length within one year.

Freshwater butterflyfishes and people: Freshwater butterflyfishes are used in home aquariums.

Conservation status: Freshwater butterflyfishes are not threatened or endangered. ∎

Freshwater butterflyfishes got their name because their large pectoral fins look like the wings of a butterfly. (Illustration by Bruce Worden. Reproduced by permission.)

FOR MORE INFORMATION

Books:

Berra, Tim M. *Freshwater Fish Distribution.* San Diego, CA: Academic Press, 2001.

Ricciuti, Edward R. *Fish.* Woodbridge, CT: Blackbirch, 1993.

Web sites:

Butler, Rhett Ayers. "Mormyridae Family." Mongabay.com. http://fish.mongabay.com/mormyridae.htm (accessed on September 4, 2004).

Butler, Rhett Ayers. "Pantodontidae Family." http://fish.mongabay.com/pantodontidae.htm (accessed on September 4, 2004).

LADYFISHES AND TARPONS
Elopiformes

Class: Actinopterygii
Order: Elopiformes
Number of families: 2 families

order CHAPTER

PHYSICAL CHARACTERISTICS

Tarpons and ladyfishes are long, silver fishes with large upturned mouths, large eyes, and deeply forked tails. They have a long, bony plate between the lower jawbones.

GEOGRAPHIC RANGE

Tarpons and ladyfishes live all over the world.

HABITAT

Tarpons and ladyfishes live in seas that are tropical, meaning that the average annual temperature is more than 68°F (20°C), and subtropical, meaning that the average annual temperature is 55°F to 68°F (13°C to 20°C). They live near the coast, often in estuaries (EHS-chew-air-eez), or the wide parts of rivers where the river meets the sea. Both tarpons and ladyfishes can live in water with a small amount of salt.

DIET

Tarpons and ladyfishes eat fish and crustaceans (krus-TAY-shuns), or water-dwelling animals with shells and jointed legs, such as crabs.

BEHAVIOR AND REPRODUCTION

Tarpons and ladyfishes are predators (PREH-duh-ters), or animals that hunt and kill other animals for food, that feed mainly in open water at middle depths. Both have small, sandpaper-like teeth, and they swallow their catches whole. Tarpons and ladyfishes often live in large schools.

These fishes spawn, or produce and release eggs, offshore in salty ocean water. They produce large numbers of eggs that float on the surface. The eggs hatch into larvae (LAR-vee), or fishes in the early stage of development before they become adults, that have long, clear bodies and fanglike teeth. Larvae of tarpons and ladyfishes reach a length of 1 to 2 inches (2.5 to 5.0 centimeters) before they undergo metamorphosis (meh-tuh-MOR-pho-sus), or change form to become adults. Metamorphosis occurs as the larvae enter coastal waters.

LADYFISHES, TARPONS, AND PEOPLE

Ladyfishes and tarpons are popular for sport fishing. They are not usually eaten.

CONSERVATION STATUS

Tarpons and ladyfishes are not threatened or endangered.

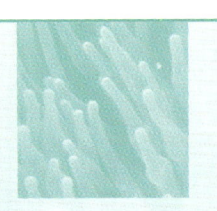

FISHING FOR TARPONS

Tarpons are known for their spectacular leaps from the water when hooked and for their willingness to enter shallow water and eat artificial (ahr-tuh-FIH-shul), or manmade, baits. Probably more than any other species, tarpons offer anglers in small boats an opportunity to pursue a large game fish. Tarpons are pursued by a large charter boat fleet in Florida.

Atlantic tarpon (*Megalops atlanticus*)

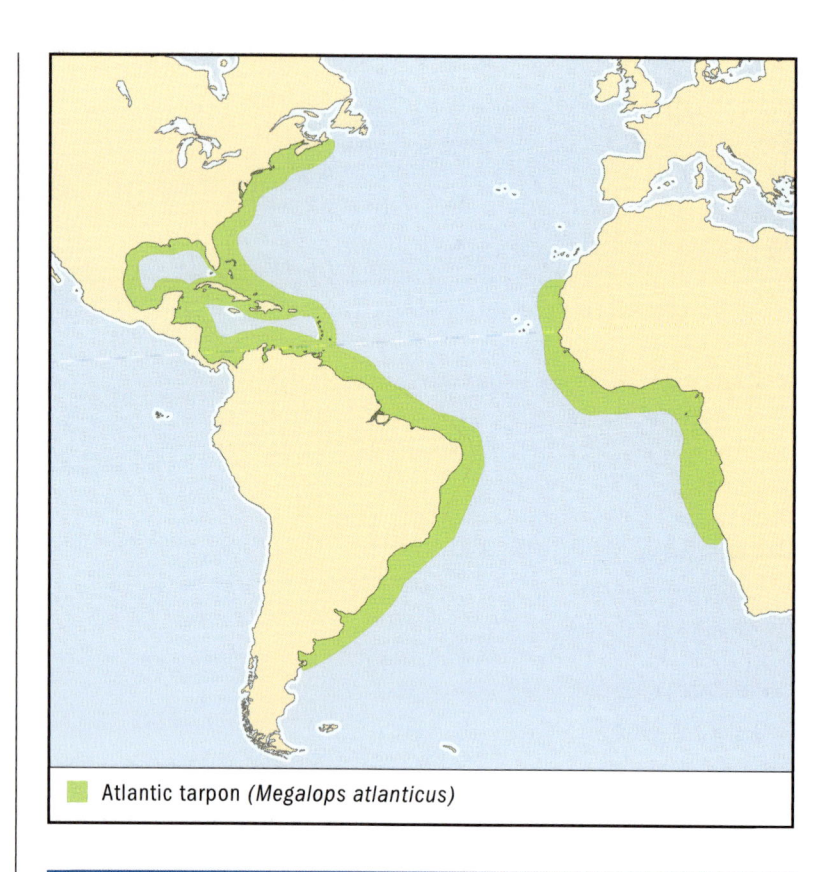

SPECIES ACCOUNT

ATLANTIC TARPON
Megalops atlanticus

Physical characteristics: Atlantic tarpons are bright silver all over, and the back is darker than the sides or belly. These fishes can weigh more than 220 pounds (100 kilograms) and can be more than 6.6 feet (2 meters) long, although the average weight of females is about 110 pounds (50 kilograms) and of males is only 66 pounds (30 kilograms). The body is long and looks flat when viewed from the top. The mouth is very large, and the lower jaw juts out beyond the upper jaw. The scales, or thin, hard plates that cover the skin, are large. The last ray, or supporting rod, of the dorsal (DOOR-suhl) fin, the fin that runs along the top of the body, is very long.

Geographic range: Atlantic tarpons live on both sides of the Atlantic Ocean.

Atlantic tarpons sometimes enter freshwater, traveling far up rivers and entering lakes far from the sea. (Illustration by Jacqueline Mahannah. Reproduced by permission.)

Habitat: Atlantic tarpons live in shallow coastal waters and estuaries. They sometimes enter freshwater, traveling far up rivers and entering lakes far from the sea. Young tarpons live in small, still pools with varying levels of salt and sometimes enter freshwater. Tarpons cannot survive water temperatures less than 55°F (12.8°C). Large numbers of tarpons die during severe cold fronts off Florida.

Diet: Young Atlantic tarpons eat microscopic crustaceans, fishes, shrimps, and mosquito larvae. Adults eat fishes, crabs, and shrimps.

Behavior and reproduction: Atlantic tarpons rise to the surface to breathe air using the swim bladder, an organ usually used for controlling their position in the water. This ability allows tarpons to live in water with small amounts of oxygen, such as hot, still, stale marshes.

Tarpons can live more than fifty years. By one year of age, tarpons are about 18 inches (46 centimeters) long. They start to reproduce at about ten years of age. Large tarpons caught in Florida are about fifteen to thirty-five years old.

In some areas Atlantic tarpons spawn all year; in others spawning takes place in spring and summer. In the western Atlantic, tarpons gather into schools at the beginning of the spawning season and then move together offshore. This behavior may be related to storms or tides. Scientists do not know how many eggs are released at each spawning, but they do know that the ovaries (OH-veh-rees), or egg-producing organs, can contain up to twenty million eggs, so the number released at one time probably is huge.

The larvae of Atlantic tarpons drift toward shore for about thirty days, reaching estuaries when they are about 1 inch (2.5 centimeters) long. During metamorphosis the fishes become smaller than the larvae, but they look like tiny versions of the giant tarpons they will become.

Atlantic tarpons and people: Atlantic tarpons are popular sport fishes, but tarpon is not considered a good food fish.

Conservation status: Atlantic tarpons are not threatened or endangered. ■

FOR MORE INFORMATION

Books:

Gilbert, Carter Rowell, and James D. Williams. *National Audubon Society Field Guide to Fishes: North America.* New York: Knopf, 2002.

Ricciuti, Edward R. *Fish.* Woodbridge, CT: Blackbirch, 1993.

Schultz, Ken. *Ken Schultz's Field Guide to Saltwater Fish.* New York: Wiley, 2004.

BONEFISHES AND RELATIVES
Albuliformes

Class: Actinopterygii
Order: Albuliformes
Number of families: 3 families

order
CHAPTER

phylum
class
subclass
● order
monotypic order
suborder
family

PHYSICAL CHARACTERISTICS

The feature shared by bonefishes and their relatives, the halosaurs (HAH-leh-sawrs) and the spiny eels, is an open canal, or a tube-shaped passage, in the lower jaw that is an extension of the series of pores and tiny tubes along each side of a fish's body used for sensing vibrations (vie-BRAY-shuns). Bonefishes have a long, thin body that tapers, or gets thinner, at each end. The relatives are eel shaped with a very long anal (AY-nuhl) fin, the fin that runs along the bottom of the body, and no tail fin. Most bonefishes and their relatives are 3.3 feet (1 meter) long or shorter.

GEOGRAPHIC RANGE

Bonefishes and their relatives live all over the world.

HABITAT

Bonefishes live in shallow tropical waters, or waters with an average annual temperature more than 68°F (20°C). Halosaurs and spiny eels live at the bottom of the ocean in water that is 3,281–9843 feet (1,000–3,000 meters) deep.

DIET

Bonefishes eat fishes and small invertebrates (in-VER-teh-brehts), or animals without backbones. Halosaurs and spiny eels eat bottom-dwelling animals, including worms; mollusks (MAH-lusks), or soft-bodied, usually hard-shelled animals such as clams; and crustaceans (krus-TAY-shuns), or water-dwelling animals without a backbone and that have jointed legs. Larger bonefishes also eat fish.

BEHAVIOR AND REPRODUCTION

Bonefishes live in small schools in sometimes extremely shallow water. They are ready to reproduce when they are about three and a half to four years old. The spawning areas of bonefishes, or the areas where they produce and release their eggs, are unknown. Bonefishes live for at least nineteen years. Spiny eel larvae (LAR-vee), or spiny eels in the early stage of development before becoming adults, can reach a length of 3.3 to 6.6 feet (1 to 2 meters).

BONEFISHES AND THEIR RELATIVES AND PEOPLE

Bonefishes are popular sport fishes. Bonefishes are not considered a food fish in Florida, and most are released when caught. Halosaurs and spiny eels are of no commercial value.

CONSERVATION STATUS

Bonefishes and their relatives are not threatened or endangered.

Bonefish (Albula vulpes)

BONEFISHES
Albula vulpes

SPECIES ACCOUNT

Physical characteristics: Bonefishes have a blue-green back with narrow, dark, horizontal lines. The sides are silver. The tail is deeply forked. The average weight of a bonefish is 2 to 5 pounds (0.9 to 2.3 kilograms), and its average length is 12 to 30 inches (30 to 76 centimeters), but these fishes can weigh as much as 10 pounds (4.5 kilograms) and be 41 inches (104 centimeters) long. The upper jaw juts out beyond the lower jaw and does not have teeth.

Geographic range: Bonefishes live all over the world.

Habitat: Bonefishes live in tropical shallow-water areas. They are most abundant at depths of less than 115 feet (35 meters) and often

Fishermen like to try to catch bonefishes because they are difficult to sneak up on, and they fight hard when they are hooked. (©Tom McHugh/Shedd Aquarium/Photo Researchers, Inc. Reproduced by permission.)

feed in water less than 3.3 feet (1 meter) deep. Bonefishes also can be found in shallow grass flats and sandy areas.

Diet: Bonefishes feed on a variety of small bottom-dwelling invertebrates and fishes. Feeding often takes place in shallow water, where bonefishes can be seen with their fins sticking out of the water as they seek food. As they forage (FOR-ihj), or search for food, bonefish schools frequently dig in the bottom and disturb the mud and sand.

Behavior and reproduction: Bonefishes are remarkable because they commonly go into water that is extremely shallow for the size of the fishes. They can use their swim bladder, an internal sac usually used to control position in the water, for breathing. These fishes usually swim in small schools of five to twenty, although they sometimes swim in large schools of one hundred or more. People fishing for bonefishes often find them by spotting their tails sticking out of the water as the fishes dig in the bottom for food.

Male bonefishes are ready to reproduce when they are about 15 inches (38 centimeters) long and about three and a half years old. Females are ready at a length of about 19 inches (48 centimeters) and about four years of age. Spawning, or the production and release of eggs, peaks from November to May. Females contain about 0.4 million to 1.7 million eggs, and the number of eggs increases with the weight of the fish. Spawning areas are not known. The long, clear larvae reach a length of about 3 inches (8 centimeters). The fishes shrink during metamorphosis (meh-tuh-MOR-pho-sus), or the changes in form that some animals make to become adults, and the fins appear during the shrinking. In about ten to twelve days, the fishes look like miniature adults. Bonefishes grow rapidly until the age of about six years, and then growth slows. Bonefishes live for at least nineteen years.

Bonefishes and people: In many areas bonefishes are important business for people who make their living running fishing trips, especially in the Florida Keys. Fishermen like to try for bonefishes because the fish are difficult to sneak up on and fight hard when they are hooked. People who fish for bonefishes in most areas need special boats that can enter shallow water with little or no noise. Bonefishes are not considered a food fish in Florida, and most bonefishes are released when caught. In some areas of the world, however, people do eat bonefish.

Conservation status: Bonefishes are not threatened or endangered. ■

FOR MORE INFORMATION

Books:

Gilbert, Carter Rowell, and James D. Williams. *National Audubon Society Field Guide to Fishes: North America.* New York: Knopf, 2002.

Nelson, Joseph S. *Fishes of the World.* New York: Wiley, 1994.

Ricciuti, Edward R. *Fish.* Woodbridge, CT: Blackbirch, 1993.

Schultz, Ken. *Ken Schultz's Field Guide to Saltwater Fish.* New York: Wiley, 2004.

Web sites:

Morey, Sean. "Biological Profiles: Bonefish." Ichthyology at the Florida Museum of Natural History. http://www.flmnh.ufl.edu/fish/Gallery/Descript/bonefish/bonefish.html (accessed on September 13, 2004).

EELS AND MORAYS
Anguilliformes

Class: Actinopterygii
Order: Anguilliformes
Number of families: 15 families

order
CHAPTER

PHYSICAL CHARACTERISTICS

Eels and morays have long, thin bodies. The color ranges from black or dark gray for eels and morays that live in the deep sea to rich colors and complex patterns in those that inhabit tropical reefs. The length ranges from about 4 inches (10 centimeters) to 13 feet (4 meters). Most eels and morays do not have scales, or thin, hard plates covering the skin. Eels and morays have as many as seven hundred vertebrae (ver-teh-BREE), the bones that make up the spinal column.

GEOGRAPHIC RANGE

Eels and morays live all over the world.

HABITAT

Eels and morays live in streams, lakes, estuaries (EHS-chew-air-eez), deep-sea waters, and coral reefs. Some spend most of their lives in freshwater and then move to the sea to spawn, or produce and release eggs. Some live in open water, but most live in small openings in coral reefs and rocks or burrow in the soft bottom.

DIET

Eels and morays eat almost any animal available, from insects to fishes. Some eels and morays feed on dead animals that lie on the ocean bottom, including whales.

BEHAVIOR AND REPRODUCTION

Eels and morays migrate (MY-grayt), or move from one place to another, for spawning. They swim by means of wavy side-to-side movements of the body and fins. They also can swim backward, which allows them to retreat rapidly into their burrows when threatened.

Eels and morays use external fertilization (FUR-teh-lih-zay-shun), or the joining of egg and sperm outside the body to start development. The eggs hatch into long (2 to 4 inches, or 5 to 10 centimeters), flat, clear, filmy larvae (LAR-vee) with sharp, fanglike teeth. The larvae can be found at varying depths, from the surface of the ocean to 1,640 feet (500 meters). The larvae undergo metamorphosis (meh-tuh-MOR-pho-sus), the changes in form that some animals make to become adults, in the open ocean six months to three years after hatching. The colder the water, the longer is the larval stage. Young eels and morays, or elvers, use ocean currents to reach the habitat they will live in as adults. They then grow and mature for as long as ten years.

A KNOTTY SITUATION

Some eels tear apart prey by tying themselves into knots to obtain leverage against the prey. The eel grabs, often by the head, a fish that is too large to swallow whole. Then the eel turns its tail back toward its body and forms a series of loops that make a knot similar to a square knot or a figure-eight knot. The knotting continues until the heads of the eel and the prey are against the knotted eel's body. The eel then pulls its own head through the knot and, with it, a mouthful of food. This action usually rips the head off the prey fish. The eel then bites onto another section of the prey, and the process continues.

EELS, MORAYS, AND PEOPLE

Freshwater eels are valued as food. Some morays and conger eels are popular in public and home aquariums.

CONSERVATION STATUS

Eels and morays are not threatened or endangered.

American eel (Anguilla rostrata) ■

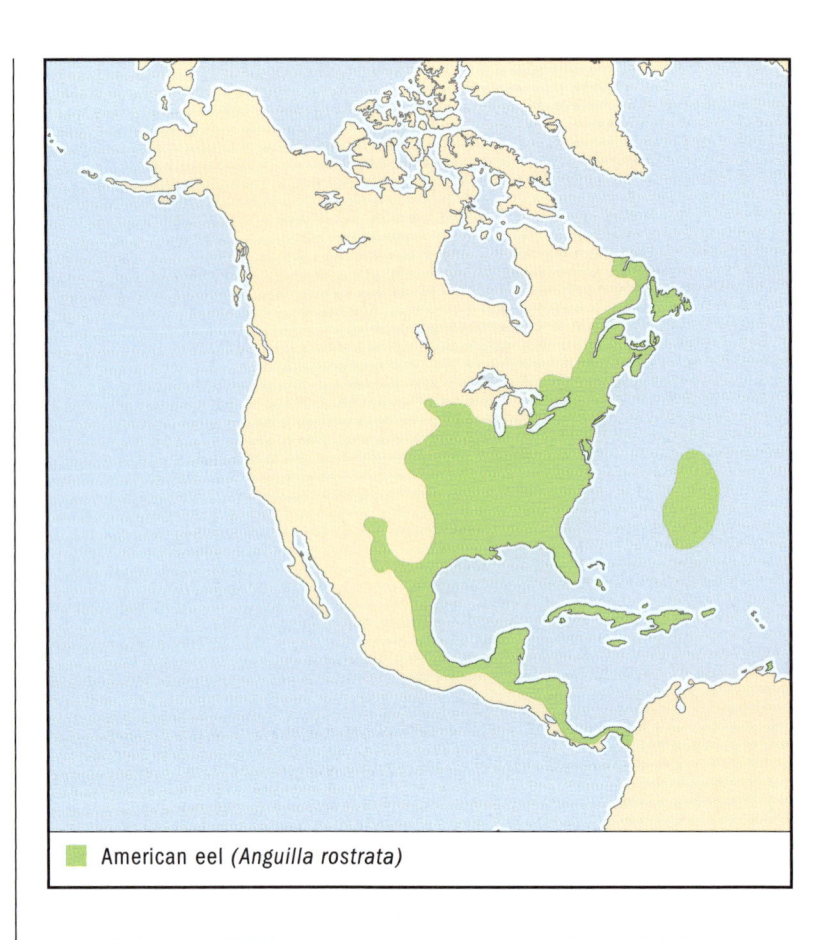

SPECIES ACCOUNTS

AMERICAN EEL
Anguilla rostrata

Physical characteristics: American eels have snakelike bodies covered with thick slime. Males grow to 5 feet (1.5 meters) and females to 4 feet (1.2 meters). These eels weigh as much as 16 pounds (7 kilograms). American eels have 103 to 111 vertebrae.

Geographic range: American eels live in the western Atlantic Ocean, the Great Lakes, the Mississippi River, and the Gulf of Mexico.

Habitat: At sea American eels live in deep water. In freshwater they live in streams with constant flow.

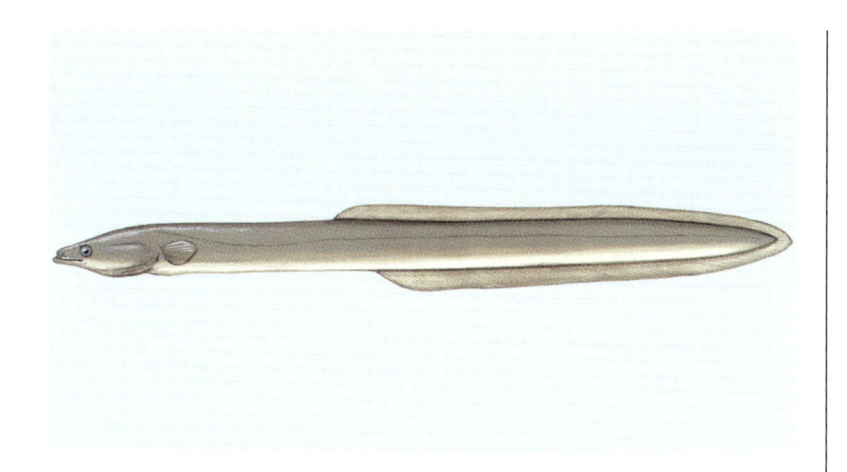

American eels have snakelike bodies covered with thick slime. (Illustration by Barbara Duperron. Reproduced by permission.)

Diet: The larvae of American eels eat plankton, which are microscopic plants and animals drifting in the water. Elvers eat water insects; small crustaceans (krus-TAY-shuns), or water-dwelling animals that have jointed legs and a hard shell but no backbone; and dead fish. Adults eat insects, crustaceans, clams, worms, fish, frogs, toads, and dead animals.

Behavior and reproduction: While in freshwater, American eels hide during the day. At night they swim near the bottom in search of food. Not much is known about reproduction among American eels. During autumn adults migrate to the western part of the Atlantic Ocean for spawning, which takes place in January. The females lay up to four million buoyant eggs, or eggs that can float on the water, and then die. After fertilizing (FUR-teh-lye-zing) the eggs, the males also die. The larvae drift toward coastal waters for as long as eighteen months. They then transform into elvers. American eels spend most of their lives, as long as twenty years, in freshwater before returning to the sea for spawning.

American eels and people: American eels are consumed as food.

Conservation status: American eels are not threatened or endangered.

Green moray (Gymnothorax funebris)

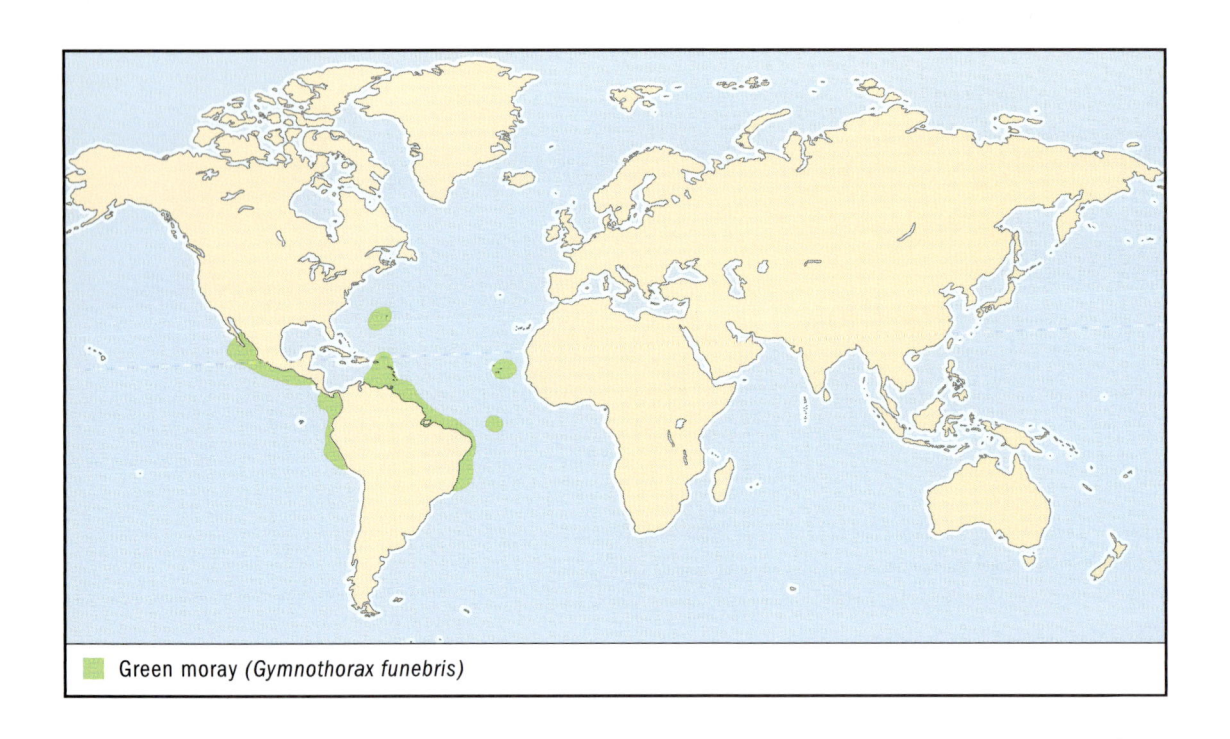

GREEN MORAY
Gymnothorax funebris

Physical characteristics: Green morays grow to 8 feet (2.4 meters) in length and weigh as much as 64 pounds (29 kilograms). Green morays are green to dark grayish green all over. The green color comes from the combination of yellow slime on dark blue skin.

Geographic range: Green morays live throughout the western and eastern Atlantic and the eastern Pacific Oceans.

Habitat: Green morays live at the bottom along rocky shorelines, in reefs, and among mangrove trees in waters shallower than about 98 feet (30 meters).

Diet: Green morays eat fishes and bottom-dwelling crustaceans.

Behavior and reproduction: Green morays attach themselves to coral or rocks or bury themselves in the bottom and allow the front half of their bodies to move with the current, keeping their mouths

Green morays grow to 8 feet (2.4 meters) in length and weigh as much as 64 pounds (29 kilograms). (©J.W. Mowbray, 1987/The National Audubon Society Collection/Photo Researchers, Inc. Reproduced by permission.)

open to catch any food animal that comes near. Green morays are cleaned by small fishes. Little is known about reproduction among green morays except that they use external fertilization and have clear, fanged larvae.

Green morays and people: Green morays are consumed as food. Large ones can cause food poisoning, however.

Conservation status: Green morays are not threatened or endangered.

Slender giant moray (*Strophidon sathete*)

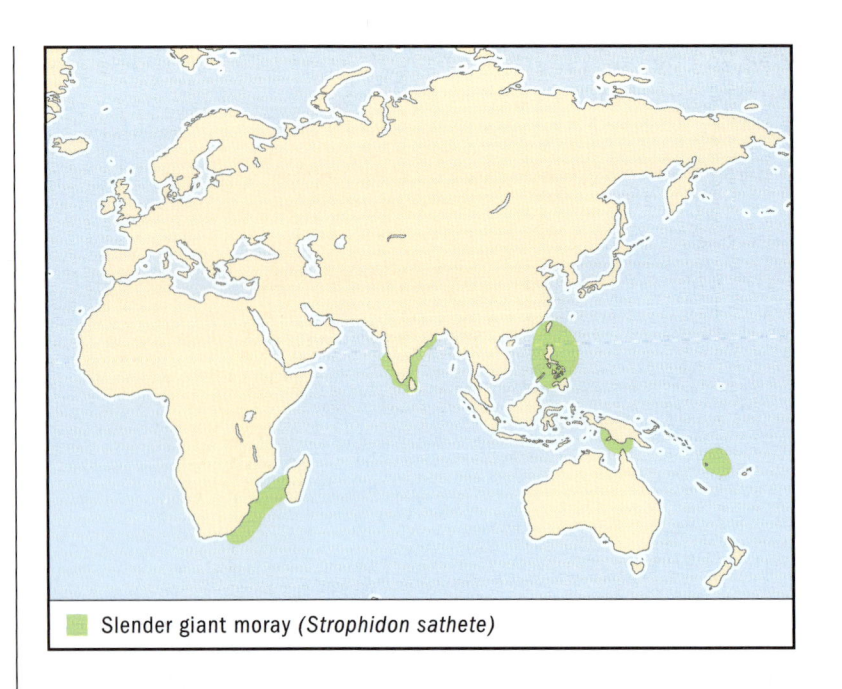

SLENDER GIANT MORAY
Strophidon sathete

Physical characteristics: Slender giant morays are the longest of the eels and morays, reaching 13 feet (4 meters). These morays are brownish gray on top and paler on the bottom.

Geographic range: Slender giant morays live in the western Pacific and Indian Oceans.

Habitat: Slender giant morays live on the muddy bottoms of coastal waters, including bays and rivers.

Diet: Slender giant morays eat crustaceans and fishes.

Behavior and reproduction: The most interesting habit of slender giant morays is that they stand straight up and down from their burrows with the head beneath the surface, rising and falling with the tide. Almost nothing is known about their reproduction.

Slender giant morays and people: Slender giant moray is a food fish.

Conservation status: Slender giant morays are not threatened or endangered. ◼

FOR MORE INFORMATION

Books:

Gilbert, Carter Rowell, and James D. Williams. *National Audubon Society Field Guide to Fishes: North America.* New York: Knopf, 2002.

Schultz, Ken. *Ken Schultz's Field Guide to Freshwater Fish.* New York: Wiley, 2004.

Schultz, Ken. *Ken Schultz's Field Guide to Saltwater Fish.* New York: Wiley, 2004.

Web sites:

"American Eel." Chesapeake Bay Program. http://www.chesapeakebay.net/info/american_eel.cfm (accessed on September 14, 2004).

"Fish in Focus: Green Moray *Gymnothorax prasinus* (Richardson, 1848)." Australian Museum Fish Site. http://www.amonline.net.au/fishes/students/focus/gymno.htm (accessed on September 14, 2004).

Slender giant morays are the longest of the eels and morays. (Illustration by Barbara Duperron. Reproduced by permission.)

> **SWALLOWERS AND GULPERS**
> **Saccopharyngiformes**
>
> **Class:** Actinopterygii
> **Order:** Saccopharyngiformes
> **Number of families:** 4 families
>
> **order CHAPTER**

phylum
class
subclass
● order
monotypic order
suborder
family

PHYSICAL CHARACTERISTICS

Swallowers and gulpers are among the most unusual fishes. They have no scales, or the thin, hard plates that cover the skin of many fishes. They also have no pelvic fins, the rear pair, corresponding to the rear legs of four-footed animals, and they have very long dorsal (DOOR-suhl) and anal (AY-nuhl) fins, the single fins that run along the top and the bottom of the body. Swallowers and gulpers are flabby to the touch and probably are poor swimmers. The mouth is quite large to enormous, and the throat and stomach can stretch to allow for the capture of large prey, or animals hunted and caught for food.

Except for a huge head and mouth, the bodies of these fishes are very long and thin. The body color varies from patchy light brown to solid black. Some of these fishes have thin white lines of unknown function that extend from the head to the tail, along the upper body. Some swallowers and gulpers have glowing bulbs at the very tip of a stringy tail, which can be half or more of the overall length of the fish. The rest of the body is no longer than 20 inches (50 centimeters).

GEOGRAPHIC RANGE

Swallowers and gulpers live in the Atlantic, Pacific, and Indian Oceans.

HABITAT

Swallowers and gulpers live in very deep, open water at depths greater than 3,281 feet (1,000 meters). Larvae (LAR-vee), a form of these fishes in the early stage of growth before becoming adults, and the young live in shallower waters.

DIET

Swallowers and gulpers are poor swimmers. It is thought that they draw prey close to them by means of glowing lures on their tails and then quickly open their mouths to suck in food. Some swallowers and gulpers eat only other fishes, but others eat fish and invertebrates (in-VER-teh-brehts), or animals without backbones. One type lures shrimps with a scent (SENT) released from glands around its mouth. When the shrimp comes close enough, the swallower bites it with a hollow fang that injects venom, or poison. The fish then swallows the dead or dying shrimp whole.

BEHAVIOR AND REPRODUCTION

Because of the extreme depths at which swallowers and gulpers live, little is known about their behavior. They have thin, ribbonlike larvae that are transparent, or see-through. In some species, or types, males and females look the same; in others they look different. It is widely believed that male gulpers locate their mates by following scent trails released by the females and that both males and females die after mating.

SWALLOWERS, GULPERS, AND PEOPLE

Swallowers and gulpers are objects of curiosity because of their strange appearance.

CONSERVATION STATUS

Swallowers and gulpers are not threatened or endangered.

Gulper eel (Saccopharynx ampullaceus)

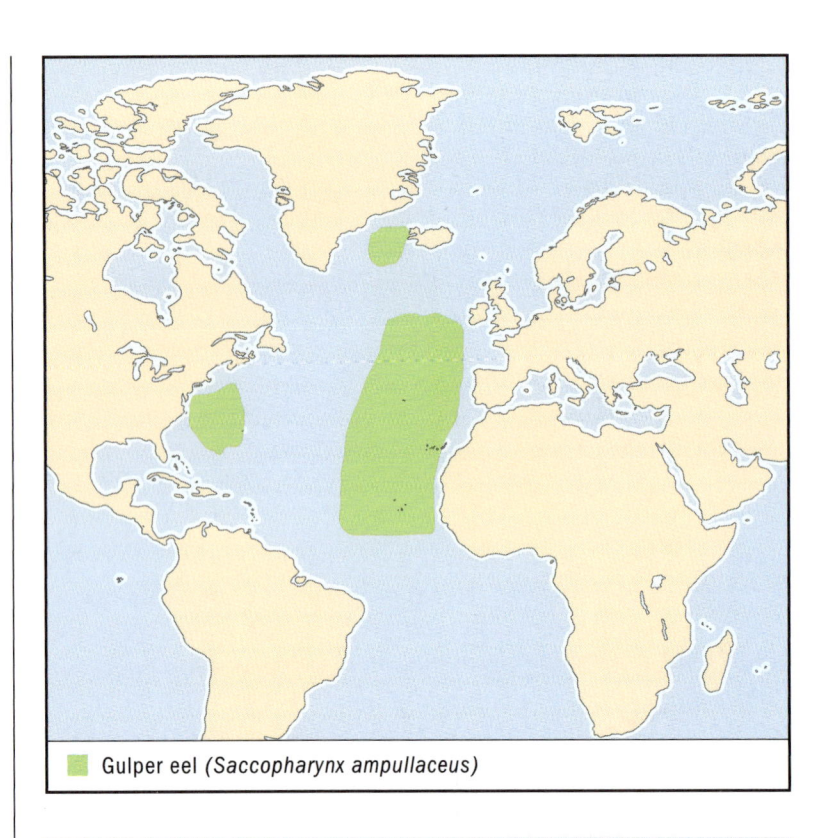

SPECIES ACCOUNTS

GULPER EEL
Saccopharynx ampullaceus

Physical characteristics: Gulper eels have a short, flabby body, with a long stomach region. They have tiny eyes that function as light detectors. They also have a huge mouth with many slightly curved teeth. The tail is extremely long, about three fourths of the total body length, and ends in a long string with a glowing bulb at the end. The body has no scales. The largest gulper eel found was 5.2 feet (1.6 meters) long, although most of that length was the long whiplike tail.

Geographic range: Gulper eels live in the northern part of the Atlantic Ocean.

Habitat: Gulper eels live in the deep, open water of the ocean. Only young gulper eels have been captured at depths of less than 2,625 feet (800 meters). It is believed that adults typically live deeper than 6,562 feet (2,000 meters).

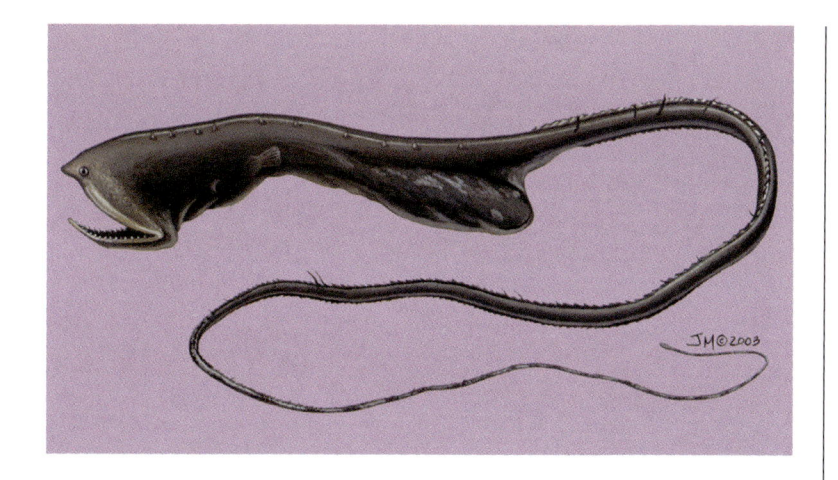

Gulper eels eat other fishes. The stomach can stretch quite far, allowing the eel to eat very large prey. (Illustration by Jacqueline Mahannah. Reproduced by permission.)

Diet: Gulper eels eat other fishes. The stomach can stretch quite far, allowing the eel to eat very large prey.

Behavior and reproduction: Because gulper eels live in such deep water, scientists can only guess at their behavior. Because of the weak skeleton and body muscles, gulper eels probably are very poor swimmers. They are believed to lure prey within range by means of the glowing bulb on the end of the tail. The eel may hang the bulb in the water near its mouth. The jaw muscles are the only well-developed muscles and probably allow the gulper eel to suck its prey into the large mouth by quickly opening the jaws. Males may locate females by tracking scent trails released by the females. Like other eels, gulpers are believed to die after reproducing. And like those of other eels, gulper eel larvae are ribbonlike and clear.

Gulper eels and people: The bizarre appearance of gulper eels fascinates people.

Conservation status: Gulper eels are not threatened or endangered.

FOR MORE INFORMATION

Books:

Hoyt, Erich. *Creatures of the Deep.* Richmond Hill, Ontario, Canada: Firefly Books, 2001.

Nelson, Joseph S. *Fishes of the World.* 3rd ed. New York: Wiley, 1994.

Web sites:

"Gulper Eel." Enhanced Learning. http://www.enchantedlearning.com/subjects/fish/printouts/Gulpereelprintout.shtml (accessed on September 7, 2004).

"Gulper Eel: *Eurypharynx pelecanoides* Vaillant, 1882." Australian Museum Fish Site. http://www.amonline.net.au/fishes/fishfacts/fish/epelecan.htm (accessed on September 7, 2004).

"Monsters of the Deep: Gulper Eel." Sea and Sky. http://www.seasky.org/monsters/sea7a1j.html (accessed on September 7, 2004).

HERRINGS
Clupeiformes

Class: Actinopterygii
Order: Clupeiformes
Number of families: 5 families

order CHAPTER

PHYSICAL CHARACTERISTICS

The herring group includes herrings, menhadens (men-HAY-dens), pilchards (PILL-churds), sardines, shads, sprats, and anchovies. Herrings are small and have streamlined bodies that aid them in swimming fast in open water. The smallest herring is the Sanaga pygmy herring, with a length of only about three-fourths inch (2.1 centimeters). Male wolf herrings are the largest herring, with an average length of 39 inches (100 centimeters). Herrings have dark shading on the back and bright silvery sides. Except for the head, the body is completely covered in large scales. Only one type of herring has a lateral (LAT-uhr-uhl) line, the series of pores and tiny tubes along each side of a fish's body used for sensing vibrations. Many herrings have a row of spiny, ridged scales along the midline of the belly.

GEOGRAPHIC RANGE

Herrings live all over the world.

HABITAT

Nearly all herrings live in open water. Four-fifths of all species live in saltwater habitats ranging from near-shore zones to nearly 100 miles (161 kilometers) offshore. Many herrings swim near the surface at night but move to deeper waters during the day. Some herrings live in inland waters or move inland to spawn, or release eggs. These species live in bays; estuaries (EHS-chew-air-eez), which is where a river meets the sea; marshes; rivers; and freshwater streams. Landlocked populations have formed as

phylum
class
subclass
● order
monotypic order
suborder
family

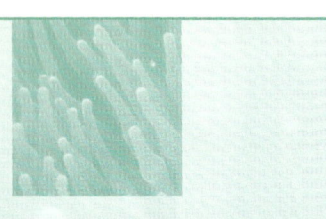

PEARL ESSENCE

Herring scales are used to give pearly lipstick and nail polish their shimmer. Researchers have not been able to make a synthetic substance that gives the same effect.

the fishes have moved into lakes or rivers and become trapped between dams.

DIET

Most herrings eat plankton, or microscopic (MY-kro-SKA-pihk) plants and animals drifting in the water that are too small to be seen with the eye. Herrings prefer plankton that consists of crustaceans (krus-TAY-shuns), or water-dwelling animals that have jointed legs and a hard shell but no backbone, and the larvae (LAR-vee) of larger crustaceans and fishes. Larvae are the early stage of an animal that must change form before becoming an adult. Some herrings visually locate and target food particles.

BEHAVIOR AND REPRODUCTION

Herrings are best known for forming large schools. Being in large groups helps the fish swim efficiently and discourages predators (PREH-duh-terz) or other fish that may hunt them for food. Herrings also form smaller, less-organized groups called shoals, particularly during spawning season. Some herrings migrate, or travel, from the ocean to streams and rivers for spawning. Many herrings make daily migrations in the water, staying deep during the day and moving to shallows at night.

Herrings produce large numbers of offspring. Some species spawn once a year, and others spawn several times a year. Most herrings spawn in shoals by releasing large numbers of small eggs that float near the surface. After fertilization (FUR-teh-lih-zay-shun), or being united with a male's sperm, the eggs and larvae drift in the current as they develop. Some herrings produce eggs that sink to the bottom, where they stick to rocks, gravel, or sand until they hatch. After hatching, larvae move to open water.

HERRINGS AND PEOPLE

Herrings are some of the most economically important fishes in the world's oceans. They have been used throughout human history, primarily for food but also as a source of oil, plant fertilizer, and animal feed. Herring fishing was one of the earliest occupations of coastal peoples.

That's a Lot of Fish!
In the ocean, schools of herring can extend for miles (kilometers) and contain four billion fish.

CONSERVATION STATUS

The World Conservation Union (IUCN) lists two herrings as Endangered, or facing very high risk of extinction in the wild in the near future, and two as Vulnerable, or facing high risk of extinction in the wild.

Bay anchovy (Anchoa mitchilli)

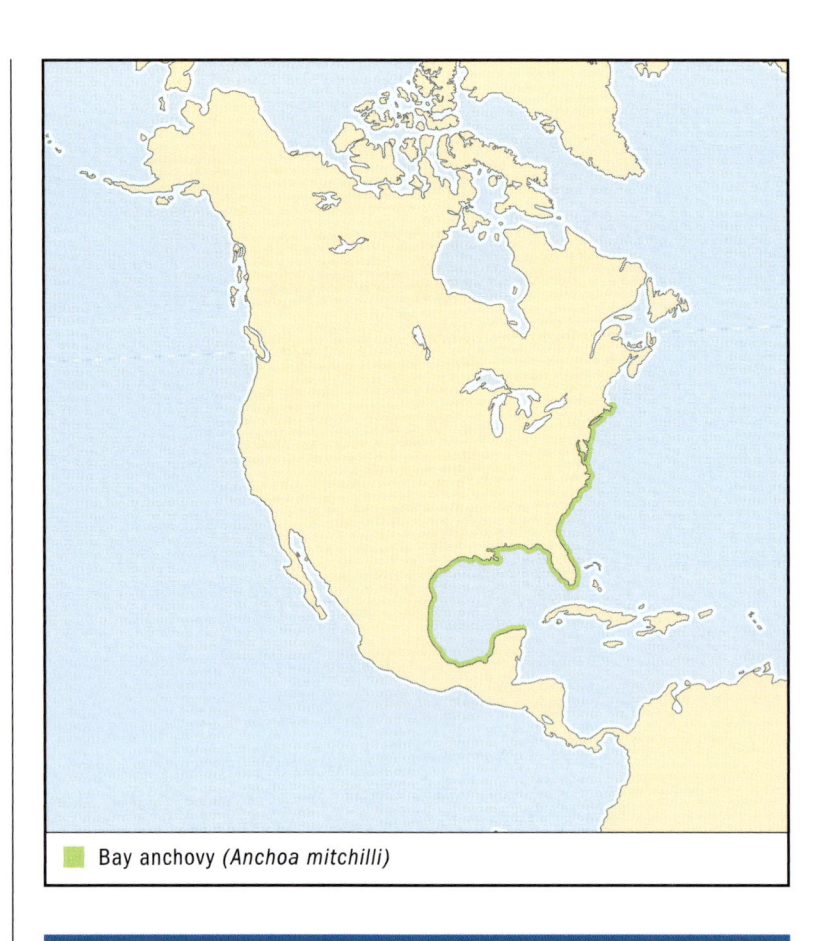

SPECIES ACCOUNT

BAY ANCHOVY
Anchoa mitchilli

Physical characteristics: Bay anchovies are typically 3 to 4 inches (7.6 to 10.2 centimeters) in total length. They are nearly transparent and greenish and have a silvery band along the sides of the body. The snout overhangs the mouth, and the lower jawbone extends well beyond the eye.

Geographic range: Bay anchovies live along the Atlantic coast of North America from Maine to the Florida Keys and westward around the Gulf of Mexico south to the Yucatán peninsula.

Habitat: Bay anchovies live along the coast in estuaries, bays, and marshes and near sandy beaches. They usually live over muddy bottoms

Bay anchovies are used as bait and for making anchovy paste. They are important in the diet of fishes caught by commercial fishermen. (Illlustration by Jonathan Higgins. Reproduced by permission.)

or among plants. Bay anchovies can handle a wide range of saltiness but are often found in water that is slightly less salty than seawater.

Diet: Bay anchovies usually eat plankton, mostly crustaceans, but sometimes they eat small fishes, snails and slugs, and crustaceans called isopods (EYE-suh-pods).

Behavior and reproduction: Bay anchovies swim in schools. They spend the winter in deep waters and migrate to shallow shores and wetlands for spawning in late spring to early summer. Spawning takes place during the evening hours. Females release the eggs into the water, where they are fertilized by males. The eggs float near the surface for approximately twenty-four hours after fertilization and then hatch. Bay anchovies mature to adults in two and one-half months.

Bay anchovies and people: Bay anchovies are used as bait and for making anchovy paste. They are important in the diet of fishes caught by commercial fishermen.

Conservation status: Bay anchovies are not threatened or endangered.

FOR MORE INFORMATION

Books:

Berra, Tim M. *Freshwater Fish Distribution.* San Diego, CA: Academic Press, 2001.

Gilbert, Carter Rowell, and James D. Williams. *National Audubon Society Field Guide to Fishes: North America.* New York: Knopf, 2002.

Niesen, Thomas M. *The Marine Biology Coloring Book.* 2nd ed. New York: HarperResource, 2000.

Ricciuti, Edward R. *Fish.* Woodbridge, CT: Blackbirch, 1993.

Schultz, Ken. *Ken Schultz's Field Guide to Freshwater Fish.* New York: Wiley, 2004.

Schultz, Ken. *Ken Schultz's Field Guide to Saltwater Fish.* New York: Wiley, 2004.

Web sites:

"Category: Anchovies and Herrings." All Science Fair Projects. http://www.all-science-fair-projects.com/science_fair_projects_encyclopedia/Category:Anchovies_and_herrings (accessed on September 23, 2004).

"FishFAQ." Northeast Fisheries Science Center. http://www.nefsc.noaa.gov/faq (accessed on September 23, 2004).

order CHAPTER

MILKFISH AND RELATIVES
Gonorynchiformes

Class: Actinopterygii
Order: Gonorynchiformes
Number of families: 3 families

phylum
class
subclass
● order
monotypic order
suborder
family

PHYSICAL CHARACTERISTICS

Milkfish are large, silver, and tapered at the ends. Of their relatives, sandfish are slender and ribbon shaped; African mudfish are tubular; and *Kneria wittei*, which has no common name, are tiny and minnow-like. The length of these fishes ranges from about three-fourths inch (1.8 centimeters) to 5 feet (1.5 meters).

GEOGRAPHIC RANGE

Milkfish and their relatives live all over the world except Antarctica.

HABITAT

Milkfish and their relatives live in saltwater and freshwater. Milkfish live in the open ocean but breed near the shore. Sandfish live in sandy areas along the coast or on the ocean bottom. *Kneria wittei* live in ponds or fast-moving streams or waterfalls. African mudfish live in quiet, shaded waters and can breathe air.

DIET

Milkfish and their relatives eat crustaceans (krus-TAY-shuns), water-dwelling animals that have jointed legs and a hard shell but no backbone; plankton, microscopic plants and animals drifting in bodies of water; plants; and algae (AL-jee), which are tiny plantlike growths that live in water and have no true roots, stems, or leaves.

BEHAVIOR AND REPRODUCTION

Milkfish form schools, both when they are young and as adults. Sandfish and African mudfish are solitary. All milkfish and their relatives use external fertilization (FUR-teh-lih-zay-shun), meaning eggs are released by the female, join with the male's sperm, and hatch outside the body.

MILKFISH AND THEIR RELATIVES AND PEOPLE

The milkfish is used for food.

CONSERVATION STATUS

Milkfish and their relatives are not threatened or endangered.

Milkfish (*Chanos chanos*)

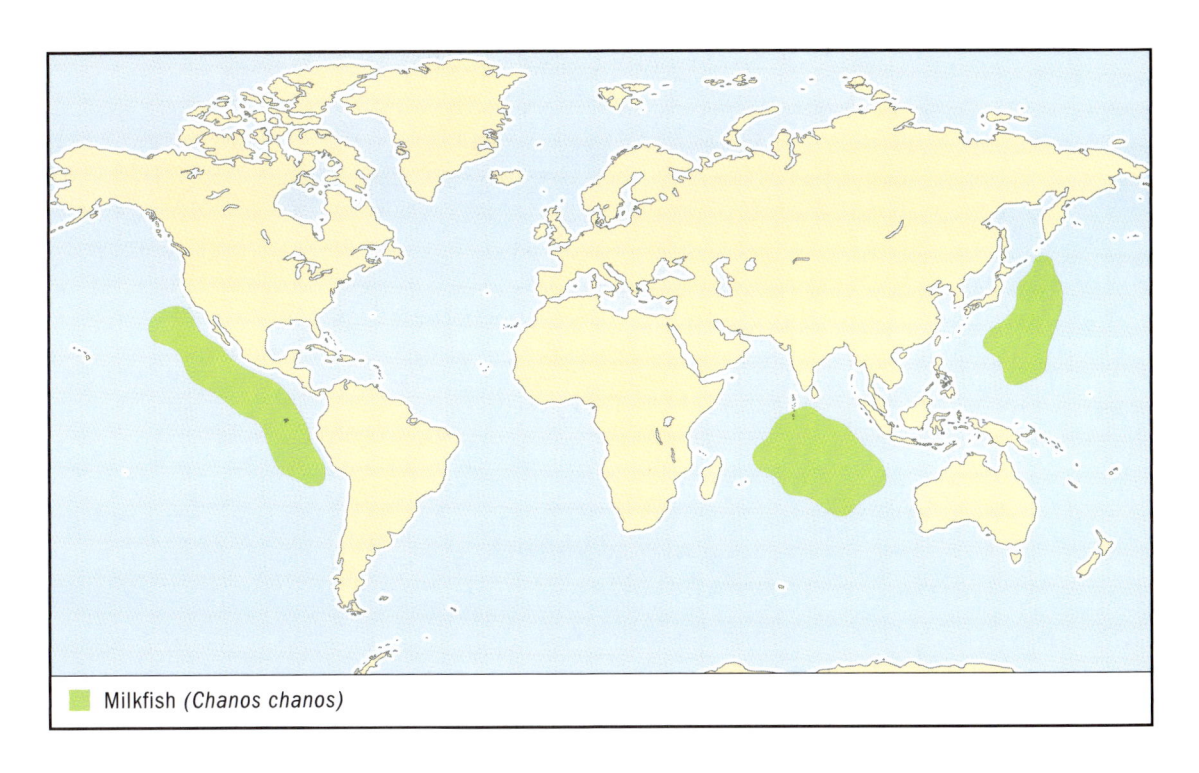

MILKFISH
Chanos chanos

SPECIES ACCOUNT

Physical characteristics: Milkfish can reach a length of about 6 feet (1.8 meters) but usually are about 5 feet (1.5 meters) long. Adults are silvery and have a forked tail, large eyes, and a pointed snout. They have a special pouch in the digestive tract for sifting plankton. The jaws are toothless. The dorsal (DOOR-suhl) fin, the one along the midline of the back, has thirteen to seventeen rays, or supporting rods; the anal (AY-nuhl) fin, the one along the midline of the belly, has six to eight rays; the pectoral (PECK-ter-uhl) fins, the front pair, have fifteen to seventeen rays; and the pelvic fins, the rear pair, have ten or eleven rays. Four or five rays support the gill covering on each side behind the head.

Geographic range: Milkfish live throughout the Indian and Pacific oceans.

Habitat: Adult milkfish live in the open ocean. Larvae (LAR-vee), or the early stage that must change form before becoming an adult,

Milkfish is one of the most important food fishes in Indonesia, the Philippines, and Taiwan. (Illustration by Patricia Ferrer. Reproduced by permission.)

live in inland ponds that have a salt content slightly less than that of seawater.

Diet: Milkfish larvae eat animal plankton. Adults eat bacteria, algae, small bottom-dwelling invertebrates (in-VER-teh-brehts), which are animals without backbones, and sometimes eat free-floating fish eggs and larvae.

Behavior and reproduction: Milkfish, both young and adults, are schooling fishes. They breed near the shore and release their eggs into open water. When the larvae are about three-eighths inch (1 centimeter) long, they enter water that has a slightly lower salt content than seawater. The young adults return to the sea.

Milkfish and people: Milkfish is one of the most important food fishes in Indonesia, the Philippines, and Taiwan. It is commercially farmed in these areas. The young are caught close to shore and then raised in coastal ponds. Milkfish also is fished extensively throughout its range. Fishermen use cormorants with rings around the birds' necks to catch the fish. The rings prevent the birds from fully swallowing the fish.

Conservation status: Milkfish are not threatened nor endangered.

FOR MORE INFORMATION

Books:

Ricciuti, Edward R. *Fish.* Woodbridge, CT: Blackbirch, 1993.

Schultz, Ken. *Ken Schultz's Field Guide to Saltwater Fish.* New York: Wiley, 2004.

Web sites:

"Milkfish." All Science Fair Projects. http://www.all-science-fair-projects.com/science_fair_projects_encyclopedia/Milkfish (accessed on September 23, 2004).

"Milkfish." SEAFDEC Aquaculture Department. http://www.seafdec.org.ph/home.html (accessed on September 24, 2004).

MINNOWS, CARPS, AND RELATIVES
Cypriniformes

Class: Actinopterygii
Order: Cypriniformes
Number of families: 5 families

order
CHAPTER

PHYSICAL CHARACTERISTICS

Minnows, carps, and loaches and their relatives have an upper jaw that can extend forward and a toothless mouth. The head is almost always scaleless. Some species have one to three rows of teeth in the throat with never more than eight teeth in any one row. Other species have more of these teeth but in only one row.

GEOGRAPHIC RANGE

Minnows, carps, and loaches and their relatives live in Europe, Asia, Africa, and North America.

HABITAT

Almost all carps, minnows, and loaches and their relatives live in freshwater.

DIET

Carps, minnows, and loaches and their relatives eat plants, insects, other fishes, plankton, and algae. Algae (AL-jee) are tiny plantlike growths that live in water and have no true roots, stems, or leaves. Plankton is made up of microscopic plants and animals drifting in the water and too small to be seen with the eye.

BEHAVIOR AND REPRODUCTION

When threatened by a predator, or an animal that hunts and kills other animals for food, some carps and minnows release a substance that causes the fishes nearby to scatter and hide. This reaction signals the rest of the group to avoid the predator. Some species of loaches use their mouths to attach themselves to the bottom and avoid being swept away by currents. Carps and minnows spawn, or release eggs, mostly in spring and summer. Many species spawn only once in a breeding season, but some spawn more than once.

MINNOW, CARPS, AND LOACHES AND THEIR RELATIVES AND PEOPLE

Carps and minnows are an important food fish. The zebrafish is one of the most important model fishes in genetics and medical research. Many carps and minnows, such as goldfish, are used in aquariums. Many loaches and their relatives are sold in pet shops because they are useful for keeping aquariums clean of algae.

CONSERVATION STATUS

The World Conservation Union (IUCN) lists seventeen species of minnows, carps, and loaches and their relatives as Extinct, one as Extinct in the Wild, forty-two as Critically Endangered; thirty-seven as Endangered; 116 as Vulnerable; seven as Lower Risk/Conservation Dependent; and thirty as Lower Risk/Near Threatened. Extinct means no longer alive at all; Extinct in the Wild means no longer alive except in captivity or through the aid of humans. Critically Endangered means facing extremely high risk of extinction in the wild in the near future. Endangered means facing very high risk of extinction in the wild in the near future. Vulnerable means facing high risk of extinction in the wild. Lower Risk/Near Threatened means at risk of becoming threatened with extinction in the future. Lower Risk/Conservation Dependent means that if the conservation program were to end, the animal would be placed in one of the threatened categories. The U.S. Fish and Wildlife Service lists twenty-six species as Endangered, or in danger of extinction throughout all or a significant portion of its range, and nineteen species as Threatened, or likely to become endangered in the near future.

BOTTOM FEEDERS

Bottom-feeding carps suck in sand and mud with their food. A basket-like structure between the mouth and gills holds the food particles but lets the dirt particles pass through. The fish spits out pebbles and sand too large to pass through the basket.

Did You Know?
Carps and minnows are the largest family of freshwater fishes.

Stoneroller (Campostoma anomalum)

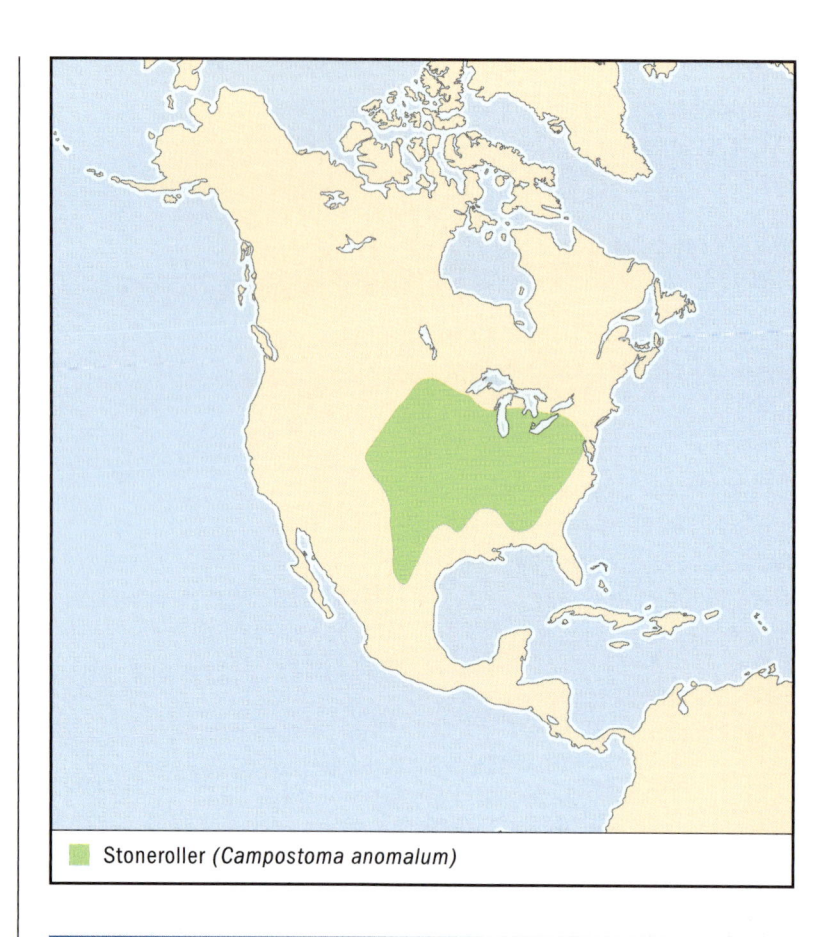

SPECIES ACCOUNTS

STONEROLLER
Campostoma anomalum

Physical characteristics: Stonerollers reach a maximum length of about 9 inches (23 centimeters) but are usually about 4 to 6 inches (10 to 15 centimeters) long. The lower jaw has a shovel-like extension. Stonerollers are brownish with a brassy luster on the back. There is a dark vertical bar behind the gill cover, and the top and bottom fins have a dark crossbar about half way up. The rest of the fin is olive in females and fiery red in males in spring. In the spring, the head and sometimes the entire body of males are covered with large round bumps.

Geographic range: Stonerollers live in the eastern and central United States, southern Canada, and northern Mexico.

In breeding season male stonerollers dig spawning pits by driving their heads into the gravel. They move gravel from the pits by nudging stones out with their snouts, which is why they are called "stonerollers." (Illustration by Emily Damstra. Reproduced by permission.)

Habitat: Stonerollers live in fast streams with sand and gravel bottoms. They prefer areas where riffles and pools alternate in rapid succession.

Diet: Stonerollers mainly eat algae but also eat waste material and aquatic insects from rock surfaces.

Behavior and reproduction: In breeding season male stonerollers dig spawning pits by driving their heads into the gravel. They move gravel from the pits by nudging stones out with their snouts, which is why they are called "stonerollers," or by moving them with their mouths. Females remain in deeper water near the spawning pits and enter the pits individually or in groups to deposit eggs. The sticky eggs become lodged in the gravel and are abandoned before hatching.

Stonerollers and people: Stonerollers are not sought by fishermen.

Conservation status: Stonerollers are not threatened or endangered. ■

Silver carp (Hypophthalmichthys molitrix)

SILVER CARP
Hypophthalmichthys molitrix

Physical characteristics: Silver carp are usually 12 to 16 inches (30 to 40 centimeters) long. They are brassy olive on the back and silver-white on the lower sides and belly. Silver carp have one row of bones in the throat that are used for crushing food.

Geographic range: Silver carp are native to China and eastern Siberia but have been introduced worldwide.

Habitat: Silver carp live in standing or flowing waters such as ponds, lakes, and rivers.

Diet: Silver carp eat plankton.

Behavior and reproduction: Silver carp are known for leaping clear of the water when disturbed. They often swim just beneath the water

In some areas silver carp are used for cleaning bodies of water where excess algae is a problem. (Illustration by Emily Damstra. Reproduced by permission.)

surface. These fish migrate to the middle or upper reaches of a river to breed. The eggs and larvae float downstream to floodplain zones.

Silver carp and people: Silver carp is an important food fish. In some areas silver carp are used mainly for cleaning bodies of water where excess algae is a problem.

Conservation status: Silver carp are not threatened or endangered. ■

Clown loach (Botia macracanthus)

CLOWN LOACH
Botia macracanthus

Physical characteristics: Clown loaches have a deep body that is orange with three black stripes. They reach a maximum length of 12 inches (30 centimeters).

Geographic range: Clown loaches live in Indonesia, Thailand, and the Philippines.

Habitat: Clown loaches live near the bottom of streams.

Diet: Clown loaches feed on bottom-dwelling algae, weeds, worms, and crustaceans (krus-TAY-shuns), water-dwelling animals that have jointed legs and a hard shell but no backbone.

Behavior and reproduction: Clown loaches are not aggressive and spend most of their time at the bottom among plants. Clown loaches breed only at the beginning of the rainy season and do so in fast-flowing rivers.

Clown loaches and people: Clown loaches are popular aquarium fishes. They sometimes are eaten.

Conservation status: Clown loaches are not threatened or endangered. ■

Clown loaches are popular aquarium fishes. (Illustration by Bruce Worden. Reproduced by permission.)

FOR MORE INFORMATION

Books:

Berra, T. M. *Freshwater Fish Distribution.* San Diego: Academic Press, 2001.

Gilbert, Carter Rowell, and James D. Williams. *National Audubon Society Field Guide to Fishes: North America.* New York: Knopf, 2002.

Schultz, Ken. *Ken Schultz's Field Guide to Freshwater Fish.* New York: Wiley, 2004.

Web sites:

"Cypriniform." All Science Fair Projects. http://www.all-science-fair-projects.com/science_fair_projects_encyclopedia/Cypriniform (accessed on September 24, 2004).

CHARACINS
Characiformes

Class: Actinopterygii
Order: Characiformes
Number of families: 11 families

order
CHAPTER

PHYSICAL CHARACTERISTICS

The size and shape of characins (CARE-uh-suhns) vary widely. Some species are quite small, and one is quite large. Most characins are silvery, but some are brightly colored. Most characins have an adipose (AE-dih-POS) fin, a short fin between the dorsal (DOOR-suhl) fin, which is the fin along the midline of the back, and the tail fin. The anal (AY-nuhl) fin, the fin along the midline of the belly, may be short or long, with as many as forty-five rays. Characins have a set of bones that connect the swim bladder, an internal sac used to control position in the water, with the inner ear.

GEOGRAPHIC RANGE

Characins live all over Central America, South America, and Africa. In North America they live only in Mexico and southern Texas.

HABITAT

Characins inhabit all types of freshwater, including weedy river edges, still ponds, rushing streams, and even underground caves.

DIET

Most characins eat fish. Some eat invertebrates (in-VER-teh-brehts), or animals that lack a backbone. Some eat only plants, fruits, and seeds. Some eat plankton, very small microscopic (MY-kro-SKA-pihk) plants and animals drifting in the water.

Some feed on waste material, mud, and algae (AL-jee), tiny plantlike growths that live in water and have no true roots, stems, or leaves. Some eat the scales or pieces of fins of other fishes.

BEHAVIOR AND REPRODUCTION

Some characins form schools when they are young but become solitary (SA-le-TER-ee) and travel alone as adults. Some travel in large groups during all life stages. When injured by a predator (PREH-duh-ter), or an animal that hunts and kills other animals for food, characins release a substance that warns others in the school to escape. Most characins scatter their eggs into the water and do not tend the eggs or the young, but some build nests.

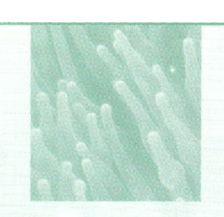

CHARACINS AND PEOPLE

Many characins are popular aquarium fishes. Others are important as food. Some are popular for sport fishing.

CONSERVATION STATUS

The World Conservation Union (IUCN) lists one characin as Endangered, or facing a very high risk of extinction in the wild in the near future.

FEEDING FRENZY

Piranhas in groups of twenty to thirty wait in plants to ambush prey. They attack the prey in a feeding frenzy intensified by the presence of blood in the water. Piranhas are not likely to attack humans unless the person is bleeding or in water near groups of prey animals.

Giant tigerfish (Hydrocynus goliath)

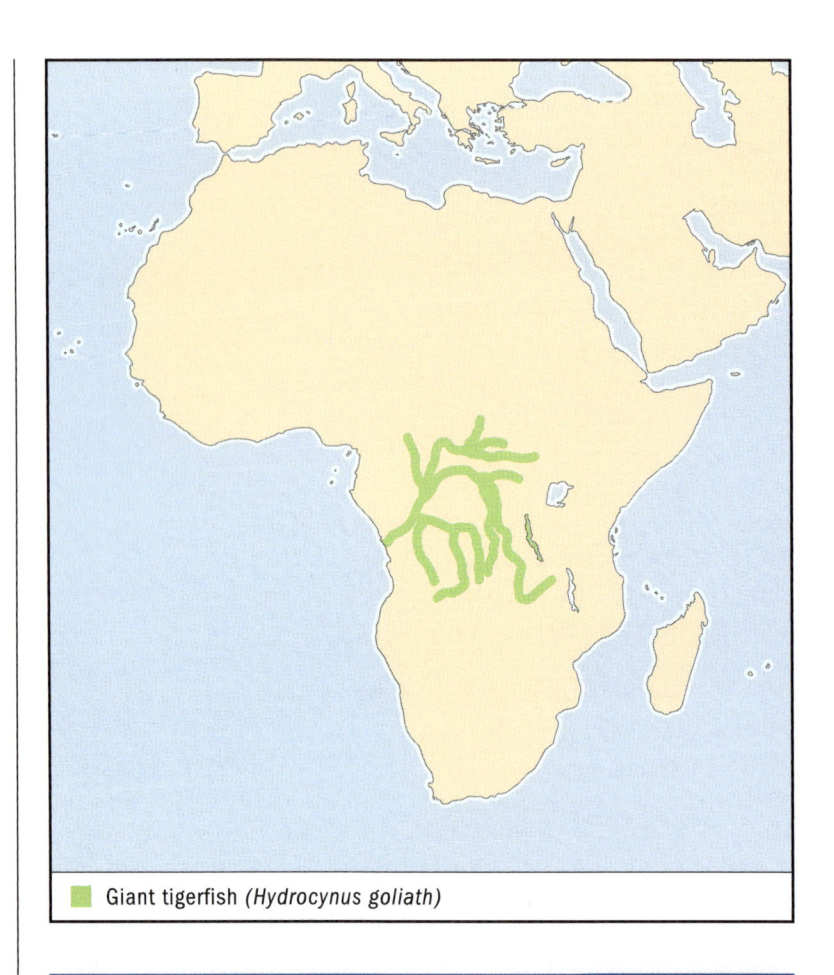

SPECIES ACCOUNTS

GIANT TIGERFISH
Hydrocynus goliath

Physical characteristics: Giant tigerfish are the largest characins, reaching a length of 4 feet, 4 inches (1.3 meters) and a weight of 110 pounds (50 kilograms). The fully scaled body is pointed at the ends and has a high dorsal fin. The body is silvery, and the back is darker gray. The fins are often orange or red, and the fish may become brightly colored during the breeding season. The teeth are sharp, and the upper teeth interlock with the lower teeth.

Geographic range: Giant tigerfish live in Africa.

Habitat: Giant tigerfish live in large rivers and near the shores of lakes.

Giant tigerfish gather with other giant tigerfish of similar size. Small fish make large groups, and large fish make small groups. (Illustration by Patricia Ferrer. Reproduced by permission.)

Diet: Adult giant tigerfish are fierce predators that consume a variety of smaller fish. The larvae (LAR-vee), the early stage that must change form before becoming an adult, eat animal plankton, but they quickly move to larger prey as they grow.

Behavior and reproduction: Giant tigerfish gather with other giant tigerfish of similar size. Small fish make large groups, and large fish make small groups. In the summer these fish migrate (MY-grayt) or move in rivers to find a place to spawn or release their eggs along the shores of lakes or the flooded banks of large rivers. Females scatter hundreds of thousands of eggs into plants, where they hatch. The adults give no parental care.

Giant tigerfish and people: Giant tigerfish attract fishermen from around the world. They also are used for food by people who live in their geographic range.

Conservation status: Giant tigerfish are not threatened or endangered.

Red-bellied piranha (*Pygocentrus nattereri*)

RED-BELLIED PIRANHA
Pygocentrus nattereri

Physical characteristics: Red-bellied piranhas have an average length of 6 to 8 inches (15 to 20 centimeters) but can grow to 12 inches (30 centimeters). The belly, the throat, the pectoral (PECK-ter-uhl) fins, or the front pair, the pelvic fins, or the rear pair, and the anal fins are bright red. The sides are often pale brown to slightly olive, and the back is bluish gray to brownish. The powerful jaws have sharp, triangular, interlocking teeth.

Red-bellied piranhas are kept as aquarium fish. This activity is illegal in some parts of the United States to prevent irresponsible hobbyists from releasing the piranhas into the wild, where they can multiply and prey on native fishes. (©David M. Schleser/Nature's Images, Inc./Photo Researchers, Inc. Reproduced by permission.)

Geographic range: Red-bellied piranhas live in South America.

Habitat: Red-bellied piranhas live in creeks and ponds. They prefer areas with dense plant life.

Diet: Red-bellied piranhas eat other fishes but also scavenge for food and eat insects, snails, worms, and plants.

Behavior and reproduction: Red-bellied piranhas look for food mainly at dusk and dawn. After a courtship display involving swimming in circles, the female deposits layers of eggs on plants in the water, and the male fertilizes them. The male guards the egg masses and fans them with his fins until the eggs hatch in nine or ten days.

Red-bellied piranhas and people: Red-bellied piranhas are kept as aquarium fish. This activity is illegal in some parts of the United States to prevent irresponsible hobbyists from releasing the piranhas into the wild, where they can multiply and prey on native fishes. People who live along the rivers inhabited by red-bellied piranhas catch and eat them.

Conservation status: Red-bellied piranhas are not threatened or endangered. ■

River hatchetfish (Gasteropelecus sternicla)

RIVER HATCHETFISH
Gasteropelecus sternicla

Physical characteristics: River hatchetfish are about 1 to 2 inches (3.8 centimeters) long. The deep body is very narrow from side to side. The belly looks like a semicircle from the side, and the chest muscles are large. The pectoral fins are long and high on the body near the head. These fish are yellow to silver with a dark stripe running along the length of the body. The fins are clear.

Geographic range: River hatchetfish live in South America.

River hatchetfish can swim very fast to rise out of the water and catch insects flying above the water level. (Illustration by Patricia Ferrer. Reproduced by permission.)

Habitat: River hatchetfish live near the surface of slow water in creeks and swamps.

Diet: River hatchetfish eat worms, crustaceans (krus-TAY-shuns), or water-dwelling animals that have jointed legs and a hard shell but no backbone, and insects on the surface of the water but also capture flying insects.

Behavior and reproduction: River hatchetfish live in groups near the surface of the water. They can be aggressive or calm. To avoid predators and capture insect prey, these fish swim very fast to rise out of the water, then fly above the surface using their long pectoral fins. River hatchetfish spawn after a lengthy courtship. The female scatters eggs in the water or onto floating plants, and the male fertilizes them. The eggs then fall to the bottom or onto plants.

River hatchetfish and people: River hatchetfish are common in aquariums.

Conservation status: River hatchetfish are not threatened or endangered. ∎

FOR MORE INFORMATION

Books:

Berra, T. M. *Freshwater Fish Distribution.* San Diego: Academic Press, 2001.

Web sites:

"Characiformes." All Science Fair Projects. http://www.all-science-fair-projects.com/science_fair_projects_encyclopedia/Characiformes. (accessed on September 25, 2004).

Weldon, Ryan. "Piranha." WhoZoo. http://www.whozoo.org/Anlife99/ryanweld/piranhaindexfinal.htm (accessed on September 25, 2004).

CATFISHES
Siluriformes

Class: Actinopterygii
Order: Siluriformes
Number of families: 34 families

order
CHAPTER

phylum
class
subclass
• order
monotypic order
suborder
family

PHYSICAL CHARACTERISTICS

More than one-tenth of living fishes are catfishes. Most catfishes have one to four pairs of barbels (BAR-buhls) around the mouth. These threadlike structures have many taste buds, which help the fish gather food efficiently. Catfishes usually have spines at the front of the dorsal (DOOR-suhl) fin, or the fin along the midline of the back, and the pectoral (PECK-ter-uhl) fins, the front pair. The spines in some catfishes are venomous and give off poison. Most catfishes are scaleless.

GEOGRAPHIC RANGE

Catfishes live all over the world except Antarctica.

HABITAT

Most catfishes live in freshwater. Some live in estuaries (EHS-chew-air-eez), or the area where a river meets the sea, and others go into even deeper ocean water.

DIET

Most catfishes are bottom feeders and mainly eat invertebrates (in-VER-teh-brehts), or animals without backbones. Some catfishes eat fish, and some feed on fallen leaves and trees as well as algae (AL-jee), which are tiny plantlike growths that live in water and have no true roots, stems, or leaves. Some catfishes eat the blood of other fish.

BEHAVIOR AND REPRODUCTION

Catfishes are generally bottom-dwelling. They are solitary, living alone, and are nocturnal (nahk-TER-nuhl) and active at

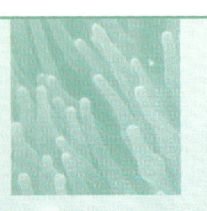

THEY DON'T SWIM IN YOUR TOILET . . .

Candirus can confuse the outward flow of nitrogen-rich water from a fish's gills with the outward flow of nitrogen-rich urine from a person urinating underwater. The candiru swims up the urinary tract, feeding on blood. The tight space and the spines of its head make it impossible for the fish to turn around or back out, and it dies inside the person, blocking urination and causing extreme pain, massive infection, shock, and often death. Humans who live on the candirus' rivers protect themselves by wearing tight clothing when swimming and by not urinating underwater.

Did You Know?

Mississippi produces 72 percent of the channel catfish farm-raised in the United States.

night. Some, however, live far away from the bottom, are active during the day, and may form schools. Catfishes usually engage in courtship activity before spawning, or releasing eggs. They then provide some parental care. Most guarding of eggs and the young is done by males. Sea catfishes carry their eggs in their mouths until they hatch.

CATFISHES AND PEOPLE

Catfishes are used as food and aquarium fishes.

CONSERVATION STATUS

The World Conservation Union (IUCN) lists one catfish species as Extinct, nine as Critically Endangered, six as Endangered, twenty-two as Vulnerable, and four as Lower Risk/Near Threatened. Extinct means no longer in existence. Critically Endangered means facing extremely high risk of extinction in the wild in the near future. Endangered means facing very high risk of extinction in the wild in the near future. Vulnerable means facing high risk of extinction in the wild. Low Risk/Near Threatened means at risk of becoming threatened with extinction in the future. The U.S. Fish and Wildlife Service lists three catfishes as Endangered, or in danger of extinction throughout all or a significant portion of its range, and two as Threatened, or likely to become endangered in the near future.

Channel catfish (*Ictalurus punctatus*)

CHANNEL CATFISH
Ictalurus punctatus

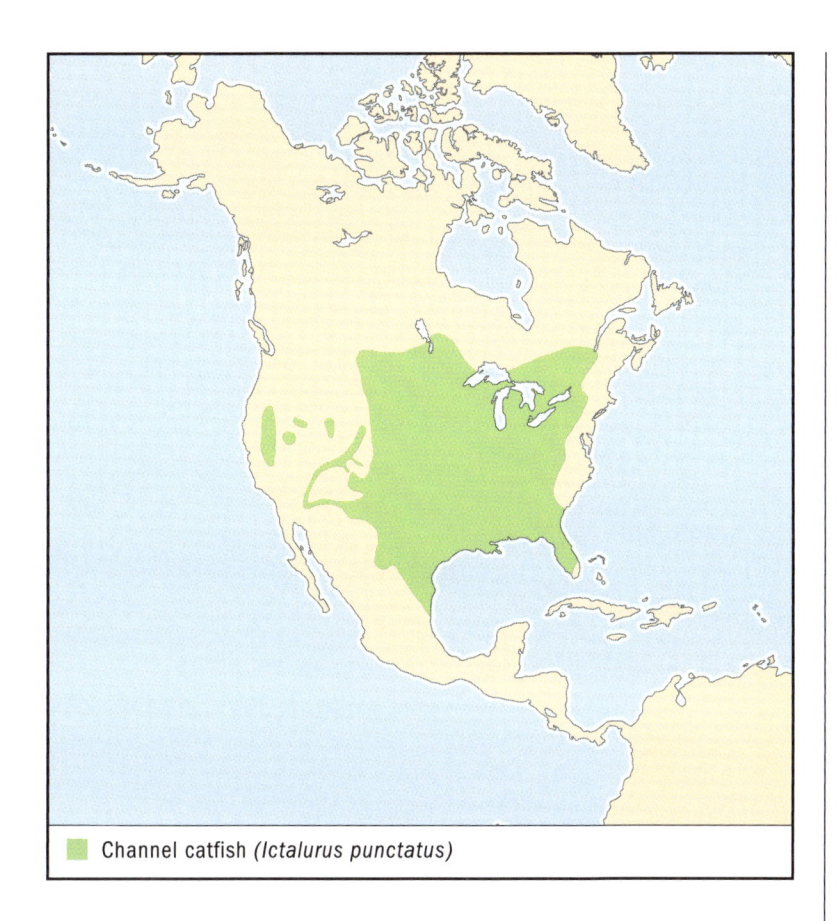

SPECIES ACCOUNTS

Physical characteristics: Channel catfish are about 3 feet, 11 inches (1.3 meters) long and weigh about 58 pounds (26 kilograms). The mouth has four pairs of barbels. The adipose fin is small and far from the caudal fin, which is deeply forked. The spine on each pectoral fin has sawlike teeth at the end. Young channel catfish are mottled and brownish on the back and whitish on the belly. Adults are mainly deep brown.

Geographic range: Channel catfish live in North America east of the Rocky Mountains.

Habitat: Channel catfish live on the sand, gravel, and rock bottoms of clear streams and medium to large rivers with swift currents. They

Catfishes 103

Channel catfish travel upstream in the spring and downstream in the fall. (Illustration by Bruce Worden. Reproduced by permission.)

also live in quiet waters of lakes, reservoirs, and ponds. They may enter waters that have a low salt content.

Diet: Channel catfish eat small fishes; crustaceans (krus-TAY-shuns), water-dwelling animals that have jointed legs and a hard shell but no backbone; insects; and mollusks (MAH-lusks), animals with a soft, unsegmented body usually covered by a hard shell.

Behavior and reproduction: Channel catfish are bottom dwellers. They travel upstream in the spring and downstream in the fall. Spawning occurs during the day in nests guarded by the male. The eggs hatch in six to ten days. Channel catfish mature in two to five years when they are about 1 foot (30 centimeters) long. They live about sixteen years.

Channel catfish and people: Channel catfish are actively farmed and are a top sport fish.

Conservation status: Channel catfish are not threatened or endangered.

Squarehead catfish (Chaca chaca)

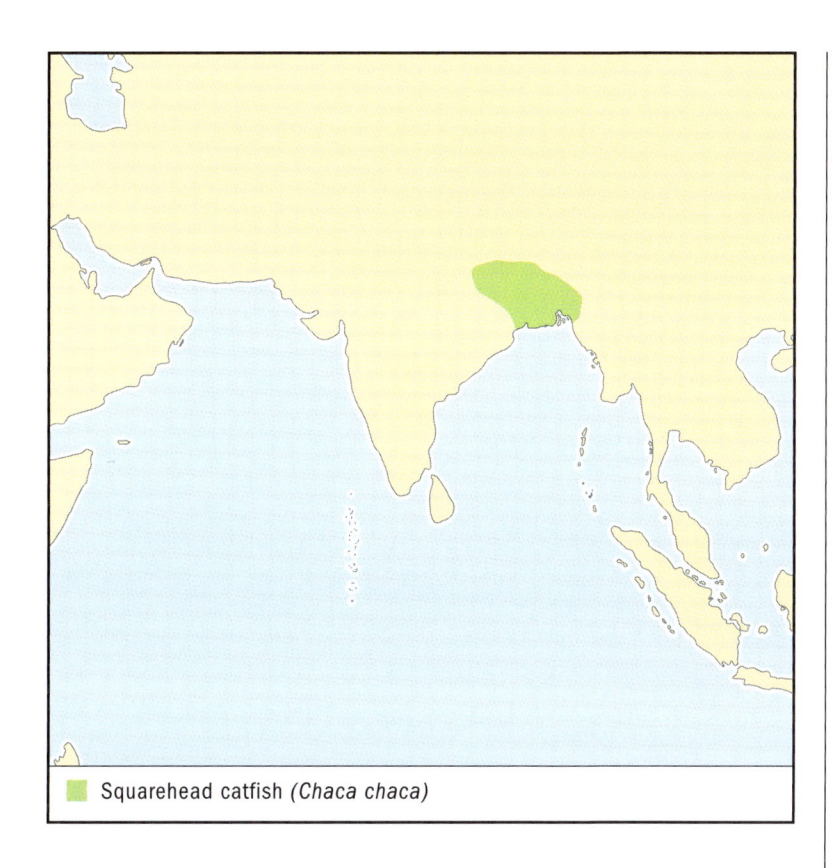

SQUAREHEAD CATFISH
Chaca chaca

Physical characteristics: Squarehead catfish are about 9 inches (23 centimeters) long. The head is broad and flat, almost square, with a deep groove on top. The mouth is very wide and has wormlike appendages that are not barbels, in addition to three pairs of small barbels. The body narrows toward the rear. The dorsal fin has a short spine. The adipose fin is a low ridge that flows into the tail fin. The pectoral fin has one notched spine. There is a row of fringe above the lateral (LAT-uhr-uhl) line, which is a series of pores and tiny tubes along each side of the body used for sensing vibrations.

Geographic range: Squarehead catfish live in India, Bangladesh, and Nepal.

Squarehead catfish are commonly fished but are not eaten, probably because they look strange. (Illustration by Bruce Worden. Reproduced by permission.)

Habitat: Squarehead catfish live on the soft bottoms of rivers, canals, ponds, and flood plains.

Diet: Squarehead catfish eat other fish, sometimes fish half as large as they are.

Behavior and reproduction: Squarehead catfish lie still on the soft bottom of the river bed. They sometimes move their barbels in a jerky motion to lure small fish near their large mouth. Scientists are not sure how squarehead catfish reproduce.

Squarehead catfish and people: Squarehead catfish are commonly fished but are not eaten, probably because they look strange. They are sometimes used in aquariums. The dorsal spine can inflict painful wounds if the fish is stepped on.

Conservation status: Squarehead catfish are not threatened or endangered. ∎

Candiru (Vandellia cirrhosa)

CANDIRU
Vandellia cirrhosa

Physical characteristics: Candirus are 1 inch (2.5 centimeters) long. The body is naked and eel-like. There are spines on the gill covers, the mouth is suckerlike, and the lower jaw is toothless. Candirus are yellowish or almost clear.

Geographic range: Candirus live in South America.

Habitat: Candirus live in freshwater. They burrow in sandy bottoms.

When a fish opens its gill cover to expel water, the candiru enters, lodges itself using its spines, bites off the tips of the host's gill filaments, gorges itself with flowing blood, and then drops off of the fish. The entire process takes 30 to 145 seconds. (Illustration by Bruce Worden. Reproduced by permission.)

Diet: Candirus eat the blood of other fishes.

Behavior and reproduction: When a fish opens its gill cover to expel water, the candiru enters, lodges itself using its spines, bites off the tips of the host's gill filaments, gorges itself with flowing blood, and drops off to the bottom. The entire process takes 30 to 145 seconds. Scientists are not sure how candirus reproduce.

Candirus and people: Candirus can swim up the urinary tracts of people.

Conservation status: Candirus are not threatened or endangered. ∎

FOR MORE INFORMATION

Books:

Berra, Tim M. *Freshwater Fish Distribution*. San Diego: Academic Press, 2001.

Gilbert, Carter Rowell, and James D. Williams. *National Audubon Society Field Guide to Fishes: North America*. New York: Knopf, 2002.

Web sites:

"Understanding Catfish." The Content Well. http://www.thecontentwell.com/Fish_Game/Catfish/Catfish_index.html (accessed on September 25, 2004).

"Vandellia Cirrhosa: Candiru." FishBase. http://www.fishbase.org/Summary/SpeciesSummary.cfm?id=8811 (accessed on September 25, 2004).

> **SOUTH AMERICAN KNIFEFISHES AND ELECTRIC EELS**
> **Gymnotiformes**
>
> **Class:** Actinopterygii
> **Order:** Gymnotiformes
> **Number of families:** 5 families

order CHAPTER

PHYSICAL CHARACTERISTICS

South American knifefishes and electric eels have a narrow ribbon-like body. Instead of a tail fin, they have a long tail. The tail is an extension of the anal (AY-nuhl) fin, the fin on the midline of the belly, which on these fishes extends the entire length of the belly. There are no pelvic fins, the rear pair, or dorsal (DOOR-suhl) fin, the fin along the midline of the back. The most outstanding feature of knifefishes and electric eels is electric organs in the skin. Electric eels give off strong electric discharges. Knifefishes produce weak electrical discharges.

GEOGRAPHIC RANGE

South American knifefishes and electric eels live in South America and Central America.

HABITAT

South American knifefishes and electric eels live in small streams, large rivers, lakes, and various types of backwaters. Many of these fishes live in deep, main-river channels. Some live in water with low oxygen content and gulp air at the water surface. Most of these fishes tolerate very warm water.

DIET

Some South American knifefishes and electric eels eat mostly young insect larvae (LAR-vee), worms, and crustaceans (krus-TAY-shuns), water-dwelling animals that have jointed legs and a hard shell but no backbone. Some have large mouths and feed

phylum
class
subclass
● order
monotypic order
suborder
family

on large prey. Some feed on scales. Some have a long, curved mouth and search for insect larvae in holes and crevices.

BEHAVIOR AND REPRODUCTION

South American knifefishes and electric eels can regrow the hind parts of their bodies. They are active at night and hide during the day among plants, in floating meadows, in crevices and holes, and under various kinds of shelter. During the day some species lie flat and motionless on the bottom, imitating leaves. Some species burrow in the sand during the day.

South American knifefishes and electric eels spawn, or release eggs, every few days to every few weeks. Knifefishes reproduce during the high-water season, and eels during the dry season. During courtship, the electrical discharges serve various purposes. Some species form pairs during reproduction, and others form complicated social groups. Some of these fishes build nests, and others lay eggs among plants. Some larvae, the early stage of an animal that must change form before becoming an adult, feed on eggs laid in another batch. Some males guard the young. Males of one type of knifefish hold the eggs in their mouths until the eggs hatch.

SOUTH AMERICAN KNIFEFISHES, ELECTRIC EELS, AND PEOPLE

Electric eels are used to study how electricity relates to biology. Some larger knifefishes are eaten by people who live in their geographic range.

CONSERVATION STATUS

South American knifefishes and electric eels are not threatened or endangered.

Electric eel (Electrophorus electricus)

ELECTRIC EEL
Electrophorus electricus

SPECIES ACCOUNTS

Physical characteristics: Electric eels can reach a length of 8 feet (2.4 meters). They have no dorsal, tail, or pelvic fins and do not have scales. The bottom part of the head and throat is yellowish to orange, and the rest of the body is dull olive to almost black. These fishes produce electric discharges as strong as 700 volts.

Geographic range: Electric eels live in northern South America.

South American Knifefishes and Electric Eels

Electric eels are active at night. They stun prey or food animals with electric shocks. (Hans Reinhard/Bruce Coleman, Inc. Reproduced by permission.)

Habitat: Electric eels live in creeks and ponds and along the shores of lakes.

Diet: Electric eels eat mostly other fishes, but they also eat amphibians (am-FIB-ee-uns), such as frogs, which spend part of their lives in water and part on land.

Behavior and reproduction: Electric eels are active at night. They stun prey or food animals with electric shocks. These eels drown if they cannot get access to air, so they swim to the surface every ten minutes or so to gulp air. They hide during the day under shelter or in holes. Electric eels breed during the dry season in small ponds. The male builds a foam nest. The larvae first eat eggs of later spawnings, then change their diet to insect larvae. These eels start eating fish when they are about 4 inches (10 centimeters) long. The males guard the young until they can eat fish.

Electric eels and people: Electric eels have been used to study how electricity works in biology.

Conservation status: Electric eels are not threatened or endangered. ■

Glass knifefish (*Eigenmannia lineata*)

GLASS KNIFEFISH
Eigenmannia lineata

Physical characteristics: Female glass knifefishes are about 8 inches (20 centimeters) long. Males are about 14 inches (36 centimeters) long. Their bodies are slender, having only pectoral fins (PECK-ter-uhl) fins, or the front pair, and a very long anal fin. Except for the head, the fish are clear. Three black stripes run lengthwise along the body. Glass knifefishes are weakly electric.

Geographic range: Glass knifefishes live in South America.

Glass knifefishes are weakly electric. Except for their heads, the fish are clear. (©Mark Smith/Photo Researchers, Inc. Reproduced by permission.)

Habitat: Glass knifefishes live near undercut banks and in old wood along rivers and streams; in the open-water areas of small creeks, lagoons, and marshes; and along rivers with dense plant life.

Diet: Glass knifefishes eat crustaceans and the larvae of water insects.

Behavior and reproduction: Glass knifefishes are social and are active at night. During the day they gather in large numbers in hiding places. They spawn during the rainy season. The dominant male spawns with a female at night, and she lays sticky eggs on floating plants. The eggs hatch on the third day after being laid.

Glass knifefishes and people: Glass knifefishes are studied by scientists.

Conservation status: Glass knifefishes are not threatened or endangered. ∎

FOR MORE INFORMATION

Books:
Berra, Tim M. *Freshwater Fish Distribution*. San Diego, CA: Academic Press, 2001.

Web sites:
"Electric Eel." All Science Fair Projects. http://www.all-science-fair-projects.com/science_fair_projects_encyclopedia/Electric_eel (accessed on September 26, 2004).

PIKES AND MUDMINNOWS
Esociformes

Class: Actinopterygii
Order: Esociformes
Number of families: 1 family

order
CHAPTER

• order

PHYSICAL CHARACTERISTICS

A striking characteristic of pikes, a group that includes muskellunge, and mudminnows is that the dorsal (DOOR-suhl) fin, the fin along the midline of the back, is quite far back on the body. The bodies of pikes and mudminnows are not tapered at the ends and are round in cross section. Some of these fishes have a long, flat snout. Although most pikes and mudminnows are small or medium-sized, the largest pikes can reach more than 5 feet (1.5 meters) in length and weigh more than 66 pounds (30 kilograms). The smallest mudminnow rarely reaches 4 inches (10 centimeters) in length and weighs less than 1 ounce (28 grams). The colors of pikes and mudminnows vary, but markings or mottled patterns on a brown or olive green background are common.

GEOGRAPHIC RANGE

Pikes and mudminnows live all over the Northern Hemisphere except Greenland.

HABITAT

Adult pikes move freely between shore and open water. All pikes and mudminnows prefer still or slow-moving water where dense plants give them a place to hide. Other than dense plant cover, mudminnows seek areas with a thick and loose muddy bottom, into which they quickly dive when startled. The digestive tract, the body parts that change food into energy, and the swim bladder, an internal sac used to control position in the water, of mudminnows are modified to extract oxygen from gulped air. This feature allows the fish to withstand the high oxygen levels of water heavy with plants.

DIET

All pikes eat fishes, including smaller fish of their own species. Larger pikes also may eat frogs, water birds, and small mammals. Mudminnows eat invertebrates (in-VER-teh-brehts), or animals without a backbone, and, very rarely, young fish.

BEHAVIOR AND REPRODUCTION

Outside the breeding season, pikes and mudminnows are solitary and swim and live alone. Pikes usually hover among plants and use small fin movements to stay in place. From this position, the fish wait for their prey, or animals hunted and killed for food, which they capture with a fast strike. Mudminnows may perch on plants or rest on the bottom, eliminating the need for fin movement. When oxygen levels in the water are low, mudminnows swim up to the water surface and gulp air.

Most pikes and mudminnows spawn, or release eggs, early in the spring when water temperatures begin to increase. Some migrate to reach their spawning grounds. Spawning most often involves one female and a few to several males. In some species, the males court the females through swimming displays or aggression. Before releasing eggs, the fish make exaggerated swimming motions and side-to-side contact. Eggs may stick to plants or drop to the bottom. The young do not receive parental care.

PIKES AND MUDMINNOWS AND PEOPLE

Pikes are popular sport fishes. Mudminnows are used for bait in some areas. Some people keep them in aquariums.

CONSERVATION STATUS

The World Conservation Union (IUCN) lists one species of pikes and minnows as Vulnerable, or facing high risk of extinction in the wild, and one as Lower Risk/Near Threatened, or at risk of becoming threatened with extinction in the future.

Muskellunge (Esox masquinongy)

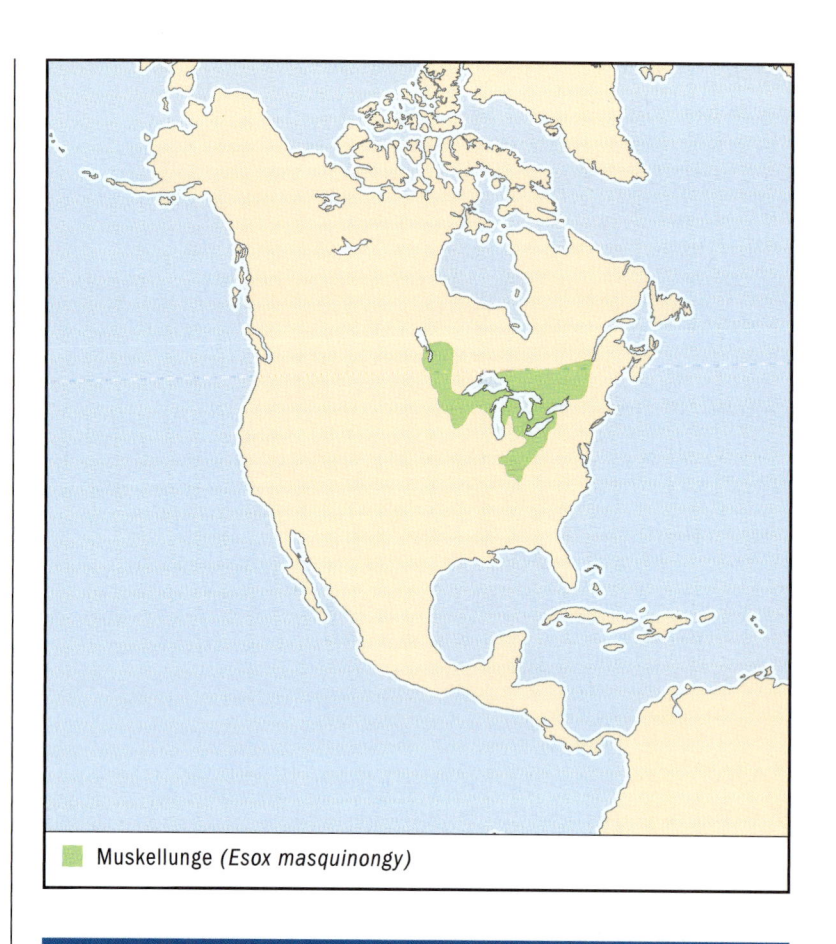

SPECIES ACCOUNT

MUSKELLUNGE
Esox masquinongy

Physical characteristics: Most muskellunge weigh 7 to 20 pounds (3 to 9 kg). The highest weight recorded is about 70 pounds (31.8 kilograms), and that fish was 6 feet (1.8 meters) long. The usual length is less than 40 inches (1 meter). The body is silver or light green with dark spots or mottled markings, but the color varies according to habitat, and markings may be absent. The cheeks and the gill covering have scales on only the upper half. Muskellunge have large pores on the lower jaw.

Geographic range: Muskellunge live in North America in the Great Lakes region.

Habitat: Muskellunge live in slow-moving or still waters with dense plant life.

Diet: Muskellunge are greedy predators (PREH-duh-ters), or animals that hunt and kill other animals for food. They feed mainly on fish but also eat crayfish, frogs, water birds, and small mammals. The young eat small invertebrates until they are able to capture larger animals.

Behavior and reproduction: Muskellunge hover among water plants, striking at prey with a fast, powerful movement. They sometimes float just beneath the water surface with their backs exposed to the air. Muskellunge spawn in spring. Males and females move close to shore or from streams to marshy areas. One female and a few smaller males swim into shallow, heavily planted areas. Females release a small number of eggs, onto which the males immediately deposit sperm. Egg release is repeated a varying number of times. Both males and females may spawn with different mates during a spawning season. Adults do not guard spawning sites or provide care to the young. Muskellunge and northern pike can breed with each other, and if they do, they produce tiger muskies, a hybrid that cannot produce its own young. Therefore, muskellunge avoid areas where northern pike spawn by releasing eggs in deeper water.

Muskellunge hover among water plants, striking at prey with a fast, powerful movement. They sometimes float just beneath the water surface with their backs exposed to the air. (©Tom McHugh/Photo Researchers, Inc. Reproduced by permission.)

Muskellunge and people: Muskellunge are popular sport fish.

Conservation status: Muskellunge are not threatened or endangered. ∎

FOR MORE INFORMATION

Books:

Berra, Tim M. *Freshwater Fish Distribution.* San Diego, CA: Academic Press, 2001.

Gilbert, Carter Rowell, and James D. Williams. *National Audubon Society Field Guide to Fishes: North America.* New York: Knopf, 2002.

Schultz, Ken. *Ken Schultz's Field Guide to Freshwater Fish.* New York: Wiley, 2004.

Web sites:

Paulson, Nicole, and Jay T. Hatch. "Central Mudminnow: *Umbra Limi* (Kirtland, 1840)." University of Minnesota. http://www.gen.umn.edu/

research/fish/fishes/central_mudminnow.html (accessed on September 26, 2004).

"Understanding Northern Pike and Muskie." The Content Well. http://www.thecontentwell.com/Fish_Game/Northern_Pike/Pike_index.html (accessed on September 26, 2004).

"What Is a Muskie? The Basics." International Muskie Home Page. http://www.trentu.ca/muskie/biology/biol01.html (accessed on September 26, 2004).

SMELTS, GALAXIIDS, AND RELATIVES
Osmeriformes

Class: Actinopterygii
Order: Osmeriformes
Number of families: 9 families

order
CHAPTER

PHYSICAL CHARACTERISTICS

Smelts, galaxiids, and their relatives are pointed at the ends. Smelts are silvery. Galaxiids and the relatives have a silvery belly but otherwise are brownish or olive with stripes or spots of various colors. These fishes are 1 to 28 inches (2.5 to 71 centimeters) long. Some have very large eyes, and some have no teeth in the upper jaw. Most galaxiids are scaleless.

GEOGRAPHIC RANGE

Smelts, galaxiids, and their relatives live all over the world except near the equator and in Antarctica.

HABITAT

Smelts, galaxiids, and their relatives live in raging mountain streams, slow-flowing rivers, ponds, lakes, estuaries (EHS-chew-air-eez), or where a river meets the sea, shallow near-shore areas of the ocean, and the deep sea, where some live in open water and others on the bottom.

DIET

Smelts, galaxiids, and their relatives eat bottom-dwelling or open-water insects; crustaceans (krus-TAY-shuns), or water-dwelling animals that have jointed legs and a hard shell but no backbone; fishes; mollusks (MAH-lusks), or animals with a soft, unsegmented body usually covered by a hard shell; and worms. One species feeds on the stinging cells and tentacles of jellyfishes.

phylum
class
subclass
● order
monotypic order
suborder
family

BEHAVIOR AND REPRODUCTION

Scientists do not know much about the behavior of smelts, galaxiids, and their relatives. They do know that some of these fishes migrate (MY-grayt) or move to another area to spawn and that others migrate at different stages of life. During upstream migrations, some of these fishes "climb" obstacles as high as 33 feet (10 meters) by jumping and wriggling in an eel-like manner, using their fins to lever themselves forward and upward. Two behavior patterns are likely in some deep-sea smelts, galaxiids, and relatives. First, those that live in the middle depths move to the surface at night to feed on animal plankton, or microscopic animals drifting in bodies of water. Second, some of these fishes have glowing organs thought to be used for attracting mates, attracting prey or food animals, and hiding from predators (PREH-duh-terz) or animals that might hunt and eat them.

Reproductive behavior varies greatly among smelts, galaxiids, and their relatives. Some undertake long migrations (my-GRAY-shunz) from coastal seas to surf beaches and estuaries. When they reach their destination, the fish often form massive spawning groups. The males press against females until they release their eggs. The males then release their sperm. Wave action buries the fertilized eggs below the sand. Other species move up into rivers and lakes to spawn.

SMELTS, GALAXIIDS, THEIR RELATIVES, AND PEOPLE

Smelts, galaxiids, and their relatives are used for commercial and recreational fishing.

CONSERVATION STATUS

The World Conservation Union (IUCN) lists one species of smelts, galaxiids, and their relatives as Extinct, four as Critically Endangered, one as Endangered, nine as Vulnerable, and five as Lower Risk/Near Threatened. Extinct means no longer in existence. Critically Endangered means facing extremely high risk of extinction in the wild in the near future. Endangered means facing very high risk of extinction in the wild in the near future. Vulnerable means facing high risk of extinction in the wild. Low Risk/Near Threatened means at risk of becoming threatened with extinction in the future. The U.S. Fish and Wildlife Services lists one species as Threatened, or likely to become endangered in the near future.

Ayu (Plecoglossus altivelis)

AYU
Plecoglossus altivelis

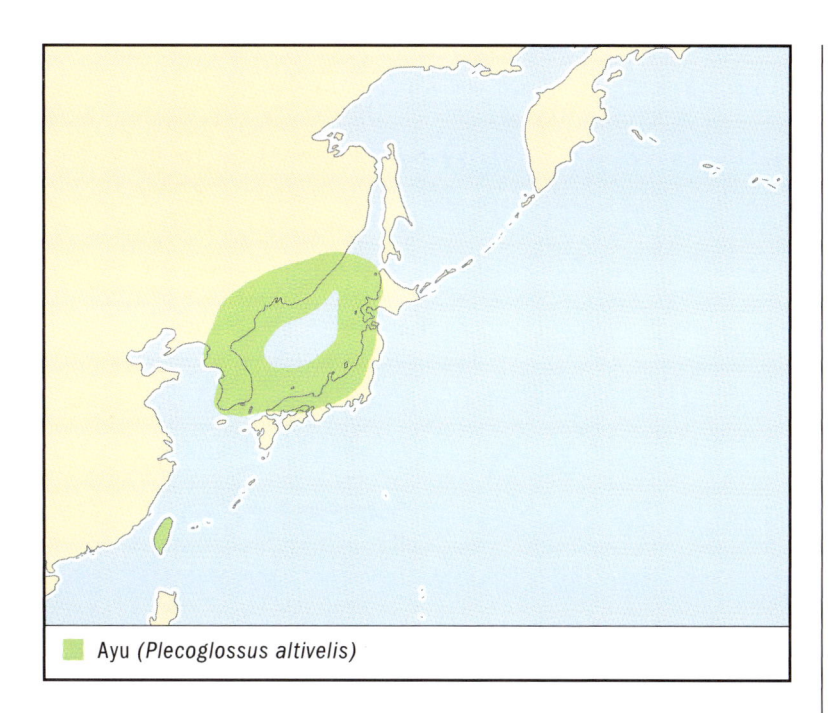

SPECIES ACCOUNTS

Physical characteristics: Ayu are about 12 inches (30 centimeters) long. The body is covered in small scales. The dorsal (DOOR-suhl) fin is midway between the head and the tail. These fish have an adipose (AE-dih-POS) fin that sits between the end of the dorsal fin and the start of the tail. Ayu are olive on the back and sides and white on the belly.

Geographic range: Ayu live in coastal seas and rivers in Japan, China, Korea, and Taiwan.

Habitat: Ayu live in both saltwater and freshwater. At different stages of life they live at the bottom of coastal seas, estuaries, rivers, streams, and lakes.

Diet: Ayu larvae (LAR-vee) and young mainly eat small bottom-dwelling crustaceans. Adults use their jaws and teeth to scrape algae (AL-jee), or tiny plantlike growths that live in water and have no true roots, stems, or leaves, from rocks.

Smelts, Galaxiids, and Relatives

Ayu live in both saltwater and freshwater. At different stages of life they live at the bottom of coastal seas, estuaries, rivers, streams, and lakes. (Illustration by Jonathan Higgins. Reproduced by permission.)

Behavior and reproduction: In rivers ayu form territories, which they guard by attacking and nipping other ayu. Ayu spawn in freshwater in the autumn, when adults move downstream to the spawning grounds. At night, the fish dig small pits in sand or gravel banks into which the female releases about ten thousand sticky eggs. The eggs hatch about two weeks later. Larger ayu spawn once and die. Smaller ones have about a 50 percent chance of surviving to spawn again two weeks later.

Ayu and people: Ayu are caught for food, raised for food, and caught for fun.

Conservation status: Ayu are not threatened or endangered. ■

Australian smelt (Retropinna semoni)

SPECIES ACCOUNTS

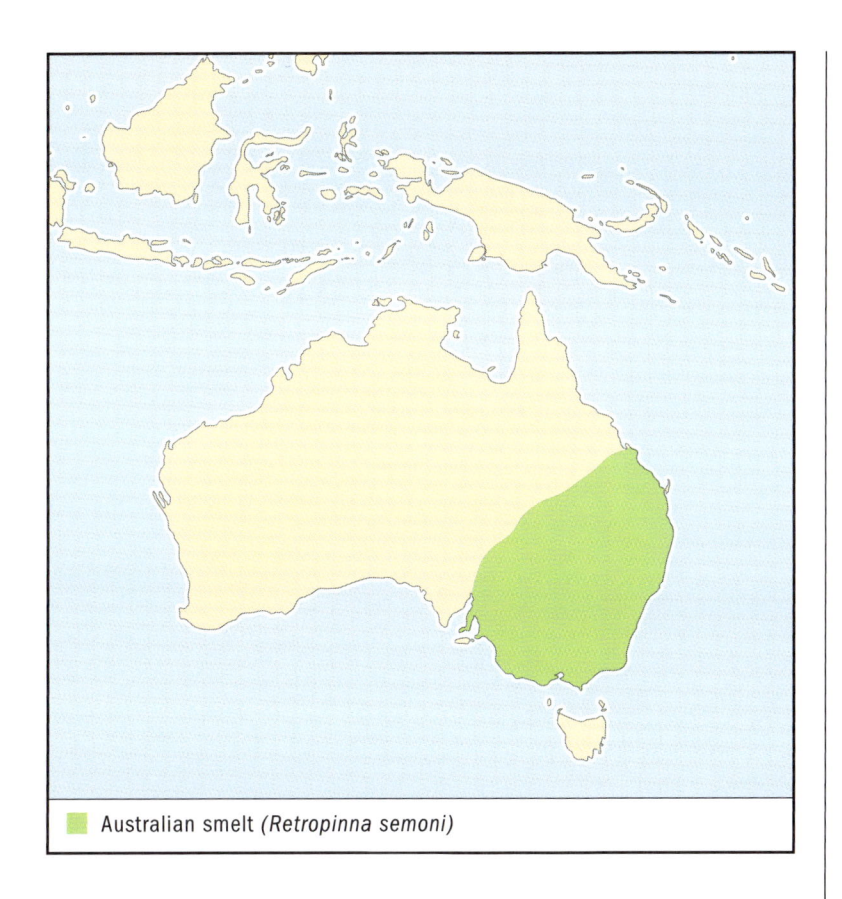

AUSTRALIAN SMELT
Retropinna semoni

Physical characteristics: Australian smelt are about 4 inches (10 centimeters) long. The dorsal fin that runs along the top of the body is toward the rear of the fish, and an adipose fin is present. There are no scales on the head. These fish are olive green on the back, golden to orange or purple on the sides, and silvery on the belly. Australian smelt often smell like cucumbers when fresh.

Geographic range: Australian smelt live in southeastern Australia.

Habitat: Australian smelt live in slow-flowing streams and rivers, lakes and ponds, and pools. They also live in waters with a low salt content. In open water these fish live at all depths.

Australian smelt live in slow-flowing streams and rivers, lakes and ponds, and pools. (Illustration by Jonathan Higgins. Reproduced by permission.)

Diet: Australian smelt eat insects, microscopic crustaceans, and algae.

Behavior and reproduction: Australian smelt form large schools from middle depths to the surface in large open bodies of water. They spawn in freshwater in the spring. Spawning fish develop bumps on their scales and fin rays. They release one hundred to one thousand sticky eggs over water plants in the stream bed. The eggs hatch after ten days.

Australian smelt and people: Australian smelt were introduced to Tasmania as forage or hunted food for introduced trouts.

Conservation status: Australian smelt are not threatened or endangered. ■

FOR MORE INFORMATION

Books:

Berra, Tim M. *Freshwater Fish Distribution.* San Diego, CA: Academic Press, 2001.

Web sites:

"Australian smelt *Retropinna semoni*." Basin Kids. http://www.mdbc.gov.au/education/basinkids/basin_fish/Australian_Smelt.htm (accessed on September 26, 2004).

"Ayu Fishing." Yamasa Institute. http://www.yamasa.org/japan/english/destinations/aichi/ayu.html (accessed on September 26, 2004).

"Osmeriformes." All Science Fair Projects. http://www.all-science-fair-projects.com/science_fair_projects_encyclopedia/Osmeriformes (accessed on September 26, 2004).

> **SALMONS**
> **Salmoniformes**
>
> **Class:** Actinopterygii
> **Order:** Salmoniformes
> **Number of families:** 1 family

order
CHAPTER

PHYSICAL CHARACTERISTICS

The salmon group includes salmons, trouts, whitefishes, and graylings. These fishes can be more than 5 feet (1.5 meters) long and weigh more than 100 pounds (45 kilograms). Salmons have streamlined bodies that are covered with small, smooth scales. Salmons have a small adipose (AE-dih-POS) fin between the dorsal (DOOR-suhl) fin, or the fin along the midline of the back, and the powerful tail fin.

GEOGRAPHIC RANGE

Salmons live in the Northern Hemisphere.

HABITAT

Many salmons spawn, or release eggs, in freshwater and migrate (MY-grayt), or move, to the sea to mature. Some salmons spawn near the ocean shore and have no real freshwater phase. Others never leave freshwater.

DIET

Some salmons eat plankton, or microscopic plants and animals drifting in bodies of water, and bottom-dwelling invertebrates (in-VER-teh-brehts), which are animals without a backbone. Other salmons eat other fishes.

BEHAVIOR AND REPRODUCTION

Some salmons are fiercely territorial and protect their living or breeding area. Others form schools soon after hatching and

phylum
class
subclass
● order
monotypic order
suborder
family

start their trip to the sea. The most remarkable characteristic of salmons is their strong swimming ability. Some can leap over obstacles, such as waterfalls, as high as 10 feet (3 meters). Salmons also are famous for returning to the stream of their birth after migrating thousands of miles in the ocean for one or more years. Salmons lay eggs that are fertilized (FUR-teh-lyezd), or penetrated by sperm to start development, outside the female.

SALMONS AND PEOPLE

Salmons are important commercial and sport fishes.

CONSERVATION STATUS

The World Conservation Union (IUCN) lists four salmons as Extinct, four as Critically Endangered, five as Endangered, and eight as Vulnerable. Extinct means no longer in existence. Critically Endangered means facing extremely high risk of extinction in the wild in the near future. Endangered means facing very high risk of extinction in the wild in the near future. Vulnerable means facing high risk of extinction in the wild. The U.S. Fish and Wildlife Services lists four species as Endangered, or in danger of extinction throughout all or a significant portion of its range, and nine as Threatened, or likely to become endangered in the near future.

Chinook salmon (Oncorhynchus tshawytscha)

CHINOOK SALMON
Oncorhynchus tshawytscha

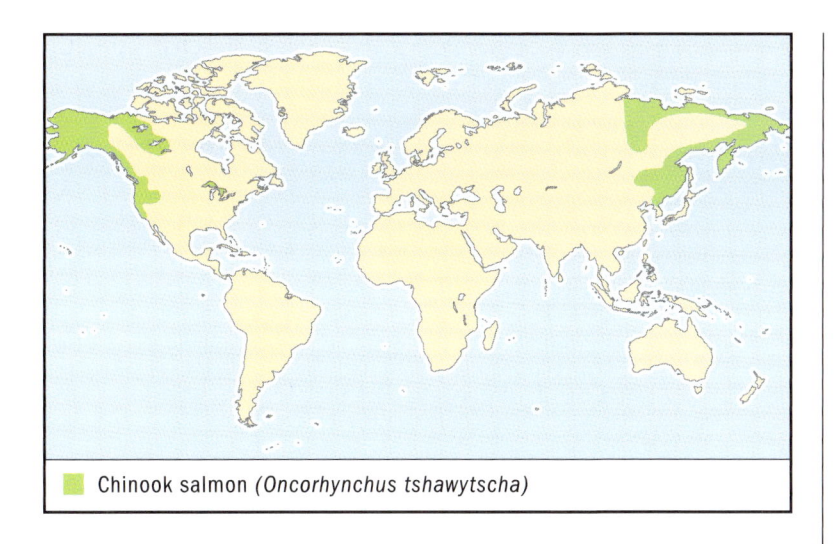

SPECIES ACCOUNTS

Physical characteristics: Chinook salmon weigh 20 to 30 pounds (9 to 14 kilograms) and are about 4 feet (1.2 meters) long. The record weight is 136 pounds (62 kilograms), and that fish was 59 inches (1.5 meters) long. The body is streamlined and narrow from side to side. There are small black spots on the back and on the tail fin. In freshwater, chinook salmon are olive brown to red or purple. At sea, adults are dark greenish to blue-black on the back and silvery to white on the belly. There are small, dark spots along the back and upper sides and on the tail fin.

Geographic range: Chinook salmon live in the Arctic and northern Pacific oceans and inland in the land bordering those waters.

Habitat: Chinook salmon spawn in freshwater and migrate to sea for feeding and maturation. In lakes they may live in water as deep as 1,230 feet (375 meters).

Diet: In streams chinook salmon mainly eat insects and small crustaceans (krus-TAY-shuns), or water-dwelling animals that have jointed legs and a hard shell but no backbone. At sea they eat fishes, crustaceans, and other invertebrates.

Salmons 129

Adult chinook salmon can migrate nearly 3,100 miles (5,000 kilometers) from the ocean upstream to spawn. (Illustration by John Megahan. Reproduced by permission.)

Behavior and reproduction: Adult chinook salmon can migrate nearly 3,100 miles (5,000 kilometers) from the ocean upstream to spawn. In December adults start to migrate from the sea, so that they reach river mouths by early spring. The female selects the spot where she will dig her nest and aggressively drives away other females competing for the same spot. When the nest is complete, the female drops into it and is joined by the dominant male. Both fish open their mouths and vibrate, and eggs and sperm are released. The female then quickly covers the eggs by moving to the upstream edge of the nest and digging small pebbles for a new nest. This process is repeated several times until the female has released all her eggs. Spent adults usually die a few days after spawning.

Chinook salmon and people: Chinook salmon are highly regarded commercial and game fishes.

Conservation status: Chinook salmon are not threatened nor endangered. ■

Atlantic salmon (*Salmo salar*)

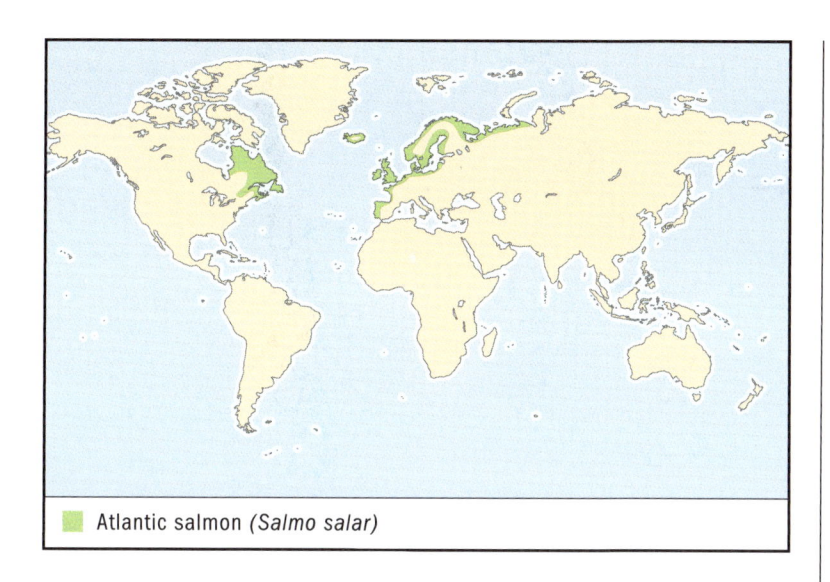

ATLANTIC SALMON
Salmo salar

Physical characteristics: Atlantic salmon weigh 7 to 12 pounds (3 to 5 kilograms) and are about 30 inches (76 cm) long, although the record is 4 feet, 5 inches (1.3 meters), 79 pounds (36 kilograms). The body is covered with black spots. In saltwater Atlantic salmon are blue-green overlaid with a silvery coating. They lose the silvery coat to become greenish or reddish brown mottled with red or orange in freshwater.

Geographic range: Atlantic salmon live on both sides of the northern part of the Atlantic Ocean and in rivers and lakes of the bordering land.

Habitat: Young Atlantic salmon live in freshwater. Adults live in saltwater except to spawn. These fish live in rocky runs and pools of large and small rivers as well as in lakes.

Diet: Young Atlantic salmon feed on mollusks (MAH-lusks), or animals with a soft, unsegmented body usually covered by a hard shell; crustaceans; insects; and fishes. Adults at sea feed on squid, shrimp, and fish.

Behavior and reproduction: Atlantic salmon are mostly active during the day. After living in freshwater for one to six years, Atlantic

Young Atlantic salmon live in freshwater. Adults live in saltwater except to spawn. (Illustration by John Megahan. Reproduced by permission.)

salmon migrate to the ocean, where they stay for one to four years before returning to their home river to spawn. The female selects a spawning site and digs a hole by turning on her side and flexing her body up and down, producing a current and never touching the bottom. Once the female releases her eggs, all males release their sperm, the greatest number of eggs being fertilized by the first male that enters the nest.

Atlantic salmon and people: Atlantic salmon are valued for their meat.

Conservation status: Atlantic salmon are not threatened or endangered. ∎

Brook trout (*Salvelinus fontinalis*)

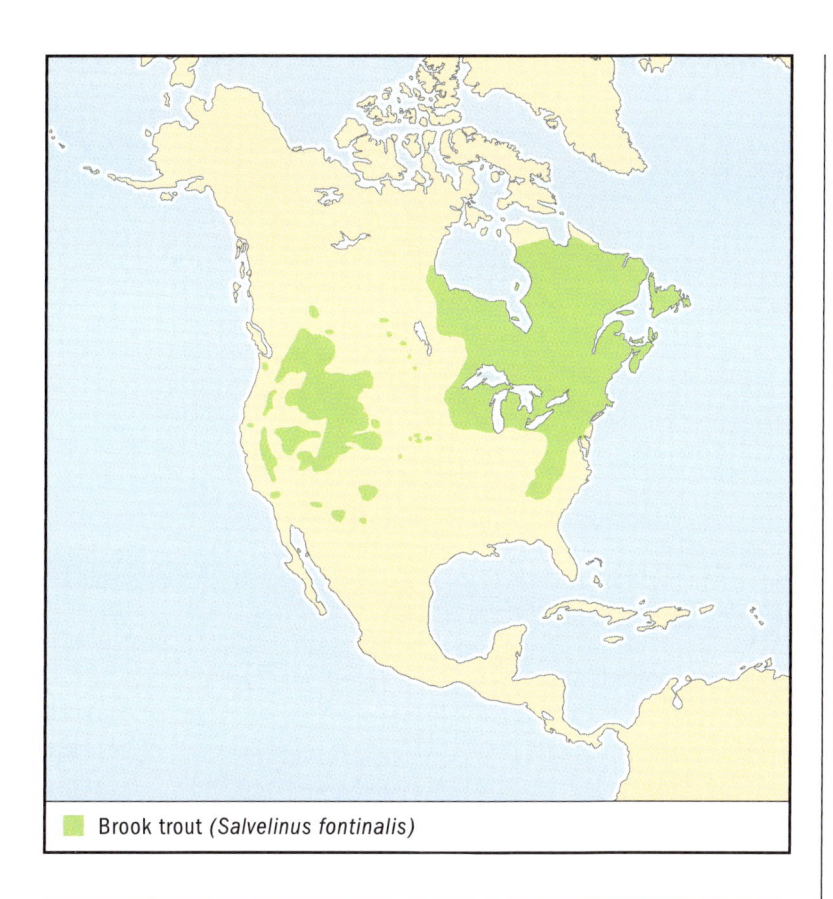

BROOK TROUT
Salvelinus fontinalis

Physical characteristics: Brook trout are 7 to 10 inches (18 to 25 centimeters) long and weigh less than 1 pound (0.45 kilogram), although the record is 14.5 pounds (6.6 kilograms), 31 inches (78.4 centimeters). These trout have a combination of dark green marbling on the back and dorsal fin and red spots with blue halos on the sides. While migrating, brook trout are dark green on the back, silvery on the sides, and white with pink spots on the belly.

Geographic range: Brook trout live in North America in eastern Canada, the Great Lakes region south to northern Georgia, and in isolated areas in western Canada and the western United States.

Habitat: Brook trout live in clear, cool creeks, in small to medium-sized rivers, and in lakes.

These brook trout are in their vibrant autumn spawning colors. Note the tail of the male, lower left, showing a bite mark received during one of the many battles between males for the right to court a female. (AP/Wide World Photos. Reproduced by permission.)

Diet: Brook trout eat worms, leeches, crustaceans, insects, mollusks, fishes, amphibians (am-FIB-ee-uns) like frogs, and even small mammals and plant matter.

Behavior and reproduction: Brook trout migrate upstream in early spring, summer, and late fall and migrate downstream in late spring and fall. A male brook trout courts females by attempting to drive them toward a suitable gravel site. If a female accepts the male, she digs the nest, then covers the eggs with small pebbles. She then moves to the upstream end of the nest and begins digging a new nest. Once the female has released all her eggs, all males release their sperm, the greatest number of eggs being fertilized by the first male that enters the nest.

Brook trout and people: Brook trout are commercially farmed. Fishermen regard these trout highly because of their fight when hooked.

Conservation status: Brook trout are not threatened or endangered. ■

FOR MORE INFORMATION

Books:

Gilbert, Carter Rowell, and James D. Williams. *National Audubon Society Field Guide to Fishes: North America.* New York: Knopf, 2002.

Montgomery, David R. *King of Fish: The Thousand-Year Run of Salmon.* Boulder, CO: Westview, 2003.

Schultz, Ken. *Ken Schultz's Field Guide to Freshwater Fish.* New York: Wiley, 2004.

Web sites:

"Fish Facts: Atlantic Salmon." U.S. Fish and Wildlife Service. http://www.fws.gov/r5crc/fish/za_sasa.html (accessed on September 27, 2004).

"Salmon." All Science Fair Projects. http://www.all-science-fair-projects.com/science_fair_projects_encyclopedia/Salmon (accessed on September 27, 2004).

"Salmon FAQs." Northeast Fisheries Science Center. http://www.nefsc.noaa.gov/faq/fishfaq2c.html#q19 (accesssed on September 27, 2004).

DRAGONFISHES AND RELATIVES
Stomiiformes

Class: Actinopterygii
Order: Stomiiformes
Number of families: 4 families

order
CHAPTER

PHYSICAL CHARACTERISTICS

Dragonfishes and their relatives are famous for having large mouths filled with enormous fanglike teeth. This feature allows the fish to efficiently capture large prey, or animals hunted and killed for food. In some cases, the prey are larger than the predator, or animal that hunts and kills other animals for food. Dragonfishes and their relatives are about 0.5 to 20 inches (1.3 to 51 centimeters) long. Some species have long, thin bodies, and others are deep-bodied and narrow from side to side.

All but one species of dragonfishes produce light. At the end of chin barbels (BAR-buhls), or long, thin feelers used for the senses of taste, touch, and smell, these fishes have bulblike glowing organs that are thought to serve as lures to other fish. These barbels range in size from less than head length to as much as ten times the length of the fish. Some of these fishes also have rows of light-producing organs along the sides of the body.

GEOGRAPHIC RANGE

Dragonfishes and their relatives live all over the world except the Arctic Ocean.

HABITAT

Dragonfishes and their relatives live in the open ocean at 660 to 3,300 feet (200 to 1,000 meters), but some live below 3,300 feet (1,000 meters).

DIET

For their size, dragonfishes and their relatives are fierce predators (PREH-duh-terz) that hunt and kill for food. They feed on other fishes, shrimps, and squid, or they feed on plankton, or microscopic plants and animals.

BEHAVIOR AND REPRODUCTION

Little is known about the behavior of dragonfishes and their relatives, mainly because most of them have never been seen alive. Most species swim from a daytime depth of 1,600 to 3,300 feet (488 to 1,000 meters) to near the surface at night and then back down again before sunrise. This upward migration or movement is thought to be mainly for feeding. Food is much more plentiful near the surface. It is thought that most dragonfishes and their relatives spawn at their deeper daytime depths. Some species have separate sexes, while others mature into males, produce sperm to fertilize (FUR-teh-lyez) eggs, or join with them to start development, and then later develop into females, producing eggs that are fertilized by younger males. In species with separate sexes, males often have a greatly developed sense of smell to help in finding females.

DRAGONFISHES, THEIR RELATIVES, AND PEOPLE

Because of their bizarre and fearsome appearance, dragonfishes and their relatives have been subjects of myth, literature, and art.

CONSERVATION STATUS

Dragonfishes and their relatives are not threatened or endangered.

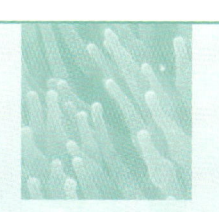

AMAZING APPETITE

Huge fangs allow dragonfishes and their relatives to take prey about one-third their own size. This meal would be equivalent to an adult human eating more than one hundred hamburgers in a single sitting.

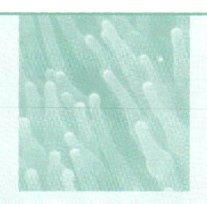

HOLD THE SCALPEL

The protein responsible for red light production by rat-trap fish has been studied for possible medical uses. This protein, if it could be synthesized and attached to an antibody, would provide a means of locating and treating tumors within a human body without the need for invasive surgery.

Viperfish (*Chauliodus sloani*)

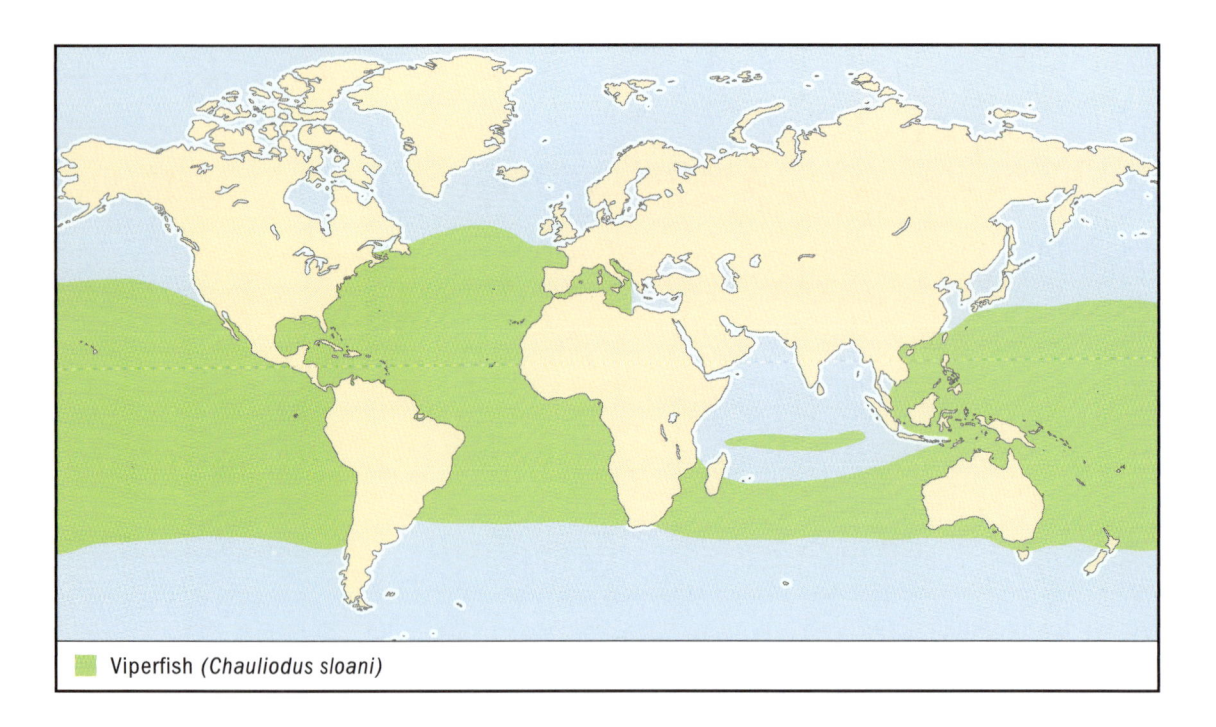

SPECIES ACCOUNTS

VIPERFISH
Chauliodus sloani

Physical characteristics: Viperfish can be as long as 14 inches (36 centimeters). The body is long and thin, and the head is large. There are five rows of large scales on each side of the body. The body is iridescent yellowish to blue-green on the sides, dark on the back, and enclosed in a jellylike sheath. This fish has more than fifteen hundred light-producing organs. The dorsal (DOOR-suhl) fin, or the fin along the midline of the back, is well forward on the body. The second ray, or supporting rod, of this fin is much longer than the others and is thought to serve as a fishing lure.

The teeth of the viperfish are so large they do not fit within the confines of the mouth. This fish sees the world through its teeth.

Geographic range: Viperfish live all over the world except the northern Indian Ocean.

Habitat: Viperfish live in the middle to deep depths of the open ocean, migrating closer to the surface at night.

The fearsome appearance of the viperfish has inspired myth, literature, and art. (Illustration by Joseph E. Trumpey. Reproduced by permission.)

Diet: Young viperfish eat small crustaceans (krus-TAY-shuns), or water-dwelling animals that have jointed legs and a hard shell but no backbone. Adults eat fishes, mainly lanternfishes, and occasionally shrimp.

Behavior and reproduction: Scientists do not know much about the behavior of viperfish except that spawning takes place year-round with a peak in late winter and early spring.

Viperfish and people: Viperfish have no commercial value. Their fearsome appearance has inspired myth, literature, and art.

Conservation status: Viperfish are not threatened or endangered.

Rat-trap fish (Malacosteus niger)

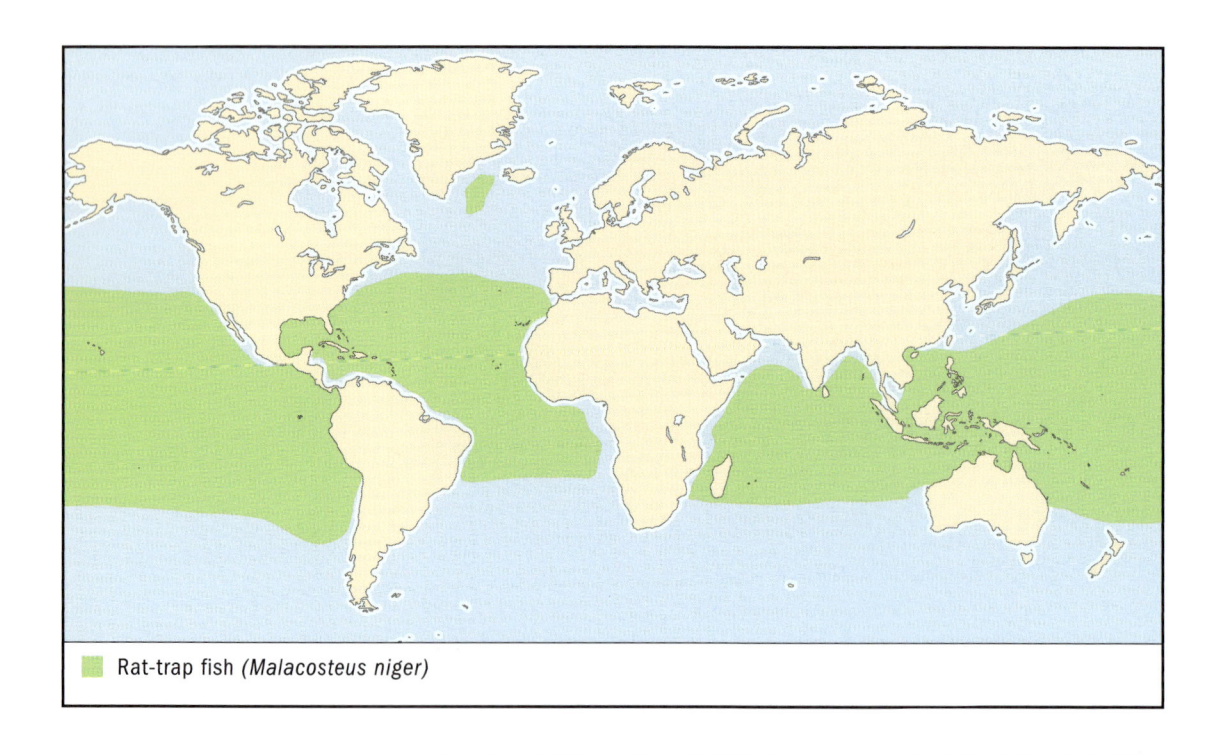

RAT-TRAP FISH
Malacosteus niger

Physical characteristics: Rat-trap fish are about 10 inches (25 centimeters) long. They are blunt on the ends, and the dorsal fin and anal (AY-nuhl) fin, or the fin along the midline of the belly, are well back near the tail fin. The body is solid black. The lower jaw is much longer than the skull and holds four pairs of large fangs. The mouths of these fish have no floor. The light organs on the body are very small. The eyes are large, and there is a large, deep-red light organ under each eye. There is no chin barbel.

Geographic range: Rat-trap fish live all over the world.

Habitat: Rat-trap fish live in the middle and deep parts of the open ocean day and night.

Diet: Rat-trap fish mainly eat small crustaceans but sometimes eat fish and shrimp.

Rat-trap fish can produce red light with the large light organs under their eyes. They can also see red light. (Illustration by Joseph E. Trumpey. Reproduced by permission.)

Behavior and reproduction: Rat-trap fish can produce red light with the large light organs under their eyes. They can also see red light. Because most deep-sea fishes can see only blue-green wavelengths, this ability helps rat-trap fish search for prey without being seen by predators. Scientists do not know much about the reproduction of rat-trap fish.

Rat-trap fish and people: Rat-trap fish have no commercial value, but they have been studied for medical purposes.

Conservation status: Rat-trap fish are not threatened or endangered.

FOR MORE INFORMATION

Books:

Hoyt, E. *Creatures of the Deep.* Buffalo, NY: Firefly, 2001.

Niesen, Thomas M. *The Marine Biology Coloring Book.* 2nd ed. New York: HarperResource, 2000.

Web sites:

"Dragonfish." All the Sea. http://www.allthesea.com/Deep-Sea-Fish-Dragonfish.html (accessed on September 27, 2004).

"Viperfish." Environmental Literacy Council. http://www.enviroliteracy.org/subcategory.php/231.html (accessed on September 27, 2004).

LIZARDFISHES AND RELATIVES
Aulopiformes

Class: Actinopterygii
Order: Aulopiformes
Number of families: 12 families

order
CHAPTER

phylum
class
subclass
● order
monotypic order
suborder
family

PHYSICAL CHARACTERISTICS

Lizardfishes are long-bodied and have a large head that looks like the head of a reptile. Some of the relatives have a first ray on the dorsal fin that is much longer than the other rays. The dorsal (DOOR-suhl) fin is the fin along the midline of the back. Rays are supporting rods in the fins. Other relatives have a series of red bars on their pelvic fins, or the rear pair, corresponding to the rear legs of four-footed animals. These fishes have yellow spots just above the lateral line and have rows of faint blue spots above and below the lateral line. The lateral (LAT-uhr-uhl) line is a series of pores and tiny tubes along each side of a fish's body and is used for sensing vibrations. The fins are pale white to clear. Some lizardfish relatives have a pencil-shaped body, a flat head with tiny eyes, and long, thick fin rays. Others have a long, sail-like dorsal fin that stretches from the head nearly to the tail. Still other relatives have tubular eyes that look like and are used as a telescope for detecting light in dim surroundings. Other relatives have fanglike teeth and lack scales.

GEOGRAPHIC RANGE

Lizardfishes and their relatives live in the Atlantic, Pacific, and Indian Oceans.

HABITAT

Lizardfishes and their relatives live at the bottom or swim freely in open water. These fishes live at depths from warm, shallow water near the shore to water so deep that light is almost absent. The bottom-dwelling fishes rest on rubble, sand, coral, rock, seaweed, or mud.

DIET

Lizardfishes and their relatives are predators (PREH-duh-terz), or animals that hunt and kill other animals for food. Bottom-dwelling species eat smaller fishes and shrimps that they ambush and capture with their large, toothy mouths. At middle depths and in deep water lizardfishes and their relatives probably capture passing fish, squid, and shrimp.

BEHAVIOR AND REPRODUCTION

Scientists know little about the behavior of lizardfishes and their relatives. They do know that the bottom-dwelling species use camouflage and make very little movement. These characteristics allow the fish to ambush prey and avoid predators. These fishes swim in short, rapid bursts and then bury themselves. The fishes that live in middle depths and deep water may swim rapidly in pursuit of prey or food animals. Smaller species may hover in the water and swim only to hunt prey or to travel to the surface at night. Some species swim with their tails down and their heads up.

Lizardfishes and their relatives have two mating systems. In one system male and female sexes are separate. Fishes that live in shallow water spawn in the open water and release eggs that when fertilized (FUR-teh-lyzed), or penetrated by sperm, drift to the bottom for development. In the other mating system the fish can be both male and female at the same time and reproduce by fertilizing themselves.

LIZARDFISHES, THEIR RELATIVES, AND PEOPLE

Although the meat of shallow-water lizardfishes and their relatives is bony, some people eat it.

CONSERVATION STATUS

Lizardfishes and their relatives are not threatened nor endangered.

Longnose lancetfish (*Alepisaurus ferox*)

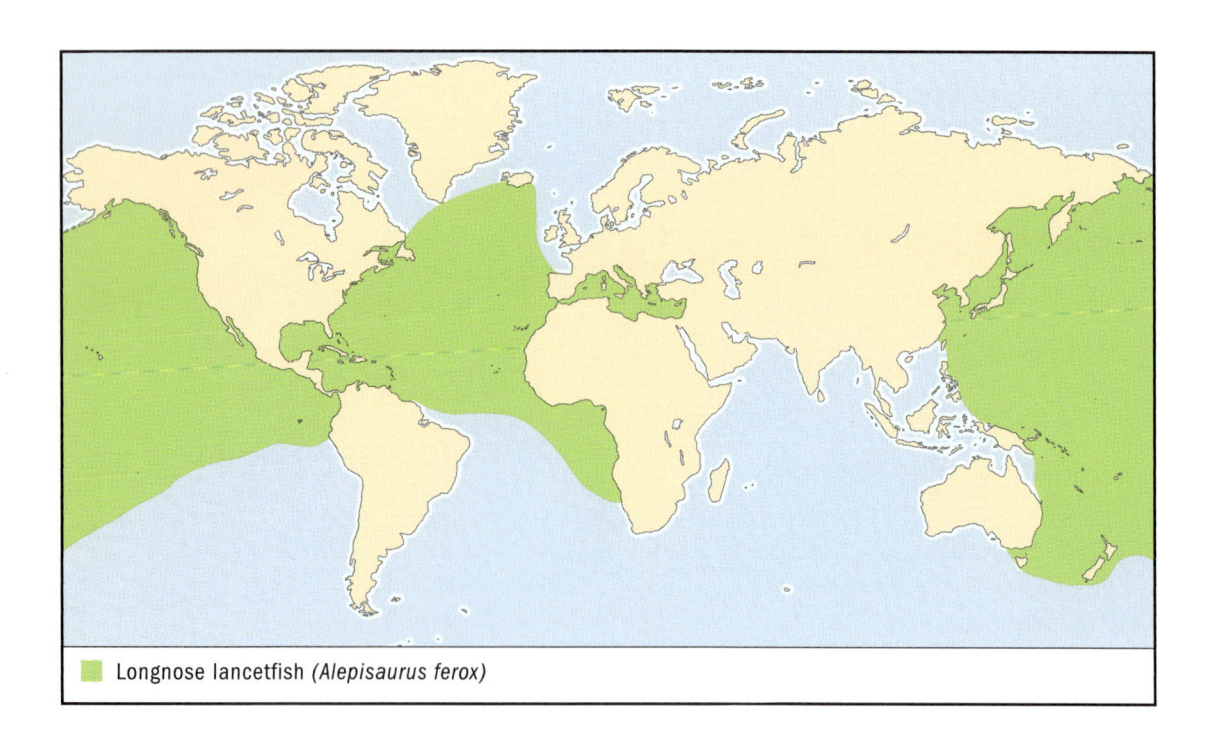

SPECIES ACCOUNTS

LONGNOSE LANCETFISH
Alepisaurus ferox

Physical characteristics: Longnose lancetfish have a long, thin body with a very long and high dorsal fin. These fish reach a length of more than 7 feet (2 meters). The mouth is large and has two fangs. The body is pale silver or shiny white or cream but is darker along the back and upper sides. At times the color has hints of light blue, green, or red. The fins are brown or black. Longnose lancetfish do not have a swim bladder, or internal sac that fishes use to control their position in the water.

Geographic range: Longnose lancetfish live in the Atlantic and Pacific oceans.

Habitat: Longnose lancetfish live in open water from the surface to the middle depths, depending on the time of day. They sometimes swim near the shore.

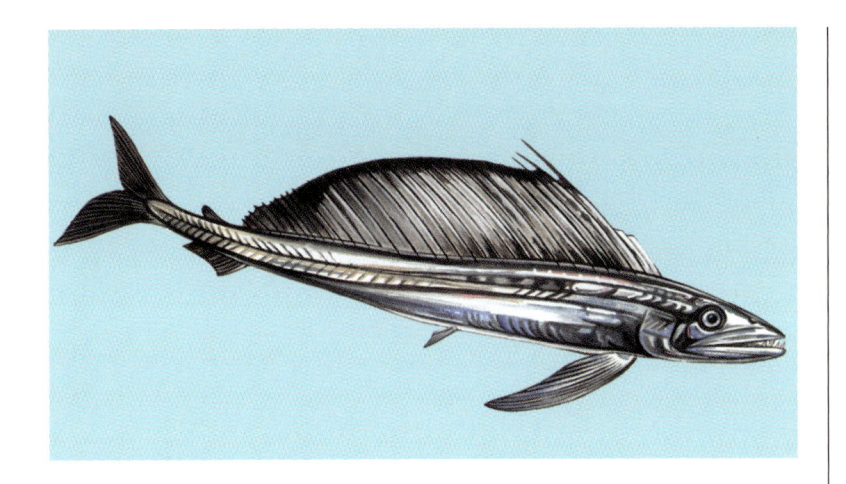

Longnose lancetfish live in open water from the surface to the middle depths, depending on the time of day. (Illustration by Patricia Ferrer. Reproduced by permission.)

Diet: Longnose lancetfish eat invertebrates (in-VER-teh-brehts), or animals without a backbone, such as squid and shrimp, and fishes. They also eat bottom-dwelling animals such as sea squirts.

Behavior and reproduction: Scientists do not know much about the behavior and reproduction of longnose lancetfish. These fish probably produce eggs in open water, and the larvae (LAR-vee) or young live in open water.

Longnose lancetfish and people: Longnose lancetfish are caught accidentally with other fishes but are not valued as a food fish.

Conservation status: Longnose lancetfish are not threatened or endangered. ■

Tripodfish (*Bathypterois quadrifilis*)

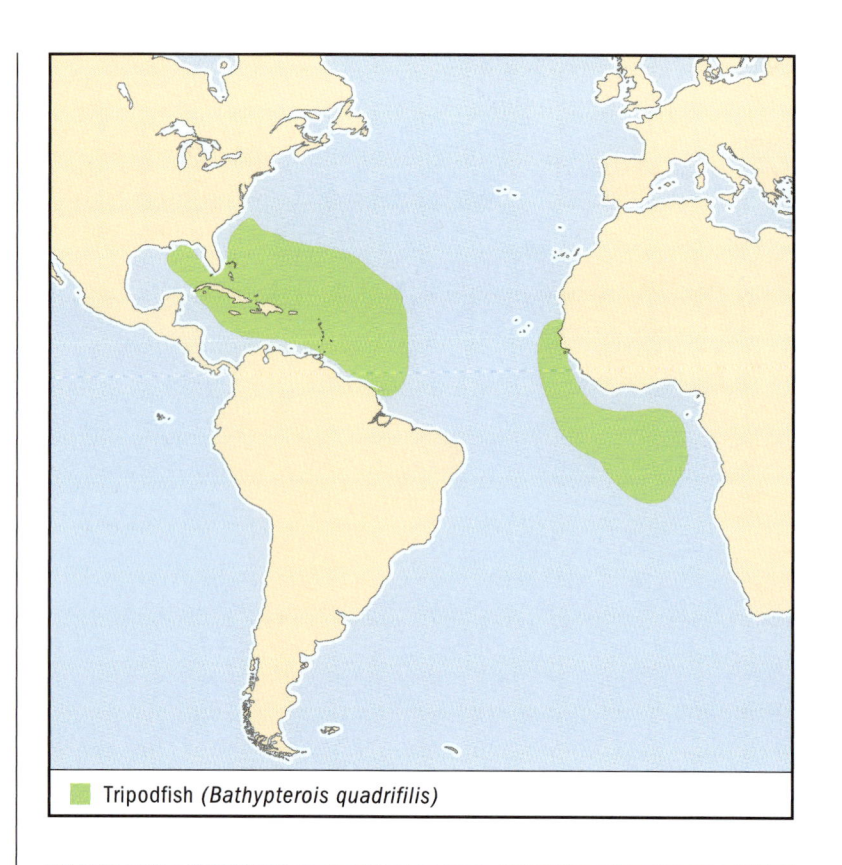

TRIPODFISH
Bathypterois quadrifilis

Physical characteristics: Tripodfish have a long, thin body and reach a length of about 7 inches (18 centimeters). The pectoral, pelvic, and tail fin rays are all very long. When erect, these rays act as a tripod on which the fish balances itself on the bottom. Tripodfish are bronze to pale with gray on the head and belly and along the lower back.

Geographic range: Tripodfish live on both sides of the Atlantic Ocean.

Habitat: Tripodfish live on sand and rubble in the deep part of the ocean.

Diet: Tripodfish eat smaller fishes and crustaceans that they ambush on the bottom. Crustaceans (krus-TAY-shuns) are water-dwelling animals that have jointed legs and a hard shell but no backbone.

Behavior and reproduction: Tripodfish can "walk" on the bottom using their tripod. To reproduce they act as both sexes at the same time. The eggs and larvae drift in open water.

Tripodfish and people: Tripodfish are of no commercial importance but are a curiosity of science.

Conservation status: Tripodfish are not threatened or endangered. ■

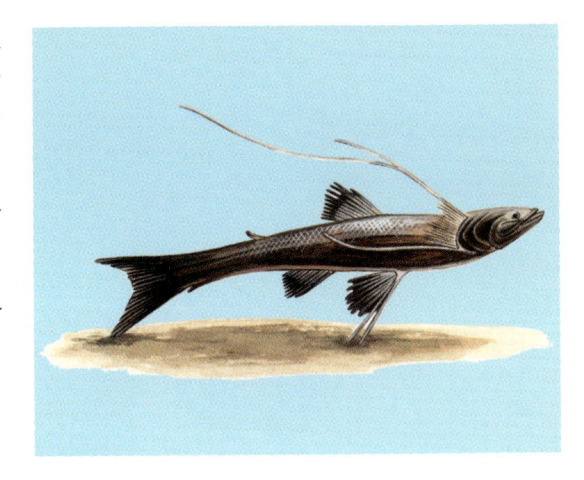

Tripodfish can "walk" on the bottom using their tripod. (Illustration by Patricia Ferrer. Reproduced by permission.)

FOR MORE INFORMATION

Books:

Byatt, Andrew, Alastair Fothergill, and Martha Holmes. *Blue Planet.* New York: DK, 2001.

Gilbert, Carter Rowell, and James D. Williams. *National Audubon Society Field Guide to Fishes: North America.* New York: Knopf, 2002.

Web sites:

"Fish of the Deep Sea Floor." Fathom. http://www.fathom.com/course/10701050/session4.html (accessed on October 4, 2004).

LANTERNFISHES
Myctophiformes

Class: Actinopterygii
Order: Myctophiformes
Number of families: 2 families

order
CHAPTER

PHYSICAL CHARACTERISTICS

Lanternfishes have many light-producing organs covering their bodies. These organs are arranged in patterns that vary according to species. In addition to light-producing organs, many lanternfishes have glowing scales and glands. Lanternfishes are small, about 3 inches (8 centimeters) long. The most common lanternfishes look like anchovies and sometimes are called glowing anchovies. The jaws of lanternfishes have many tiny teeth. These fishes have two general body types. One is a strong, firmly muscled body, and the other is a watery, flabby body with a weak skeleton and muscles.

Lanternfishes are brilliant metallic bronze to dark blue-black on the back and have mirrorlike silvery sides and belly. Some deep-dwelling lanternfishes are dark brown or black. The light-producing organs on freshly captured lanternfishes appear silver, reddish, or deep blue.

All lanternfishes have an adipose (ADD-uh-pohs) fin, which is a short fin between the dorsal fin and the tail fin. The dorsal (DOOR-suhl) fin is the fin along the midline of the back. Some species have long, sweeping pectoral (PECK-ter-uhl) fins, which are the front pair, corresponding to the front legs of four-footed animals. The pectoral fins of the flabby-bodied species are so small and delicate that they are almost unnoticeable. The rays, or supporting rods, of all lanternfish fins are soft.

GEOGRAPHIC RANGE

Lanternfishes live all over the world except the Arctic Ocean.

HABITAT

As adults most lanternfishes live in the middle depths of the open ocean, usually between 660 and 3,330 feet (200 and 1,000 meters). Some may enter the upper part of the deep-water region. Several lanternfishes are thought to live near, but not in contact with, the bottom at some point in life. Larval or young lanternfishes live near the surface, mainly between about 160 and 800 feet (50 to 250 meters).

DIET

Scientists do not know much about the feeding habits of lanternfishes. Some eat crustacean (krus-TAY-shun) plankton. Crustaceans are water-dwelling animals that have jointed legs and a hard shell but no backbone. Plankton are microscopic plants and, in this case, animals drifting in water.

BEHAVIOR AND REPRODUCTION

Little is known about the behavior of lanternfishes. They move from middle depths into very shallow surface waters at night to feed and to lay their eggs. These surface waters, usually above 330 feet (100 meters), are rich in food. The trips up and down take about two hours each, depending on conditions such as solar eclipses, the degree of moon fullness, the clearness of the night sky, and the presence of strong currents.

Swimming behavior among lanternfishes takes two forms depending on the body type. Strong-bodied species swim in short bursts, propelled by rapid closing of the tail fin rays and a flick of the tail. In general, these fishes are the strongest migrators and move around for food. The flabby-bodied forms tend to move with a slow eel-like wriggling of the entire body. These species usually live in the deeper middle zone of the ocean and travel shorter distances.

In warmer waters, lanternfishes spawn year-round. In cooler waters they spawn once a year. Warm-water species live one year or less, whereas cooler-water species may live three or four years.

LANTERNFISHES AND PEOPLE

Lanternfishes are processed to form fish meal, which is used as poultry feed and as crop fertilizer. Like sardines and anchovies, lanternfishes can be bought packed in oil. Lanternfishes are very important to the ocean environment. Damage to or loss of lanternfish populations would be harmful to many other animals in the food web of the open ocean.

CONSERVATION STATUS

Lanternfishes are not threatened or endangered.

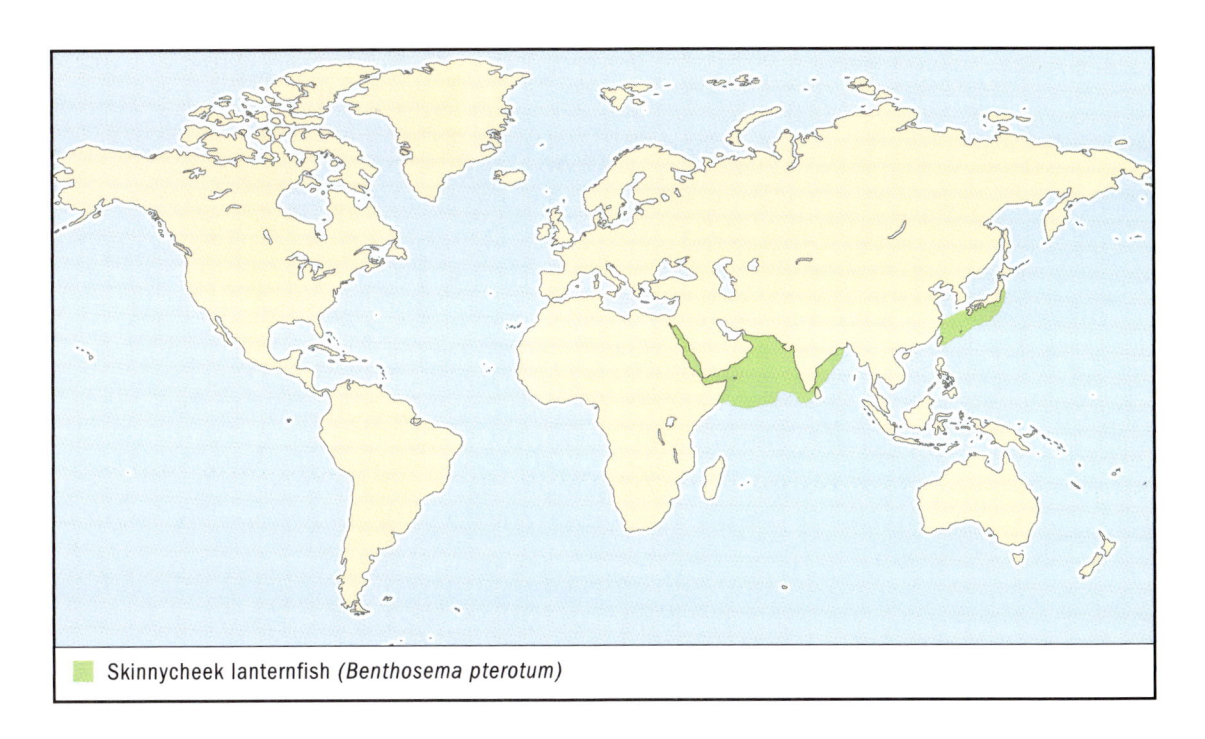

Skinnycheek lanternfish (*Benthosema pterotum*)

SKINNYCHEEK LANTERNFISH
Benthosema pterotum

SPECIES ACCOUNT

Physical characteristics: Skinnycheek lanternfish have a large head and very large eyes. They are among the smaller lanternfishes, reaching a maximum length of about 2 inches (5 centimeters). These fish are mirrorlike silver on the sides and belly and blue-black on the back.

Geographic range: Skinnycheek lanternfish live in the northern Indian Ocean, the Arabian Sea, and the Pacific Ocean near Japan.

Habitat: Skinnycheek lanternfish live in open water in the middle depths of the ocean, near the continental shelf edges, and around islands.

Diet: Skinnycheek lanternfish eat crustacean plankton. As they grow larger, these fish eat larger crustaceans. They eat at night.

Behavior and reproduction: Skinnycheek lanternfish travel up and down in the water for feeding. They form extremely dense groups. In

Skinnycheek lanternfish live in open water in the middle depths of the ocean, near the continental shelf edges, and around islands. (Illustration by Marguette Dongvillo. Reproduced by permission.)

the northern Arabian Sea commercial open-water trawlers, or fishing boats using nets, have captured these fish at a rate of 88 tons (80 metric tons) per hour.

Female lanternfish can reproduce when they are about 1 inch (2.5 centimeters) long. The eggs are fertilized (FUR-teh-lyzed), or united with the male's sperm, outside the female's body. Spawning occurs in the late afternoon and evening as the fish are traveling upward. Skinnycheek lanternfish release two hundred to three thousand eggs per batch, depending on body size. They spawn from the time they reach sexual maturity until death. These fish live slightly less than one year.

Skinnycheek lanternfish and people: Skinnycheek lanternfish are processed for fertilizer.

Conservation status: Skinnycheek lanternfish are not threatened or endangered. ∎

FOR MORE INFORMATION

Books:

Byatt, Andrew, Alastair Fothergill, and Martha Holmes. *Blue Planet.* New York: DK, 2001.

Niesen, Thomas M. *The Marine Biology Coloring Book.* 2nd ed. New York: HarperResource, 2000.

Web site:

"Lanternfishes in General." Iziko: South African Museum. http://www.museums.org.za/sam/resources/marine/lantern.htm (accessed on October 4, 2004).

OPAHS AND RELATIVES
Lampridiformes

Class: Actinopterygii
Order: Lampridiformes
Number of families: 7 families

order CHAPTER

phylum
class
subclass
● **order**
monotypic order
suborder
family

PHYSICAL CHARACTERISTICS

Opahs are almost round when viewed from the side, but their relatives are long and slender. Opahs and their relatives have red fins and brightly colored bodies. The jaw structure allows these fishes suddenly to open their mouths to forty times the closed size and use enormous suction to capture plankton, or microscopic plants and animals drifting in water.

GEOGRAPHIC RANGE

Opahs and their relatives live in all oceans except in polar waters.

HABITAT

Opahs and their relatives are strictly saltwater fishes. Some live near the shore, and some live in the deep ocean, from surface waters to depths of hundreds of feet.

DIET

Opahs and their relatives eat crustacean (krus-TAY-shun) plankton, small to medium-sized squid, and small to medium-sized fishes. Crustaceans are water-dwelling animals that have jointed legs and a hard shell but no backbone.

BEHAVIOR AND REPRODUCTION

Scientists do not know much about opahs and their relatives. The long forms hold themselves straight up and down in the water. The other forms swim belly down and head forward the

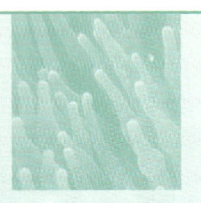

SEA SERPENT

The oarfish is a fabled species whose tremendous length, bright crimson fins, long dorsal rays, silvery form, and tendency to appear suddenly at the ocean surface after wind storms brought fearful cries of "sea monster!" from sailors 100 years ago.

way most fish do. Opahs are powerful swimmers, using their large pectoral (PECK-ter-uhl) fins to move themselves forward. The pectoral fins are the front pair, corresponding to the front legs of four-footed animals. One opah relative delivers a mild electric shock when handled. Other species release ink when disturbed.

Opahs and their relatives probably scatter their eggs. The eggs are large and brightly colored, usually red, pink, or amber. Fertilized (FUR-teh-lyzed) eggs, or those that have been penetrated by sperm, develop in surface waters for approximately three weeks. At hatching, larvae (LAR-vee), or the early stage that must change form before becoming an adult, have fully developed mouths and digestive tracts, are able to take in food, and begin immediately to feed on plankton.

OPAHS, THEIR RELATIVES, AND PEOPLE

Opahs and their relatives, especially the large, long species, attract considerable public attention when they are stranded or beached, because of their rarity and unusual appearance. Opahs have excellent meat and are prized when they are caught by commercial fishermen going for other fish. The relatives are considered inedible by those who have tasted them.

CONSERVATION STATUS

Opahs and their relatives are not threatened or endangered.

Oarfish (Regalecus glesne)

OARFISH
Regalecus glesne

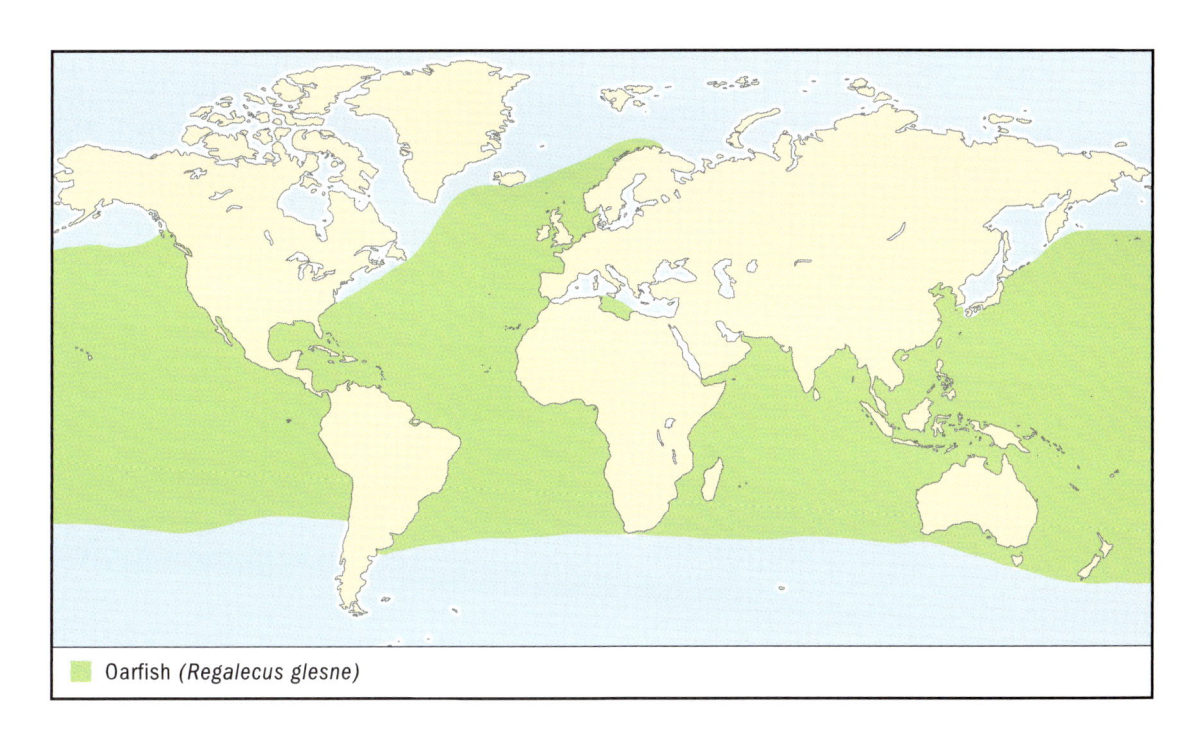

SPECIES ACCOUNT

Physical characteristics: Oarfish are spectacular animals with long, slender, usually silver bodies, brilliant red fins, a large plume of dorsal fin rays on the head, and long pelvic or back fins. Often attaining a length of 26–33 feet (8–10 meters), oarfish are the longest of all bony fishes. The pelvic fin ray has a large red swelling at its tip that looks like the blade of an oar. The tail fin is tiny, but it has very long rays that are covered in small spines. Oarfish have about four hundred dorsal (DOOR-suhl) fin rays and 150 vertebrae (ver-teh-BREE), which are the small bones that make up the spinal column. The dorsal fin is the fin along the midline of the back. The pelvic fins are the rear pair, corresponding to the rear legs of four-footed animals. Rays are the supporting rods in fins.

Geographic range: Oarfish live in all oceans, including the Mediterranean Sea, but not in polar seas.

Oarfish are spectacular animals with long, slender, usually silver bodies, brilliant red fins, a large plume of dorsal fin rays on the head, and long pelvic or back fins. (Illustration by Wendy Baker. Reproduced by permission.)

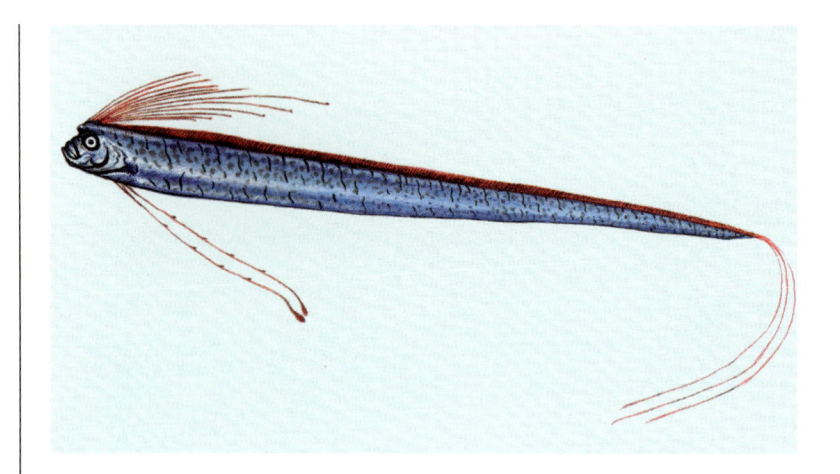

Habitat: Oarfish live in open water near the surface to depths of about 656 feet (200 meters).

Diet: Oarfish eat crustacean plankton and small fishes.

Behavior and reproduction: Oarfish move by wavy movement of the dorsal fin. The natural body position is head up with the dorsal fin rays and pelvic rays extended outward; the fish swim up and down in the water this way. The pelvic fin may allow oarfish to "taste" the surrounding habitat. Scientists know little about the reproduction of oarfish. The eggs drift in open water and have been found in plankton collections. Researchers report that eggs can take up to three weeks to hatch and that the larvae are close to their adult form at hatching.

Oarfish and people: Sightings of oarfish usually stir considerable public attention, but the species has no commercial value, and its meat is reported to be inedible.

Conservation status: Oarfish are not threatened or endangered. ∎

FOR MORE INFORMATION

Books:

Gilbert, Carter Rowell, and James D. Williams. *National Audubon Society Field Guide to Fishes: North America.* New York: Knopf, 2002.

Periodicals:

Skerry, B. "Eye-to-Eye with the Sea Serpent: First Photos of the Mysterious Oarfish." *Sport Diver* (August 1997): 40–43.

Web sites:

"Oarfish: *Regalecus glesne* Ascanius, 1772." Australian Museum Fish Site. http://www.amonline.net.au/fishes/fishfacts/fish/rglesne.htm (accessed on October 4, 2004).

"Strange but True." Divernet. http://www.divernet.com/biolog/oarf198.htm (accessed on October 4, 2004).

BEARDFISHES
Polymixiiformes

Class: Actinopterygii
Order: Polymixiiformes
Number of families: 1 family

order CHAPTER

phylum
class
subclass
● order
monotypic order
suborder
family

PHYSICAL CHARACTERISTICS

Beardfishes have a pair of barbels (BAR-buhls), which are long, thin feelers on the chin, used for the senses of taste, touch, and smell, that look like a beard. The body is pointed at the ends. The dorsal (DOOR-suhl) and anal fins have well-developed spines. The dorsal fin is the fin along the midline of the back, and the anal (AY-nuhl) fin is the fin along the midline of the belly.

GEOGRAPHIC RANGE

Beardfishes live in the Atlantic, Indian, and western Pacific oceans.

HABITAT

Very little is known about the habitat of beardfishes, but because they have chin barbels these fishes are believed to be bottom dwellers, probably over sand or mud.

DIET

The stomach of beardfishes is thick walled and muscular, often with more than one hundred pouches. These fishes eat crustaceans (krus-TAY-shuns), squid, and small fishes. Crustaceans are water-dwelling animals that have jointed legs and a hard shell but no backbone.

BEHAVIOR AND REPRODUCTION

Scientists know little about the behavior of beardfishes and nothing about their reproduction. Beardfish eggs have not been found.

BEARDFISHES AND PEOPLE

Beardfishes are marketed for human consumption in most regions. Commercial catches are small but growing.

CONSERVATION STATUS

Beardfishes are not threatened or endangered.

Stout beardfish (*Polymixia nobilis*)

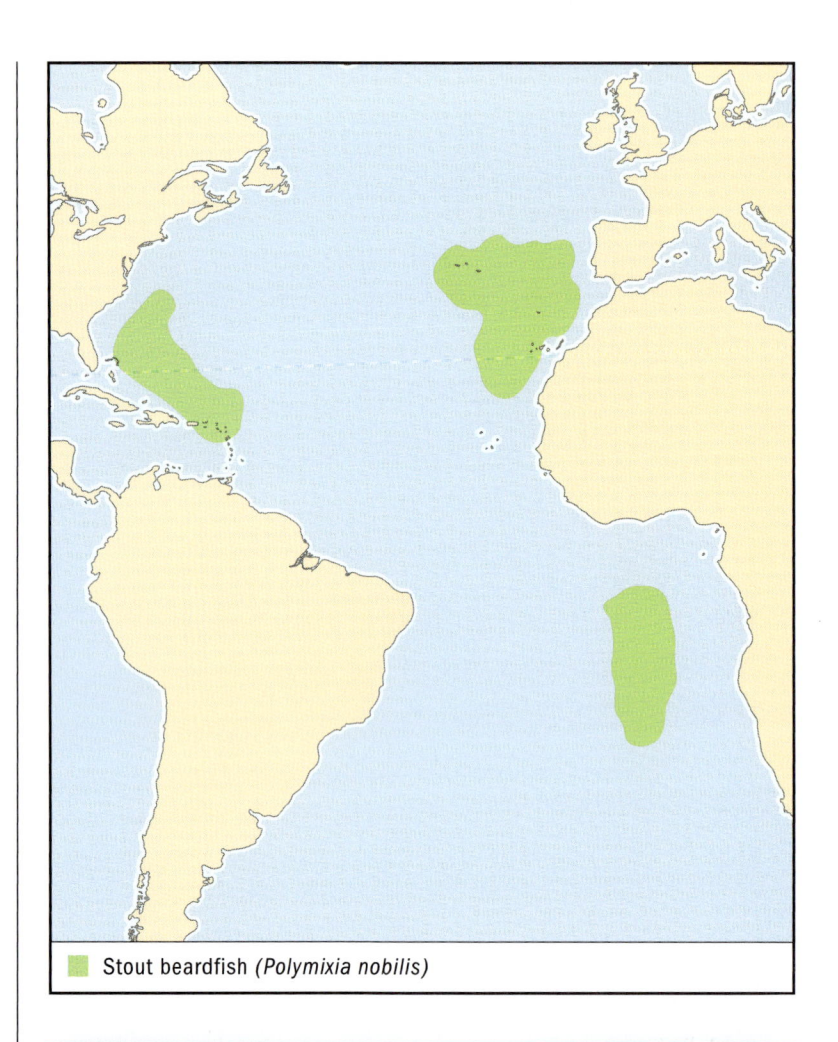

SPECIES ACCOUNT

STOUT BEARDFISH
Polymixia nobilis

Physical characteristics: Stout beardfish reach a maximum length of about 20 inches (50 centimeters). They are dark bronze-gray on the back and silvery on the belly. The scales have rows of tiny teeth. The chin barbels are long and threadlike.

Geographic range: Stout beardfish live on both sides of the Atlantic Ocean.

Habitat: Stout beardfish live on gravel and sandy bottoms.

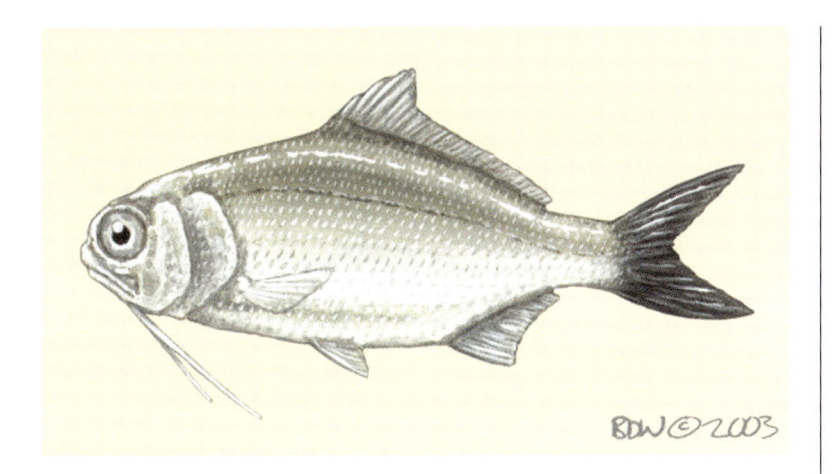

Scientists do not know how stout beardfish behave or reproduce. (Illustration by Bruce Worden. Reproduced by permission.)

Diet: Stout beardfish feed on crustaceans, squid, and small fishes.

Behavior and reproduction: Scientists do not know how stout beardfish behave or reproduce. Eggs have not been found.

Stout beardfish and people: Stout beardfish are marketed fresh and frozen.

Conservation status: Stout beardfish are not threatened or endangered. ■

FOR MORE INFORMATION

Web site:

"Polymixia nobilis: Stout Beardfish." FishBase. http://www.fishbase.org/Summary/SpeciesSummary.cfm?genusname=Polymixia&speciesname=nobilis (accessed on October 4, 2004).

TROUTPERCHES AND RELATIVES
Percopsiformes

Class: Actinopterygii
Order: Percopsiformes
Number of families: 3 families

order
CHAPTER

PHYSICAL CHARACTERISTICS

Troutperches and their relatives are less than 8 inches (20 centimeters) long and have an adipose (ADD-uh-pohs) fin, a short fin between the dorsal (DOOR-suhl) fin and the tail fin. The dorsal fin is the fin along the midline of the back. If pelvic fins are present, they are located on the belly and farther back from the head than they are on other fishes. Pelvic fins, the rear pair, correspond to the rear legs of four-footed animals. The body is covered with smooth or rough scales.

GEOGRAPHIC RANGE

Troutperches and their relatives live in Alaska, Canada, and the eastern United States.

HABITAT

Troutperches and their relatives live in freshwater. Some live in swamps, and some live in caves.

DIET

Troutperches and their relatives are predators (PREH-duh-ters), or animals that hunt and kill other animals for food. They eat a variety of animals. Some eat members of their own species.

BEHAVIOR AND REPRODUCTION

All troutperches and their relatives live alone, but little else is known about their behavior. At least two of the species that do not live in caves are active at night. These fishes lay eggs that are penetrated by sperm and hatch outside the female's body, but little else is known about their reproduction. At least for the species that do not live in caves, spawning, or the release of eggs, takes place in the spring.

TROUTPERCHES, THEIR RELATIVES, AND PEOPLE

Some troutperches and their relatives can be found in both home and public aquariums.

CONSERVATION STATUS

The World Conservation Union (IUCN) lists one species of troutperches and their relatives as Critically Endangered, or facing extremely high risk of extinction in the wild in the near future, and three as Vulnerable, or facing high risk of extinction in the wild. The U.S. Fish and Wildlife Service lists one species as Endangered, or in danger of extinction throughout all or a significant portion of its range, and one as Threatened, or likely to become endangered in the near future.

Did You Know?
Troutperches are neither trouts nor perches.

Environmental Engineer
Pirate perch are considered an indicator of good water quality by the Arkansas Department of Environmental Quality for the Gulf Coastal Ecoregion.

Pirate perch (Aphredoderus sayanus)

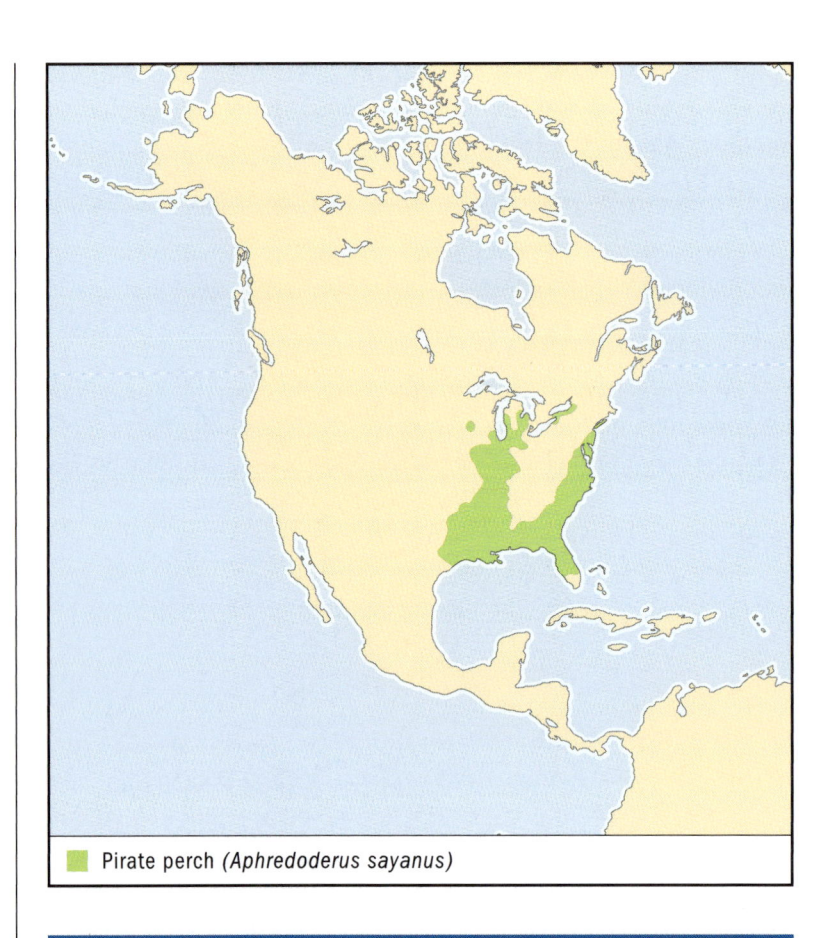

SPECIES ACCOUNT

PIRATE PERCH
Aphredoderus sayanus

Physical characteristics: Pirate perch grow to a length of 5½ inches (14 centimeters). The head and mouth are large, and the bottom jaw juts beyond the top jaw. The lateral (LAT-uhr-uhl) line, a series of pores and tiny tubes along each side of a fish's body used for sensing vibrations, is either absent or incomplete. The sides of the head are covered by rough scales. As pirate perch mature, the anus moves forward from about the middle of the belly to the throat area.

Geographic range: Pirate perch live along the Atlantic and Gulf coasts of the United States and in the Mississippi Valley.

Pirate perch usually live over mud in quiet bodies of water, such as swamps, ponds, ditches, and pools of creeks and in small to large rivers on mud and sandy bottoms. (Illustration by Emily Damstra. Reproduced by permission.)

Habitat: Pirate perch usually live over mud in quiet bodies of water, such as swamps, ponds, ditches, and pools of creeks and in small to large rivers on mud and sandy bottoms. Adults usually live on bottoms that are covered with leaf litter.

Diet: Pirate perch feed on insects, blue-green algae (AL-jee), which are plantlike growths that live in water and have no true roots, stems, or leaves, and small crustaceans (krus-TAY-shuns) and fishes. Crustaceans are water-dwelling animals that have jointed legs and a hard shell but no backbone.

Behavior and reproduction: Pirate perch live alone and are active at dusk. They release sticky eggs over leaf litter and woody debris. They live for about four years.

Pirate perch and people: Pirate perch are used for testing the quality and cleanliness of water.

Conservation status: Pirate perch are not threatened or endangered.

FOR MORE INFORMATION

Books:

Berra, Tim M. *Freshwater Fish Distribution.* San Diego, CA: Academic Press, 2001.

Gilbert, Carter Rowell, and James D. Williams. *National Audubon Society Field Guide to Fishes: North America.* New York: Knopf, 2002.

Schultz, Ken. *Ken Schultz's Field Guide to Freshwater Fish.* New York: Wiley, 2004.

Web sites:

"Indicator Species." U.S. Environmental Protection Agency Biological Indicators of Watershed Health. http://www.epa.gov/bioindicators/html/indicator.html (accessed on October 16, 2004).

"Pirate Perch, *Aphredoderus sayanus*." The Virtual Aquarium. http://www.cnr.vt.edu/efish/families/aphredoderidae.html (accessed on October 4, 2004).

CUSK-EELS AND RELATIVES
Ophidiiformes

Class: Actinopterygii
Order: Ophidiiformes
Number of families: 5 families

order CHAPTER

PHYSICAL CHARACTERISTICS

Most cusk-eels and their relatives are long and thin. The dorsal (DOOR-suhl) and anal (AY-nuhl) fins are very long, reaching the tail fin in some species. The dorsal fin is the fin along the midline of the back. The anal fin is the fin along the midline of the belly. The tail fin of these fishes is small, sometimes just a bony point. Cusk-eels and their relatives are about $1\frac{1}{2}$ inches (4 centimeters) to 6 feet, 6 inches (2 meters) long. Some species have long, thick barbels (BAR-buhls) on the chin. Barbels are feelers used for the senses of taste, touch, and smell. Cusk-eels often have black or brown markings or bands extending the length of the body. Some relatives are covered with small spots, and others are colorless. Some species have long pectoral (PECK-ter-uhl) fins, which are the front pair and correspond to the front legs of four-footed animals. Scales can be absent, but when present, they generally are small. The pelvic fins are either very small or absent. The pelvic fins are the rear pair and correspond to the rear legs of four-footed animals.

GEOGRAPHIC RANGE

Cusk-eels and their relatives live all over the world.

HABITAT

Cusk-eels and their relatives live in the ocean, some in very deep water and some in shallow seas and estuaries (EHS-chew-air-eez), or the areas where rivers meet the sea. Most of these fishes are bottom dwellers that live in mucus-lined mud or sand

phylum
class
subclass
● order
monotypic order
suborder
family

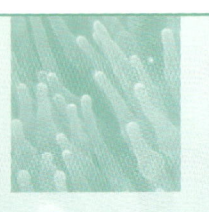

HOME SWEET CUCUMBER

The pearlfish uses its snout to locate the anus of the sea cucumber. Holding its head in the anus, the pearlfish curves its body and tracks the tip of its tail along the sea cucumber until the tail reaches the cucumber's anus. Once it has the tip of its tail aligned and pointed into the anus, the pearlfish turns abruptly and forces its way tail first into the sea cucumber.

burrows, rock or coral crevices, or sea caves. Some live with communities of bottom-dwelling invertebrates (in-VER-teh-brehts), or animals without backbones, such as tube worms. Some species live in the body cavity of invertebrate hosts, such as pearl oysters, giant clams, and sea cucumbers. Some species live in freshwater caves.

DIET

Most cusk-eels and their relatives look for bottom-dwelling animals during evening hours. They eat invertebrates and small bottom fishes.

BEHAVIOR AND REPRODUCTION

Many cusk-eels and their relatives produce sound with their swim bladder, forward vertebrae (ver-teh-BREE), and the ligaments and muscles attached to those vertebrae. The swim bladder is an internal sac that fishes use to control their position in the water. Vertebrae are the bones that make up the spinal column. In some cusk-eels and their relatives, the swim bladder is hard and serves as an echo chamber. Some species make the sound just before mating.

Cusk-eels and their relatives usually hide in burrows or crevices or in or around invertebrate hosts during daylight hours and then exit at night to look for food. Some never leave the host and constantly feed on its internal organs.

Cusk-eels and their relatives either release eggs or bear live young. Eggs are released in open water and float individually or are deposited in a gummy raft. The egg rafts float at the ocean surface until they hatch, usually within several days. Larvae (LAR-vee) of some species float near the surface and sometimes travel great distances from their hatching place. Larvae are animals in an early stage and must change form before becoming adults.

CUSK-EELS, THEIR RELATIVES, AND PEOPLE

Cusk-eels are large; their meat is tasty, and they are fished commercially.

CONSERVATION STATUS

The World Conservation Union (IUCN) lists seven species of cusk-eels and their relatives as Vulnerable, or facing high risk of extinction in the wild.

Pearlfish (*Carapus bermudensis*)

SPECIES ACCOUNT

PEARLFISH
Carapus bermudensis

Physical characteristics: Pearlfish are long, slender, and eel-like. The skin is cloudy, almost clear, with silvery bands along the sides and black along the back. The cheeks are silver, and there are blotches of color at the bases of the dorsal and anal fins and on the head. The dorsal and anal fins extend almost the length of the body. There are

Pearlfish live in the bodies of sea cucumbers during the day and exit at night to look for food. (©Chesher/Photo Researchers, Inc. Reproduced by permission.)

no pelvic fins and usually no tail fin. The teeth on the upper jaw are small, and some are heart-shaped. The teeth on the lower jaw are larger and cone shaped. The swim bladder is separated into two parts.

Geographic range: Pearlfish live in the western Atlantic Ocean from Bermuda to Brazil.

Habitat: Pearlfish live in sea cucumbers, which usually live in shallow waters to about 98 feet (30 meters) on sandy bottoms or grass beds in warm lagoons near reefs.

Diet: Pearlfish eat crustaceans (krus-TAY-shuns), or water-dwelling animals that have jointed legs and a hard shell but no backbone, such as small shrimps and crabs.

Behavior and reproduction: Pearlfish live in the bodies of sea cucumbers during the day and exit at night to look for food and perhaps to spawn, or release eggs. Pearlfish deposit their eggs into a jellylike blob that floats at the surface. Eggs hatch in one to two days. Pearlfish larvae are remarkable in that they undergo two separate growth phases. In the first phase the larvae have a long, showy thread in front of the dorsal fin. These larvae are very long, about 7 inches (18 centimeters). In the second phase the larvae shrink to about half their original length.

Pearlfish and people: Pearlfish are rarely seen and are not fished commercially.

Conservation status: Pearlfish are not threatened or endangered.

FOR MORE INFORMATION

Books:

FAO Species Catalogue: Ophidiiform Fishes of the World. Rome, Italy: Food and Agriculture Organization of the United Nations, 1999.

Gilbert, Carter Rowell, and James D. Williams. *National Audubon Society Field Guide to Fishes: North America.* New York: Knopf, 2002.

Web sites:

"The Cusk Eel Is All Talk, Some Slime." *Points East.* http://www.pointseast.com/thegulf/040701eel-ad.shtml (accessed on October 6, 2004).

"Cusk eel *Lepophidium cervinum* (Goode and Bean) 1885." Fishes of the Gulf of Maine. http://www.gma.org/fogm/Default.htm (accessed on October 6, 2004).

GRENADIERS, HAKES, CODS, AND RELATIVES
Gadiformes

Class: Actinopterygii
Order: Gadiformes
Number of families: 11 families

order
CHAPTER

PHYSICAL CHARACTERISTICS

Some fishes in the group that includes grenadiers, hakes, cods, and their relatives have three separate dorsal (DOOR-suhl) fins and two separate anal fins. The dorsal fin is the fin along the midline of the back. The anal (AY-nuhl) fin is the fin along the midline of the belly. Other fishes in this group have two dorsal fins. The front one is small and may have a long spine. The rear dorsal fin in these fishes is quite long, extending from just behind the first dorsal fin all the way to the tail. Some fishes in this group have two anal fins. Others have one long anal fin that extends almost the length of the body. Still others have one small anal fin. Other fishes in this group have long bodies that get thinner toward the tail and have a long thin tail rather than a tail fin. Some fishes in this group have a large chin barbel (BAR-buhl), or a feeler used for the senses of taste, touch, and smell. Cods that live in open water are small, about 6 inches (15 centimeters) long. Bottom-dwelling fishes in this group have a well-developed swim bladder, which is an internal sac that fishes use to control their position in the water. The open-water species do not have a swim bladder.

GEOGRAPHIC RANGE

Grenadiers, hakes, cods, and their relatives live all over the world.

HABITAT

Grenadiers, hakes, cods, and their relatives live in the open ocean at all depths, the deepest-occurring species living deeper

phylum
class
subclass
● order
monotypic order
suborder
family

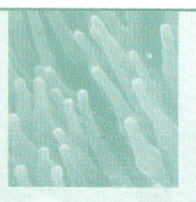

COD IN HISTORY

The Vikings crossed the Atlantic Ocean in pursuit of cod. In medieval times the Basques, people from an area between Spain and France, turned cod into a commercial product. Cape Cod, Massachusetts, was named in honor of the cod in 1602. Cod have been the cause of wars between countries from American colonial times to a twentieth-century conflict between Iceland and Great Britain. Newfoundland, Canada, was settled by Irish and English natives in the early eighteenth century, largely because of opportunities for cod fishing. Throughout most of the nineteenth century, cod fishing was the most important source of employment and income for people in eastern Canada.

---

than 3,000 feet (900 meters). Fishes in this group also live in estuaries (EHS-chew-air-eez), or the areas where rivers meet the sea, sometimes in eel grass beds; in shallow waters near the coast; on bottoms consisting of rock, sand, mud, gravel, or broken shells; and on the bottoms of rivers and lakes. Some fishes in this group migrate (MY-grayt) or travel from one habitat to another to spawn, or reproduce, and then continue to change habitats as they change life stages. A fish may move from an estuary, across the continental shelf, to the upper part of the continental slope, and from the surface to the bottom.

DIET

Bottom-dwelling grenadiers, hakes, cods, and their relatives use their chin barbels to find bottom-dwelling prey, or animals hunted and killed for food. Open-water species eat krill, which are tiny crustaceans (krus-TAY-shuns). Crustaceans are water-dwelling animals that have jointed legs and a hard shell but no backbone. Some of the fishes in this group eat other fishes such as Atlantic herring.

BEHAVIOR AND REPRODUCTION

Many grenadiers, hakes, cods, and their relatives travel with the changes of seasons to reproduce or to find important prey. Some of these fishes stop feeding during spawning season. Most grenadiers, hakes, cods, and their relatives release masses of eggs into the open water, and the eggs are fertilized (FUR-teh-lyzed), or penetrated by sperm to start development, outside the body.

GRENADIERS, HAKES, CODS, THEIR RELATIVES, AND PEOPLE

Some grenadiers, hakes, cods, and their relatives are among the world's most important food fishes.

CONSERVATION STATUS

The World Conservation Union (IUCN) lists one species of grenadiers, hakes, cods, and relatives as Critically Endangered, or facing extremely high risk of extinction in the wild in the near future, and two as Vulnerable, or facing high risk of extinction in the wild.

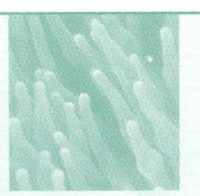

OVERFISHING

In 1992 cod nearly became extinct in waters off eastern Canada, and cod fishing was banned. This ban removed the main source of employment and income for thousands of fishermen from hundreds of small fishing communities and devastated the Canadian economy. The effects have been compared to the Great Depression of the 1930s in the United States.

Atlantic cod *(Gadus morhua)*

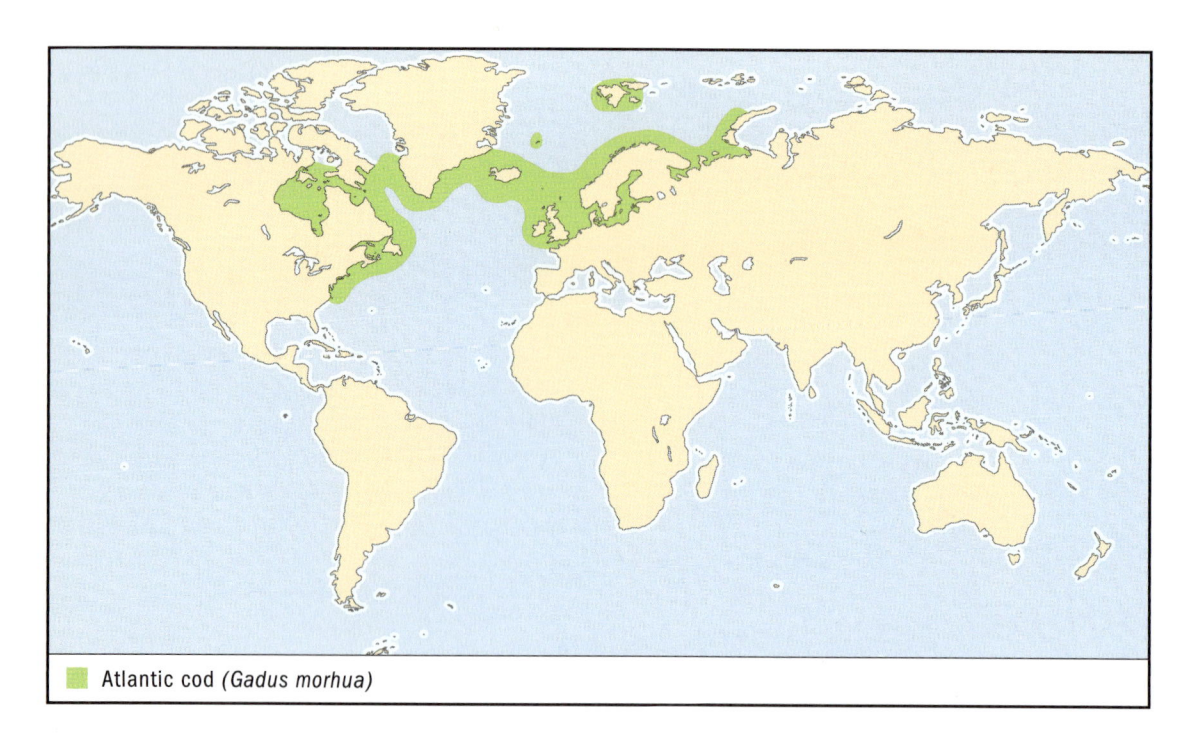

SPECIES ACCOUNTS

ATLANTIC COD
Gadus morhua

Physical characteristics: Atlantic cod have three separate dorsal fins and two separate anal fins. They also have chin barbels. The pelvic fins sometimes have one long ray. Pelvic fins are the rear pair and correspond to the rear legs of four-footed animals. Atlantic cod are usually about 2 feet (60 centimeters) long and weigh about 10 pounds (4.5 kilograms), although they can reach a length of 4 feet (120 centimeters) and a weight of 60 pounds (27 kilograms). The record is 6 feet (1.8 meters), 209 pounds (95 kilograms). These fish are brownish to greenish gray on the upper sides and paler toward the belly. The body is covered with spots.

Geographic range: Atlantic cod live in the northern part of the Atlantic Ocean from Hudson Bay in Canada south to the coast of the Carolinas in the United States to the Barents Sea, which is north of Norway and Russia.

Habitat: The habitat of Atlantic cod changes with the life stages. The fertilized eggs drift in open water. Larvae (LAR-vee) also live in

Atlantic cod is an extremely important food fish for humans. The annual catch is tens of thousands of tons. (Illustration by Emily Damstra. Reproduced by permission.)

open water and drift slowly away from spawning areas as they develop. Larvae are animals in an early stage and must change form before becoming adults. The young sink to the bottom when they are about 2 inches (5 centimeters) long and settle on pebble and gravel deposits. After settlement, young fish live in habitats such as eel grass in protected coastal waters, where they avoid being eaten by older cod and other predators. One- and two-year-old fish join the adults. Adult cod travel into shallower waters during summer and deeper waters with rock, pebble, sand, or gravel bottoms for the winter.

Diet: The diet of Atlantic cod changes with life stage. Cod are greedy eaters and eat any plant or meat available. Adult Atlantic cod feed at dawn and dusk, but young fish feed almost continuously. Larvae feed on plankton, which are microscopic plants and animals drifting in water. Young Atlantic cod feed on invertebrates, or animals without a backbone, especially small crustaceans. Older fish feed on invertebrates and fishes, including young cod.

Behavior and reproduction: Huge schools of Atlantic cod leave their wintering areas in deep, oceanic waters and follow tongues of deep, relatively warm, oceanic waters across the continental shelf to summer feeding areas nearer to the coast. Spawning occurs in dense groups as the fish begin their travels. As it moves toward shore, the huge mass of cod encounters groups of important prey animals such as shrimp and breaks up to feed. The mass is led by the largest fish, or scouts, and the smallest bring up the rear. After reaching nearshore waters, the fish turn and move northward along the coast in late summer, then eventually return to their deep-water wintering areas.

Atlantic cod produce more eggs than almost any other fish. A female weighing 11 pounds (5 kilograms) can produce 2.5 million eggs. These fish start reproducing when they are about two years old and 15 inches (38 centimeters) long. Reproduction peaks in winter and spring but continues sporadically throughout the year. Eggs and larvae live in open water, and young Atlantic cod begin moving to the bottom when they are between 1 and 2 inches (2.5 and 6.0 centimeters) long.

Atlantic cod and people: Atlantic cod is an extremely important food fish. The annual catch is tens of thousands of tons.

Conservation status: The IUCN lists Atlantic cod as Vulnerable or facing a high risk of extinction in the wild. ∎

Haddock (Melanogrammus aeglefinus)

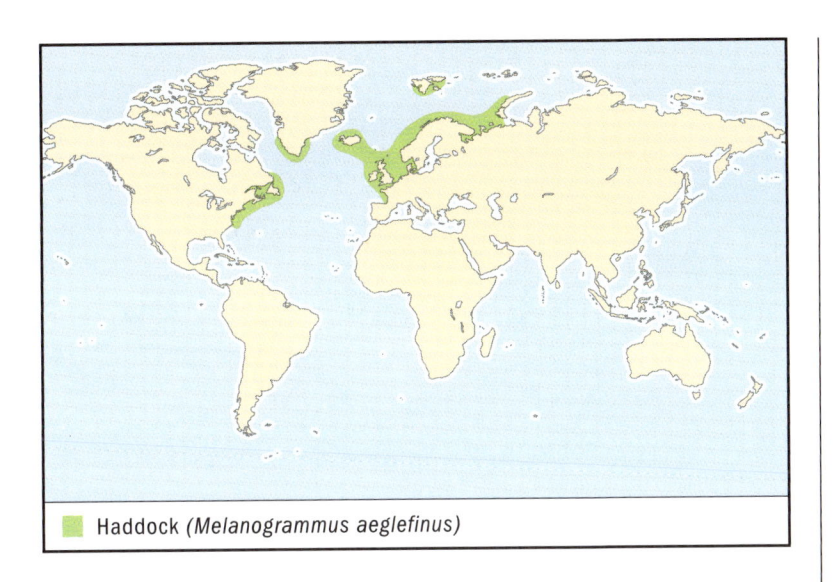

HADDOCK
Melanogrammus aeglefinus

Physical characteristics: Haddock have three separate dorsal fins and two separate anal fins. They also have a small chin barbel. The pelvic fins sometimes have one long ray. The lateral (LAT-uhr-uhl) line is dark. The lateral line is a series of pores and tiny tubes along each side of a fish's body and is used for sensing vibrations. Haddock have a large dark blotch over the pectoral fin on each side. The pectoral (PECK-ter-uhl) fins are the front pair and correspond to the front legs of four-footed animals.

Geographic range: Haddock live in the northern part of the Atlantic Ocean from off the coast of Virginia to the Barents Sea, which is north of Norway and Russia.

Habitat: Haddock live near the bottom of cool water 148–443 feet (45–135 meters) deep. They prefer bottoms of rock, sand, gravel, or broken shells. Haddock shift habitat depending on their life stage. The young live in shallower water in bank and shoal areas. Larger adults live in deeper water.

Diet: Haddock eat crabs, sea urchins, worms, and clams. They rarely eat other fish.

Haddock eat crabs, sea urchins, worms, and clams. They rarely eat other fish. (Illustration by Emily Damstra. Reproduced by permission.)

Behavior and reproduction: Adult haddock do not undertake long travels to reproduce. Spawning occurs between January and June, peaking in late March and early April. Depending on size, females produce 850,000 to three million eggs each year.

Haddock and people: Haddock is an extremely important food fish.

Conservation status: The IUCN lists haddock as Vulnerable or facing a high risk of extinction in the wild. ∎

FOR MORE INFORMATION

Books:

Gilbert, Carter Rowell, and James D. Williams. *National Audubon Society Field Guide to Fishes: North America.* New York: Knopf, 2002.

Kurlansky, M. *Cod: A Biography of the Fish That Changed the World.* New York: Walker, 1997.

Schultz, Ken. *Ken Schultz's Field Guide to Saltwater Fish.* New York: Wiley, 2004.

Web sites:

"Atlantic Cod." Fisheries and Oceans Canada. http://www.dfo-mpo.gc.ca/zone/underwater_sous-marin/atlantic/acod_e.htm (accessed on October 7, 2004).

"Cod War." All Science Fair Projects. http://www.all-science-fair-projects.com/science_fair_projects_encyclopedia/Cod_War (accessed on October 7, 2004).

"Empty Oceans, Empty Nets." PBS. http://www.pbs.org/emptyoceans/cod (accessed on October 7, 2004).

> **TOADFISHES**
> **Batrachoidiformes**
>
> **Class:** Actinopterygii
> **Order:** Batrachoidiformes
> **Number of families:** 1 family
>
> order CHAPTER

phylum
class
subclass
● order
monotypic order
suborder
family

PHYSICAL CHARACTERISTICS

Toadfishes have a broad, flat head and a wide mouth, which usually has thick barbels or flaps of skin around it. Barbels (BAR-buhls) are feelers used for the senses of taste, touch, and smell. The eyes are on the top of the head and face upward. Some toadfishes have light organs along their sides and belly. Other toadfishes have hollow, venomous spines in the first dorsal (DOOR-suhl) fin and gill cover. The dorsal fin is the one along the midline of the back.

The fin arrangement of toadfishes is unusual in that the pelvic fins, which correspond to the hind legs of four-footed animals, are forward of the pectoral (PECK-ter-uhl) fins, which correspond to the forelegs of four-footed animals. The pectoral fins of toadfishes are large. There are two separate dorsal fins. The first is small and has two or three spines, and the second is long, almost the length of the body. The anal (AY-nuhl) fin is a bit shorter than the second dorsal fin. The anal fin is the one on the midline of the belly.

Toadfishes are small to medium sized, about 2 to 20 inches (5 to 51 centimeters) long. They are usually rather drab, often brownish with darker saddles, bars, or spots. Some, however, are brightly colored.

GEOGRAPHIC RANGE

Toadfishes live all over the world.

Toadfishes 181

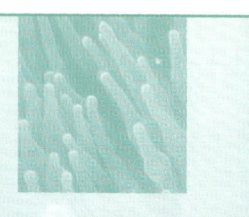

THE RIGHT STUFF: THE SENATOR AND THE TOADFISH

Two oyster toadfish accompanied the former senator John Glenn and several other astronauts on space shuttle mission STS-95 in October 1998. Glenn, one of the original Mercury astronauts in the 1960s, was the first American to orbit Earth.

A Helpful Fish

Oyster toadfish are used in studies of hearing, dizziness, and motion sickness, of insulin and diabetes, and of the effects of drugs.

HABITAT

Toadfishes live in saltwater from shoreline waters with a low salt content down to deep sea water, about 1,200 feet (366 meters). These fishes sometimes enter rivers. Their camouflage allows toadfishes to blend with the bottom, where they bury themselves and ambush their prey, or animals caught for food. One species lives in the sand under coral heads.

DIET

In addition to ambushing their prey, toadfishes move about feeding on invertebrates, or animals without backbones, such as crabs, shrimps, mollusks (MAH-lusks), and sea urchins. Some eat fish, and some eat plankton. Mollusks are animals with a soft, unsegmented body usually covered by a hard shell, such as snails and clams. Plankton are microscopic plants and animals drifting in water.

BEHAVIOR AND REPRODUCTION

Toadfishes produce sound by contracting muscles on their swim bladder, which is an internal sac that fishes use to control their position in the water. Both males and females produce grunts, but only males make longer courtship calls, which sound like boat whistles or humming.

Male toadfishes prepare nests, usually under rocks or shells but sometimes under objects discarded by humans, such as cans and bottles. Males attract females by making their sounds, and then females lay large, sticky eggs and leave the area. Males guard and fan the eggs until after hatching. Fanning is using the fins to move water over the eggs to clean them and make sure they have plenty of oxygen. The young may remain in the nest after hatching. One species of toadfish has two types of males, larger nest-holding ones and smaller sneaker males that dart into nests attempting to fertilize (FUR-teh-lyze), or place sperm on, eggs of a nesting pair.

TOADFISHES AND PEOPLE

Large toadfishes are eaten. One species is collected and sold in the aquarium business. Another species is used in laboratory studies. Venomous toadfishes can inflict pain if handled.

CONSERVATION STATUS

The World Conservation Union (IUCN) lists five species of toadfishes as Vulnerable, or facing high risk of extinction in the wild.

Oyster toadfish (Opsanus tau)

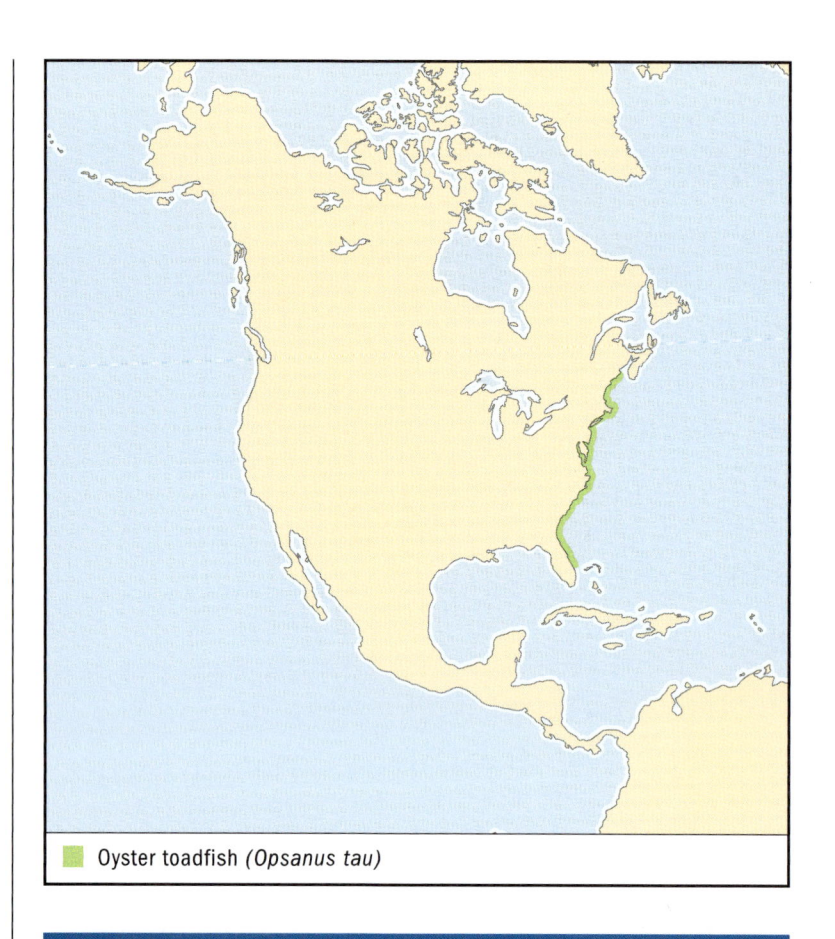

SPECIES ACCOUNT

OYSTER TOADFISH
Opsanus tau

Physical characteristics: Oyster toadfish grow as long as 15 inches (38 centimeters). They have three dorsal-fin spines, no scales, and a spine under the gill cover. The second dorsal fin has 23 to 27 soft rays, and the anal fin has 19 to 23 soft rays. The body is dark and has no spots. The pectoral fin has cross bars.

Geographic range: Oyster toadfish live along the Atlantic coast of the United States.

Habitat: Oyster toadfish usually live over rock, sand, mud, or oyster shell bottoms in estuaries (EHS-chew-air-eez), areas where a river meets the sea.

Oyster toadfish make a grunting noise by rubbing muscles across their swim bladder. (©David Hall/Photo Researchers, Inc. Reproduced by permission.)

Diet: Oyster toadfish feed mainly on small crabs and other crustaceans (krus-TAY-shuns), which are water-dwelling animals that have jointed legs and a hard shell but no backbone.

Behavior and reproduction: Oyster toadfish make a grunting noise by rubbing muscles across their swim bladder. Males use a boatwhistle call to attract females to nesting sites. Males establish nesting sites from April through October.

Oyster toadfish and people: Oyster toadfish are helpful to people because they are used for medical studies.

Conservation status: Oyster toadfish are not threatened or endangered. ■

FOR MORE INFORMATION

Books:

Gilbert, Carter Rowell, and James D. Williams. *National Audubon Society Field Guide to Fishes: North America.* New York: Knopf, 2002.

Niesen, Thomas M. *The Marine Biology Coloring Book.* 2nd ed. New York: HarperResource, 2000.

Web sites:

"Toadfish." All Science Fair Projects. http://www.all-science-fair-projects.com/science_fair_projects_encyclopedia/Toadfish (accessed on October 8, 2004).

"Toadfish Song May Help Heal Humans." CNN.com. http://www.cnn.com/2003/TECH/science/12/19/toadfish.song.ap (accessed on October 8, 2004).

"Toadfish in Space." Marine Biological Laboratory. http://www.mbl.edu/publications/LABNOTES/8.2/toadfish.html (accessed on October 8, 2004).

> **ANGLERFISHES**
> **Lophiiformes**
>
> **Class:** Actinopterygii
> **Order:** Lophiiformes
> **Number of families:** 18 families
>
> order CHAPTER

PHYSICAL CHARACTERISTICS

The first spine of the dorsal (DOOR-suhl) fin of anglerfishes serves as a fishing, or angling, rod and lure for attracting prey, animals hunted and caught for food. The dorsal fin is the one along the midline of the back. The fishes use muscles at the base of the rod to move it rapidly, thrashing the lure above or in front of the anglerfish's mouth. In some anglerfishes the lure may be a simple bulb, but in others it is quite elaborate. In many deep-sea anglerfishes, the lure glows. In forms that live in sunlit regions, the lure may resemble a shrimp or even a fish. The bases of the pectoral (PECK-ter-uhl) fins of anglerfishes are so long that the fins appear to be at the end of long, jointed arms. The pectoral fins are the front pair and correspond to the front legs of four-footed animals. The color and size of anglerfishes vary greatly. Many bottom-dwelling anglerfishes have camouflage coloring, but the midwater forms are usually very dark brown or black. The length ranges from a few inches (centimeters) to several feet (about 2 meters).

GEOGRAPHIC RANGE

Anglerfishes live all over the world.

HABITAT

Most anglerfishes live in the deep ocean. Some live in open water in middle depths. Others are bottom dwellers. A few anglerfishes enter shallows, and many live in coral reefs.

phylum
class
subclass
● order
monotypic order
suborder
family

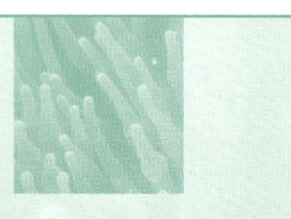

WHY IS FISHING CALLED ANGLING?

In the old days in England the word *angle* meant "fish hook." Angling is the sport of catching fish with a hook, as opposed to a net or one's hands. Anglers are people who like this sport.

DIET

Anglerfishes eat fishes and other animals attracted by the lure. A few anglerfishes feed mainly on bottom-dwelling invertebrates, animals without backbones.

BEHAVIOR AND REPRODUCTION

Anglerfishes ambush their prey. During a typical ambush, the anglerfish remains motionless (either on the bottom or in open water) until it detects prey. When it senses prey, the anglerfish uses its fishing rod to attract the prey to within reach. When the prey reaches the strike zone, the anglerfish opens its mouth rapidly and widely, creating strong suction, which draws in the prey. The entire open, suck, and swallow takes four to seven milliseconds.

Little is known about the reproduction and early life of anglerfishes. Scientists believe that the larvae (LAR-vee) of all anglerfishes drift in open water.

Larvae are animals in an early stage and must change form before becoming adults. Eggs are released from female anglerfishes embedded in a long ribbonlike veil of mucus. This veil can be as long as 39 feet (12 meters) and as wide as 5 feet (1.5 meters) and has been estimated to contain more than 1.3 million eggs. The males of some deep-sea anglerfishes are tiny and permanently attach themselves to the bodies of females.

THE SARGASSO SEA

The Sargasso Sea is a huge floating island of seaweed (2 million square miles) in a calm area of the Atlantic Ocean near Bermuda.

ANGLERFISHES AND PEOPLE

Some anglerfishes are caught for their meat and for the liver.

CONSERVATION STATUS

The World Conservation Union (IUCN) lists one species of anglerfish as Critically Endangered, or facing extremely high risk of extinction in the wild in the near future.

Sargassumfish (*Histrio histrio*)

SARGASSUMFISH
Histrio histrio

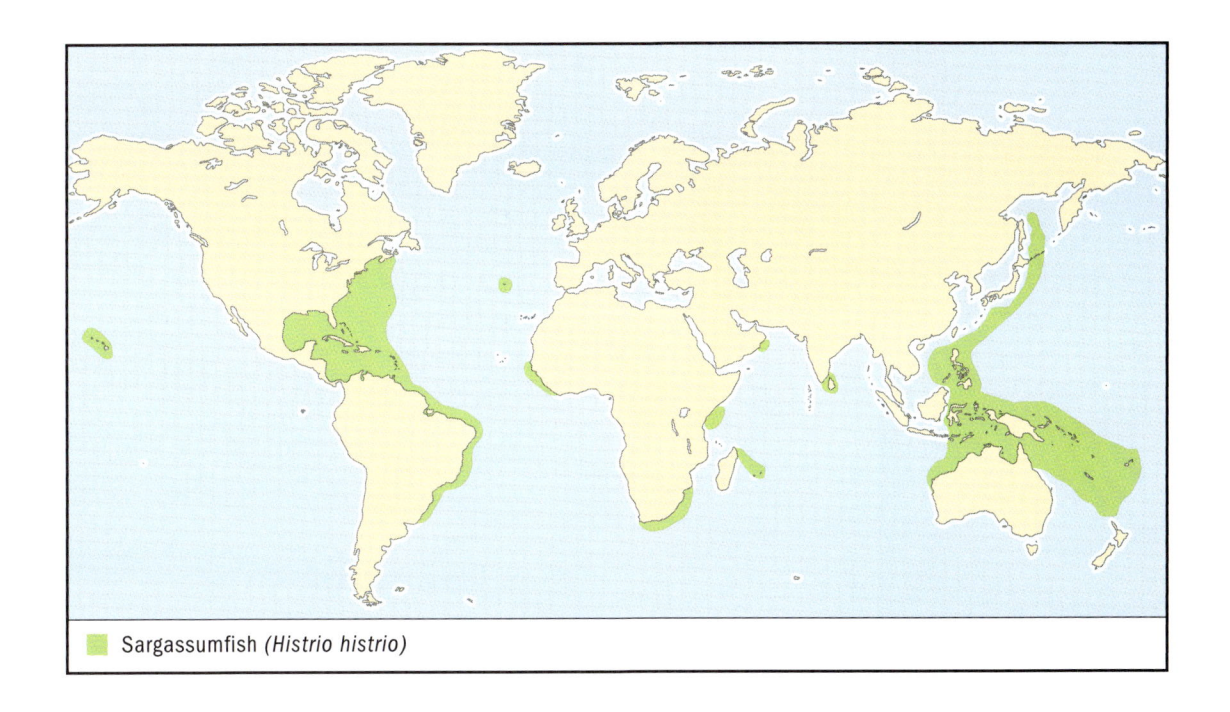

SPECIES ACCOUNTS

Physical characteristics: Sargassumfish have a short fishing rod and smooth skin. The fish are usually camouflaged with streaks, spots, and mottling of brown, olive, and yellow, making them nearly impossible to detect in the seaweed in which they hide.

Geographic range: Sargassumfish live in the western Atlantic, western Pacific, and Indian oceans.

Habitat: Sargassumfish live only in open warm water on the surface in sargassum. Sargassum is a brown seaweed that is a type of algae (AL-jee), plantlike growths that live in water and have no true roots, stems, or leaves.

Diet: Sargassumfish eat anything they can swallow, including fishes as long as or longer than they are. They even eat other sargassumfish.

Behavior and reproduction: Sargassumfish release eggs in an egg veil 35 to 47 inches (90 to 120 centimeters) long and 2 to 4 inches (5 to 10 centimeters) wide.

Anglerfishes

Sargassumfish eat anything they can swallow, including fishes as long as or longer than they are. (Illustration by Joseph E. Trumpey. Reproduced by permission.)

Sargassumfish and people: Sargassumfish have no importance to people.

Conservation status: Sargassumfish are not threatened or endangered. ∎

Monkfish (Lophius americanus)

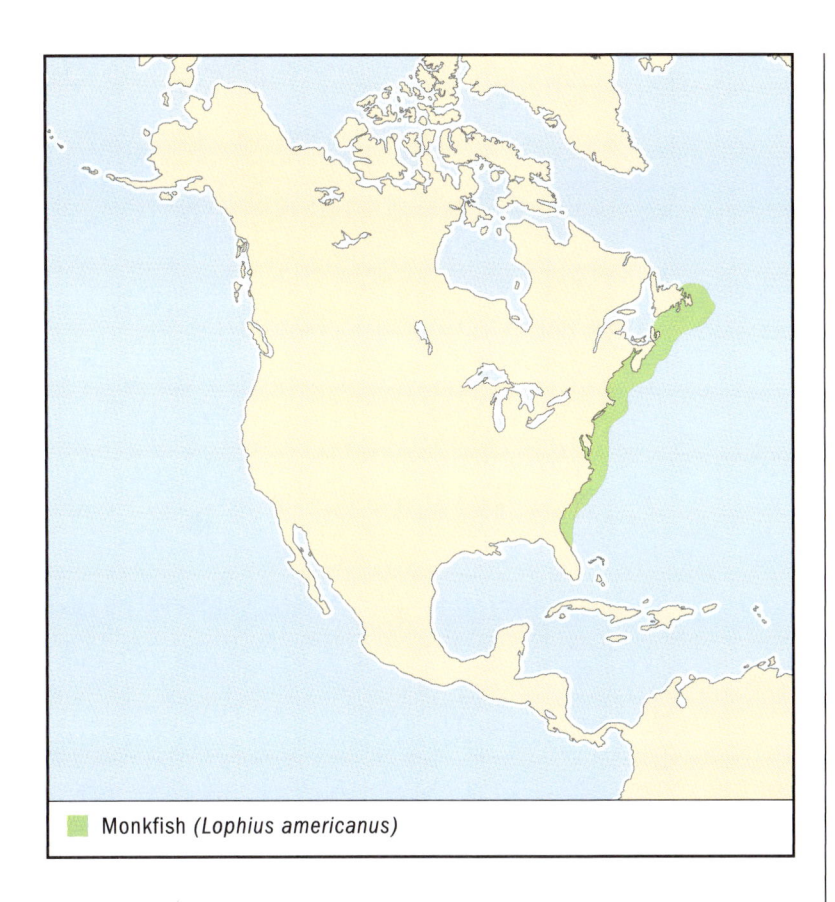

MONKFISH
Lophius americanus

Physical characteristics: Monkfish have a very large, wide, flattened head and an enormous mouth armed with long, sharp, cone-shaped teeth. Monkfish have hairlike threads hanging in front of their eyes that act as fishing line. The lines have knoblike lures at the end. Monkfish have a large number of dorsal and anal fin rays and vertebrae (ver-teh-BREE), which are the bones that make up the spinal column.

Geographic range: Monkfish live in the western Atlantic Ocean.

Habitat: Monkfish live on soft and hard bottoms, including mud, sand, pebbles, gravel, and broken shells from just below the tide line to depths of about 2,625 feet (800 meters).

Monkfish have been known to eat birds such as cormorants, herring gulls, loons, and auks. (Illustration by Joseph E. Trumpey. Reproduced by permission.)

Diet: Monkfish are greedy ambushers that eat any prey large enough to engulf, including fishes nearly as long as they are. Monkfish have been known to engulf birds such as cormorants, herring gulls, loons, and auks. Smaller monkfish feed on a variety of invertebrates.

Behavior and reproduction: Small fish that come in range of the fishing line and lures of monkfish and strike at them are led down the line into the monkfish's huge mouth. Except for the facts that monkfish have long egg veils and the early larvae drift in open water, scientists do not how these fish reproduce.

Monkfish and people: Monkfish is a popular food fish. Some people call it goosefish.

Conservation status: Monkfish are not threatened or endangered. ■

FOR MORE INFORMATION

Books:

Byatt, Andrew, Alastair Fothergill, and Martha Holmes. *Blue Planet.* New York: DK, 2001.

Gilbert, Carter Rowell, and James D. Williams. *National Audubon Society Field Guide to Fishes: North America.* New York: Knopf, 2002.

Web sites:

"City Boat Joins Monkfish Study." *South Coast Today.* http://www.s-t.com/daily/02-01/02-28-01/a01lo002.htm (accessed on October 8, 2004).

"Frequently Asked Questions about Monkfish." Northeast Fisheries Science Center. http://www.nefsc.noaa.gov/read/popdy/monkfish/Survey2004/2004_index.html (accessed on October 10, 2004).

"Sargassum Anglerfish: *Histrio histrio* (Linnaeus, 1758)." Australian Museum Fish Site. http://www.amonline.net.au/fishes/fishfacts/fish/hhistrio.htm (accessed on October 10, 2004).

MULLETS
Mugiliformes

Class: Actinopterygii
Order: Mugiliformes
Number of families: 1 family

order
CHAPTER

phylum
class
subclass
● order
monotypic order
suborder
family

PHYSICAL CHARACTERISTICS

Most mullets reach about 8 inches (20 centimeters) in total length, but some may be as long as 31 to 39 inches (80 to 100 centimeters). The head is broad and flat on top. In most species, the teeth are very small or may even be absent. In many species, the teeth are on the lips. The eyes of mullets may be partially covered by fat. There is no lateral (LAT-uhr-uhl) line, a series of pores and tiny tubes along each side of the body, used for sensing vibrations. Mullets usually are grayish green or blue on the back, and the sides are silvery, often with dark stripes. The belly is pale or yellowish. Mullets have two short, well-separated dorsal (DOOR-suhl) fins and a short anal fin. The pectoral fins are high on the body, and the tail fin is slightly forked. The dorsal fin is the one along the midline of the back. The anal (AY-nuhl) fin is the one along the midline of the belly. The pectoral (PECK-ter-uhl) fins are the front pair, corresponding to the front legs of four-footed animals.

GEOGRAPHIC RANGE

Mullets live all over the world.

HABITAT

Most mullets live in shallow near-shore saltwater habitats, such as bays, reef flats, tide pools, and harbor pilings and in habitats with a low salt content, such lagoons, mangrove forests, and estuaries (EHS-chew-air-eez), which are areas where rivers meet the sea. Mullets usually swim over sandy or muddy bottoms and sea grass meadows in relatively still waters. They commonly live in water depths of 66 feet (20 meters). Many species move between saltwater and the freshwater environments of rivers and flooded rice fields. Some species sometimes swim far upriver, and a few species spend their entire adult lives in rivers.

DIET

Young mullets eat plankton, which are microscopic plants and animals drifting in water. Larger mullets eat microscopic plants and animals from submerged surfaces and eat small invertebrates, or animals without backbones.

BEHAVIOR AND REPRODUCTION

The feeding behavior of mullets follows daily cycles, which may change through the seasons according to water temperature and the availability of prey, animals hunted and caught for food. Several species form schools, particularly at night. Schooling adults may leap, especially in the evening. Mullets spawn, or release eggs, in shallow open areas or offshore, forming large schools before moving out to the spawning grounds. Some freshwater species move downstream to spawn in water with a low salt content. Others spawn upstream, and the young are swept downstream for a short time before traveling back upriver.

MULLETS AND PEOPLE

Mullets are important food fishes. They are both caught and farmed.

CONSERVATION STATUS

Mullets are not threatened or endangered.

Flathead mullet (*Mugil cephalus*)

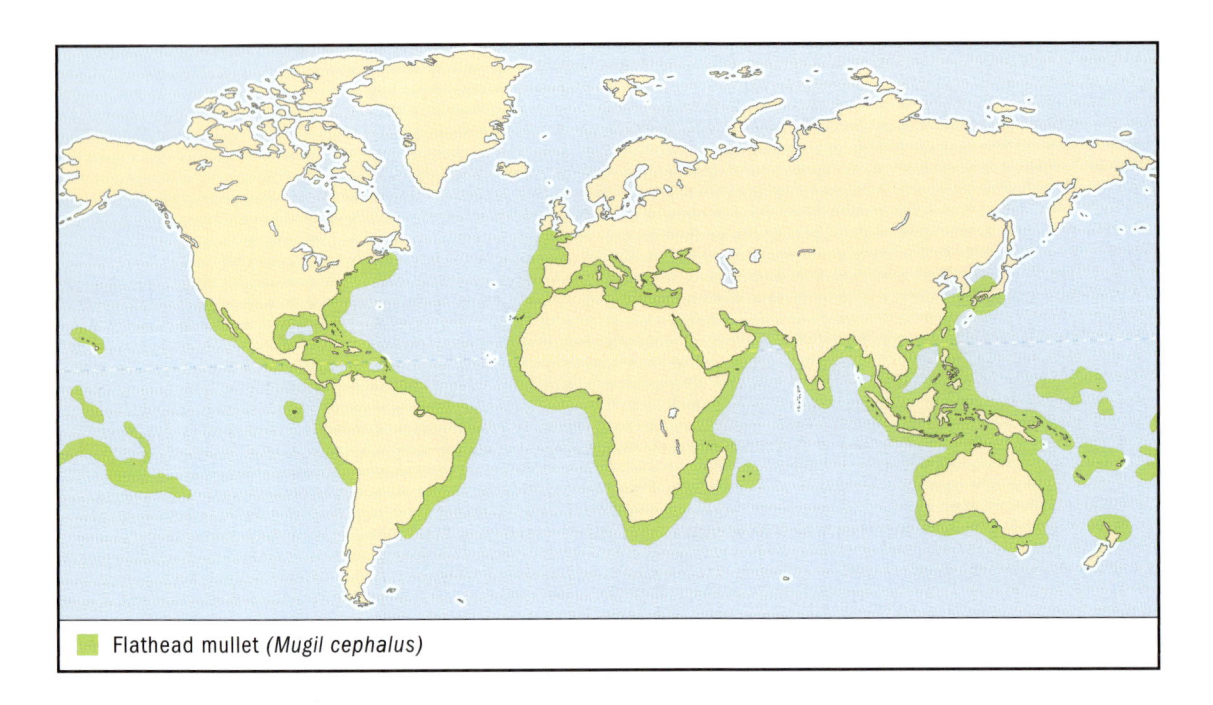

SPECIES ACCOUNT

FLATHEAD MULLET
Mugil cephalus

Physical characteristics: Flathead mullets commonly reach a length of 14 inches (35 centimeters) from the tip of the snout to the end of the body but may reach 47 inches (120 centimeters) from the tip of the snout to the end of the tail. Fat covers a large portion of the eyes. Flathead mullets have several rows of teeth on the edges of the lips. The body is olive green on the back and silvery on the sides and belly, and there are about seven dark stripes along the sides. The pelvic fin, anal fin, and lower lobe of the tail fin are yellowish in some fish. The pelvic fins are the rear pair, corresponding to the rear legs of four-footed animals.

Geographic range: Flathead mullets live all over the world in warm water.

Habitat: Flathead mullets live in inshore marine waters, estuaries, lagoons, and rivers, usually in shallow water, rarely moving deeper than 656 feet (200 m). Adults may move far upriver.

Diet: Larvae and young flathead mullets feed on plankton.

Flathead mullets live in warm water all over the world. (Illustration by Barbara Duperron. Reproduced by permission.)

Larvae (LAR-vee) are animals in an early stage and must change form before becoming adults. Adults feed on invertebrates and algae (AL-jee), plantlike growths that live in water and have no true roots, stems, or leaves. These fish may gulp and filter sediment, browse over submerged surfaces, or feed at the surface.

Behavior and reproduction: Adult flathead mullets form schools and sometimes jump. Adults move offshore in unorganized groups to spawn, usually at night, before returning to near-shore waters with a low salt content or freshwater. The young remain in sheltered bays, lagoons, and estuaries until they are old enough to reproduce.

Flathead mullets and people: Flathead mullets are important food fish in many parts of the world.

Conservation status: Flathead mullets are not threatened or endangered. ∎

FOR MORE INFORMATION

Books:

Berra, Tim M. *Freshwater Fish Distribution.* San Diego, CA: Academic Press, 2001.

Gilbert, Carter Rowell, and James D. Williams. *National Audubon Society Field Guide to Fishes: North America.* New York: Knopf, 2002.

Schultz, Ken. *Ken Schultz's Field Guide to Freshwater Fish.* New York: Wiley, 2004.

Web sites:

"Production of Mullet Fish Larvae in UAE." Government of United Arab Emirates. http://www.uae.gov.ae/uaeagricent/FISHERIES/beyahfish_en.stm (accessed on October 10, 2004).

RAINBOWFISHES AND SILVERSIDES
Atheriniformes

Class: Actinopterygii
Order: Atheriniformes
Number of families: 8 families

order
CHAPTER

PHYSICAL CHARACTERISTICS

Silversides are long and narrow from side to side. They have two dorsal (DOOR-suhl) fins, a single anal (AY-nuhl) fin spine, usually smooth scales, and no lateral line. Most are silvery and have a stripe along each side of the body. Male rainbowfishes are brilliantly colored with patterns in shades of red, yellow, orange, blue, and green. The anal and dorsal fins sometimes have thread-like extensions or elaborate fanlike shapes. The anal fin is the one along the midline of the belly. The dorsal fin is the one along the midline of the back. A lateral line is a series of pores and tiny tubes along each side of the body, used for sensing vibrations.

GEOGRAPHIC RANGE

Rainbowfishes and silversides live all over the world.

HABITAT

Rainbowfishes and silversides live in coastal areas of seas; estuaries (EHS-chew-air-eez), areas where rivers meet the sea; reefs; lagoons, and the surf along beaches. Only a few species live in the open water. Freshwater species live in lakes and streams, rainforest pools, spring-fed desert waterholes, and mountain lakes.

DIET

Rainbowfishes and silversides eat invertebrates, which are animals without backbones; algae; and plankton. Some species eat fish larvae. Algae (AL-jee) are plantlike growths that live in water and have no true roots, stems, or leaves. Plankton are microscopic plants and animals drifting in the water. Larvae (LAR-vee) are animals in an early stage that must change form before becoming adults.

BEHAVIOR AND REPRODUCTION

Rainbowfishes and silversides form schools of various sizes. Some saltwater silversides form schools numbering in the thousands and cruise just below the surface, constantly feeding on plankton. Some schools are more than 328 feet (100 meters) long and 66 feet (20 meters) wide. At night silversides are attracted to bright lights and are caught easily by fishermen for use as bait.

Rainbowfishes and silversides are known for their unusual reproductive behaviors. These fishes have large eggs with sticky filaments that are used to anchor the eggs to plants or other materials at the bottom of the water. Female rainbowfishes spawn, or release eggs, day after day for a long time. The eggs attach themselves by a thread to underwater plants. Grunions time their spawning to take advantage of the tides.

RAINBOWFISHES, SILVERSIDES, AND PEOPLE

Most rainbowfishes and silversides are not eaten by humans. Saltwater silversides are important to commercial fishing because they are an important food source for fishes that people do eat. Silversides that are fished are used as bait or are converted into pet food. Because of their extraordinary colors, rainbowfishes are valued in the aquarium business. Most of the rainbowfishes sold in pet stores are bred in captivity, but some have been fished heavily to satisfy the demands of aquarium owners.

CONSERVATION STATUS

The World Conservation Union (IUCN) lists one species of rainbowfishes and silversides as Extinct, six species as Critically Endangered, five as Endangered, thirty-one as Vulnerable, and eight as Near Threatened. Extinct means no longer in existence. Critically Endangered means facing an extremely high risk of extinction in the wild. Endangered means facing a very high risk of extinction in the wild. Vulnerable means facing a high risk of extinction in the wild. Near Threatened means at risk of becoming threatened with extinction in the near future. The U. S. Fish and Wildlife Service lists one species as Threatened, or likely to become endangered in the near future.

California grunion (Leuresthes tenuis)

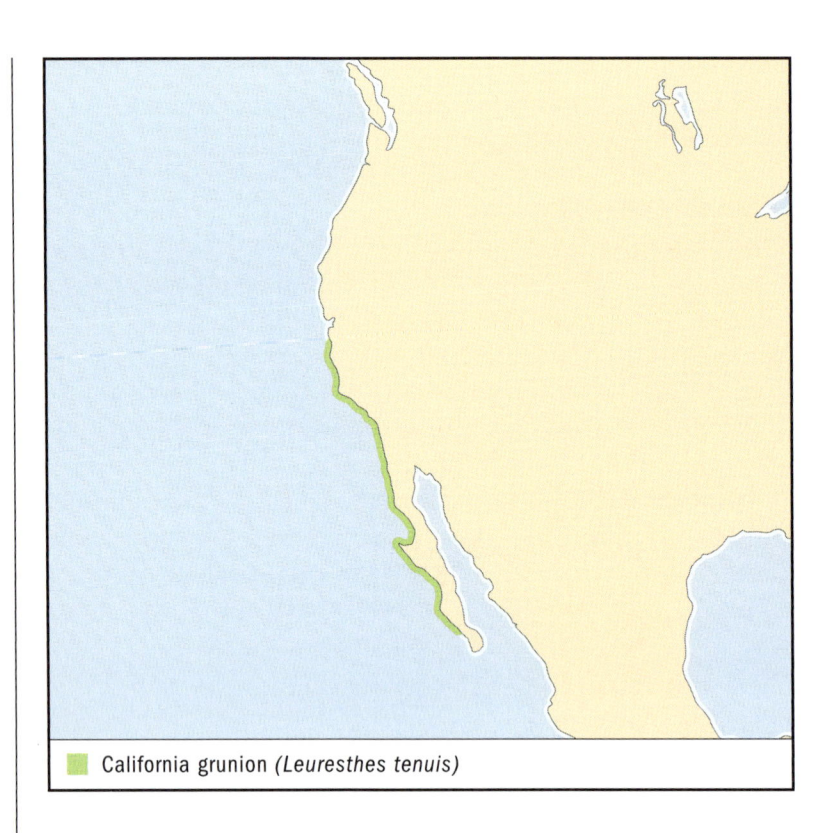

SPECIES ACCOUNT

CALIFORNIA GRUNION
Leuresthes tenuis

Physical characteristics: California grunion grow to 7½ inches (19 centimeters). They are long silversides with a prominent silvery band on the sides and bluish green on the back.

Geographic range: Grunion live on the coast of North America from Monterey Bay, California, in the United States to the southern part of the Baja Peninsula in Mexico.

Habitat: California grunion live in coastal ocean waters.

Diet: California grunion eat animal plankton.

Behavior and reproduction: California grunion are known for their spawning behavior. They emerge from the surf in large groups to spawn on beaches during the highest tides of the spring and summer

California grunion are known for their spawning behavior. They emerge from the surf in large groups to spawn on beaches during the highest tides of the spring and summer months. (Illustration by Patricia Ferrer. Reproduced by permission.)

months. Both males and females ride in on waves and are left exposed on the sand when the water recedes. Females burrow tail first into the sand to deposit their eggs, and males place sperm on the eggs as they are released. The eggs are left buried in the sand a few inches below the surface and hatch in about two weeks, when they are agitated by another high tide. After spawning, adults return to the sea. They can spawn numerous times.

California grunion and people: California grunion are collected by hand during spawning runs.

Conservation status: California grunion are not threatened or endangered. ∎

FOR MORE INFORMATION

Books:

Berra, T. M. *Freshwater Fish Distribution.* San Diego: Academic Press, 2001.

Gilbert, Carter Rowell, and James D. Williams. *National Audubon Society Field Guide to Fishes: North America.* New York: Knopf, 2002.

Schultz, Ken. *Ken Schultz's Field Guide to Saltwater Fish.* New York: Wiley, 2004.

Web sites:

"The Amazing Grunion." California Department of Fish and Game, Marine Region. http://www.dfg.ca.gov/mrd/grnindx3.html (accessed on October 11, 2004).

"The California Grunion." Dr. C's Remarkable Ocean World. http://www.oceansonline.com/index.htm (accessed on October 11, 2004).

NEEDLEFISHES AND RELATIVES
Beloniformes

Class: Actinopterygii
Order: Beloniformes
Number of families: 5 families

order
CHAPTER

PHYSICAL CHARACTERISTICS

Needlefishes and their relatives, the flyingfishes, halfbeaks, sauries, and rice fishes, are long fishes. The dorsal (DOOR-suhl) and anal (AY-nuhl) fins are far back on the body. The dorsal fin is the one along the midline of the back. The anal fin is the one along the midline of the belly. The lateral (LAT-uhr-uhl) line is on the belly. This line, a series of pores and tiny tubes used for sensing vibrations is usually along the sides of a fish's body.

Needlefishes have a sleek body and very long upper and lower jaws studded with sharp teeth. In halfbeaks the lower jaw is much longer than the upper jaw. Flyingfishes are streamlined and have very large pectoral (PECK-ter-uhl) fins, which are the front pair, corresponding to the front legs of four-footed animals. Rice fishes do not look like the other members of this group. They have a less streamlined body, large eyes, an upturned mouth, and a long anal fin.

GEOGRAPHIC RANGE

Needlefishes and their relatives live all over the world.

HABITAT

Some needlefishes and their relatives live in the surface waters of the open ocean and in coastal habitats such as estuaries (EHS-chew-air-eez), the areas where rivers meet the sea. The freshwater species live in lakes and rivers.

WATCH OUT FOR THIS FISH

In rare cases needlefishes can cause injury or death. In one such case, a surfer was killed when the snout of a fast-swimming needlefish went through his eye socket and into his brain.

HOW DO THEY DO IT?

A flyingfish swimming at a speed of about 33 feet (10 meters) per second breaks the surface at an angle and taxis for 16 to 82 feet (5 to 25 m) by rapidly beating its tail fin in the water. Then it breaks into free flight for as far as 164 feet (50 meters) at a height that can reach 26 feet (8 meters). Once it loses altitude, the fish can taxi again with its tail fin without returning to the water, so flights can be stretched to about 1,300 feet (400 meters).

DIET

Needlefishes and their relatives eat small fishes, animal plankton, water and land insects, algae, sea grasses, and waste material. Plankton are microscopic plants and, in this case, animals drifting in water. Algae (AL-jee) are plantlike growths that live in water and have no true roots, stems, or leaves.

BEHAVIOR AND REPRODUCTION

Some fishes in the needlefish group can fly or glide through the air. Another unusual characteristic is a strong attraction to lights at night. The eggs of many open-water species of needlefishes and their relatives have sticky threads used to attach the eggs to floating debris or seaweed. The larvae (LAR-vee) can feed as soon as they hatch. Larvae are animals in an early stage and must change form before becoming adults. Some species in the needlefish group bear live young rather than releasing eggs. Other species release eggs that have been fertilized (FUR-teh-lyzed), or penetrated by sperm, inside the female.

NEEDLEFISHES, THEIR RELATIVES, AND PEOPLE

Needlefishes are caught at night by fishermen using lights. In areas where there are many flyingfishes, fishermen leave a light suspended all night over a canoe partially filled with water and return in the morning to a boat full of fish. Freshwater halfbeaks, rice fishes, and needlefishes are used in aquariums. In Thailand, halfbeaks are sold as fighting fish. Rice fish are bred in captivity for use in research.

CONSERVATION STATUS

The World Conservation Union (IUCN) lists two species of needlefishes and their relatives as Critically Endangered, three as Endangered, eight as Vulnerable, and one species as Near Threatened. Critically Endangered means facing extremely high risk of extinction in the wild. Endangered means facing a very high risk of extinction in the wild. Vulnerable mean facing a high risk of extinction in the wild. Near Threatened means likely to become threatened with extinction in the future.

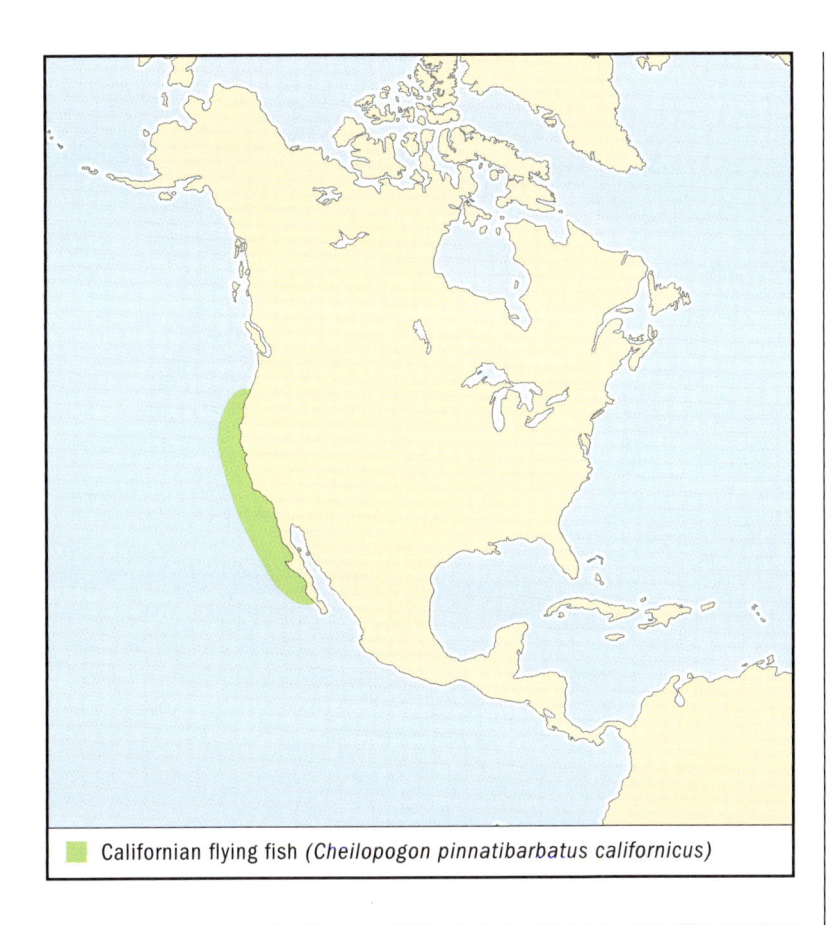

Californian flying fish *(Cheilopogon pinnatibarbatus californicus)*

CALIFORNIA FLYINGFISH
Cheilopogon pinnatibarbatus californicus

SPECIES ACCOUNTS

Physical characteristics: California flyingfish reach a length of 15 inches (38 centimeters). They are four-winged flyingfishes, meaning both the pectoral and the pelvic fins are enlarged. The pelvic fins are the rear pair, corresponding to the rear legs of four-footed animals. The lower part of the tail fin is much larger than the upper part. These fish are bluish gray on the back and silver on the belly.

Geographic range: California flyingfish live off the coast of North America from Oregon to southern Baja California.

Habitat: California flyingfish live near the surface in open water.

Diet: California flyingfish eat animal plankton and small fish.

California flyingfish are four-winged flyingfishes, meaning both the pectoral and the pelvic fins are enlarged. (Illustration by Wendy Baker. Reproduced by permission.)

Behavior and reproduction: California flyingfish can leap out of the water and glide for long distances, possibly to evade predators (PREH-duh-ters), animals that hunt and kill other animals for food. These fish live in schools and spawn, or reproduce, in summer. The eggs drift in open water and stick to floating seaweed and other debris.

California flyingfish and people: California flyingfish are sometimes used as bait.

Conservation status: California flyingfish are not threatened or endangered. ∎

Californian needlefish (*Strongylura exilis*)

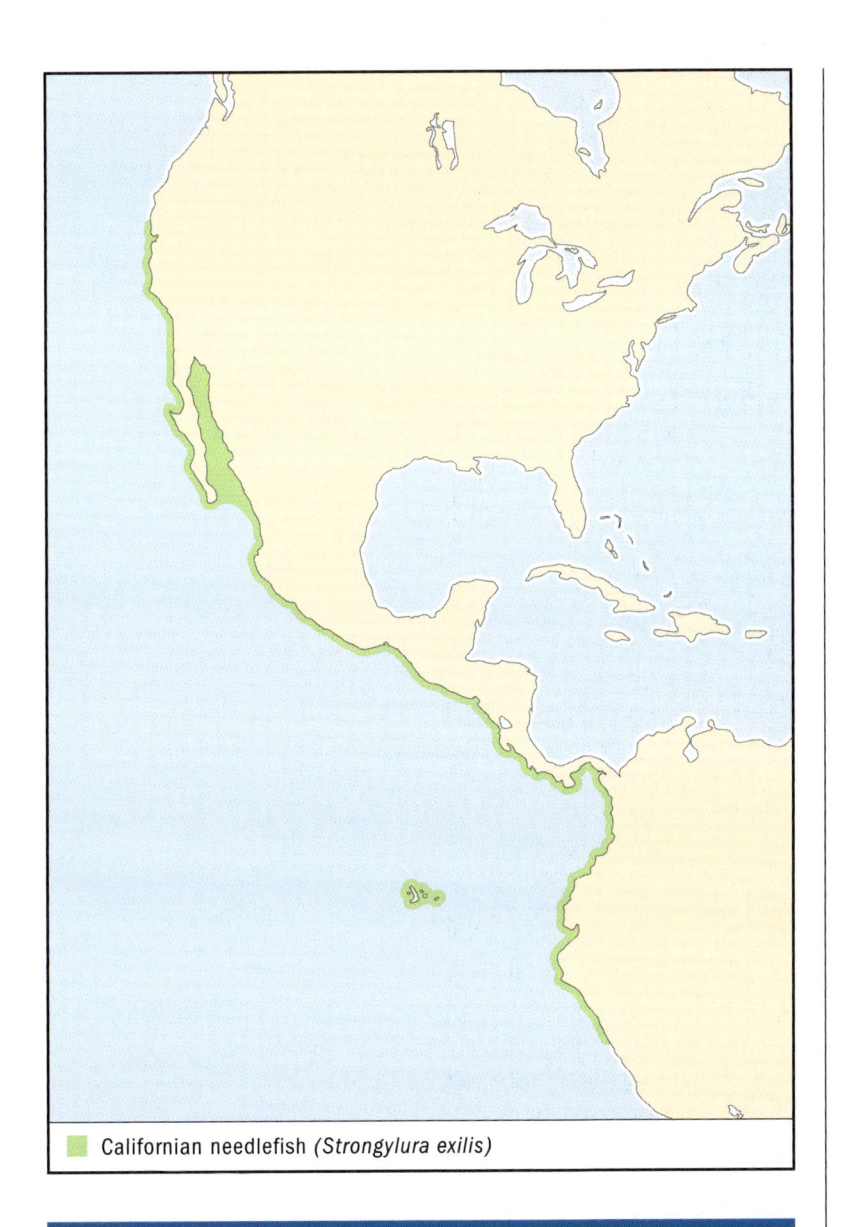

CALIFORNIAN NEEDLEFISH
Strongylura exilis

Physical characteristics: Californian needlefish reach a length of about 39 inches (1 meter). The body is very thin and has a long snout and sharp teeth. The tail fin is notched but does not have a deep fork.

Californian needlefish sometimes form large schools. They leap out of the water when threatened. (Illustration by Wendy Baker. Reproduced by permission.)

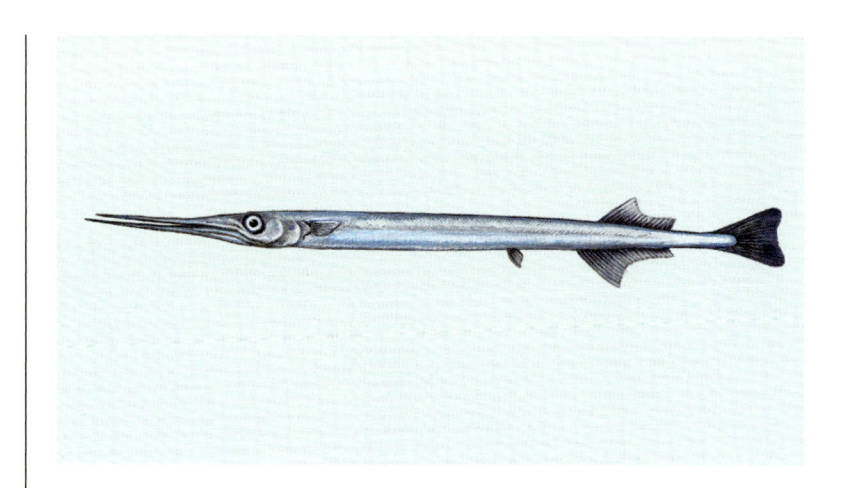

Geographic range: Californian needlefish live along the coast of North and South America from California to Peru. They also live around the Galápagos Islands.

Habitat: Californian needlefish live in lagoons, harbors, and coastal areas. They frequent mangrove forests and enter freshwater.

Diet: Californian needlefish feed on small fishes.

Behavior and reproduction: Californian needlefish sometimes form large schools. They leap out of the water when threatened. The eggs of these fish are attached to floating plants by long threads. The larvae drift in surface waters. The eggs hatch about two weeks after being released.

Californian needlefish and people: Californian needlefish are sold fresh in fish markets. In rare cases, these fish cause injury or death by impalement.

Conservation status: Californian needlefish are not threatened or endangered. ■

FOR MORE INFORMATION

Books:

Byatt, Andrew, Alastair Fothergill, and Martha Holmes. *Blue Planet.* New York: DK, 2001.

Gilbert, Carter Rowell, and James D. Williams. *National Audubon Society Field Guide to Fishes: North America.* New York: Knopf, 2002.

Web sites:

"Flying Fish!!!" OceanLink. http://oceanlink.island.net/oinfo/biodiversity/flyingfish/flyingfish.html (accessed on October 11, 2004).

Scott, Susan. "Needlefish." Hawaiian Lifeguard Association. http://www.aloha.com/lifeguards/needle.html (accessed on October 11, 2004).

KILLIFISHES AND LIVE-BEARERS
Cyprinodontiformes

Class: Actinopterygii
Order: Cyprinodontiformes
Number of families: 9 families

order
CHAPTER

PHYSICAL CHARACTERISTICS

Killifishes and live-bearers vary greatly in length from about half an inch (1 centimeter) to nearly 13 inches (33 centimeters). Some of these fishes are sleek, and others are blunt at the ends and flat-topped. Males may be brightly colored, but most females are plain. The fins may have fancy extensions. There is no lateral (LAT-uhr-uhl) line system along the sides, but there is around the head. The lateral line is a series of pores and tiny tubes used for sensing vibrations and usually found along the sides of the body.

GEOGRAPHIC RANGE

Killifishes live all over the world. Live-bearers live in North, Central, and South America.

HABITAT

Killifishes and live-bearers live in heavily planted streams, rivers, lakes, ponds, swamps, desert springs, salt marshes, estuaries (EHS-chew-air-eez) or areas where a river meets the sea, and coastal waters. Some live in temporary bodies of water such as puddles and ditches.

DIET

Killifishes and live-bearers eat fish, plants, invertebrates (in-VER-teh-brehts) or animals without a backbone, animal plankton, waste material, and algae. Plankton are microscopic plants and, in this case, animals drifting in water. Algae (AL-jee) are plantlike growths that live in water and have no true roots, stems, or leaves. Some species of live-bearers eat members of their own species.

BEHAVIOR AND REPRODUCTION

Males of some species of killifishes and live-bearers are aggressively territorial, defending their breeding sites against other males. The fishes that live in temporary habitats such as ditches lay eggs on the bottom and die when the water evaporates. The eggs go into a resting state and hatch in the next rainy season. Killifishes that live in permanent waters spawn, or release eggs, in plants. The eggs stick to the plants. When the young hatch, they are fully capable of swimming and feeding.

KILLIFISHES AND LIVE-BEARERS AND PEOPLE

Some killifishes and live-bearers are eaten. Others are sold as bait. They all help people by eating mosquitos. Aquarium hobbyists keep many species of killifishes and live-bearers. These fishes also are used in medical research.

CONSERVATION STATUS

The World Conservation Union (IUCN) lists ten species of killifishes and live-bearers as Extinct, five as Extinct in the Wild, eighteen as Critically Endangered, twenty as Endangered, twenty-five as Vulnerable, and three species as Near Threatened. Extinct means no longer in existence. Extinct in the Wild means no longer alive except in captivity or through the aid of humans. Critically Endangered means facing an extremely high risk of extinction in the wild. Endangered means facing a very high risk of extinction in the wild. Vulnerable means facing a high risk of extinction in the wild. Near Threatened means likely to become threatened with extinction in the future. The U.S. Fish and Wildlife Service lists fifteen species as Endangered and one species as Threatened. Endangered means in danger of extinction throughout all or a significant portion of its range. Threatened means likely to become endangered in the near future.

PRETTY AND PRACTICAL

The beauty of many killifishes and live-bearers has led to their being featured on the postage stamps of several countries, which aids in stimulating an interest in conservation efforts.

Largescale foureyes (Anableps anableps)

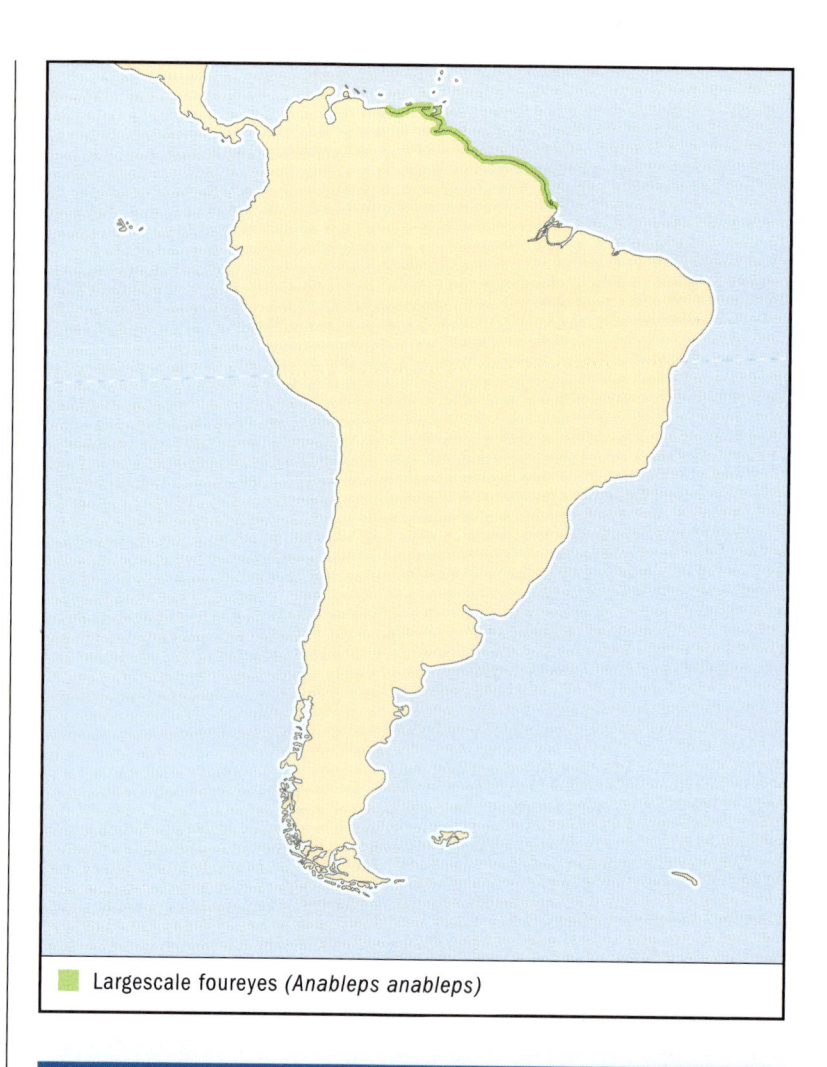

SPECIES ACCOUNTS

LARGESCALE FOUREYES
Anableps anableps

Physical characteristics: Largescale foureyes have large, bulging, froglike eyes set far forward and divided by a black band into upper and lower portions that see above and below the waterline. These fish grow to 12 inches (30 centimeters). They are long and narrow and have a flat head. The dorsal (DOOR-suhl) fin, the one along the midline of the back, is far toward the rear of the body. Three to five blue to purple lines run along the sides of the body. The back is brownish with a whitish line that divides into a Y at the gill cover, each arm ending at an eye.

Largescale foureyes see well both above and below the waterline. Because they swim with the upper half of their eyes above the water, they bob their heads up and down to keep their eyes wet. (Illustration by Emily Damstra. Reproduced by permission.)

Geographic range: Largescale foureyes live along the northeast coast of South America.

Habitat: Largescale foureyes live in rivers, streams, and estuaries near beaches.

Diet: Largescale foureyes jump out of the water at low tides to gulp down mud, which is rich in algae, tiny animals, and worms. These fish leap from the water to catch low-flying insects. They also eat small fishes.

Behavior and reproduction: Largescale foureyes see well both above and below the waterline. Because they swim with the upper half of their eyes above the water, they bob their heads up and down to keep their eyes wet. These fish ride breaking waves near sandy beaches, sometimes being tossed onto the beach by the waves. They just jump back into the water. These fish form schools of as many as hundreds of fish.

Largescale foureyes are live-bearers that use internal fertilization (FUR-teh-lih-zay-shun), meaning egg and sperm unite inside the female's body. About twenty weeks after fertilization, ten to twenty young are born. These young fish are as large as 2 inches (5 centimeters) at birth. This size is remarkable because the parents may be only 3½ inches (9 centimeters) long.

Largescale foureyes and people: Largescale foureyes are eaten. To a limited extent, they are sold for aquariums.

Conservation status: Largescale foureyes are not threatened or endangered. ■

Green swordtail (*Xiphophorus hellerii*)

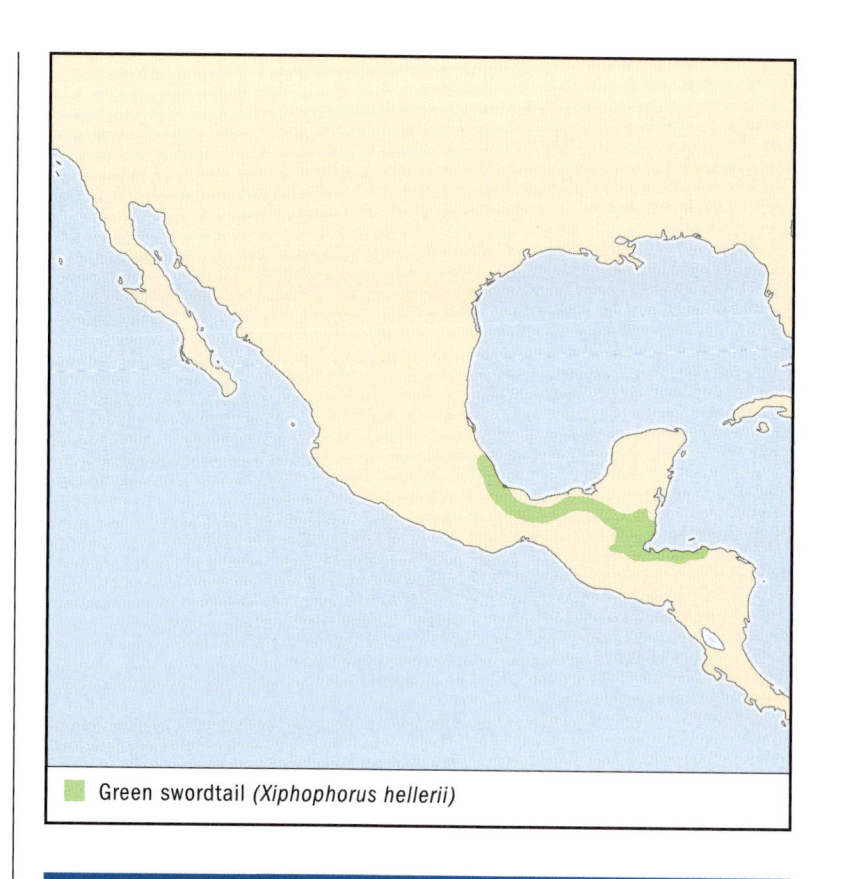

GREEN SWORDTAIL
Xiphophorus hellerii

Physical characteristics: Male green swordtails have a long extension on the bottom of the tail fin that forms a sword. Males grow to 5½ inches (14 centimeters) in total length, the sword being 1½ to 3 inches (4 to 8 centimeters) long. Females grow to 6 inches (16 centimeters). Both sexes have a grayish green background color. Males have two lines of reddish dots on a squared-off dorsal fin and a line of bright to dark red along the entire body. The sword is shiny yellowish green bordered in black.

Geographic range: The native home of green swordtails is Mexico and northwestern Honduras.

Habitat: Green swordtails live in rivers, streams, warm springs and their runoffs, canals, and ponds with heavy plant life.

Diet: Green swordtails eat plants and insects.

Behavior and reproduction: The dominant male in a group of green swordtails drives off rivals in a feeding area or an area where females have grouped. These fish are live-bearers. Males insert their sperm into females. The females can store sperm and produce several broods from a single mating.

Green swordtails and people: Green swordtails are used in the aquarium business and are frequently used in medical research.

Conservation status: Green swordtails are not threatened or endangered. ∎

The dominant male in a group of green swordtails drives off rivals in a feeding area or an area where females have grouped. (Hans Reinhard/Bruce Coleman, Inc. Reproduced by permission.)

Blackfin pearl killifish (Austrolebias nigripinnis)

BLACKFIN PEARL KILLIFISH
Austrolebias nigripinnis

Physical characteristics: Blackfin pearl killifish are rarely more than 2 inches (5 centimeters) long. The fins are blue-black with shiny metallic-green borders. There are pearly whitish to greenish spots on all fins and the body.

Geographic range: Blackfin pearl killifish live in Uruguay and Argentina.

Blackfin pearl killifish live in Uruguay and Argentina. They are found in temporary waters, such as flooded meadows, shallow ponds, and roadside ditches. (Illustration by Emily Damstra. Reproduced by permission.)

Habitat: Blackfin pearl killifish live in temporary waters, such as flooded meadows, shallow ponds, and roadside ditches.

Diet: Blackfin pearl killifish eat insects, worms, and other water-dwelling invertebrates.

Behavior and reproduction: A male blackfin pearl killifish takes over an area that it defends against other males. A female moves in and signals she is ready to reproduce by tilting herself down. The pair spawns on the bottom of the pond or ditch. The eggs laid go into a resting state. When the water evaporates, the adults die, but the eggs survive and then hatch in the next rainy season, within hours of getting wet.

Blackfin pearl killifish and people: Blackfin pearl killifish are exchanged among aquarium hobbyists but are sold only rarely.

Conservation status: Blackfin pearl killifish are not threatened or endangered. ∎

FOR MORE INFORMATION

Books:

Berra, Tim M. *Freshwater Fish Distribution.* San Diego: Academic Press, 2001.

Gilbert, Carter Rowell, and James D. Williams. *National Audubon Society Field Guide to Fishes: North America.* New York: Knopf, 2002.

Web sites:

Bayan, Ruby. "Introducing: Livebearers." Freshwater Aquaria. http://oursimplejoys.com/freshwateraquaria/article1005.html (accessed on October 11, 2004).

"Killifish FAQ." American Killifish Association. http://www.aka.org/pages/beginners/faq.html (accessed on October 11, 2004).

WHALEFISHES AND RELATIVES
Stephanoberyciformes

Class: Actinopterygii
Order: Stephanoberyciformes
Number of families: 9 families

order CHAPTER

PHYSICAL CHARACTERISTICS

Most whalefishes and their relatives have a large head with bony ridges that give the fish a highly armored look. These fishes are rarely longer than 10 inches (25 centimeters) and usually are shorter than 5 inches (12 centimeters). The colors usually are drab brown or grayish black, but some fishes are reddish. Many whalefishes and their relatives look velvety because they have small outgrowths on the skin or because they have many spines on their scales. Some fishes in this group lack scales. Others have large, smooth scales. Numerous pores are usually visible on the head and lateral line. The lateral (LAT-uhr-uhl) line is a series of pores and tiny tubes along each side of a fish's body and is used for sensing vibrations. Some species have glowing tissues. All fishes in this group have a single dorsal (DOOR-suhl) fin with very few spines or no spines. The pelvic fins can be well developed, small, absent, or even winglike. The dorsal fin is the one along the midline of the back. The pelvic fins are the rear pair, corresponding to the rear legs of four-footed animals. The tail fin may have spines.

GEOGRAPHIC RANGE

Whalefishes and their relatives live all over the world.

HABITAT

Whalefishes and their relatives live in open water down to about 13,100 feet (4,000 meters). Some species travel close to the surface.

phylum
class
subclass
● order
monotypic order
suborder
family

Whalefishes and Relatives

DIET

Little is known about the diet of whalefishes and their relatives. Tiny crustaceans (krus-TAY-shuns) have been found in the stomachs of a few fish. Crustaceans are water-dwelling animals that have jointed legs and a hard shell but no backbone.

BEHAVIOR AND REPRODUCTION

Whalefishes and their relatives travel from deep to shallower water. The reproductive biology of whalefishes and their relatives is largely unknown, but both eggs and larvae (LAR-vee) drift in open water. Larvae are animals in an early stage and must change form before becoming adults. In general, larvae and the young appear to live in shallower water than adults, which live in the deep sea. The larvae of some species have very long streamers on their tails.

WHALEFISHES AND THEIR RELATIVES AND PEOPLE

Whalefishes and their relatives are not eaten. Whalefishes are probably important food for fishes that are caught and sold, such as orange roughy.

CONSERVATION STATUS

Whalefishes and their relatives are not threatened or endangered.

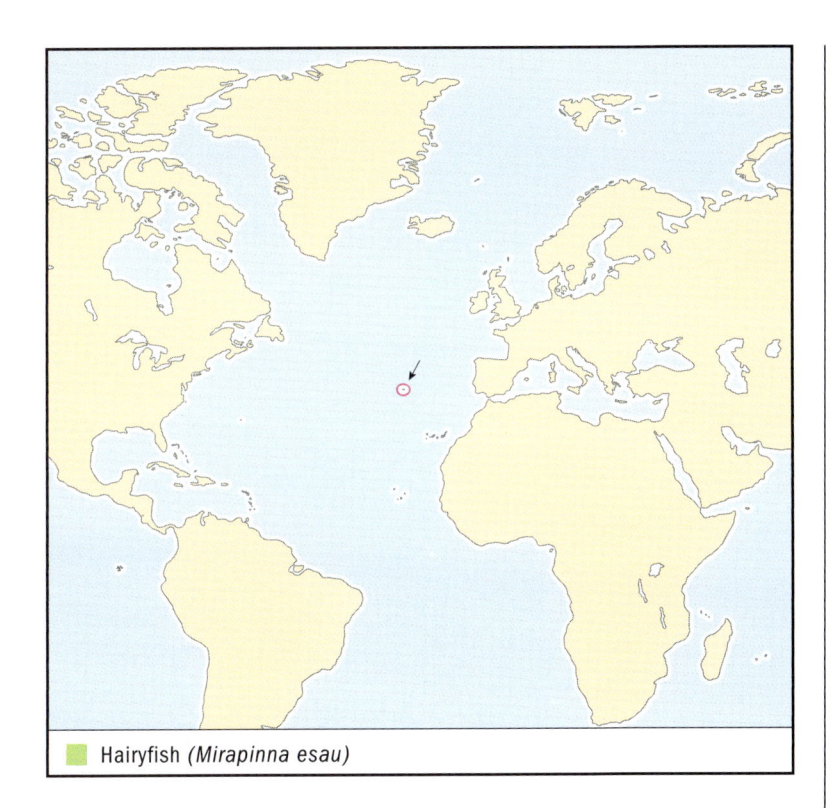

Only one hairyfish has been caught, and that was in the eastern part of the Atlantic Ocean. (Illustration by Brian Cressman. Reproduced by permission.)

■ Hairyfish (*Mirapinna esau*)

HAIRYFISH
Mirapinna esau

SPECIES ACCOUNT

Physical characteristics: The skin of hairyfish is covered in hair-like outgrowths. These fish have huge pelvic fins that are located near the fish's throat and stick up like wings. The tail fin is divided into two distinct parts that overlap. The single dorsal fin is located far toward the rear of the body. The anal (AY-nuhl) fin is on the belly directly below the dorsal fin. The fish is dark brown.

Geographic range: Only one hairyfish has been caught, and that was in the eastern part of the Atlantic Ocean.

Habitat: The only known hairyfish was caught at the surface.

Diet: Animal plankton was found in the stomach of the only known hairyfish. Plankton are microscopic plants and, in this case, animals drifting in water.

Only one hairyfish has been caught, and that was in the eastern part of the Atlantic Ocean. (Illustration by Brian Cressman. Reproduced by permission.)

Behavior and reproduction: Scientists do not know anything about the behavior and reproduction of hairyfish.

Hairyfish and people: Hairyfish have no known importance to people.

Conservation status: Hairyfish are not threatened or endangered. ∎

FOR MORE INFORMATION

Books:

Nelson, Joseph S. *Fishes of the World.* 3rd ed. New York: Wiley, 1994.

Web sites:

"Flabby Whalefish." All Science Fair Projects. http://www.all-science-fair-projects.com/science_fair_projects_encyclopedia/Flabby_whalefish (accessed on October 12, 2004).

ROUGHIES, FLASHLIGHTFISHES, AND SQUIRRELFISHES

Beryciformes

Class: Actinopterygii
Order: Beryciformes
Number of families: 7 families

order CHAPTER

PHYSICAL CHARACTERISTICS

Roughies, flashlightfishes, and squirrelfishes are spiny-rayed fishes 3 to 24 inches (8 to 61 centimeters) long. Some have colorful scales. Squirrelfishes and soldierfishes are reddish orange from head to forked tail. Flashlightfishes have a glowing organ under each eye. Pineapplefishes and pineconefishes have large, beautiful scales. Usually yellow, each scale has its own dark outline, which makes the fish look armored. These fishes also have spines poking backward from each scale. Orange roughies have mucus cavities just beneath the skin of the head. Sometimes they are called slimeheads.

GEOGRAPHIC RANGE

Roughies, flashlightfishes, and squirrelfishes live all over the world.

HABITAT

Squirrelfishes live in shallow, tropical reefs. Roughies live in dark ocean waters 1 mile (1,600 meters) deep. The fishes that live in shallow waters usually hide under a coral overhang, in a cave, or under another structure during the day.

DIET

Roughies, flashlightfishes, and squirrelfishes eat small fish and various invertebrates (in-VER-teh-brehts), which are animals without a backbone. The shallows dwellers feed mainly at night, although some feed on invertebrates passing through their daytime retreats.

phylum
class
subclass
● order
monotypic order
suborder
family

THAT'S OLD!

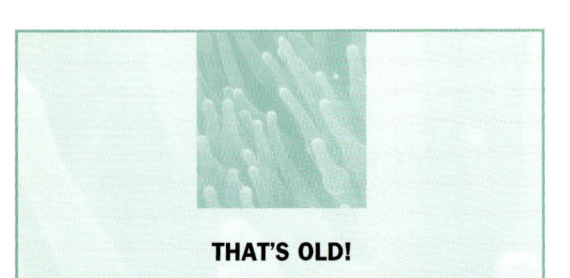

Orange roughies live as long as 149 years. They are the longest-living fish.

BEHAVIOR AND REPRODUCTION

Perhaps the most notable characteristic of flashlightfishes, pineapplefishes, pineconefishes, and a few other fishes in this group is their ability to produce light and in some cases control it. The light is produced by glowing bacteria that live in pockets just below the skin of the fish. These fishes use the light to find and attract prey, or animals hunted and killed for food, during their nightly feeding. Some of these fishes alter the blinking pattern of the light to communicate with other fish in their species and as a method of confusing predators (PREH-duh-ters), or animals that hunt and kill other animals for food.

Little is known about the reproduction of roughies and flashlightfishes. Scientists believe that all these fishes use external fertilization (FUR-teh-lih-zay-shun), meaning egg and sperm are united outside the body. More is known about the reproduction of squirrelfishes and soldierfishes because these fishes are common in reefs, where they are frequently observed by divers. During mating male and female squirrelfish grunt and click, align themselves side by side, and place their tails together while fanning out their heads to the left and right.

ROUGHIES, FLASHLIGHTFISHES, AND SQUIRRELFISHES AND PEOPLE

Roughies, flashlightfishes, and squirrelfishes are important in the pet business. Orange roughy is fished commercially for food.

CONSERVATION STATUS

Roughies, flashlightfishes, and squirrelfishes are not threatened or endangered.

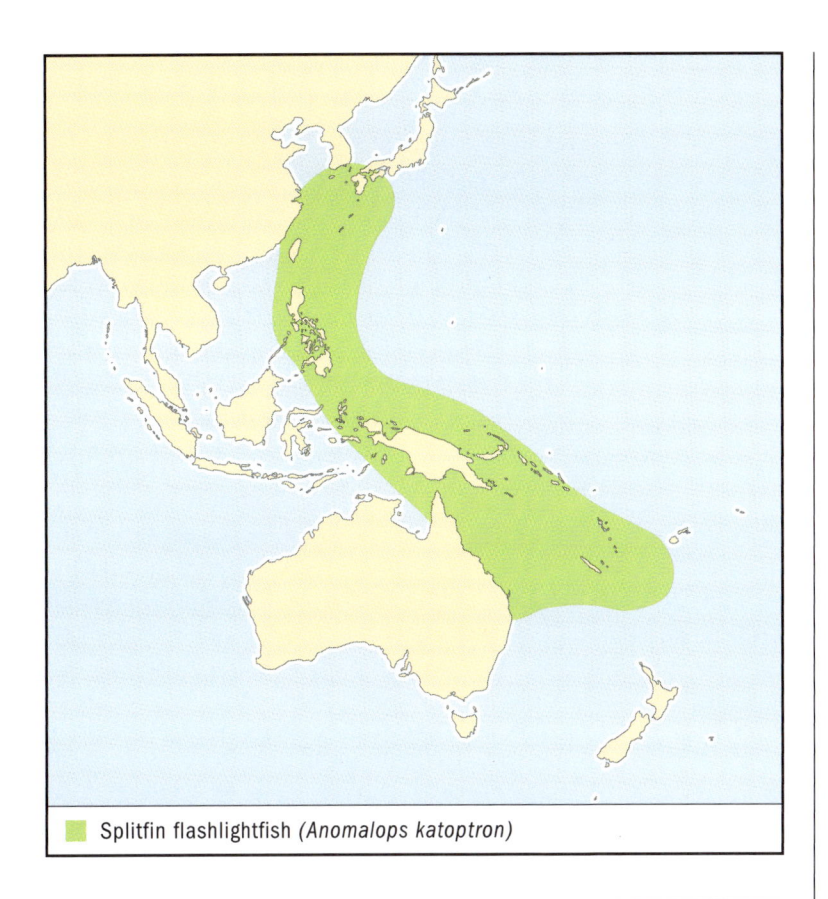

Splitfin flashlightfish (Anomalops katoptron)

SPLITFIN FLASHLIGHTFISH
Anomalops katoptron

SPECIES ACCOUNTS

Physical characteristics: Splitfin flashlightfish are 4 to 12 inches (10 to 30 centimeters) long. These fish have large eyes with light-producing organs below them. They have two dorsal (DOOR-suhl) fins, which are the fins along the midline of the back. The rear dorsal fin is triangular and much larger than the front one.

Geographic range: Splitfin flashlightfish live in the western part of the Pacific Ocean from the Great Barrier Reef to southern Japan.

Habitat: Splitfin flashlightfish live in reef areas 66 to 1,300 feet (20 to 400 meters) deep. During the day these fish remain hidden from sunlight, either in deep water or in dark caves. In winter, the fish gather in the warm, shallow waters of the Philippines.

Splitfin flashlightfish use their large light organ during feeding, which is done primarily at night. One of these fishes has its light off. (©Fred McConnaughey/Photo Researchers, Inc. Reproduced by permission.)

Diet: Splitfin flashlightfish use their large light organ during feeding, which is done primarily at night. These fish shun even dim light, searching for food before or after the moon has risen and set or on nights of a new moon. Their diet is mainly animal plankton. Plankton are microscopic plants and animals drifting in water.

Behavior and reproduction: Splitfin flashlightfish have a light-producing organ and control it with muscles that rotate the organ either to allow the glowing bacteria to shine forth or to hide the glow from view. The fish use the light to communicate with one another. Splitfin flashlightfish often travel in schools of twenty-four to forty-eight fish. Little is known about the reproduction of these fish except that they probably do not guard eggs.

Splitfin flashlightfish and people: Splitfin flashlightfish are used in the aquarium business. Sometimes they are used for bait.

Conservation status: Splitfin flashlightfish are not threatened or endangered. ■

Blackbar soldierfish (*Myripristis jacobus*)

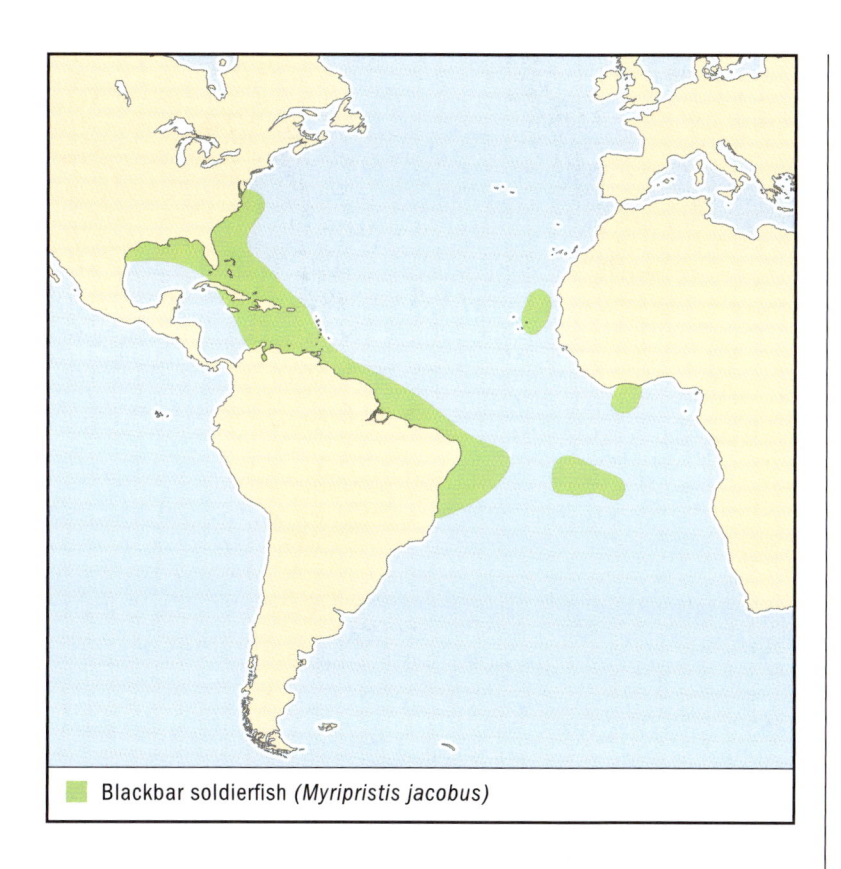

BLACKBAR SOLDIERFISH
Myripristis jacobus

Physical characteristics: Blackbar soldierfish grow to 10 inches (25 centimeters) in length. They are red and have large eyes, two dorsal fins, and a forked tail fin. They sport a brownish black, vertical bar behind the gill cover.

Geographic range: Blackbar soldierfish live in the Gulf of Mexico and the eastern Atlantic Ocean from North Carolina to Brazil.

Habitat: Blackbar soldierfish live in reefs and around structures such as piers. They are commonly seen by divers in very shallow waters but also are found at depths to 330 feet (100 meters).

Diet: Blackbar soldierfish feed at night on shrimp and animal plankton.

Blackbar soldierfish feed at night on shrimp and animal plankton. (Illustration by Wendy Baker. Reproduced by permission.)

Behavior and reproduction: Blackbar soldierfish usually live alone but sometimes form schools of as many as thirty-six fish. Under stress, blackbar soldierfish make clicking and grunting noises with their swim bladder, an internal sac that fishes use to control their position in the water. Blackbar soldierfish often swim upside down. These fish use external fertilization on the days that follow a full moon. Although the adults prefer shallower reefs, the larvae (LAR-vee) may travel well out to sea. Larvae are animals in an early stage and must change form before becoming adults.

Blackbar soldierfish and people: Blackbar soldierfish are used as pets. They are sometimes sold for food.

Conservation status: Blackbar soldierfish are not threatened or endangered. ∎

FOR MORE INFORMATION

Books:

Ferrari, Andrea, and Antonella Ferrari. *Reef Life.* Buffalo, NY: Firefly, 2002.

Gilbert, Carter Rowell, and James D. Williams. *National Audubon Society Field Guide to Fishes: North America.* New York: Knopf, 2002.

Web sites:

"Flashlightfish." Shedd Aquarium. http://www.sheddaquarium.org/sea/fact_sheets.cfm?id=99 (accessed on October 12, 2004).

"Myripristis jacobus." New Jersey State Aquarium. http://www.njaquarium.org/species/index3.php3?exhibit=2&tank=35&animal=96 (accessed on October 12, 2004).

"Orange Roughy (*Hoplostethus atlanticus*)." Oceans Alive. http://www.oceansalive.org/eat.cfm?subnav=fishpage&fish=70 (accessed on October 12, 2004).

> **DORIES**
> **Zeiformes**
>
> **Class:** Actinopterygii
> **Order:** Zeiformes
> **Number of families:** 6 families

order
CHAPTER

PHYSICAL CHARACTERISTICS

Dories are oval to disk shaped and very thin when viewed from the front. The size ranges from 4 inches (10 centimeters) for the dwarf dory to 3 feet (91 centimeters), 12 pounds (5.4 kg) for the South African Cape dory. Most dories are silver, bronze, brown, or red. Dories can change color in seconds from silver to dark brown or gray.

GEOGRAPHIC RANGE

Dories live on both sides of the Atlantic Ocean and its connecting seas, in the Indian Ocean, and on both sides of the Pacific Ocean.

HABITAT

Most dories live near the bottom of water 115 to 5100 feet (35 to 1500 meters) deep. Some live in middle depths or near the surface. Some species have a young open-water stage and live near the surface in the open ocean. Adults live on sandy, muddy, rocky bottoms.

DIET

Dories feed mainly on a variety of fishes but also eat shell-less mollusks (MAH-lusks) and crustaceans (krus-TAY-shuns). Mollusks are animals with a soft, unsegmented body that may or may not have a shell. Crustaceans are water-dwelling animals that have jointed legs and a hard shell but no backbone. Young dories of the larger species, adult dwarf dories,

phylum
class
subclass
● order
monotypic order
suborder
family

Dory Not a Dory

In the animated film *Finding Nemo*, Dory is a regal tang, not a dory.

and tinselfishes eat animal plankton. Plankton are microscopic plants and animals drifting in water.

BEHAVIOR AND REPRODUCTION

Little is known of the behavior of dories. Adult John dories are mainly solitary. Buckler dories often live in small groups. Female dories grow larger than males. Dories apparently release eggs and sperm into the water, and fertilization (FUR-teh-lih-zay-shun), or the joining of egg and sperm to start development, takes place in the sea. The eggs and larvae (LAR-vee) drift in open water and float near the surface. Larvae are animals in an early stage and must change form before becoming adults.

DORIES AND PEOPLE

Larger dories are of commercial importance as food fishes. Most dories are caught by trawlers, which are fishing boats dragging nets, but a few of the larger species are caught with hook and line.

CONSERVATION STATUS

Dories are not threatened or endangered.

Red boarfish (Antigonia rubescens)

RED BOARFISH
Antigonia rubescens

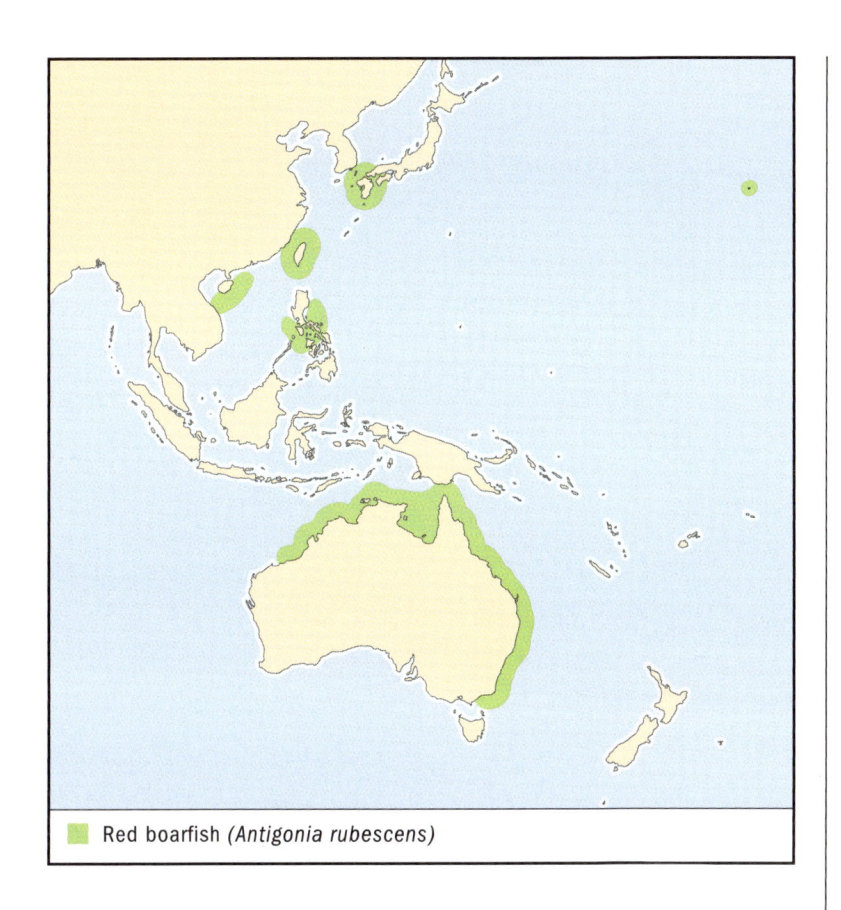

SPECIES ACCOUNT

Physical characteristics: Red boarfish are about 6 inches (15 centimeters) long from the tip of the snout to the end of the tail fin. The head and body are shaped like a disk or diamond and are very narrow when viewed from the front. The body, cheeks, and gill covers are coated with small, rough scales. The body is pale, silvery red with a dark red bar that starts at the dorsal (DOOR-suhl) fin, goes along the back and across the tail, and ends at the front of the anal (AY-nuhl) fin. The dorsal fin is the one along the midline of the back. The anal fin is the one along the midline of the belly. Another red bar lies above and below the eyes. The belly and lower rear part of the head are silvery white.

Geographic range: Red boarfish live in the western part of the Pacific Ocean.

Habitat: Red boarfish live at the bottom at depths of 330 to 3,000 feet (100 to 900 meters).

Diet: Scientists are not sure what red boarfish eat. They believe it is probably plankton and small invertebrates, or animals without backbones.

Behavior and reproduction: Scientists do not know much about the behavior and reproduction of red boarfish because these fish live too deep to be observed easily. It is known that the fish live in large groups, because many fish are caught in a single trawl haul. Red boarfish probably scatter their eggs in the open water, and the larvae probably drift in open water.

Scientists do not know much about the behavior and reproduction of red boarfish because these fish live too deep to be observed easily. (Illustration by John Megahan. Reproduced by permission.)

Red boarfish and people: Red boarfish are of no known importance to people.

Conservation status: Red boarfish are not threatened or endangered. ∎

FOR MORE INFORMATION

Books:

Nelson, Joseph S. *Fishes of the World.* 3rd ed. New York: Wiley, 1994.

Web site:

"John Dory: *Zeus faber* Linnaeus, 1758." Australian Museum Fish Site. http://www.amonline.net.au/fishes/fishfacts/fish/zfaber.htm (accessed on October 13, 2004).

STICKLEBACKS, SEAHORSES, AND RELATIVES
Gasterosteiformes

Class: Actinopterygii
Order: Gasterosteiformes
Number of families: 11 families

order CHAPTER

PHYSICAL CHARACTERISTICS

Most sticklebacks, seahorses, and their relatives have a long snout. The mouth usually is very small and has no teeth. These fishes have enlarged protective plates on their bodies. Seahorses and their relatives have extreme camouflage coloring. Many species can change color at will. Most pipefishes and seahorses have no tail fin. Many have a grasping tail like that of a monkey.

GEOGRAPHIC RANGE

Sticklebacks, seahorses, and their relatives live all over the world.

HABITAT

Sticklebacks, seahorses, and their relatives live in coral reefs, sea grass meadows, kelp forests, tide pools, bays, lagoons, and estuaries (EHS-chew-air-eez), areas where a river meets the sea. Many species hide among rocks and crevices in reefs or blend in with coral or sea grass. Others live over sandy or muddy bottoms. The young of many species live in open water and settle closer to the bottom as adults. Some species live in lakes, coastal rivers, creeks, marshes, and protected coastal inlets.

DIET

Most pipefishes and seahorses eat small invertebrates (in-VER-teh-brehts), or animals without a backbone, and the larvae (LAR-vee) of other fishes. Larvae are animals in an early stage that must change form before becoming adults.

phylum
class
subclass
● order
monotypic order
suborder
family

Sticklebacks, Seahorses, and Relatives

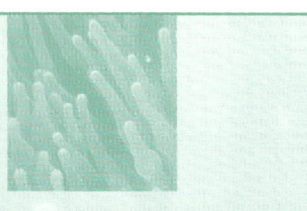

> **BEYOND DADDY DAYCARE**
>
> Many male fishes tend their young, but male seahorses actually give birth to their young. The female transfers her eggs to a pouch on the male's belly, where they are fertilized by the male and stay until they hatch.

> **EATS LIKE A HORSE**
>
> Seahorses eat constantly because they have no stomach in which to store food. They have no teeth, so they use their long jaws as a straw to suck up prey, which they swallow whole.

The larger species eat other fishes. Most sticklebacks, seahorses, and their relatives suck in prey, or animals killed for food, by quickly opening their mouths to produce a strong inward current.

BEHAVIOR AND REPRODUCTION

Sticklebacks, seahorses, and their relatives are active during the day. They live alone, in pairs, in small groups, or in groups as large as thousands. Many species change color according to their background, using this ability to sneak up on prey or to hide from predators (PREH-duh-ters), or animals that hunt and kill other animals for food. Many pipefishes and seahorses appear to hover in one location, controlling their position by co-ordinated movements of their fins.

Sticklebacks, seahorses, and their relatives are famous for their reproductive behaviors. In some species females carry fertilized (FUR-teh-lyzed) eggs, which are those that have been penetrated by sperm, on the outside of their bodies, protecting them with their fins. In other species the male carries the eggs. Many species use complex courtship dances.

STICKLEBACKS, SEAHORSES, AND THEIR RELATIVES AND PEOPLE

Many sticklebacks, seahorses, and their relatives are sought out by recreational divers. Many are aquarium fishes and are raised in captivity.

CONSERVATION STATUS

The World Conservation Union (IUCN) lists one species of sticklebacks, seahorses, and their relatives as Critically Endangered and one as Vulnerable. Critically Endangered means facing an extremely high risk of extinction in the wild. Vulnerable means facing a high risk of extinction in the wild. The U.S. Fish and Wildlife Service lists one species as Endangered, or in danger of extinction throughout all or a significant portion of its range.

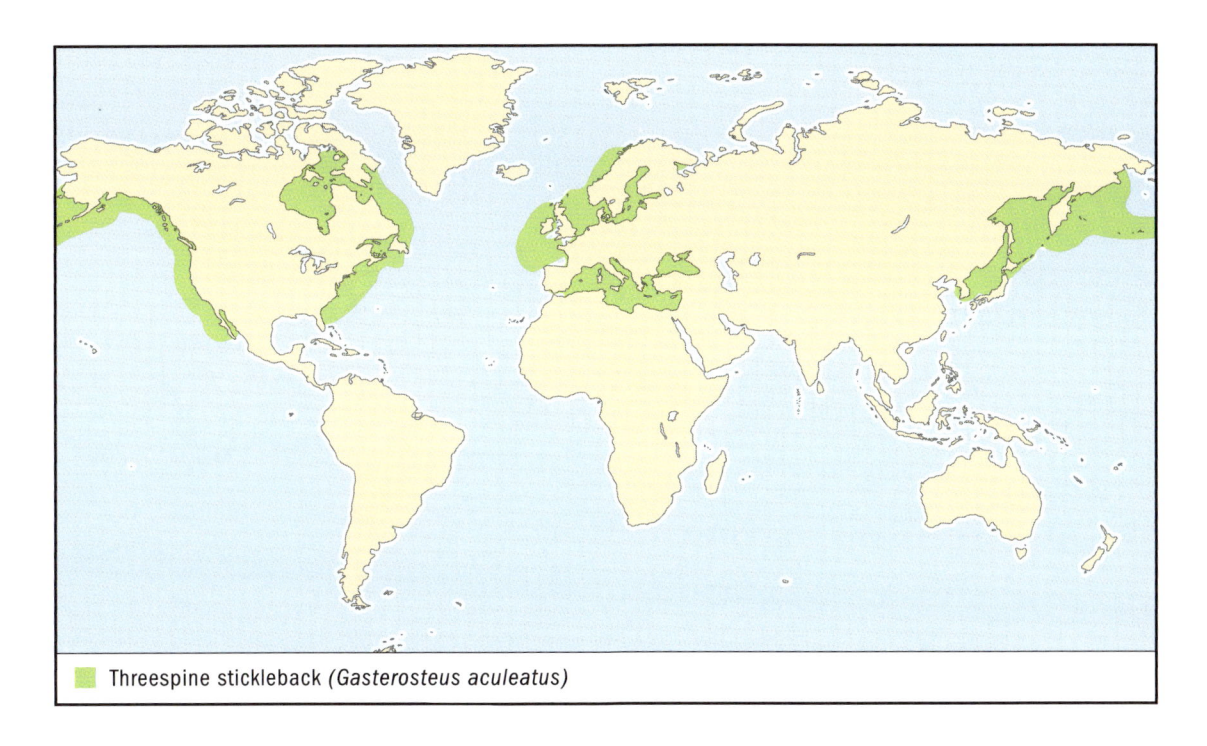

Threespine stickleback (*Gasterosteus aculeatus*)

THREESPINE STICKLEBACK
Gasterosteus aculeatus

SPECIES ACCOUNTS

Physical characteristics: Threespine sticklebacks have three strong, widely spaced spines in front of the first dorsal (DOOR-suhl) fin, the one along the midline of the back. The first two spines are very tall. These fish reach a length of about 3½ inches (9 centimeters). The body is pointed at the ends, and the eyes are large. The fish are silvery on the sides, bluish black on the back, and orange on the belly. Males become more reddish when courtship begins and drab when it ends.

Geographic range: Threespine sticklebacks live in the Northern Hemisphere on both sides of the Atlantic and Pacific Oceans.

Habitat: Threespine sticklebacks live in tidal pools, coastal rivers and creeks, lakes, salt marshes, protected coastal inlets, and the open ocean. Adults live near plants such as eel grass.

Diet: Threespine sticklebacks eat small invertebrates and their larvae and sometimes the eggs of other sticklebacks.

Sticklebacks, Seahorses, and Relatives

Threespine sticklebacks swim by "rowing" with their pectoral fins and are strong enough to swim upriver. (Illustration by Joseph E. Trumpey. Reproduced by permission.)

Behavior and reproduction: Many populations of threespine sticklebacks live in the open sea but enter coastal habitats to spawn, or reproduce, and die. They swim by "rowing" with their pectoral (PECK-ter-uhl) fins and are strong enough to swim upriver. The pectoral fins are the front pair, corresponding to the front legs of four-footed animals. During spawning periods, males become strongly territorial.

Before spawning, male threespine sticklebacks establish a territory and build a nest. When an egg-filled female enters the territory, the male performs a zigzagging courtship dance. Once a female is impressed, the male leads her to the nest and points to it with his open mouth. The female enters the nest and releases her eggs. The male then fertilizes the eggs and forces the female out. After the eggs hatch, the male destroys the nest and guards the young.

Threespine sticklebacks and people: Threespine sticklebacks are kept in aquariums. They also are studied intently by scientists who specialize in fish behavior.

Conservation status: The U.S. Fish and Wildlife Service lists the unarmored threespine stickleback as Endangered, or in danger of extinction throughout all or a significant portion of its range. ∎

Leafy seadragon (*Phycodurus eques*)

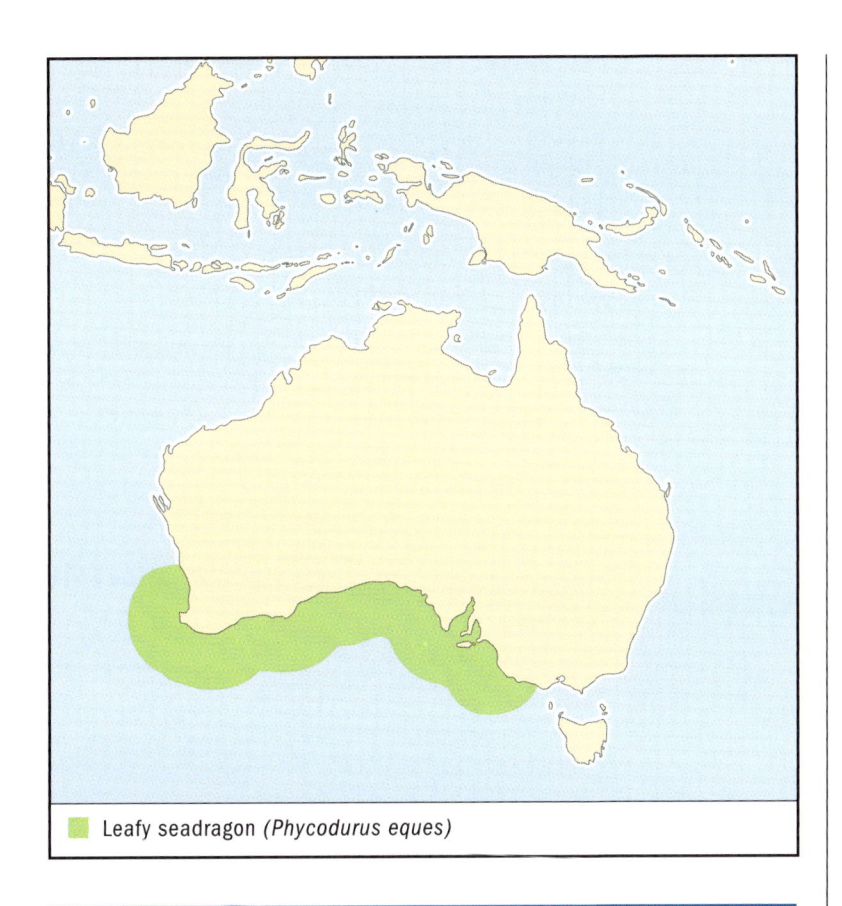

LEAFY SEADRAGON
Phycodurus eques

Physical characteristics: The back, belly, head, and tail of leafy seadragons are covered with spines that support flowing skin that looks like leaves. These fish are greenish brown or yellow with stripes along the trunk. The head has a slight mask and dark blotches on the "leaves." These fish are about 14 inches (35 centimeters) long. The body is long and slender and is encased in ringlike bony plates. The head is long and is almost at a right angle to the body. The snout is very long. The tail is slender and grasping, like that of a monkey. Leafy seadragons have no pelvic or tail fins, lateral line, or scales. Pelvic fins, the rear pair, correspond to the rear legs of four-footed animals. The lateral (LAT-uhr-uhl) line is a series of pores and tiny tubes along each side of a fish's body and is used for sensing vibrations.

Leafy seadragons appear to float aimlessly in kelp beds, protected by their elaborate camouflage. (Illustration by Joseph E. Trumpey. Reproduced by permission.)

Geographic range: Leafy seadragons live along the southern coast of Australia.

Habitat: Leafy seadragons live in shallow water and down to about 98 feet (30 meters), usually sheltered among seaweed and reefs but also over sandy areas.

Diet: Leafy seadragons eat shrimp and lobster.

Behavior and reproduction: Leafy seadragons appear to float aimlessly in kelp beds, protected by their elaborate camouflage. They may move rhythmically back and forth in a manner similar to seaweed being swept by currents. Adults may gather in shallow bays in late winter to pair and mate.

When a male leafy seadragon is ready to mate, his tail becomes swollen and turns bright yellow, and he releases sperm onto his belly. The female deposits her eggs onto the male's belly, pushing them into place. Egg pockets then form on the male to fasten the eggs securely in place under his tail. After about eight weeks, the eggs hatch and the male deposits the young over a wide area.

Leafy seadragons and people: Leafy seadragons are aquarium fishes that also attract recreational divers who want to see them up close.

Conservation status: Leafy seadragons are not threatened or endangered. ∎

Lined seahorse (Hippocampus erectus)

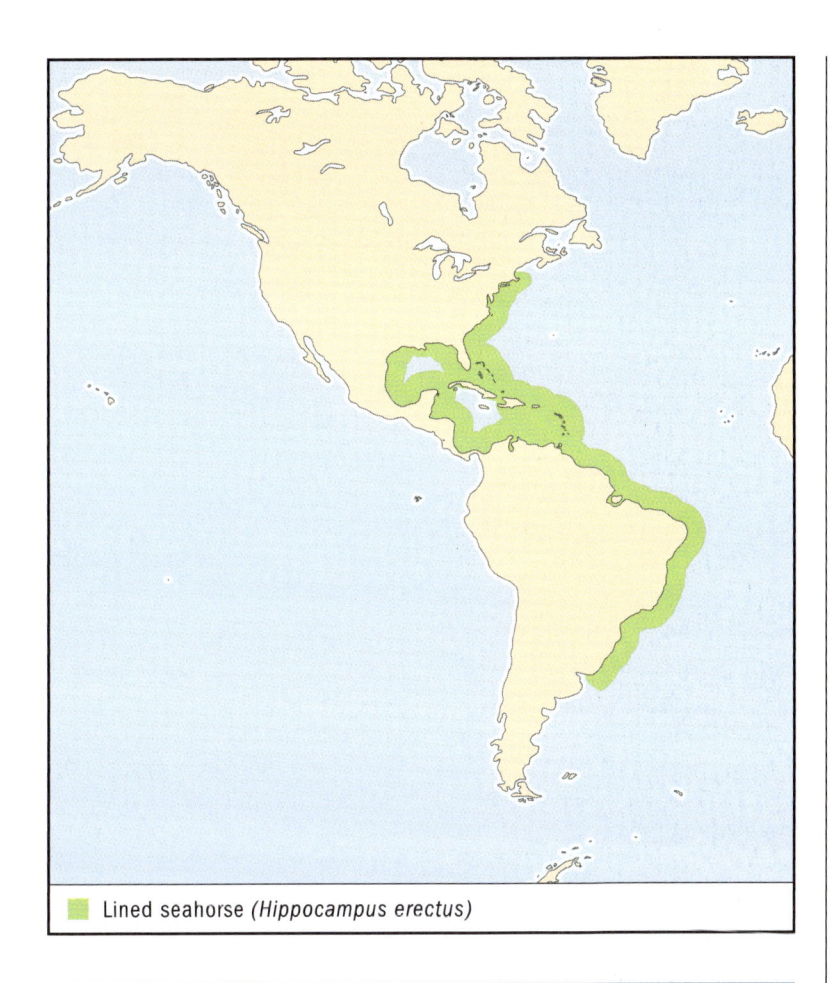

LINED SEAHORSE
Hippocampus erectus

Physical characteristics: The belly of lined seahorses faces forward rather than down. The head is at a right angle to the trunk and tail. The snout is long, and the mouth has no teeth. There are pairs of spines behind the eyes. There is one dorsal fin just in front of the tail. The pectoral and anal (AY-nuhl) fins are small, and there are no pelvic fins. The anal fin is the one along the midline of the belly. The grasping tail tapers into a slender stalk without a tail fin. The body is encased in ten to twelve bony rings, each with four spines. The tail has about thirty-five rings. The color can be light brown, black, gray, yellow, or red covered with small blotches, stripes, and spots. Small white

The eggs develop in the male lined seahorse's pouch for twelve to fourteen days. The young seahorses look like tiny adults when they are born. (©Gregory G. Dimijian/Photo Researchers, Inc. Reproduced by permission.)

stripes extend from the eyes. Lined seahorses grow to a length of about 8 inches (20 centimeters).

Geographic range: Lined seahorses live in the western part of the Atlantic Ocean.

Habitat: Lined seahorses live in shallow waters and waters as deep as 240 feet (73 meters). They live in bays, near beaches, in salt marshes, in oyster beds, around piers, and in other environments with plants and shelter. They can withstand great variations in temperature and salt content.

Diet: Lined seahorses eat small crustaceans (krus-TAY-shuns) and larvae. Crustaceans are water-dwelling animals that have jointed legs and a hard shell but no backbone.

Behavior and reproduction: Lined seahorses swim slowly, belly forward, by making wavelike movements of the dorsal and pectoral fins. They use their tails to cling to plants and coral. These fish produce sounds to communicate with one another. Younger lined seahorses live in open water, sometimes swimming in groups.

After courting, male and female lined seahorses meet belly to belly and twine their tails together. The female then transfers her eggs to the male a few at a time until there are 250 to 400 eggs in his pouch. As eggs are being transferred, both seahorses rise in the water and may change color. The eggs develop in the pouch for twelve to fourteen days. The young seahorses look like tiny adults when they are born.

Lined seahorses and people: Lined seahorses are common in aquariums.

Conservation status: The IUCN lists lined seahorses as Vulnerable or facing a high risk of extinction in the wild. ■

FOR MORE INFORMATION

Books:

Burton, Jane. *Coral Reef.* New York: DK, 1992.

Byatt, Andrew, Alastair Fothergill, and Martha Holmes. *The Blue Planet: Seas of Life.* New York: DK, 2001.

Gilbert, Carter Rowell, and James D. Williams. *National Audubon Society Field Guide to Fishes: North America.* New York: Knopf, 2002.

Web sites:

"About Seahorses." Project Seahorse. http://www.projectseahorse.org (accessed on October 13, 2004).

"Leafy Seadragon." Shedd Aquarium. http://www.sheddaquarium.org/ani_bios_19.html (accessed on October 15, 2004).

"Lined Seahorse." Shedd Aquarium. http://www.sheddaquarium.org/ani_bios_20.html (accessed on October 15, 2004).

SWAMP AND SPINY EELS
Synbranchiformes

Class: Actinopterygii
Order: Synbranchiformes
Number of families: 3 families

order
CHAPTER

PHYSICAL CHARACTERISTICS

Swamp and spiny eels reach a length of 8 to 48 inches (20 to 150 centimeters). Although they look like eels, these fishes are not related to true eels. Scales are either absent or very small. These fishes do not have a swim bladder, an internal sac that fishes use to control their position in the water. The dorsal (DOOR-suhl) and anal (AY-nuhl) fins are low and join each other at the tip of the tail. The pelvic fins, if present, are small and on the throat. The dorsal fin is the one along the midline of the back. The anal fin is the one along the midline of the belly. The pelvic fins, the rear pair, correspond to the rear legs of four-footed animals.

GEOGRAPHIC RANGE

Swamp and spiny eels are native to Africa, Asia, Australia, South America, and North America only as far north as Mexico. They have been introduced in Florida, Georgia, and Hawaii in the United States.

HABITAT

Swamp and spiny eels live in swamps, caves, and sluggish freshwater and in water with a low salt content. They live in leaf litter and mats of fine tree roots along the banks. Swamp eels can move overland, and some can live out of water for a long time. Some species are burrowers and dig holes in which to live. Four species are found only in caves.

DIET

Swamp and spiny eels eat bottom-dwelling fishes and invertebrates (in-VER-teh-brehts), or animals without a backbone, especially larvae (LAR-vee), which are animals in an early stage that must change form before becoming adults.

BEHAVIOR AND REPRODUCTION

Some swamp and spiny eels can breathe air with special structures in the throat. They usually are active only at night. In some species of swamp eels, adult males grow a head hump and are larger than females. These fishes lay about forty eggs at a time. The eggs have a pair of long threads for attaching themselves to the bottom material. Reproduction takes place during the wet season. Females probably spawn, or release eggs, more than once but only in one season. These fishes do not have a long life span.

SWAMP AND SPINY EELS AND PEOPLE

In some parts of Asia, swamp eels and one species of spiny eel are valued as food and are sometimes kept in ponds or rice fields.

CONSERVATION STATUS

The World Conservation Union (IUCN) lists one species of swamp and spiny eels as Endangered, or facing a very high risk of extinction in the wild.

SPECIES ACCOUNT

Marbled swamp eel (*Synbranchus marmoratus*)

MARBLED SWAMP EEL
Synbranchus marmoratus

Physical characteristics: Marbled swamp eels grow to about 59 inches (150 centimeters). They have a long cylindrical body, no pectoral or pelvic fins, and very small dorsal and anal fins. The pectoral (PECK-ter-uhl) fins, the front pair, correspond to the front legs of four-footed animals.

Geographic range: Marbled swamp eels live in North and South America from Mexico to central Argentina.

Marbled swamp eels are active at night, usually at the edge of the water. (Sullivan & Rogers. Bruce Coleman, Inc. Reproduced by permission.)

Habitat: Marbled swamp eels live in clear or murky freshwater and in water with a low salt content in a variety of habitats, including streams, canals, ponds, and rice fields.

Diet: Marbled swamp eels eat fish and invertebrates and are considered aggressive predators (PREH-duh-ters), or animals that hunt and kill other animals for food.

Behavior and reproduction: Marbled swamp eels are active at night, usually at the edge of the water. They can travel over land for long distances. They also burrow, especially during the dry season. During the time in the burrow the metabolism slows, but the fish still may flee if disturbed. After the first rains, marbled swamp eels return to larger bodies of water. Many marbled swamp eels function first as a female and then as a male. Others remain young females. Marbled swamp eels use external fertilization (FUR-teh-lih-zay-shun), meaning egg and sperm unite outside the body.

Marbled swamp eels and people: Marbled swamp eels sometimes appear in public aquariums, although they do not make a good exhibit because of their burrowing behavior.

Conservation status: Marbled swamp eels are not threatened or endangered. ■

FOR MORE INFORMATION

Books:

Berra, Tim M. *Freshwater Fish Distribution*. San Diego, CA: Academic Press, 2001.

Web sites:

Bricking, Erica M. "Asian Swamp Eel (Monopterus Albus)." Introduced Species Summary Project. http://www.columbia.edu/itc/cerc/danoff-burg/invasion_bio/inv_spp_summ/Monopterus_albus.html (accessed on October 14, 2004).

"Frequently Asked Questions about the Asian Swamp Eel." United States Geological Survey. http://cars.er.usgs.gov/Nonindigenous_Species/Swamp_eel_FAQs/swamp_eel_faqs.html (accessed on October 14, 2004).

> **GURNARDS, FLATHEADS, SCORPIONFISHES, AND RELATIVES**
> **Scorpaeniformes**
>
> **Class:** Actinopterygii
> **Order:** Scorpaeniformes
> **Number of families:** 33 families
>
> order CHAPTER

PHYSICAL CHARACTERISTICS

The characteristic that gurnards, flatheads, scorpionfishes, greenlings, and sculpins have in common is a bone that connects the bones under the eye with the front of the gill cover. In all but one species, a bony ridge below the eyes makes the head look armored. Flatheads and flying gurnards have large pectoral (PECK-ter-uhl) fins, the pair that corresponds to the front legs of four-footed animals. These fishes use the rays, or supporting rods, of these fins to "walk" on the sea floor. All scorpionfishes have sharp spines on their bodies. Some of these fishes display bright warning colors and are highly venomous, venom being poison made by the animals. Greenlings and sculpins have a flat head and large pectoral fins. They have no swim bladder, an internal sac that fishes use to control their position in the water.

GEOGRAPHIC RANGE

Gurnards, flatheads, scorpionfishes, greenlings, and sculpins live in the Indian, Pacific, and Atlantic oceans.

HABITAT

Most gurnards, flatheads, scorpionfishes, greenlings, and sculpins live near the shore, but some live in deep water. Some of these fishes live in mud or sandy bottoms. Others live in rocky habitats and coral reefs.

DIET

Gurnards, flatheads, scorpionfishes, greenlings, and sculpins eat crustaceans, such as crabs and shrimp, and smaller fishes.

phylum
class
subclass
● order
monotypic order
suborder
family

FIRST AID

Scorpionfish venom affects both the nervous system and the blood vessels and has caused many human deaths. The effects of the venom are lessened if the wounded area is soaked in very hot, but not boiling, water.

HOW DID THEY GET THERE?

The first red lionfish to live in the Atlantic Ocean were swept there when a home aquarium in Florida was shattered by Hurricane Andrew in 1992.

Crustaceans (krus-TAY-shuns) are water-dwelling animals that have jointed legs and a hard shell but no backbone. Some sculpins eat seaweed.

BEHAVIOR AND REPRODUCTION

Gurnards and flatheads lie and wait to ambush their prey, or animals hunted and killed for food. Little is known about the reproduction of flatheads and gurnards. They produce free-floating eggs. Some flatheads begin life as males and become females as they grow older.

Scorpionfishes can disguise themselves as leaves or rocks. Some scorpionfishes bury themselves in the sand. Most scorpionfishes live alone except to form mating groups. In many species the male places sperm in the female, and then the female squeezes out the eggs in a jellylike mass that floats at the surface. Other scorpionfishes scatter their eggs, which hatch into free-floating larvae. Larvae (LAR-vee) are animals in an early stage and must change form before becoming adults.

Sculpins and greenlings feed by pouncing on and swallowing their prey whole or by sucking in the prey with a stream of water. Most greenlings and sculpins lay masses of eggs that always stick to each other but not always to the surface on which they land. Male sculpins and greenlings guard their egg masses.

GURNARDS, FLATHEADS, SCORPIONFISHES, GREENLINGS, SCULPINS, AND PEOPLE

Flatheads, greenlings, and sculpins are eaten. Lionfishes, scorpionfishes, and sculpins are popular in aquariums.

CONSERVATION STATUS

The World Conservation Union (IUCN) lists one species of gurnards, flatheads, scorpionfishes, greenlings, and sculpins as Extinct, three as Critically Endangered, two as Endangered, and five as Vulnerable. Extinct means no longer in existence. Critically Endangered means facing an extremely high risk of extinction in the wild. Endangered means facing a very high risk of extinction in the wild. Vulnerable means facing a high risk of extinction in the wild. The U.S. Fish and Wildlife Service lists one species as Threatened, or likely to become endangered in the near future.

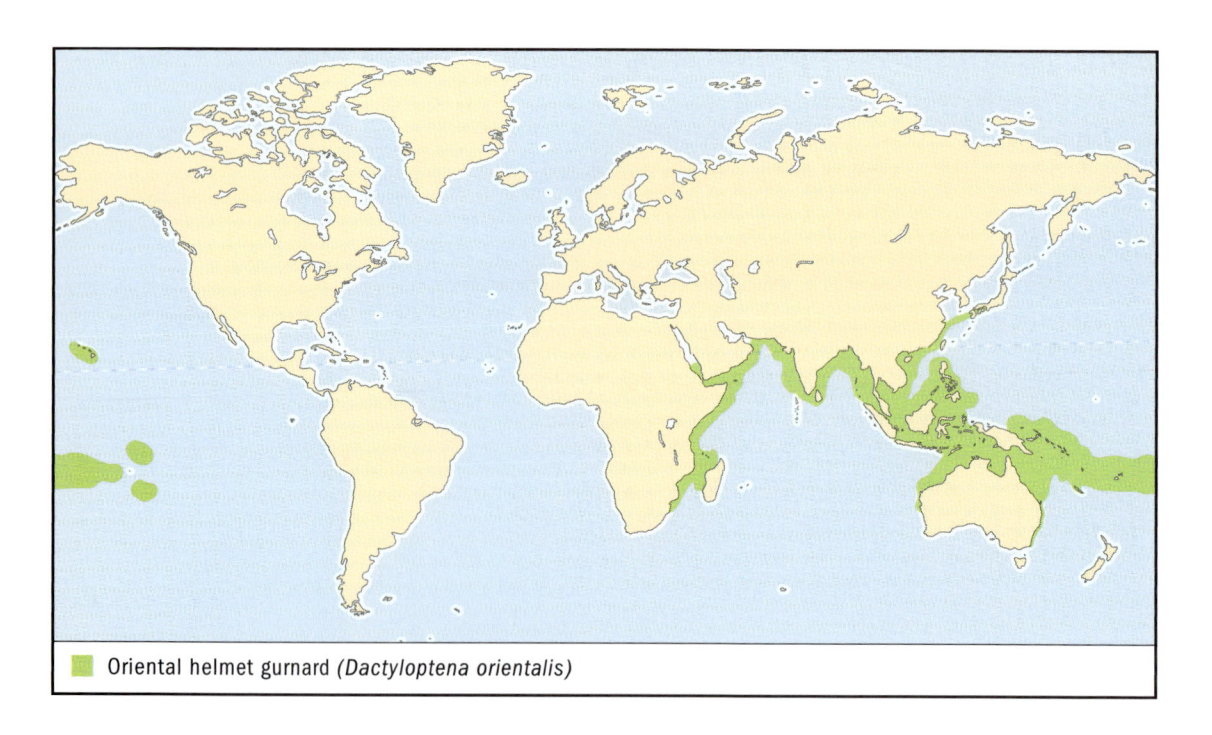

Oriental helmet gurnard (Dactyloptena orientalis)

SPECIES ACCOUNTS

ORIENTAL HELMET GURNARD
Dactyloptena orientalis

Physical characteristics: Oriental helmet gurnards have a long thin body and grow to about 16 inches (40 centimeters) in length. The head is heavily armored. The body is gray to light brown, and there are dark brown and black spots on the back and sides. A long spine just behind the head is followed by a much smaller spine and then two dorsal (DOOR-suhl) fins, which are the fins along the midline of the back. The huge winglike pectoral fins are spotted and have striking blue wavy lines near the edges.

Geographic range: Oriental helmet gurnards live in the Indian Ocean and Red Sea and the Pacific Ocean east to the Hawaiian Islands.

Habitat: Oriental helmet gurnards live on sandy bottoms.

Diet: Oriental helmet gurnards eat bottom-dwelling crustaceans, clams, and fishes.

Oriental helmet gurnards "walk" along the sea floor stirring up and eating prey. (©Fred McConnaughey/Photo Researchers, Inc. Reproduced by permission.)

Behavior and reproduction: Oriental helmet gurnards "walk" along the sea floor stirring up and eating prey. To defend themselves oriental helmet gurnards quickly expand their large winglike pectoral fins. Scientists know little about how oriental flying gurnards reproduce in the wild.

Oriental helmet gurnards and people: Oriental helmet gurnards are caught for the aquarium business.

Conservation status: Oriental helmet gurnards are not threatened or endangered. ■

■ Red lionfish (Pterois volitans)

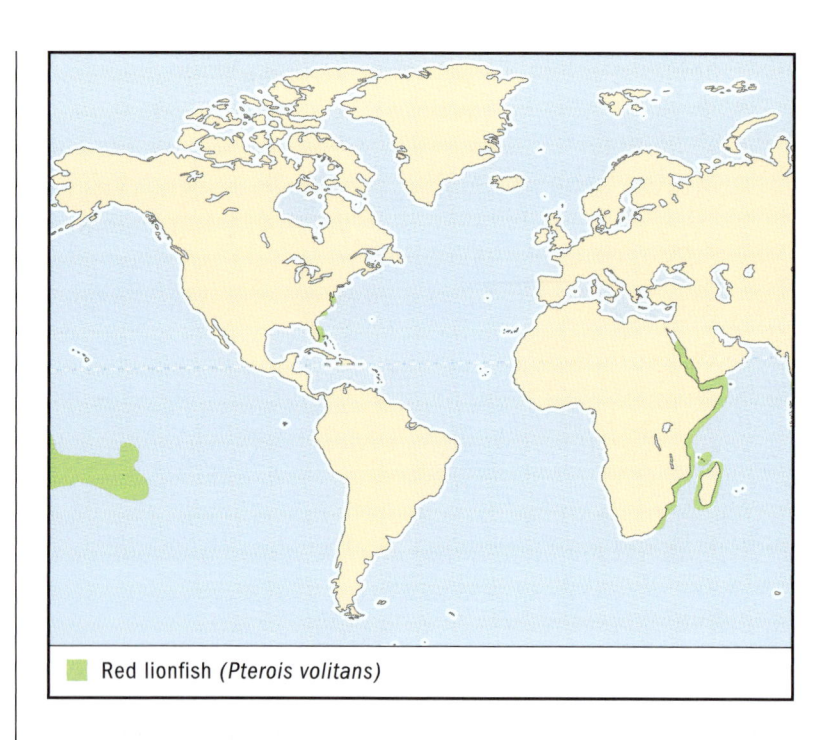

RED LIONFISH
Pterois volitans

Physical characteristics: Red lionfish have dark red bands on the head and body and have pectoral fins that look like long feathers. The dorsal and anal fins are covered with dark rows of spots on a clear to yellowish background. The anal (AY-nuhl) fin is the fin along the midline of the belly. The fin spines are venomous. Red lionfish reach a length of about 14 inches (35 centimeters).

Geographic range: Red lionfish are native to the Indian and Pacific oceans. A small number live in the Atlantic Ocean along the coast of the United States.

Habitat: Red lionfish live on reefs, usually in shallow water.

Diet: Red lionfish are fierce predators (PREH-duh-ters). They hunt other animals for food and feed primarily on small fishes, shrimps, and crabs.

Behavior and reproduction: Red lionfish feed at night and hide among rocks or in caves during the day. They use their fanned-out

Lionfish use their venomous spines for protection. They charge attackers and pierce them with the dorsal spines. (JLM Visuals. Reproduced by permission.)

pectoral fins to trap prey in a corner then suck in the animal whole. Lionfish use their venomous spines for protection. They charge attackers and pierce them with the dorsal spines. After the puncture, glands at the base of the spines shoot venom along the spines and into the attacker. The bright color of the lionfish is a warning for predators to stay away.

Red lionfish usually live alone, but a single male forms groups with females for mating. Females produce two tubes made of mucus and eggs. Soon after release, the egg tubes swell with seawater and are penetrated by the male's sperm. Larvae hatch after thirty-six to forty-eight hours.

Red lionfish and people: Red lionfish are collected for the aquarium business. Even though they are venomous, red lionfish also are caught for food.

Conservation status: Red lionfish are not threatened or endangered.

Lingcod (Ophiodon elongatus)

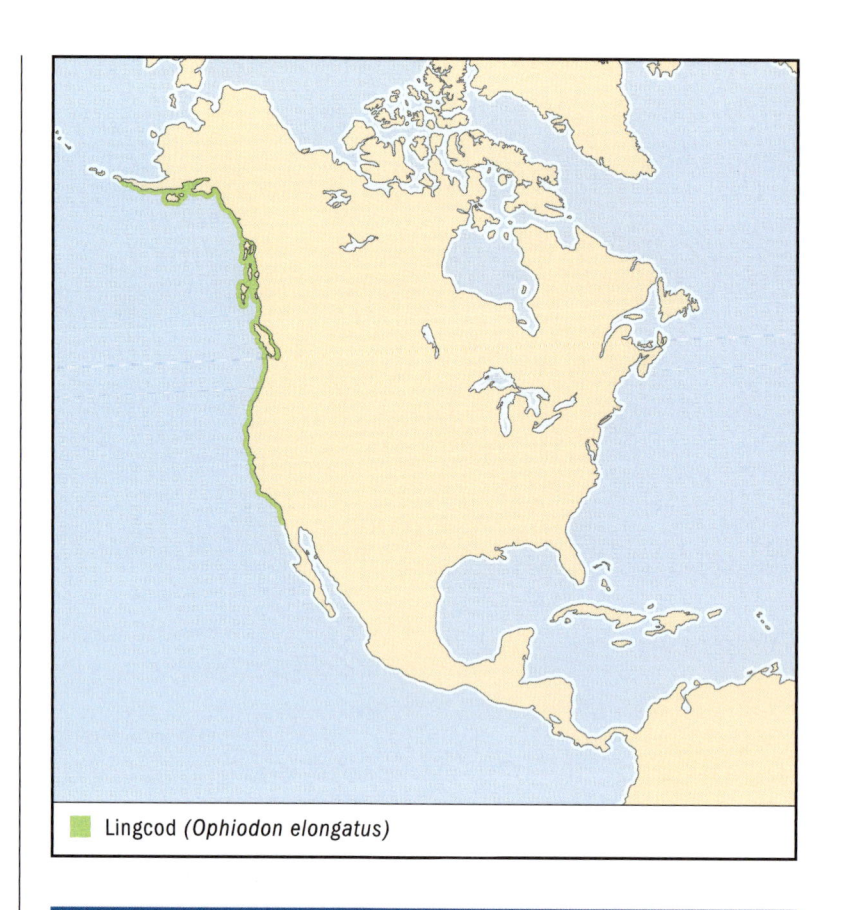

LINGCOD
Ophiodon elongatus

Physical characteristics: Lingcod are large, up to 5 feet (1.5 meters) long and weighing 100 pounds (45 kilograms). The mouth has large teeth. The dorsal fin runs the entire length of the body and looks like two fins. Most lingcod are brown; some are blue-green. They all have staggered black blotches along the sides of the body and the back. Males become all black in the winter just before mating.

Geographic range: Lingcod live in the Pacific Ocean along the west coast of North America from Alaska to Mexico.

Habitat Lingcod spawn, or release eggs, on rocky reefs along the shoreline. After spawning the females move to sand and mud bottoms in deeper water. Males stay on the spawning reefs.

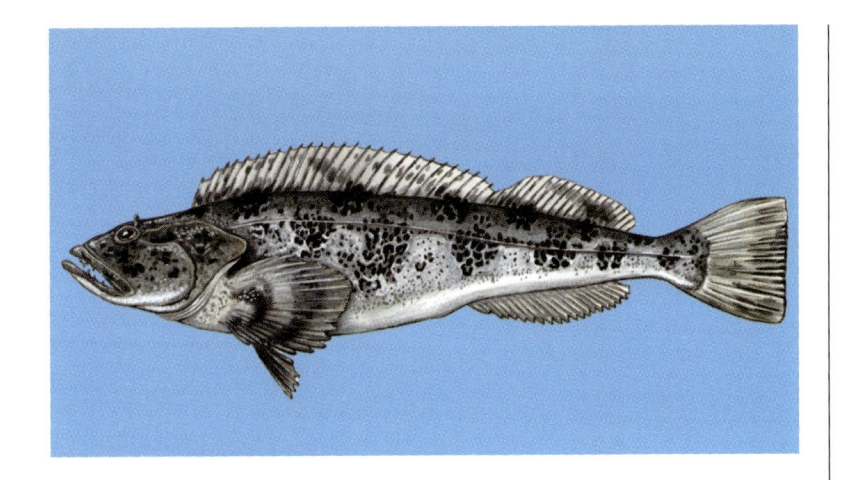

Lingcod mainly eat fish, including young lingcod, by swallowing them head first. (Illustration by Gillian Harris. Reproduced by permission.)

Diet: Lingcod mainly eat fish, including young lingcod, by swallowing them head first.

Behavior and reproduction: Lingcod rest near rocks and wait for prey to come close. Males spawn with one female after another, guarding up to three egg masses at a time.

Lingcod and people: Lingcod is valued as a food fish.

Conservation status: Lingcod are not threatened or endangered. ∎

FOR MORE INFORMATION

Books:

Allen, Missy, and Michel Peissel. *Dangerous Water Creatures.* New York: Chelsea House, 1992.

Gilbert, Carter Rowell, and James D. Williams. *National Audubon Society Field Guide to Fishes: North America.* New York: Knopf, 2002.

Web site:

"Lionfish Invade Eastern US Coast." *Neuroscience for Kids.* http://faculty.washington.edu/chudler/lion.html (accessed on November 10, 2004).

PERCHES, BASSES, AND RELATIVES
Perciformes

Class: Actinopterygii
Order: Perciformes
Number of families: 139 families

order
CHAPTER

phylum
class
subclass
● **order**
monotypic order
suborder
family

PHYSICAL CHARACTERISTICS

When people close their eyes and picture a fish, they probably see a member of Perciformes (puhr-sih-FOR-mehs), the largest order not only of fishes but also of invertebrates (in-VER-teh-brehts), or animals without backbones. There are about seven thousand species in the order Perciformes. Fishes in Perciformes vary from tiny gobies and darters to huge marlins and swordfishes. The body shape varies from long and thin like that of wolf-eels to short and round like that of yellow tangs. Most fish in this order, however, are the familiar "fish" shape of perch, bass, tuna, and bluegill.

The traits that most fishes in Perciformes have in common are spines on the front parts of the dorsal and anal fins; pelvic fins made up of one spine and five rays, or supporting rods; rough scales; and the presence of a lateral line. The dorsal (DOOR-suhl) fin is along the midline of the back, and the anal (AY-nuhl) fin is along the midline of the belly. The pelvic fins correspond to the rear legs of four-footed animals. The lateral (LAT-uhr-uhl) line is a series of pores and tiny tubes along each side of a fish's body and is used for sensing vibrations.

GEOGRAPHIC RANGE

Fishes in Perciformes live all over the world from just below the Arctic Circle to Antarctica.

HABITAT

Fishes in Perciformes live in freshwater or saltwater. Some live near the shore; others live far out at sea. Some live in open water;

others are bottom dwellers over sand, mud, or rocks. Some live on rock or coral reefs, and some live among plants such as sea grass. Some Perciformes fishes live in still water; others, in fast-moving water. Some live in cold water, but most live in warm or cool water.

DIET

Fishes in Perciformes eat everything from algae and plankton to other fish. Some even eat land animals. Algae (AL-jee) are plantlike growths that live in water and have no true roots, stems, or leaves. Plankton are microscopic plants and animals drifting in water.

BEHAVIOR AND REPRODUCTION

Some fishes in Perciformes are active during the day; others, at night. Some are fierce hunters, and others eat whatever floats their way. Some fishes live alone, and others form schools. In some species of Perciformes, eggs are fertilized (FUR-teh-lyzed), or united with sperm to start development, after the female releases them into the water or a nest. In other species the eggs are fertilized inside the female and then either are laid, or develop inside the female, then giving birth to larvae or to young that look like adults. Larvae (LAR-vee) are animals in an early stage that must change form before becoming adults. Some Perciformes guard their eggs and young. In some species the young develop in a parent's mouth.

PERCIFORMES AND PEOPLE

Some Perciformes fishes are caught or farmed for food, fish oil, fish meal, or bait. Others are used in aquariums. People in some areas, such as the Amazon, support themselves by catching and selling aquarium fishes. Many Perciformes fishes are popular for sport fishing. Some Perciformes fishes are used for scientific research.

CONSERVATION STATUS

The World Conservation Union (IUCN) lists forty-three species in Perciformes as Extinct, five as Extinct in the Wild, fifty-five as Critically Endangered, twenty-eight as Endangered, 135 as Vulnerable, five as Conservation Dependent, and forty

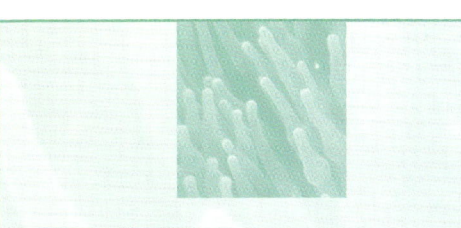

WHAT IS AN ORDER?

An order is one of the groups used to classify natural things. From most general to having the most in common, these groups are kingdom, phylum, class, order, family, genus, and species. The kingdoms are animal, vegetable, and mineral. Animals in the same species have enough traits in common to produce young with one another.

as Near Threatened. Extinct means no longer in existence. Extinct in the Wild means no longer alive except in captivity or through the aid of humans. Critically Endangered means facing extremely high risk of extinction in the wild. Endangered means facing very high risk of extinction in the wild. Vulnerable means facing high risk of extinction in the wild. Conservation Dependent means if the conservation program were to end, the animal would be placed in one of the threatened categories. Near Threatened means at risk of becoming threatened with extinction in the future.

The U.S. Fish and Wildlife Service lists fourteen Perciformes species as Endangered and seven as Threatened. Endangered means in danger of extinction throughout all or a significant portion of its range. Threatened means likely to become endangered in the near future.

FOR MORE INFORMATION

Books:

Gilbert, Carter Rowell, and James D. Williams. *National Audubon Society Field Guide to Fishes: North America.* New York: Knopf, 2002.

Web sites:

"Perciform." All Science Fair Projects. http://www.all-science-fair-projects.com/science_fair_projects_encyclopedia/Perciform (accessed on November 11, 2004).

PERCHES, DARTERS, AND RELATIVES
Percoidei

Class: Actinopterygii
Order: Perciformes
Suborder: Percoidei
Number of families: 77 families

suborder
CHAPTER

PHYSICAL CHARACTERISTICS

Fishes in the suborder Percoidei (puhr-COI-dee-ee) have the following characteristics in common: spines in the dorsal (DOOR-suhl), anal (AY-nuhl), and pelvic fins; two dorsal fins; rough scales; pelvic fins in the chest area; a spine and soft rays, or supporting rods, in the pelvic fin; and no more than seventeen rays in the tail fin. The dorsal fins are the ones along the midline of the back. The anal fin is along the midline of the belly. The pelvic fins correspond to the rear legs of four-footed animals.

GEOGRAPHIC RANGE

Fishes in Percoidei live all over the world except for polar waters.

HABITAT

Fishes in Percoidei live in freshwater or saltwater. The freshwater fishes live in lakes, ponds, ditches, swamps, and fast- and slow-moving streams. Saltwater fishes live near the shore or out at sea.

DIET

Some fishes in Percoidei eat algae, plants, animal plankton, invertebrates, which are animals without backbones, and fish. Algae (AL-jee) are plantlike growths that live in water and have no true roots, stems, or leaves. Plankton is microscopic plants and animals drifting in water.

phylum
class
subclass
order
monotypic order
○ **suborder**
family

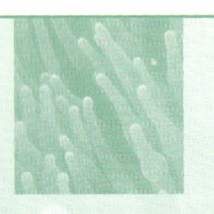

CIGUETERA

Ciguetera poison comes from a one-cell plant eaten by plankton, which is eaten by fish, which are eaten by other fish. The strength of the poison increases ten times every time it is taken in by a new animal. Humans who eat fish with ciguatera suffer nerve damage that can be fatal.

Ready, Aim, Fire
Archerfish can spit water up to 5 feet (1.5 meters) to knock insects into the water for a meal.

BEHAVIOR AND REPRODUCTION

Some fishes in Percoidei are active during the day, and some are active at night. Some form schools; others live alone. Some fishes rest on the bottom. Some move up and down in the water. Some fishes travel for spawning, or releasing eggs. Some spawn in groups and scatter their eggs; others build nests to mate. Many fishes guard their eggs and young.

PERCHES, DARTERS, THEIR RELATIVES, AND PEOPLE

Some fishes in Percoidei are caught for food, and some are farmed. Many are prized sport fishes, and many are used in aquariums.

CONSERVATION STATUS

The World Conservation Union (IUCN) lists one species in Percoidei as Extinct, eight as Critically Endangered, eleven as Endangered, fifty-six as Vulnerable, one as Conservation Dependent, and twenty as Near Threatened. Extinct means no longer in existence. Critically Endangered means facing an extremely high risk of extinction in the wild. Endangered means facing a very high risk of extinction in the wild. Vulnerable means facing a high risk of extinction in the wild. Conservation Dependent means if the conservation program were to end, the animal would be placed in one of the threatened categories. Near Threatened means at risk of becoming threatened with extinction in the future.

The U.S. Fish and Wildlife Service lists thirteen species as Endangered and seven as Threatened. Endangered means in danger of extinction throughout all or a significant portion of its range. Threatened means likely to become endangered in the near future.

Largemouth bass *(Micropterus salmoides)*

LARGEMOUTH BASS
Micropterus salmoides

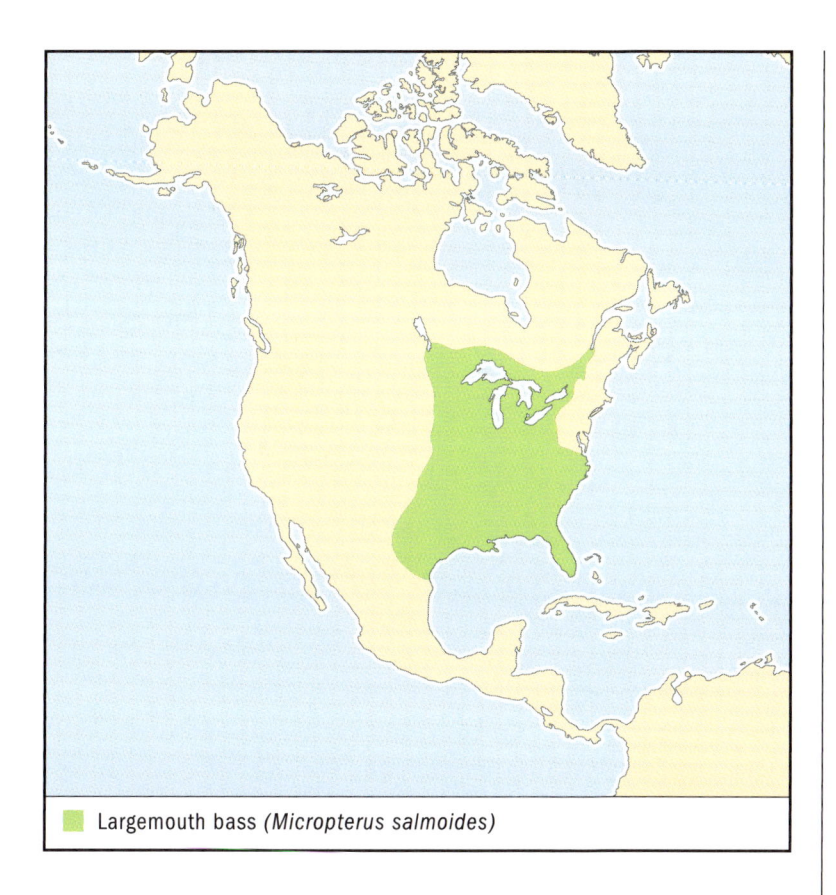

SPECIES ACCOUNTS

Physical characteristics: Largemouth bass reach a length of about 38 inches (97 centimeters). The mouth is so large it extends back past the eyes. These fish are light green to light brown on the back and upper part of the sides and white on the lower sides and belly. A dark stripe runs along each side of the body.

Geographic range: Largemouth bass are native to the eastern half of the United States and southern Canada but have been introduced worldwide.

Habitat: Largemouth bass live in lakes, ponds, and rivers that have many hiding places.

The mouth of a largemouth bass is so large it extends back past the eyes. (Illustration by Emily Damstra. Reproduced by permission.)

Diet: Largemouth bass mainly eat crustaceans and fishes. Crustaceans (krus-TAY-shuns) are water-dwelling animals that have jointed legs and a hard shell but no backbone.

Behavior and reproduction: Adult largemouth bass live alone. The young form schools. At spawning time males become territorial and dig a nest in a weedy area at the bottom of the water. A female may lay eggs over several nests. Both males and females guard their eggs and young.

Largemouth bass and people: Largemouth bass are popular sport fish.

Conservation status: Largemouth bass are not threatened or endangered. ∎

Common dolphinfish (*Coryphaena hippurus*)

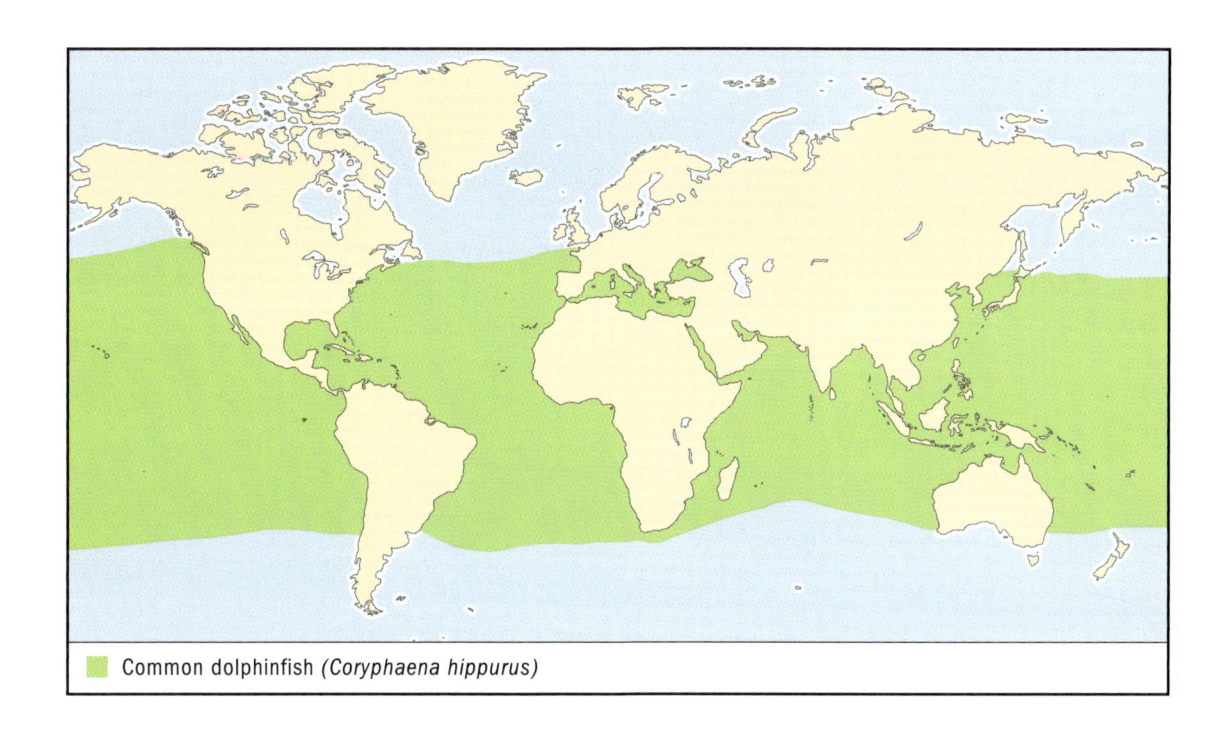

COMMON DOLPHINFISH
Coryphaena hippurus

Physical characteristics: Common dolphinfish are about 83 inches (2 meters) long. Males have a high, block-like forehead, but females have a rounded forehead. The dorsal fin extends from head to tail. The anal fin extends from the center of the body to the tail. The tail fin is deeply forked. Dolphinfish are brilliant metallic green and blue on the back and upper sides, gold on the lower sides, and yellow and white on the belly.

Geographic range: Common dolphinfish live in the Atlantic, Pacific, and Indian oceans.

Habitat: Common dolphinfish live in open water near the surface but sometimes go near shore to look for food.

Diet: Common dolphinfish mainly eat smaller fish and squid.

Behavior and reproduction: Common dolphinfish form traveling schools. They are attracted to boats and floating objects. These fish

Perches, Darters, and Relatives

Common dolphinfish males have a high, block-like forehead, but females have a rounded forehead. (A. Kerstitch/Bruce Coleman, Inc. Reporduced by permission.)

can reproduce when they are only four to five months old. They release free-floating eggs in open water, and the eggs hatch in about thirty-six hours. Common dolphinfish live for about five years.

Dolphinfish and people: Common dolphinfish are highly prized for food and sport. They can cause ciguatera (see-gwuh-TEHR-uh), a form of food poisoning.

Conservation status: Common dolphinfish are not threatened or endangered. ■

Golden perch (Macquaria ambigua)

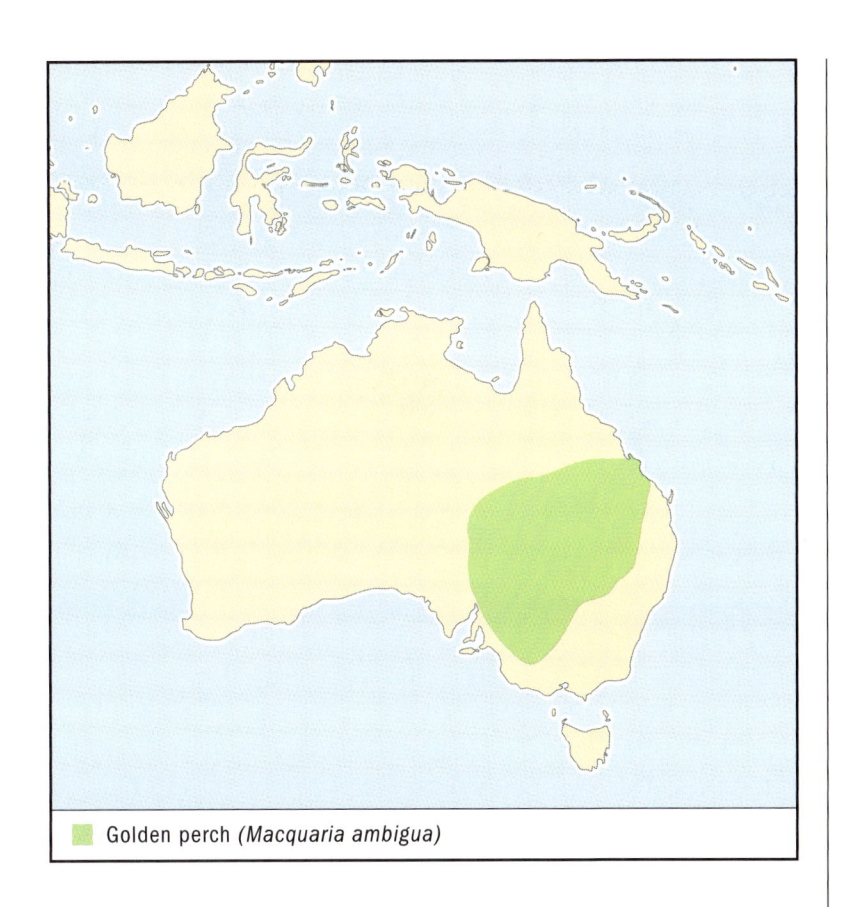

GOLDEN PERCH
Macquaria ambigua

Physical characteristics: Golden perch reach a length of 30 inches (75 centimeters) and a weight of 53 pounds (24 kilograms), but most are smaller. They are olive green, bronze, or brownish and have a yellow belly. The body is somewhat broad from back to belly and narrow from side to side. The pelvic fins have long strings.

Geographic range: Golden perch live in Australia.

Habitat: Golden perch live near fallen or submerged trees, overhanging banks, and rocky ledges in muddy, slow-flowing rivers and clear, fast-flowing rivers.

Golden perch live near fallen or submerged trees, overhanging banks, and rocky ledges. (Illustration by Marguette Dongvillo. Reproduced by permission)

Diet: Golden perch eat crustaceans, mollusks, and fish. Mollusks (MAH-lusks) are animals with a soft, unsegmented body that may or may not have a shell.

Behavior and reproduction: Golden perch live alone. Females can reproduce when they are four years old, males when they are two years old. Golden perch travel more than 1,200 miles (2,000 kilometers) to reach their spawning grounds. Eggs float after spawning and hatch in a little more than a day. The larvae drift downstream.

Golden perch and people: Golden perch are mainly game fish.

Conservation status: Golden perch are not threatened or endangered.

Banded archerfish (Toxotes jaculatrix)

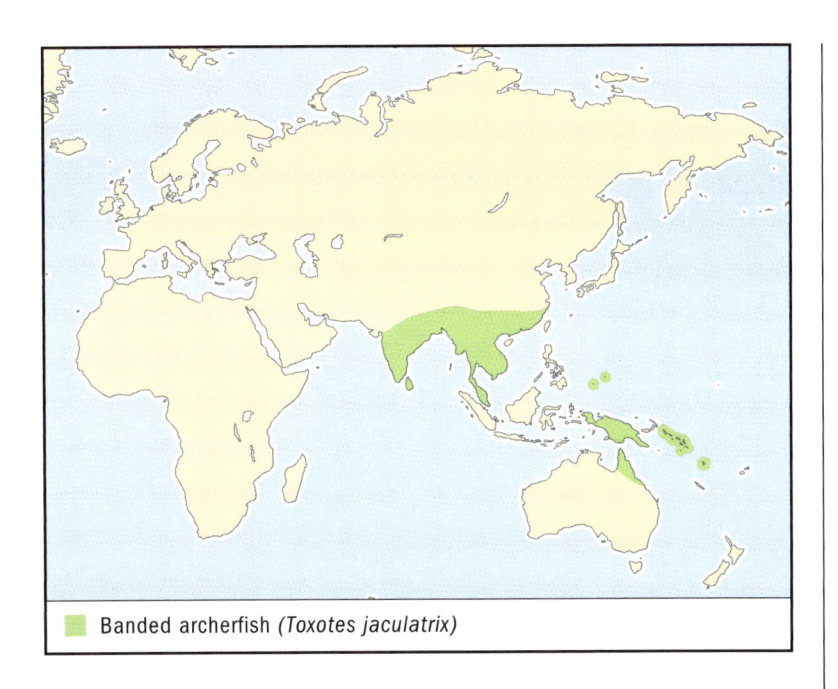

BANDED ARCHERFISH
Toxotes jaculatrix

Physical characteristics: Banded archerfish are silvery white and have five black bands across the upper sides of the body, the dorsal fin, and the tail. There is yellow on the fins. The body is broad from back to belly. These fish grow to a length of about 8 inches (20 centimeters).

Geographic range: Banded archerfish live in India, Southeast Asia, and Australia.

Habitat: Banded archerfish live in bays and the parts of rivers and creeks that are closest to the sea.

Diet: Banded archerfish eat insects and floating fruits and flowers.

Behavior and reproduction: Banded archerfish live alone or in small groups around shelter. They swim slowly as they hunt for food both below and above the surface of the water. Banded archerfish spawn in pairs and release eggs near the bottom. The larvae (LAR-vee), or young, float in open water.

Banded archerfish eat insects and floating fruits and flowers. (Illustration by Joseph E. Trumpey. Reproduced by permission.)

Banded archerfish and people: Banded archerfish are mainly used in aquariums.

Conservation status: Banded archerfish are not threatened or endangered. ∎

Nassau grouper (*Epinephelus striatus*)

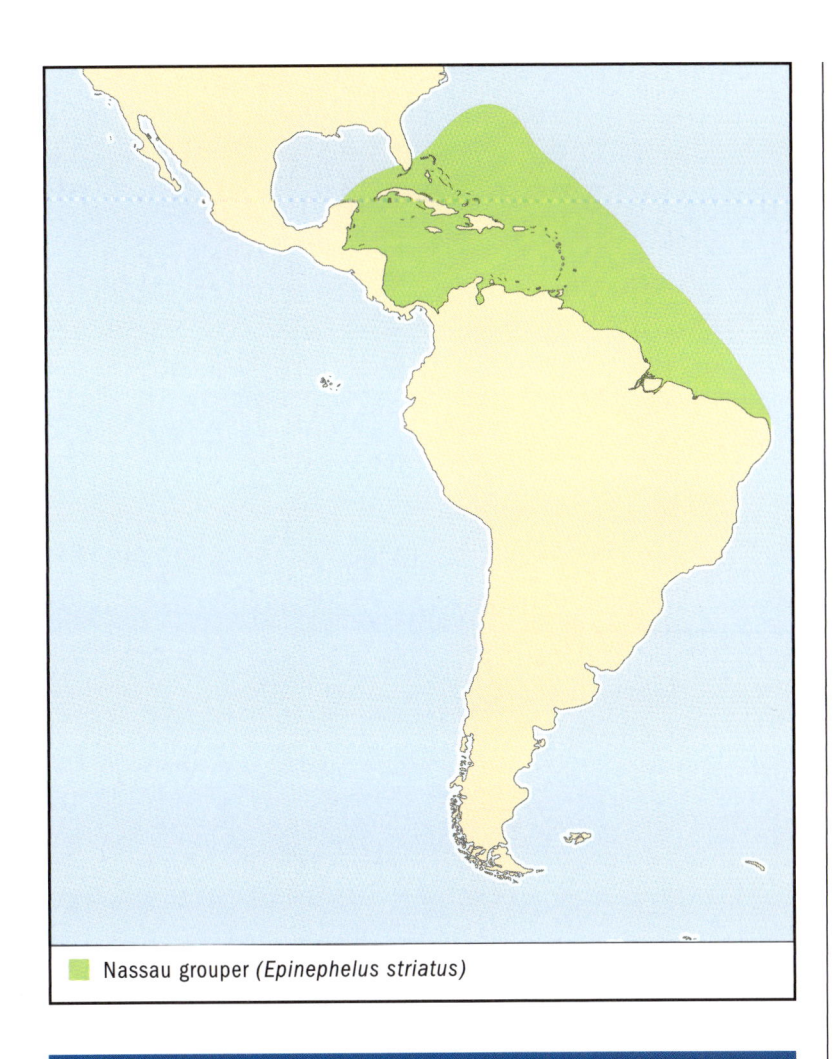

NASSAU GROUPER
Epinephelus striatus

Physical characteristics: Nassau groupers have a thick body with a sloping forehead and large fins. The third spine of the dorsal fin is the longest. The body is light brown in shallow water and pinkish brown or red in deeper water. There are dark and pale bands along the sides and the dorsal fin. A dark saddle on the upper part of the tail and dark spots around the eyes are present no matter what color the rest of the fish is. Nassau groupers grow to a length of about 47 inches (120 centimeters).

Nassau groupers can change colors, from light to dark, very rapidly. (Illustration by Emily Damstra. Reproduced by permission.)

Geographic range: Nassau groupers live in the western part of the Atlantic Ocean from Bermuda to northern Brazil.

Habitat: Adult Nassau groupers live in coral and rocky reefs. The young usually live in sea grass beds.

Diet: Nassau groupers mainly eat crabs and large mollusks.

Behavior and reproduction: Nassau groupers can change color rapidly, from dark to light shades. They usually live alone, although they may form groups for spawning. They ambush their prey. Nassau groupers can reproduce when they are four to eight years old and function first as a female and then as a male. They spawn in open water in large groups. The eggs and larvae float in open water.

Nassau groupers and people: Nassau groupers are important food and game fish. They can cause ciguatera in humans who eat this fish. They also are collected for large aquariums.

Conservation status: The World Conservation Union (IUCN) lists Nassau groupers as Endangered. Endangered means they are facing a very high risk of extinction in the wild. ■

FOR MORE INFORMATION

Books:

Gilbert, Carter Rowell, and James D. Williams. *National Audubon Society Field Guide to Fishes: North America.* New York: Knopf, 2002.

Nelson, Joseph S. *Fishes of the World.* 3rd ed. New York: Wiley, 1994.

Schultz, Ken. *Ken Schultz's Field Guide to Freshwater Fish.* New York: Wiley, 2004.

Schultz, Ken. *Ken Schultz's Field Guide to Saltwater Fish.* New York: Wiley, 2004.

Web sites:

"Lesson 1: Refraction at a Boundary—The Secret of the Archer Fish." The Physics Classroom. http://www.physicsclassroom.com/Class/refrn/U14L1f.html (accessed on October 26, 2004).

"Mahimahi (*Coryphaena hippurus*)." Oceans Alive. http://www.oceansalive.org/eat.cfm?subnav=fishpage&group=mahimahi (accessed on October 26, 2004).

"Nassau Grouper (*Epinephelus striatus*)." Oceans Alive. http://www.oceansalive.org/eat.cfm?subnav=fishpage&fish=38 (accessed on October 26, 2004).

CICHLIDS, SURFPERCHES, AND RELATIVES
Labroidei

Class: Actinopterygii
Order: Perciformes
Suborder: Labroidei
Number of families: 6 families

suborder
CHAPTER

PHYSICAL CHARACTERISTICS

Cichlids (SIH-cluhds), surfperches, damselfishes, wrasses, parrotfishes, and rock whitings have a second set of jaws in the throat. These fishes have a dorsal fin that extends the length of the fish's back. The dorsal (DOOR-suhl) fin is the one along the midline of the back.

GEOGRAPHIC RANGE

Cichlids live in South America, Africa, Asia, and North America. Surfperches live in coastal areas of the northern part of the Pacific Ocean. Parrotfishes, wrasses, and damselfishes live in the Atlantic, Pacific, and Indian oceans. Rock whitings live in Australia and New Zealand.

HABITAT

Cichlids live in freshwater in lakes, swamps, streams, and rivers, including rapids. Surfperches live in saltwater near sandy beaches, sea grass beds, rocky outcroppings, and piers. Damselfishes, wrasses, parrotfishes, and rock whitings live on reefs, although a few species live in the open sea.

DIET

Many cichlids hunt other fishes and eat them whole. Some scrape algae from rocks. Some eat animal plankton. One species eats plant plankton. Many cichlids have special teeth for crushing the shells of snails. Surfperches eat crustaceans, mollusks, and worms. Damselfishes, parrotfishes, and rock whitings eat plants and animals. Some wrasses eat hard-shelled invertebrates, or animals without a backbone. Others eat plankton. Cleaner wrasses eat parasites and waste they find on other fishes. Crustaceans (krus-TAY-shuns) are water-dwelling animals that have jointed legs and a hard shell but no backbone. Mollusks (MAH-lusks) are animals with a soft, unsegmented body that may or may not have a shell. Algae (AL-jee) are plantlike growths that live in water and have no true roots, stems, or leaves. Parasites (PAIR-uh-sites) are animals or plants that live on other animals or plants without helping them and often harming them.

BEHAVIOR AND REPRODUCTION

Some cichlids form pairs in which both parents guard eggs laid on the bottom. Some change sex. Some cichlids are mouth brooders, meaning the eggs and young develop inside the mouth of one or both parents. Many cichlids build huge, cone-shaped sand nests, sometimes in groups as large as fifty thousand stretched over several miles (kilometers) of sand.

> **FISH WASH**
>
> Cleaner wrasses set up sites for providing cleaning services to other fishes. Fish come to the cleaning stations and announce their desire to be cleaned by moving their mouths or bodies. The cleaner wrasses strike a deal by brushing the "customer" with their fins, and the cleaning begins. The wrasses pick over the body, fins, and head of the customer and may even enter the gill chamber and mouth to remove parasites, mucus, dead skin, loose scales, and other waste. Both the customer and the wrasse benefit from the arrangement: The cleaner is fed, and the customer is cleaned.

Surfperches give birth to live young. Damselfishes, wrasses, parrotfishes, and rock whitings change colors and sexes according to life stage. Damselfishes are territorial of their mating sites and viciously attack intruders. Rock whitings change sex from female to male and live in small groups of one male and several females. Females lay their eggs directly into a plankton mass.

CICHLIDS, SURFPERCHES, THEIR RELATIVES, AND PEOPLE

Cichlids and surfperches are caught or farmed for food. Cichlids, damselfishes, wrasses, parrotfishes, and rock whitings are used in aquariums.

CONSERVATION STATUS

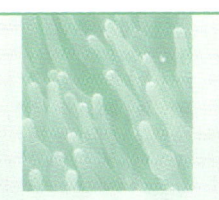

The World Conservation Union (IUCN) lists forty-two species of cichlids, surfperches, damselfishes, wrasses, parrotfishes, and rock whitings as Extinct, five as Extinct in the Wild, thirty-seven as Critically Endangered, twelve as Endangered, forty-three as Vulnerable, and one as Conservation Dependent. Extinct means no longer in existence. Extinct in the Wild means no longer alive except in captivity or through the aid of humans. Critically Endangered means facing an extremely high risk of extinction in the wild. Endangered means facing a very high risk of extinction in the wild. Vulnerable means facing a high risk of extinction in the wild. Conservation Dependent means if the conservation program were to end, the animal would be placed in one of the threatened categories.

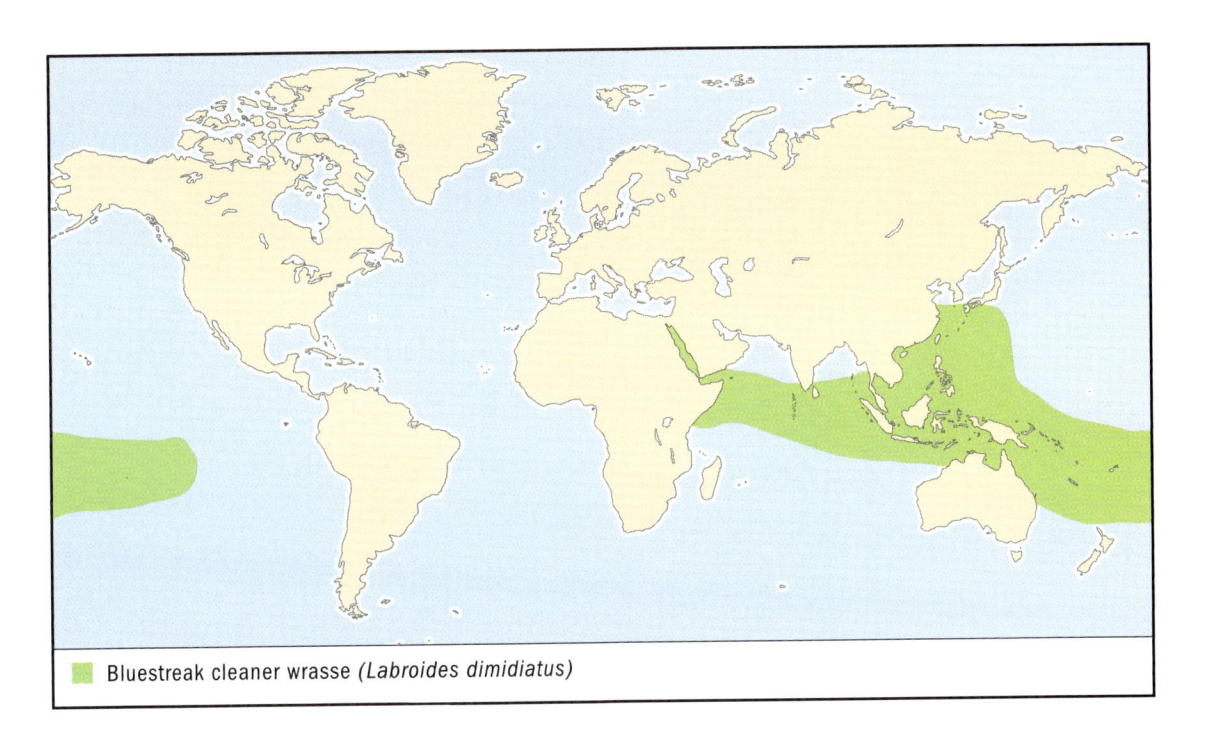

Bluestreak cleaner wrasse (*Labroides dimidiatus*)

BLUESTREAK CLEANER WRASSE
Labroides dimidiatus

SPECIES ACCOUNTS

Physical characteristics: Bluestreak cleaner wrasses are about 4½ inches (12 centimeters) long. Adults are mostly light blue. A long black stripe along each side of the body widens as it approaches the tail. The young are black with a blue stripe on the back.

Geographic range: Bluestreak cleaner wrasses live in the Indian and Pacific oceans.

Habitat: Bluestreak cleaner wrasses live on coral reefs.

Diet: Bluestreak cleaner wrasses eat what they find on other fishes.

Behavior and reproduction: Bluestreak cleaner wrasses clean other fishes. They sometimes lives in pairs but frequently live in groups of one male and six to ten females. If the male leaves the group, one of the females takes his place and in about two weeks starts functioning as a male.

Cichlids, Surfperches, and Relatives

Bluestreak cleaner wrasses and people: Bluestreak cleaner wrasses are common aquarium fish.

Conservation status: Bluestreak cleaner wrasses are not threatened or endangered. ■

Bluestreak cleaner wrasses clean other fishes. (Illustration by Joseph E. Trumpey. Reproduced by permission.)

Striped parrotfish (Scarus iseri)

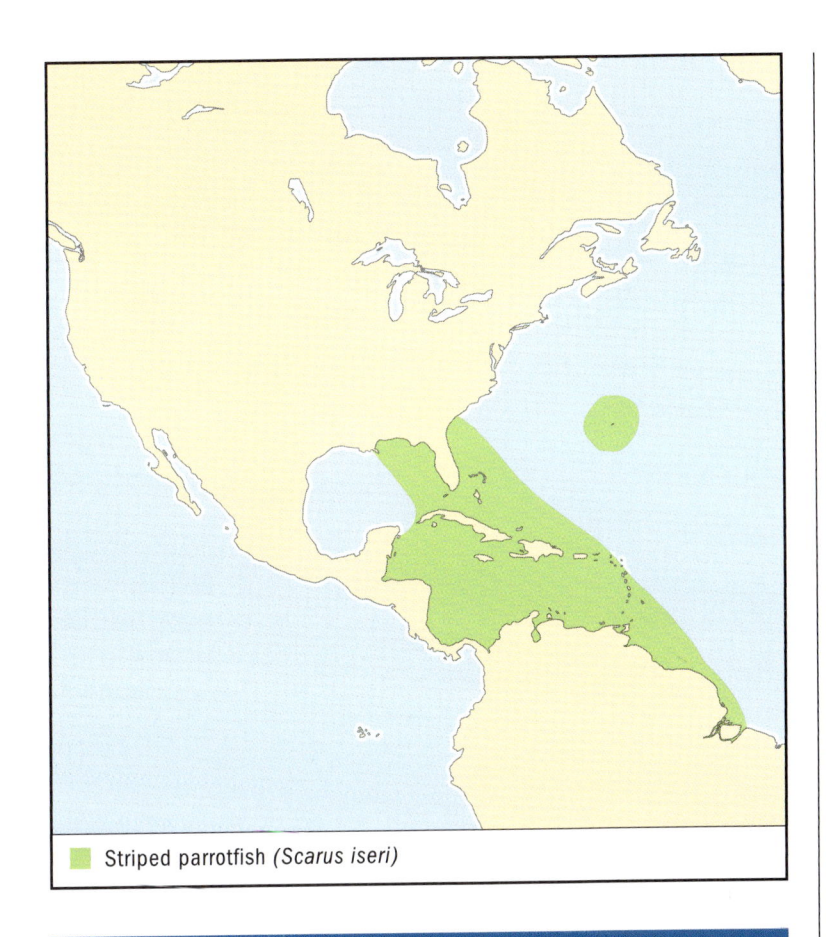

STRIPED PARROTFISH
Scarus iseri

Physical characteristics: Striped parrotfish reach a length of about 14 inches (35 centimeters). In their first phase of life, these fish have dark stripes extending from head to tail. The most prominent stripe goes through the eye and nearly to the tail. Males in the final life stage are turquoise.

Geographic range: Striped parrotfish live in the eastern part of the Atlantic Ocean from Florida to Brazil.

Habitat: Striped parrotfish live on reefs.

Diet: Striped parrotfish eat algae, which they scrape from rocks and other surfaces.

Parrotfish prepare for sleep by making a tube of mostly clear mucus that surrounds the body. (Illustration by Patricia Ferrer. Reproduced by permission.)

Behavior and reproduction: Parrotfish prepare for sleep by making a tube of mostly clear mucus that surrounds the body. The tube forms in about thirty to sixty minutes. The mucus tube hides the parrotfish from predators and may be an unpleasant-tasting barrier. Striped parrotfish form schools. They also change sex from female to male. These fish mate year-round in pairs or in groups, scattering their eggs, which float in open water.

Striped parrotfish and people: Striped parrotfish sometimes are fished and sold for food and sometimes are used in aquariums.

Conservation status: Striped parrotfish are not threatened or endangered. ∎

Freshwater angelfish (Pterophyllum scalare)

FRESHWATER ANGELFISH
Pterophyllum scalare

Physical characteristics: Freshwater angelfish are about 3 inches (7.5 centimeters) long. The combination of large triangular dorsal and anal fins above and below a round body gives the fish a diamond-shaped profile. The body is very narrow from side to side. Adults are silver with four dark stripes that extend from the top to the belly of the fish. The young have seven dark bars.

Geographic range: Freshwater angelfish live in South America.

Habitat: Freshwater angelfish live in lakes, swamps, and flooded forests with dense plant life and little current.

Diet: Freshwater angelfish eat bottom-dwelling crustaceans, such as shrimp.

Behavior and reproduction: Freshwater angelfish are peaceful fishes that hide in plants. They form pairs for mating. Females spawn on thick leaves, and both parents care for the eggs and young.

Freshwater angelfish and people: Freshwater angelfish are extremely popular for aquariums. Millions are sold every year.

Conservation status: Freshwater angelfish are not threatened or endangered. ■

Freshwater angelfish are peaceful fishes that hide in plants. (Illustration by Barbara Duperron. Reproduced by permission.)

FOR MORE INFORMATION

Books:

Gilbert, Carter Rowell, and James D. Williams. *National Audubon Society Field Guide to Fishes: North America.* New York: Knopf, 2002.

Web sites:

Coleman, Ron. "Introducing the Cichlids." Cichlid Research Home Page. http://www.cichlidresearch.com/introducingcichlids.html (accessed on October 26, 2004).

Smith, Richard. "Cleaner Wrasse." *Catalyst—ABC TV Science.* http://www.abc.net.au/catalyst/default.htm (accessed on October 27, 2004).

EELPOUTS AND RELATIVES
Zoarcoidei

Class: Actinopterygii
Order: Perciformes
Suborder: Zoarcoidei
Number of families: 9 families

suborder CHAPTER

PHYSICAL CHARACTERISTICS

Most eelpouts and their relatives are shaped like eels. They usually are less than 16 inches (40 centimeters) long, but some reach a length of 24 inches (60 centimeters). The wolf-eel is the largest fish in this group, reaching a length of 80 inches (2 meters). Eelpouts are usually gray, brown, black, or purple and have spots of various colors.

GEOGRAPHIC RANGE

Eelpouts and their relatives live all over the world from the Arctic to Antarctica.

HABITAT

Some eelpouts and their relatives live above the high tide line in rock pools, burrowing in sand or gravel beaches. Some live in rocky reefs in seaweed and keep well hidden by day. Other species live as far as 2 miles (4,000 meters) deep in the ocean.

DIET

Most eelpouts and their relatives hunt for worms, clams, sea urchins, smaller fishes, sea snails, crabs, hermit crabs, starfish, jellyfishes, and plankton, which is microscopic plants and animals drifting in water. Some eat only algae (AL-jee), which are plantlike growths that live in water and have no true roots, stems, or leaves.

BEHAVIOR AND REPRODUCTION

Most eelpouts and their relatives live alone and hide but may gather for a short time in shelters or around food sources.

phylum
class
subclass
order
monotypic order
○ **suborder**
family

During the winter in colder regions species that live near the shore may travel into deeper water to avoid freezing. Scientists know little about the reproduction of eelpouts and their relatives. In some species eggs are fertilized (FUR-teh-lyzed), or joined to sperm to start development, inside the female and then are laid. In other species, eggs are fertilized as they are laid in clusters. Most of the nearshore eelpouts and their relatives spawn during the day, when they can see one another for courting. Some eelpout relatives guard their nests.

EELPOUTS, THEIR RELATIVES, AND PEOPLE

Except for wolf-eels, eelpouts and their relatives are not fished for food or fun.

CONSERVATION STATUS

Eelpouts and their relatives are not threatened or endangered.

Wolf-eel (Anarrhichthys ocellatus)

WOLF-EEL
Anarrhichthys ocellatus

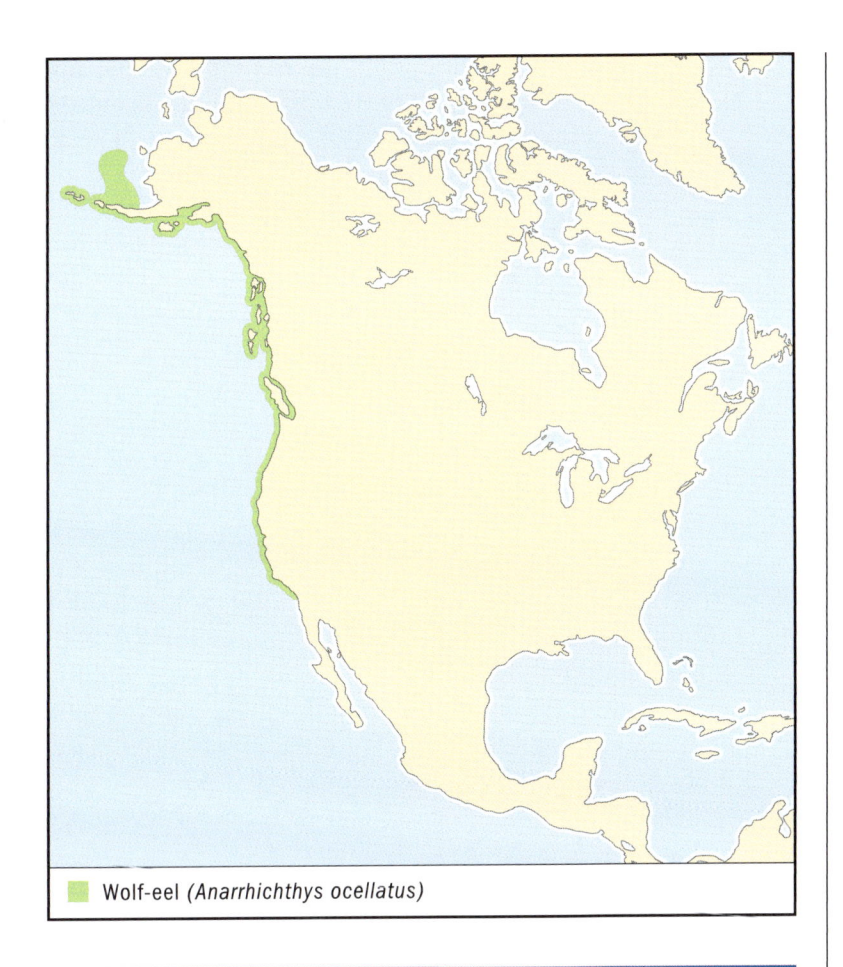

SPECIES ACCOUNTS

Physical characteristics: Wolf-eels have a long, snake-like body and reach a length of about 6 feet (2 meters). The background color is blue, greenish brown, or grayish brown. The body and head are covered with white-lined black spots. The scales are small and rounded and embedded in the skin. The dorsal (DOOR-suhl) and anal (AY-nuhl) fins are very long and low; the pectoral fins, large and fanlike. There are no pelvic fins. The dorsal fin is the one along the midline of the back. The anal fin is the one along the midline of the belly. The pectoral (PECK-ter-uhl) fins correspond to the front legs of four-footed animals. The pelvic fins correspond to the rear legs of four-footed animals. The mouth

Eelpouts and Relatives

is large and has big lips. The front teeth are like dog or wolf teeth. The back teeth are molars like those of people.

Geographic range: Wolf-eels live along the coast of North America from Alaska to California.

Habitat: Wolf-eels live on deep rocky reefs in caves or crevices. The young live in open water.

Diet: Wolf-eels eat crabs, clams, mussels, sea urchins, sand dollars, and snails. The young eat plankton.

Wolf-eels hide and live alone or with a lifelong mate in a den. (Illustration by Marguette Dongvillo. Reproduced by permission.)

Behavior and reproduction: Wolf-eels hide and live alone or with a lifelong mate in a den. They hunt at dusk and dawn but also feed during the day. Wolf-eels grab their prey, or animal hunted and killed for food, with their large front teeth and crush it with their molars.

Wolf-eels form pairs when they are about four years old and first lay eggs when they are about seven years old. In courtship the male repeatedly bumps the female's belly. When the female is ready, the male coils around her. The eggs are fertilized as they are laid in clumps, and the female gathers the clumps up into a ball and wraps around them, turning them once in a while so that they all get enough oxygen. Both parents guard the nest, and one always stays with the nest while the other looks for food. Young wolf-eels swim freely for up to two years then settle on the bottom until they begin their den life.

Wolf-eels and people: Wolf-eel tastes good and is caught by scuba divers and fishermen. Wolf-eels have been known to snap at fishermen and can inflict serious bites on scuba divers who spear them.

Conservation status: Wolf-eels are not threatened or endangered.

Ocean pout (Zoarces americanus) ▮

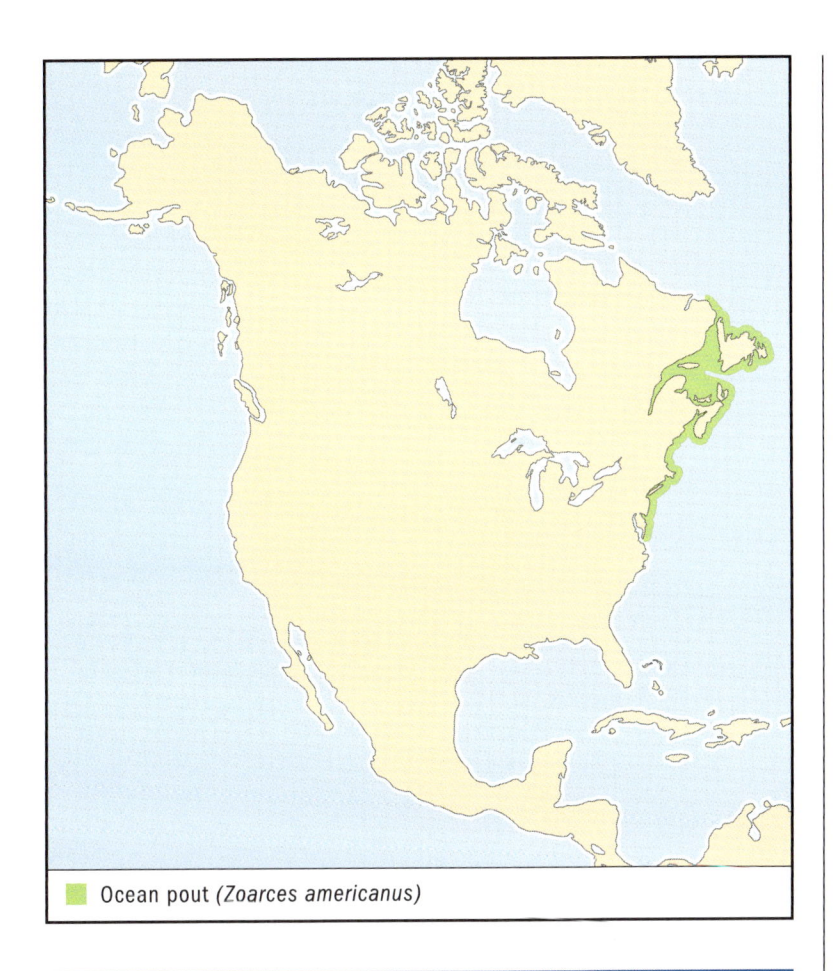

OCEAN POUT
Zoarces americanus

Physical characteristics: Ocean pouts have a body that is eel-like but rather stout. The background color usually is muddy yellow tinged with brown but becomes darker with age. The belly is yellow or olive green. There are brown splotches on the sides. The dorsal and anal fins are long and low. The pectoral fins large and fanlike. Some ocean pouts have green teeth because they eat sea urchins. Ocean pout scales are tiny and round and do not overlap.

Geographic range: Ocean pouts live along the coast of North America from Labrador, Canada, to Virginia, United States.

Ocean pouts graze on the sea floor for crabs, hermit crabs, sea urchins, worms, clams, sea snails, and sea stars. (©Andrew J. Martinez/Photo Researchers, Inc. Reproduced by permission.)

Habitat: Adult ocean pouts live off shore on sandy or muddy bottoms. The young may come closer to shore and live among seaweed and rocks.

Diet: Ocean pouts graze on the sea floor for crabs, hermit crabs, sea urchins, worms, clams, sea snails, and sea stars.

Behavior and reproduction: Scientists know little about the behavior of ocean pouts. These fish probably live alone and gather only for spawning. Spawning males approach females and roll on their sides or even upside down under the female. The eggs are fertilized inside the female and then laid in rocky areas. After laying her egg mass the female fans the eggs with her fins and wipes her skin over the eggs for about thirty minutes, coating them with protective mucus. She then wraps herself tightly around the mass, helping it stick together in a ball.

Ocean pouts and people: Ocean pouts once were fished for food.

Conservation status: Ocean pouts are not threatened or endangered.

FOR MORE INFORMATION

Books:

Gilbert, Carter Rowell, and James D. Williams. *National Audubon Society Field Guide to Fishes: North America.* New York: Knopf, 2002.

Web sites:

Kruse, Katrina. "Wolf-eel *Anarrhichthys ocellatus*." North American Native Fishes Association. http://www.nanfa.org/fif/wolfeel.shtml (accessed on February 11, 2005).

"The Ocean Pouts and Wolf Eels: Family Zoarcidae." Gulf of Main Research Institute, *Fishes of the Gulf of Maine.* http://octopus.gma.org/fogm/Zoarcidae.htm (accessed on October 28, 2004).

> **SOUTHERN COD-ICEFISHES**
> Notothenioidei
>
> **Class:** Actinopterygii
> **Order:** Perciformes
> **Suborder:** Notothenioidei
> **Number of families:** 8 families
>
> **suborder CHAPTER**

phylum
class
subclass
order
monotypic order
● **suborder**
family

PHYSICAL CHARACTERISTICS

Most southern cod-icefishes are about 1 foot (30 centimeters) long, but some species are as short as 4 inches (10 centimeters) or as long as 6 feet (1.8 meters). Most of these fishes have black, brown, or gray mottling on a pale background. They have two or three lateral lines. The lateral (LAT-uhr-uhl) line is a series of pores and tiny tubes along each side of a fish's body and is used for sensing vibrations. Southern cod-icefishes do not have a swim bladder, an internal sac that fishes use to control their position in the water. To help them maintain their position in the water, these fishes have lighter bones than most bottom dwellers and a large amount of oil in their muscles.

GEOGRAPHIC RANGE

All but one species of southern cod-icefishes live just north of Antarctica. One species lives in Antarctica.

HABITAT

Southern cod-icefishes live in streams and estuaries (EHS-chew-air-eez), the areas where rivers meet the sea. Most live on or near the bottom, but some live in open water.

DIET

Some southern cod-icefishes eat anything that comes their way. Others ambush small crustaceans and mollusks. Crustaceans (krus-TAY-shuns) are water-dwelling animals that have jointed legs and a hard shell but no backbone. Mollusks (MAH-lusks) are animals with a soft, unsegmented body that may or may not have a shell.

BEHAVIOR AND REPRODUCTION

Southern cod-icefishes tend to stay on the bottom and rarely swim. Many southern cod-icefishes breed every two years, releasing eggs on or near the bottom. Most larvae hatch six to twelve months after the eggs are released and then live in open water, settling to the bottom after feeding on plankton for six to nine months. Larvae (LAR-vee) are animals in an early stage that must change form before becoming adults. Plankton is microscopic plants and animals drifting in the water.

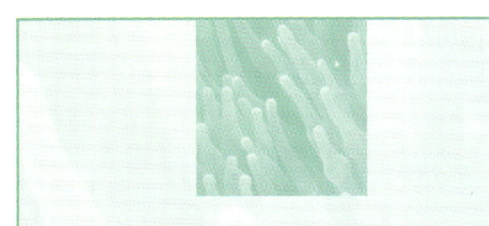

SOUTHERN COD-ICEFISHES AND PEOPLE

Some southern cod-icefishes have been harvested for fish meal and oil but are most important as food fish.

CONSERVATION STATUS

Southern cod-icefishes are not threatened or endangered.

NATURAL ANTIFREEZE

Many southern cod-icefishes live in seawater that is near its freezing point of about 28.6°F (−1.89°C). They protect themselves by making antifreeze in their bodies.

Emerald notothen (*Trematomus bernacchii*)

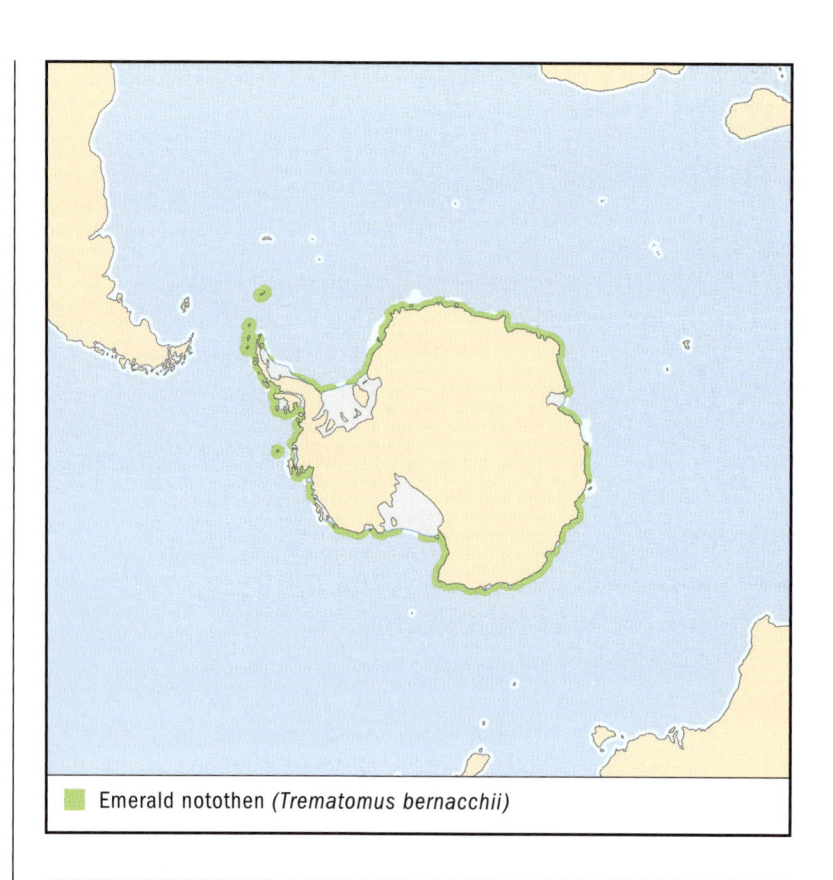

SPECIES ACCOUNT

EMERALD NOTOTHEN
Trematomus bernacchii

Physical characteristics: Emerald notothen reach a length of about 12 inches (30 centimeters) and a weight of about 12 ounces (350 grams). They are thick-bodied and light brown to pinkish brown on the sides and have dark blotches. The belly is silvery gray. There may be a solid or interrupted white band across the neck and gill cover. These fish are covered with rough scales, except for a patch between the eyes, where there may be a single row of scales.

Geographic range: Emerald notothen live in Antarctica.

Habitat: Emerald notothen live on boulder, rock, or gravel bottoms or in sponge beds. Young fish live in shallow water, and mature fish live in deeper water.

Emerald notothen live in Antarctica. (Illustration by Michelle Meneghini. Reproduced by permission.)

Diet: Emerald notothen eat whatever they can find, mainly bottom-dwelling invertebrates, or animals without backbones.

Behavior and reproduction: Emerald notothen spend most of their time staying still on the bottom. If they swim, it is slowly. These fish live eight to ten years. They can reproduce when they are five years old. Females spawn every two years. The eggs attach to rocks, seaweed, or sponges. Emerald notothen may tend egg masses in sponges.

Emerald notothen and people: Emerald notothen are important in the study of how living things survive in the Antarctic environment.

Conservation status: Emerald notothen are not threatened or endangered. ■

FOR MORE INFORMATION

Books:

Nelson, Joseph S. *Fishes of the World*. 3rd ed. New York: Wiley, 1994.

Web sites:

"Emerald Notothen or Emerald Rockcod *Trematomus bernacchii*." University of California, San Diego. http://scilib.ucsd.edu/sio/nsf/fguide/chordata8.html (accessed on October 28, 2004).

WEEVERFISHES AND RELATIVES
Trachinoidei

Class: Actinopterygii
Order: Perciformes
Suborder: Trachinoidei
Number of families: 13 families

suborder
CHAPTER

PHYSICAL CHARACTERISTICS

Weeverfishes and their relatives are only loosely related to one another, so they do not have many physical characteristics in common. They can be about 2 inches (5 centimeters) to about 30 inches (76 centimeters) long. Some have snakelike bodies, and some have a familiar "fish" shape. Some have a large mouth with huge teeth. Some have no scales. Some have light-producing organs. Some have electric organs. Some have eyes on the tops of their heads and a venomous spine on the gill cover. Some have two dorsal fins and some only one very long dorsal fin. Some have one short and one long dorsal fin. Most have long anal fins. Some have large pectoral fins. The dorsal (DOOR-suhl) fin is the one along the midline of the back. The anal (AY-nuhl) fin is the one along the midline of the belly. The pectoral (PECK-ter-uhl) fins correspond to the front legs of four-footed animals.

GEOGRAPHIC RANGE

Weeverfishes and their relatives live in the Arctic, Atlantic, Indian, and Pacific oceans. One species lives only in New Zealand.

HABITAT

Most weeverfishes and their relatives live in the sea close to shore and in estuaries (EHS-chew-air-eez), or the areas where rivers meet the sea, on sandy to muddy bottoms. Some live in burrows under coral. Others live in the deep ocean. Some hug the bottom of fast-flowing freshwater streams.

DIET

Weeverfishes and their relatives eat fishes, animal plankton, small crustaceans, and worms. Plankton is microscopic plants and animals drifting in water. Crustaceans (krus-TAY-shuns) are water-dwelling animals that have jointed legs and a hard shell but no backbone.

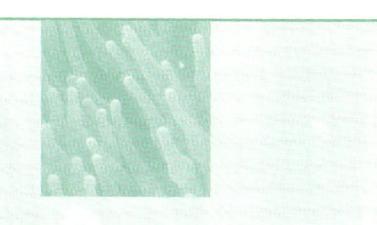

BEHAVIOR AND REPRODUCTION

Most weeverfishes and their relatives live alone. Some form schools of hundreds to several thousand fish. Some weeverfish relatives hide in the sand or mud and suck in their prey, or animals hunted and killed for food. Others chase down their prey. Some fishes in this group are active during the day; others, at night. Some move from deep water to the surface at night. Scientists know little about the reproduction of weeverfishes and their relatives. Some fishes change sex from female to male. Most probably scatter their eggs, which sink to the bottom.

DID YOU KNOW?

The name "weeverfish" probably comes from the Anglo-Saxon word *wivere*, which means "viper." Weeverfish venom causes severe pain and sometimes fever, vomiting, and heart failure.

WEEVERFISHES AND THEIR RELATIVES AND PEOPLE

Only a few weeverfishes and their relatives are caught and sold for food. Some are caught for fishmeal and oil. People can be injured if they step on the sharp spines of weeverfishes and stargazers.

CONSERVATION STATUS

The World Conservation Union (IUCN) lists one species of weeverfishes and their relatives as Endangered and one species as Vulnerable. Endangered means facing a very high risk of extinction in the wild. Vulnerable means facing a high risk of extinction in the wild.

Inshore sand lance (*Ammodytes americanus*)

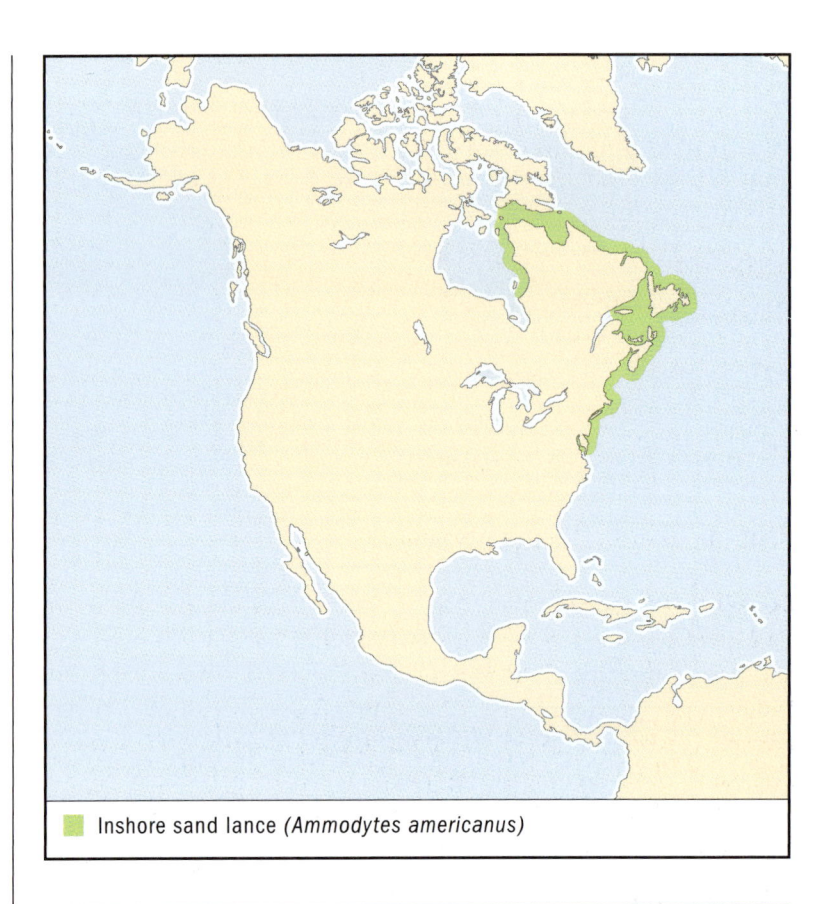

SPECIES ACCOUNTS

INSHORE SAND LANCE
Ammodytes americanus

Physical characteristics: Inshore sand lances are long and thin. They have no teeth, and the lower jaw juts far beyond the upper jaw. The dorsal and anal fins are very long. Tiny folds of skin all along the body have smooth scales underneath them. The body is olive, brownish, or bluish green on top with silvery sides and a white belly. These fish grow to a length of about 6 inches (16 centimeters).

Geographic range: Inshore sand lances live on the Atlantic coast of North America.

Habitat: Inshore sand lances burrow in sand or gravel in shallow water along the coast and in estuaries.

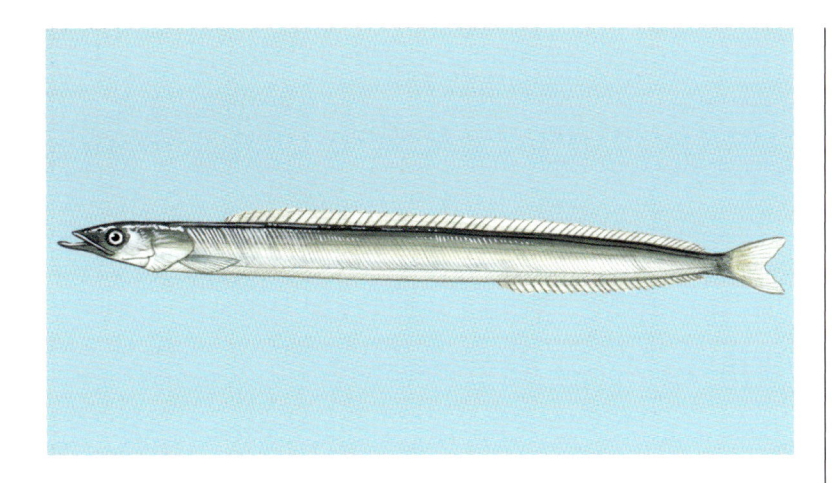

Inshore sand lances form schools of up to several thousand fish. (Illustration by Barbara Duperron. Reproduced by permission.)

Diet: Inshore sand lances eat animal plankton.

Behavior and reproduction: Inshore sand lances form schools of up to several thousand fish. At high tide they burrow into the sand and remain there until the next tide. Scientists have never observed inshore sand lances spawning. These fish can reproduce when they are about two years old. They release eggs that sink to the bottom and hatch into freely swimming larvae (LAR-vee), or animals in an early stage that must change form before becoming adults. Inshore sand lances live about twelve years.

Inshore sand lances and people: Inshore sand lances have little direct importance to humans. They are important as food for fish that are caught and sold.

Conservation status: Inshore sand lances are not threatened or endangered. ■

Northern stargazer (Astroscopus guttatus)

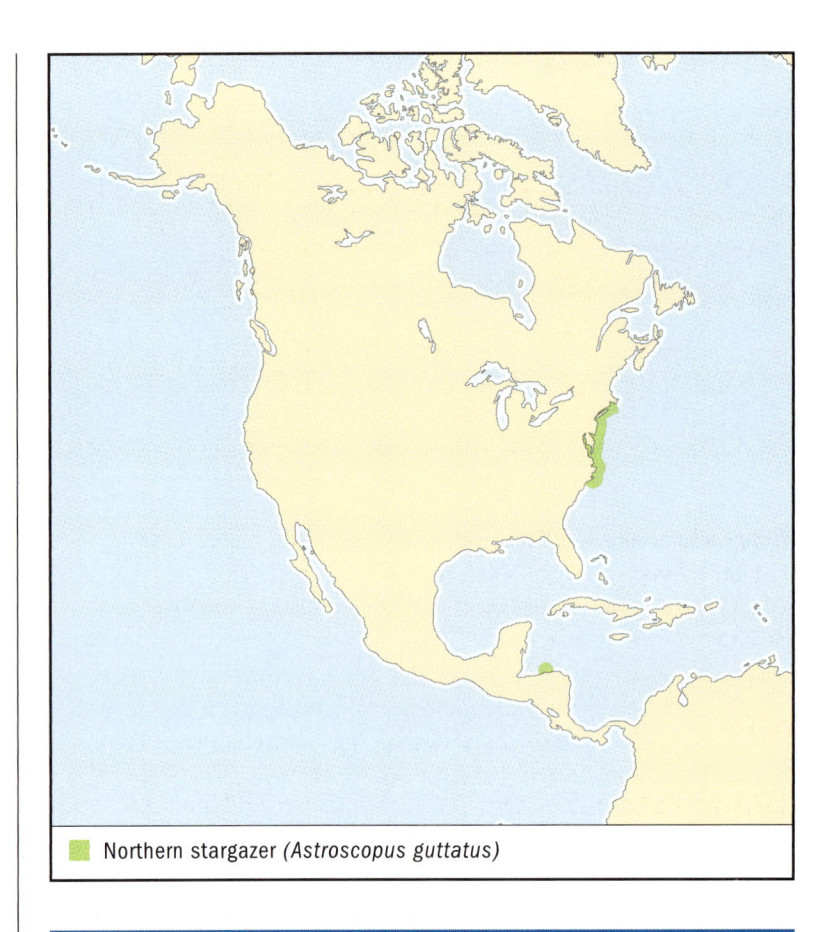

NORTHERN STARGAZER
Astroscopus guttatus

Physical characteristics: Northern stargazers have a squarish head with a flattened top and a large mouth with fringed lips. The eyes are on the top of the head, and there are electric organs in pouches behind the eyes. The first of the two dorsal fins has four or five spines. The anal fin has one spine. The pectoral fins are large, and there is a spine just above each one. The fish's back is dark brown with small white spots. The belly is gray. The first dorsal fin is solid brown, and the second has black and white stripes. The pectoral fins are dark with a pale edge. Northern stargazers grow to a length of 22 inches (56 centimeters) and a weight of 20 pounds (9 kilograms).

Northern stargazers lie buried on the bottom with only the top of the head, eyes, and mouth exposed waiting for prey, at which they lunge aggressively and suck into their large mouths. (Illustration by Barbara Duperron. Reproduced by permission.)

Geographic range: Northern stargazers live on the Atlantic coast of North America from New York to North Carolina.

Habitat: Northern stargazers live on sandy bottoms in coastal waters.

Diet: Northern stargazers eat small fishes and crustaceans.

Behavior and reproduction: Northern stargazers lie buried on the bottom with only the top of the head, eyes, and mouth exposed waiting for prey, at which they lunge aggressively and suck into their large mouths. These fish release their eggs into open water. The larvae settle on sandy bottoms until they are about 8 inches (20 centimeters) long and then move farther offshore.

Northern stargazers and people: Northern stargazers are not fished for food or sport. If caught, they should be handled with care, because of the sharp pectoral spines and the electric organs.

Conservation status: Northern stargazers are not threatened or endangered. ∎

FOR MORE INFORMATION

Books:

Allen, Missy, and Michel Peissel. *Dangerous Water Creatures*. New York: Chelsea House, 1992.

Gilbert, Carter Rowell, and James D. Williams. *National Audubon Society Field Guide to Fishes: North America.* New York: Knopf, 2002.

Web sites:

"Northern Stargazer." Florida Museum of Natural History. http://www.flmnh.ufl.edu/fish/Gallery/Descript/StarGazerNorth/StarGazeNorth.htm (accessed on October 28, 2004).

"Sand Lance." *Fisheries and Oceans Canada.* http://www.dfo-mpo.gc.ca/zone/underwater_sous-marin/SandLance/sandlanc_e.htm (accessed on October 28, 2004).

> **BLENNIES**
> **Blennioidei**
>
> **Class:** Actinopterygii
> **Order:** Perciformes
> **Suborder:** Blennioidei
> **Number of families:** 6 families

suborder CHAPTER

phylum
class
subclass
order
monotypic order
○ **suborder**
family

PHYSICAL CHARACTERISTICS

Blennies have a variety of body types from short and stout and covered in scales to long and blunt-headed and entirely lacking scales. Most have short fringe on their heads, and some have large spines on their heads. The color ranges from drab, mottled brown and tan to brilliant red, yellow, and blue. Blennies are small, usually less than 4 inches (10 centimeters) long.

GEOGRAPHIC RANGE

Blennies live all over the world except in the Arctic.

HABITAT

Blennies live in almost every underwater habitat, and some even climb out of the water onto rocks. Most are bottom dwellers on coral and rocky reefs. A few blennies live in freshwater streams and rivers.

DIET

Most blennies eat small, bottom-dwelling invertebrates (in-VER-teh-brehts), or animals without a backbone. Some eat algae (AL-jee), or plantlike growths that live in water and have no true roots, stems, or leaves.

BEHAVIOR AND REPRODUCTION

Blennies usually sit on rocks or coral rubble and use their pelvic fins, the pair that corresponds to the rear legs of four-footed animals, to lift their head off the bottom. Some blennies sit just above the waterline and when threatened leap from the rock and skip across the surface of the water to the next rock.

Some male blennies guard a small territory, often an empty shell or a rock crevice. The female enters the male's territory; lays eggs that stick to the shell or rock as they are fertilized (FUR-teh-lyzed), or joined with the male's sperm, and then leaves. The male then guards the eggs and fans water over them until they hatch. Newly hatched young swim toward the surface and feed on plankton, or microscopic plants and animals drifting in water, before returning to the bottom.

BLENNIES AND PEOPLE

Although they are eaten in some areas, blennies are used mainly as aquarium fish.

CONSERVATION STATUS

The World Conservation Union (IUCN) lists one species of blennies as Vulnerable, or facing a high risk of extinction in the wild.

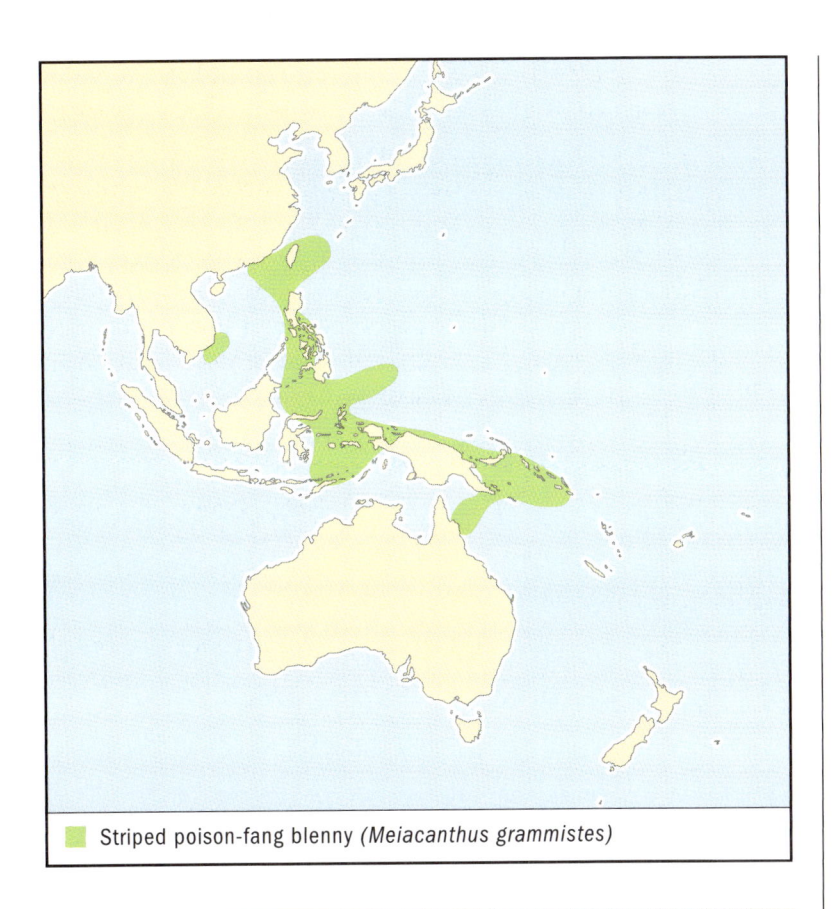

Striped poison-fang blenny *(Meiacanthus grammistes)*

STRIPED POISON-FANG BLENNY
Meiacanthus grammistes

SPECIES ACCOUNTS

Physical characteristics: Striped poison-fang blennies reach a length of 3½ inches (9 centimeters). They have a poison-producing gland in the base of each lower-jaw fang. Black and white stripes run the length of the body from the snout almost to the tail, where they break up into small black spots. The dorsal and anal fins have a black stripe. The dorsal (DOOR-suhl) fin is the one along the midline of the back. The anal (AY-nuhl) fin is the one along the midline of the belly.

Geographic range: Striped poison-fang blennies live in the western part of the Pacific Ocean.

Habitat: Striped poison-fang blennies live on or near coral reefs, seeking shelter in holes.

Diet: Striped poison-fang blennies eat small, bottom-dwelling invertebrates.

Behavior and reproduction: Striped poison-fang blennies inject venom using fangs in the lower jaw. Scientists know little about the reproduction of these blennies. The male tries to entice one or more females to lay eggs in a hole in the reef and probably guards the eggs until they hatch.

Striped poison-fang blennies and people: Striped poison-fang blennies are sold as aquarium fish.

Conservation status: Striped poison-fang blennies are not threatened or endangered. ∎

Striped poison-fang blennies inject venom using fangs in the lower jaw. (Illustration by Patricia Ferrer. Reproduced by permission.)

Miracle triplefin (*Enneapterygius mirabilis*)

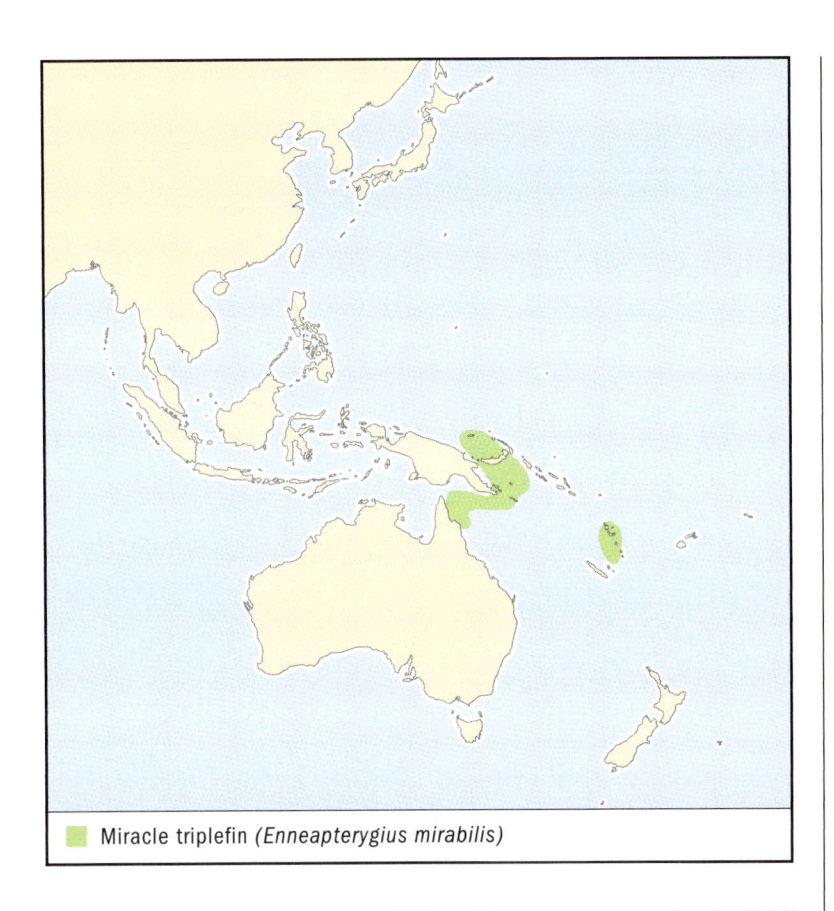

MIRACLE TRIPLEFIN
Enneapterygius mirabilis

Physical characteristics: Miracle triplefins are a little more than an inch (3 centimeters) long. They are light red with lighter spots. These fish have long spines in the first dorsal fin. The second dorsal is divided so that it looks like two fins, thus the name "triplefin."

Geographic range: Miracle triplefins live in the western part of the Pacific Ocean near Australia.

Habitat: Miracle triplefins live on coral reefs.

Diet: Scientists know little about the diet of miracle triplefins. The tooth structure suggests these fish eat small, bottom-dwelling invertebrates.

The second dorsal fin of the miracle triplefin is divided so that it looks like two fins, thus the name "triplefin." (Illustration by Patricia Ferrer. Reproduced by permission.)

Behavior and reproduction: Miracle triplefins have not been observed alive underwater. The eggs are probably fertilized outside the female.

Miracle triplefins and people: Miracle triplefins are not used by humans.

Conservation status: Miracle triplefins are not threatened or endangered. ∎

FOR MORE INFORMATION

Books:

Gilbert, Carter Rowell, and James D. Williams. *National Audubon Society Field Guide to Fishes: North America.* New York: Knopf, 2002.

Web sites:

Webster, Mark. "The Pussycat Factor." *Divernet.* http://www.divernet.com/biolog/0602blennies.htm (accessed on October 30, 2004).

suborder CHAPTER

RAGFISH
Icosteoidei

Class: Actinopterygii
Order: Perciformes
Suborder: Icosteoidei
Number of families: 1 family

PHYSICAL CHARACTERISTICS

Young ragfish have limp bodies. The body is broad from back to belly and narrow from side to side. It is smooth-skinned and scaleless, except along the lateral line, where the scales have small spines. The lateral (LAT-uhr-uhl) line is a series of pores and tiny tubes along each side of a fish's body and is used for sensing vibrations. The snout is blunt and looks like that of a calf. The dorsal (DOOR-suhl) fin that runs along the midline top of the body has one spine. The tail fin is rounded and fanlike. The pelvic fins, the pair that corresponds to the rear legs of four-footed animals, have one spine. All fins have tiny spines on the surface.

When ragfish become adults, the body lengthens and becomes less broad from back to belly, and a ridge develops along the midline of the belly. The lateral line spines, the spines on the fins, and the pelvic fins disappear. The color turns to solid dark brown over the entire body and fins. Ragfish have been reported to reach a length of about 7 feet (2.1 meters).

GEOGRAPHIC RANGE

Ragfish live in the northern part of the Pacific Ocean.

HABITAT

Ragfish usually live offshore in deeper water.

DIET

Ragfish probably eat small fish, squid, octopuses, and jellyfish.

phylum
class
subclass
order
monotypic order
○ suborder
family

WHAT'S IN A NAME?

The Latin name of the ragfish, *Icosteus aenigmaticus*, means "puzzling fish with yielding bones." Ragfish have cartilage rather than bones, so they are limp and raglike when out of the water.

BEHAVIOR AND REPRODUCTION

Ragfish have never been observed in their natural habitat. They probably live alone. Large ragfish sometimes are found stranded on the shore. Ragfish are ready to spawn when they are seven to nine years of age. The eggs probably are fertilized (FUR-teh-lyzed), or joined by sperm to start development, outside the female. The eggs and larvae drift in the water. Larvae (LAR-vee) are animals in an early stage that must change form before becoming adults.

RAGFISH AND PEOPLE

Ragfish are not caught for food or sport.

CONSERVATION STATUS

Ragfish are not threatened or endangered.

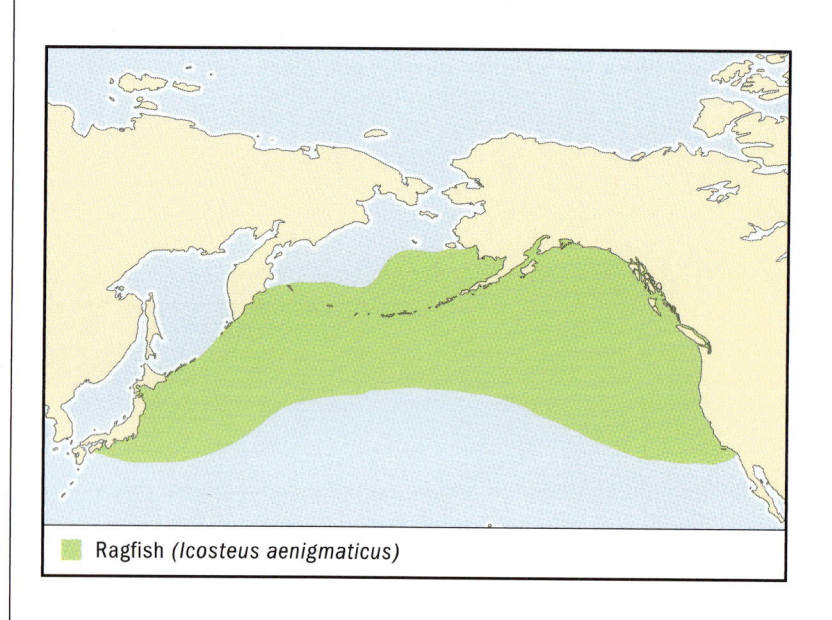

Ragfish (*Icosteus aenigmaticus*)

Ragfish have never been observed in their natural habitat. (Illustration by Michelle Meneghini. Reproduced by permission.)

FOR MORE INFORMATION

Books:

Nelson, Joseph S. *Fishes of the World.* 3rd ed. New York: Wiley, 1994.

Web sites:

Nokkentved, N. S. "Unusual Deep-Water Fish Causes a Stir on Shore. *The Olympian.* http://www.theolympian.com/home/specialsections/Critters/20020806/26894.shtml (accessed on February 8, 2005.)

CLINGFISHES AND SINGLESLITS

Gobiesocoidei

Class: Actinopterygii
Order: Perciformes
Suborder: Gobiesocoidei
Number of families: 1 family

suborder
CHAPTER

PHYSICAL CHARACTERISTICS

Instead of pelvic fins, or the pair that corresponds to the rear legs of four-footed animals, clingfishes have a sucking disk they use to cling to rocks, plants, and even sea urchins. Most clingfishes have a tadpole-shaped body, but one species has a long, thin body that mimics the long spines of a sea urchin. Clingfishes have no scales but shield themselves with mucus. They also have no swim bladder, an internal sac that fishes use to control their position in the water. The colors of clingfishes vary from black to orange, brown, green, or red. The fishes also may have stripes, bars, or spots of yellow, blue, green, brown, gray, or white. Most clingfishes are about 2 inches (5 centimeters) long, but some reach a length of 12 inches (30 centimeters). Clingfishes have one dorsal and one anal fin. The dorsal (DOOR-suhl) fin is the one along the midline of the back. The anal (AY-nuhl) fin is the one along the midline of the belly.

Singleslits have an eel-like shape. The pelvic fins are very small. These fishes have a sucking disk, but it does not function. The dorsal and anal fins look like those of eels. Only the tail fin has rays, or supporting rods. The colors vary from frosty pink or green to light green, brown, gray, or black. Spots or bars of black, gray, brown, or yellow may be present. Singleslits are usually smaller than 2 inches (5 centimeters) long, but one species reaches a length of 5 inches (12 centimeters).

GEOGRAPHIC RANGE

Clingfishes live in the Atlantic, Indian and Pacific oceans. Singleslits live off the southern coast of Australia.

HABITAT

Clingfishes cling to the bottom. They can withstand breaking waves and surging waters. Many species live on or under boulders and rocks, in crevices, and on rocky slopes and rock faces. Species that live in tide pools can stay out of water for several days, if they stay moist and out of sunlight. Some species live with coral, sponges, sea squirts, and sea urchins. Others cling to the blades of sea grasses and seaweed. Singleslits live in the sea near the shore, usually in shallow tide pools and often under stones or in seaweed.

DIET

Clingfishes eat algae, body parts of sea urchins, small fishes, and small invertebrates (in-VER-teh-brehts), or are animals without backbones. Some are cleaner fishes that remove parasites from other fishes. Singleslits feed mainly on small, bottom-dwelling invertebrates. Algae (AL-jee) are plantlike growths that live in water and have no true roots, stems, or leaves. Parasites (PAIR-uh-sites) are animals or plants that live on other animals or plants without helping them and often harming them.

BEHAVIOR AND REPRODUCTION

Clingfishes use their sucking disk to cling to rocks, plants, or even sea urchins. Clingfishes and singleslits tend to be secretive and probably are territorial. In mating the male nudges the female's belly. If the female accepts him, the male moves parallel to her and quivers. The female then quivers and deposits eggs on stones, algae, or other bottom material while the male places sperm on them. Egg laying may last several minutes to a few hours. The eggs then are guarded by the male or abandoned by the pair. Larvae (LAR-vee), the early stage that must change form before becoming adults, probably drift in the water.

CLINGFISHES AND SINGLESLITS AND PEOPLE

Some clingfishes and singleslits are collected for aquariums.

CONSERVATION STATUS

Clingfishes and singleslits are not threatened or endangered.

Sonora clingfish (Tomicodon humeralis)

SONORA CLINGFISH
Tomicodon humeralis

SPECIES ACCOUNT

Physical characteristics: Sonora clingfish have a long thin body with a broad head and a large sucking disk. There are light diagonal stripes along the entire body and a pair of spots just behind the head. Sonora clingfish grow to a length of about 3 inches (8 centimeters).

Geographic range: Sonora clingfish live in the Gulf of California, off Mexico.

Habitat: Sonora clingfish live under rocks, to which they cling, and in little or no water. If kept moist, these fish can withstand extreme temperatures when exposed to air.

Sonora clingfish live under rocks, to which they cling, and in little or no water. (Illustration by Bruce Worden. Reproduced by permission.)

Diet: Sonora clingfish hunt during the day for small crustaceans and mollusks, such as barnacles and limpets. Crustaceans (krus-TAY-shuns) are water-dwelling animals that have jointed legs and a hard shell but no backbone. Mollusks (MAH-lusks) are animals with a soft, unsegmented body that may or may not have a shell.

Behavior and reproduction: Sonora clingfish are secretive, clinging to the undersides of rocks and moving over rocky surfaces to feed. Their movements are related to tidal movements. Activity is greater at high tide, and there is little or no activity at low tide. Males are territorial. Both males and females produce large amounts of mucus, which coats their bodies and protects the fish from drying out.

Sonora clingfish form pairs to mate at the bottom of their habitat. A single male may mate with more than one female. Eggs are sticky and are laid on the underside of rocks, where they are guarded by the male, sometimes with the aid of one or more females. During low tide, the parents secrete mucus that protects the eggs from exposure. The larvae drift in the water.

Sonora clingfish and people: Sonora clingfish sometimes are collected for aquariums.

Conservation status: Sonora clingfish are not threatened or endangered. ∎

FOR MORE INFORMATION

Books:
Gilbert, Carter Rowell, and James D. Williams. *National Audubon Society Field Guide to Fishes: North America.* New York: Knopf, 2002.

Web sites:

"Eastern Cleaner-Clingfish: *Cochleoceps orientalis* Hutchins, 1991." Australian Museum Fish Site. http://www.amonline.net.au/fishes/students/focus/cochleo.htm (accessed on October 31, 2004).

> **DRAGONETS AND RELATIVES**
> **Callionymoidei**
>
> **Class:** Actinopterygii
> **Order:** Perciformes
> **Suborder:** Callionymoidei
> **Number of families:** 2 families

suborder CHAPTER

phylum
class
subclass
order
monotypic order
○ **suborder**
family

PHYSICAL CHARACTERISTICS

Dragonets and their relatives are small and have a long flat body with a broad flat head. Dragonets usually have two dorsal fins, the first having one to four spines. The dorsal fins of some males are large and high and have long rays, or supporting rods. Dragonets also have large pelvic and pectoral fins. The dorsal (DOOR-suhl) fin is the one along the midline of the back. The pelvic fins correspond to the rear legs and the pectoral (PECK-ter-uhl) fins to the front legs of four-footed animals.

The bone in front of the gill cover of dragonets has spines. The body has no scales. Many species of dragonets have camouflage coloring, but others are brilliantly colored. Some species produce a bitter-tasting slime that covers their bodies and may serve as protection from predators (PREH-duh-ters), or animals that hunt and kill other animals for food.

Draconetts have small, long, tubular bodies, large pectoral fins, and long pelvic fins. They have no scales. These fishes have large eyes. There are two dorsal fins, with the first having three spines. There are strong spines around the gill covers.

GEOGRAPHIC RANGE

Dragonets and their relatives live in the Atlantic, Indian, and Pacific oceans.

HABITAT

Most dragonets live on coral, rubble, sand, mud, and other soft bottoms. Some live among algae-covered rocks or mangrove roots in water with a low salt content. Little is known about the habitats of draconetts. They probably live in rubble and sand or among rocks. Algae (AL-jee) are plantlike growths that live in water and have no true roots, stems, or leaves.

DIET

Dragonets and their relatives eat small, bottom-dwelling invertebrates, or animals without backbones. Larger species eat larger animals.

BEHAVIOR AND REPRODUCTION

Male dragonets use their long first dorsal fins for male-to-male fights and male-to-female courtship. Almost nothing is known about the behavior of draconetts. Their large eyes probably aid them in movement, feeding, and reproductive behavior in deep bottom habitats.

Males dragonets defend their territory when they are reproducing. In courtship a male approaches a female, displays his spread-out fins to her, and, as if carrying her, rises with her a short distance in the water, where free-floating eggs are released and fertilized (FUR-teh-lyzed), or united with sperm to start development. Almost nothing is known about reproduction of draconetts. Mating is probably paired and takes place in open water with a rapid, short rise in the water, where eggs and sperm are released.

DRAGONETS, THEIR RELATIVES, AND PEOPLE

Dragonets are important aquarium fish. Draconetts do not appear to have any importance to humans.

CONSERVATION STATUS

The World Conservation Union (IUCN) lists one species of dragonets and their relatives as Critically Endangered, or facing an extremely high risk of extinction in the wild.

Lancer dragonet (*Paradiplogrammus bairdi*)

LANCER DRAGONET
Paradiplogrammus bairdi

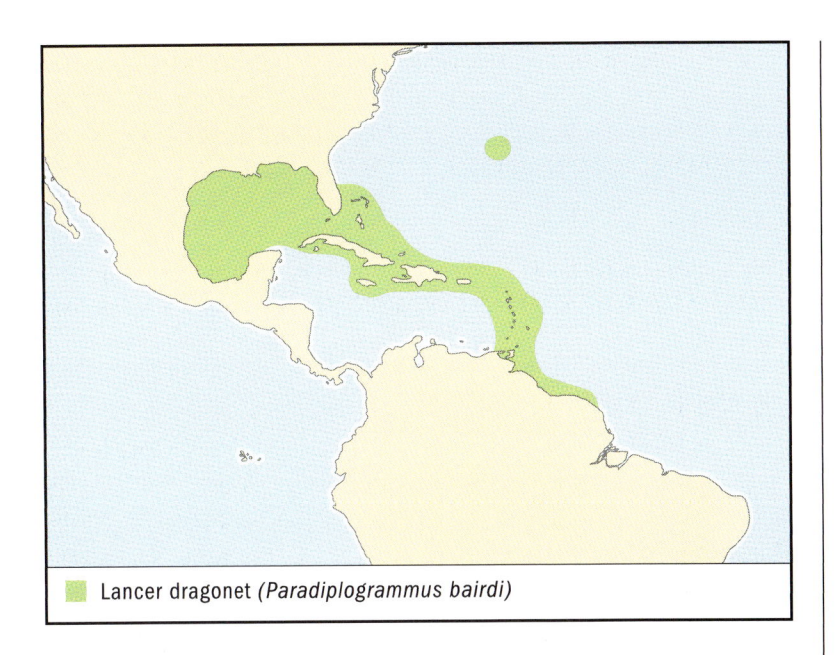

SPECIES ACCOUNT

Physical characteristics: Lancer dragonets reach a total length of about 4 inches (11 centimeters). Males are larger than females, have larger fins, an extended dorsal fin, and bolder color patterns on the body and fins. The body is long and has no scales. These fish have four spines on the first dorsal fin. The color pattern varies between sexes. The top half of the body has marbling and mottling in shades of brown, black, and white. There are white, roundish blotches between narrow brown bars on the bottom half of the body. The first dorsal fin of males has a yellow swirl, and the second dorsal fin has a downward-pointing pattern of dark bands. Males also have blue lines and rows of spots on the first dorsal fin; blue bars with narrow orange edges on the first bone of the gill cover; orange spots, small blue lines, and crescent-shaped markings on the top half of the body; and blue spots around the bottom half of the body and the eyes.

Geographic range: Lancer dragonets live in the western part of the Atlantic Ocean near Bermuda and from southern Florida, United States, to northern South America and west into the Gulf of Mexico.

Lancer dragonets have coloring that is good camouflage as they forage for food along the bottom. (Illustration by Marguette Dongvillo. Reproduced by permission.)

Habitat: Lancer dragonets are bottom dwellers. They live on sand patches on shallow reefs, rocky shorelines, and sea-grass flats at depths of 3 to 300 feet (1 to 91 meters).

Diet: Lancer dragonets eat small bottom-dwelling invertebrates.

Behavior and reproduction: Lancer dragonets take advantage of their camouflage coloring as they forage for food along the bottom. Males defend their territories and females by displaying their fins. Males also begin courtship by displaying their fins to females. These fish spawn in pairs after rising a short distance in the water, where the eggs are fertilized. Eggs drift in a mass in the water. The egg mass breaks up before hatching.

Lancer dragonets and people: Lancer dragonets are collected for aquariums.

Conservation status: Lancer dragonets are not threatened or endangered. ■

FOR MORE INFORMATION

Books:

Allen, Gerald. *Reef Fish Identification: Tropical Pacific.* Jacksonville, FL: New World, 2003.

Gilbert, Carter Rowell, and James D. Williams. *National Audubon Society Field Guide to Fishes: North America.* New York: Knopf, 2002.

Web sites:

"Dragonets." *Life at the Edge of Reef.* http://www.edge-of-reef.com/callionimidi/callionimidien.htm (accessed on November 1, 2004).

> **GOBIES**
> **Gobioidei**
>
> **Class:** Actinopterygii
> **Order:** Perciformes
> **Suborder:** Gobioidei
> **Number of families:** 9 families
>
> suborder
> CHAPTER

phylum
class
subclass
order
monotypic order
○ **suborder**
family

PHYSICAL CHARACTERISTICS

Gobies are small fishes with a body that is tubular or is narrow from side to side. Most are about 1½ to 4 inches (4 to 10 centimeters) long. Gobies have a short broad head that may be flat on top. The eyes are near the top of the head. There are usually two separate dorsal fins. The pectoral fins are broad and rounded but may be pointed in some species. Each pelvic fin has one spine. The dorsal (DOOR-suhl) fin is the one along the midline of the back. The anal (AY-nuhl) fin is the one along the midline of the belly. The pectoral (PECK-ter-uhl) fins correspond to the front legs and the pelvic fins to the rear legs of four-footed animals. Some gobies have no scales, and some have them only on the rear part of the body. Some gobies are brightly colored, but others are brown or off white. In many gobies the pelvic fins are united to form a suction disk.

GEOGRAPHIC RANGE

Gobies live all over the world except the polar regions.

HABITAT

Most gobies live near the coast and in estuaries (EHS-chew-air-eez), or the areas where rivers meet the sea. About half of known species live in coral reefs. Some gobies live in caves, and some live in rivers and streams.

DIET

Gobies eat invertebrates (in-VER-teh-brehts), or animals without backbones. (Vertebrates are animals with backbones.)

SIZE COUNTS

The small size of gobies places them at risk from many predators. For example, gobies hiding under sea urchins are eaten by long-snouted predators that probe between the spines of the urchin, and shrimp can overpower small gobies.

WORLD'S SMALLEST

The stout infantfish, a goby 8.4 millimeters long and weighing 1 milligram, in July 2004 replaced the dwarf goby as the world's smallest fish and world's smallest vertebrate. Both fishes are smaller than a raisin but larger than a ladybug.

Some coral-dwelling gobies feed on the coral on which they live. Species that live in open water feed on plankton, or microscopic plants and animals drifting in water. Large gobies may feed on other, smaller fish. Some gobies scrape algae off rocks. Algae (AL-jee) are plantlike growths that live in water and have no true roots, stems, or leaves. Cleaner gobies pick parasites (PAIR-uh-sites) off other fishes. Parasites are animals or plants that live on other animals or plants without helping them and often harming them. Some gobies eat the tube feet of sea urchins.

BEHAVIOR AND REPRODUCTION

Some open-water species of gobies form schools. Many gobies are territorial, especially during the breeding season. Males often care for developing eggs. Females lay a few to several hundred small eggs, attaching them to the underside of rocks or onto plants or coral. The eggs usually hatch in a few days, and the young are dispersed by water currents. In freshwater species, the larvae (LAR-vee), or young, are swept downstream by the water current. The young spend a few weeks to months at sea before returning to freshwater.

GOBIES AND PEOPLE

In some areas gobies are eaten by the local people. They also are used in aquariums.

CONSERVATION STATUS

The World Conservation Union (IUCN) lists five species of gobies as Critically Endangered, twenty-six as Vulnerable, one as Conservation Dependent, and twenty as Near Threatened. Critically Endangered means facing an extremely high risk of extinction in the wild. Vulnerable means facing a high risk of extinction in the wild. Conservation Dependent means if the conservation program were to end, the animal would be placed in one of the threatened categories. Near Threatened means at risk of becoming threatened with extinction in the future. The U.S. Fish and Wildlife Service lists one species as Endangered, or in danger of extinction throughout all or a significant portion of its range.

Fire goby (*Nemateleotris magnifica*)

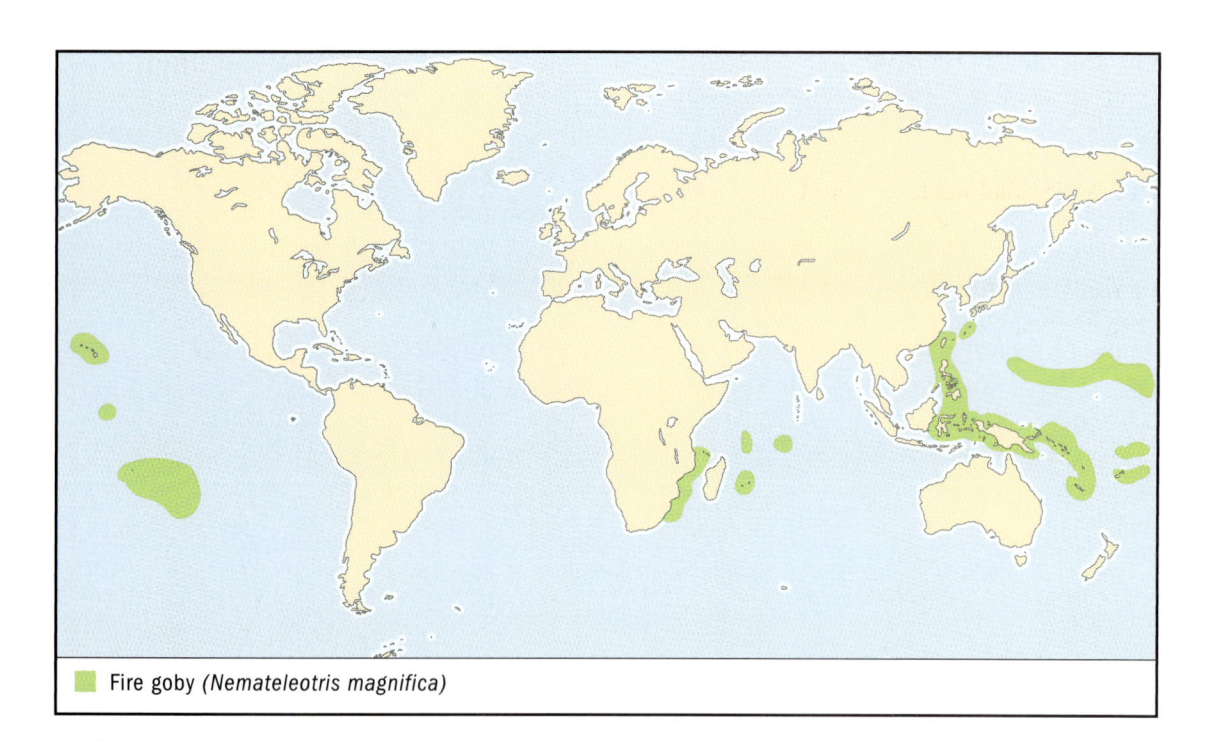

SPECIES ACCOUNTS

FIRE GOBY
Nemateleotris magnifica

Physical characteristics: Fire gobies reach a length of 3½ inches (9 centimeters). The front of the first dorsal fin is extremely long, almost as long as the fish itself. The second dorsal and the anal fins are long and look like the tail of an arrow. The head has a yellow mask over the snout and eyes. The front half of the fish is white, and the rear half goes from orange to red with green streaks.

Geographic range: Fire gobies live in the Indian and Pacific oceans.

Habitat: Fire gobies live on coral reefs over sand or gravel.

Diet: Fire gobies eat animal plankton.

Behavior and reproduction: Fire gobies hover, alone or in small groups, in the water just above the bottom. They usually have a small territory around a hole, cave, or burrow into which they retreat at the threat of danger. These fish flick their first dorsal spine up and down when threatened or defending territory. Mating occurs in burrows.

Fire gobies and people: Fire gobies are important saltwater aquarium species.

Conservation status: Fire gobies are not threatened or endangered. ■

Fire gobies usually have a small territory around a hole, cave, or burrow into which they retreat at the threat of danger. (©Fred McConnaughey/Photo Researchers, Inc. Reproduced by permission.)

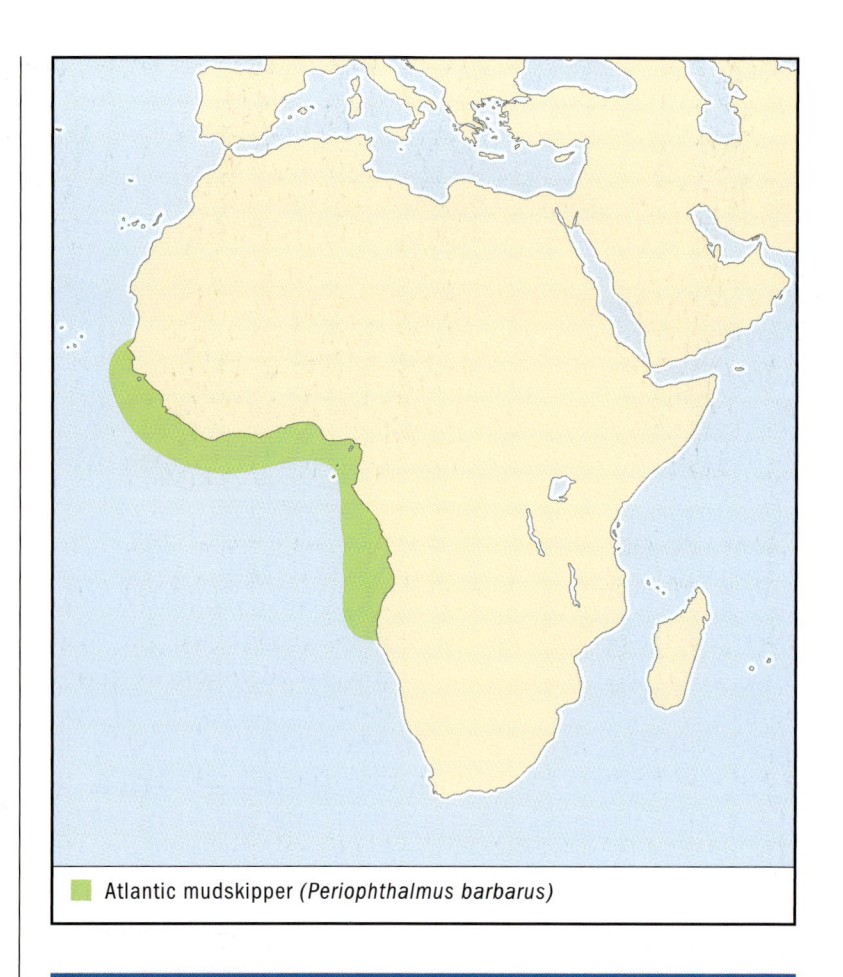

Atlantic mudskipper (*Periophthalmus barbarus*)

ATLANTIC MUDSKIPPER
Periophthalmus barbarus

Physical characteristics: Atlantic mudskippers grow to a length of about 6 inches (15 centimeters). Large eyes stick out of a large head. There are two dorsal fins. The body is tan but is lighter on the belly. There are black diagonal bars on the back and upper parts of the sides and pearly spots on the head and forward part of the trunk. A light edge on the first dorsal fin may be tinged with light blue. The second dorsal fin has a dark band over a light band.

Geographic range: Atlantic mudskippers live along the western coast of Africa.

Atlantic mudskippers live near the seashore in mangrove estuaries and muddy tidal flats, where they live in burrows. (Illlustration by Amanda Humphrey. Reproduced by permission.)

Habitat: Atlantic mudskippers live near the seashore in mangrove estuaries and muddy tidal flats, where they live in burrows.

Diet: Atlantic mudskippers eat crustaceans, worms, and insects. Crustaceans (krus-TAY-shuns) live in water and have a soft segmented body covered by a hard shell.

Behavior and reproduction: Atlantic mudskippers use their muscular pectoral and pelvic fins for crawling and climbing. They flee from predators (PREH-duh-ters), or animals that hunt and kill other animals for food, by skipping or hopping across mudflats and into mangrove forests or into their burrows. On land, mudskippers keep a mouthful of water for extracting oxygen through the gills, and they can breathe through their skin. Spawning occurs in burrows.

Atlantic mudskippers and people: Atlantic mudskippers are not fished for food or sport. They are not widely used in aquariums.

Conservation status: Atlantic mudskippers are not threatened or endangered. ∎

Marble sleeper (Oxyeleotris marmorata)

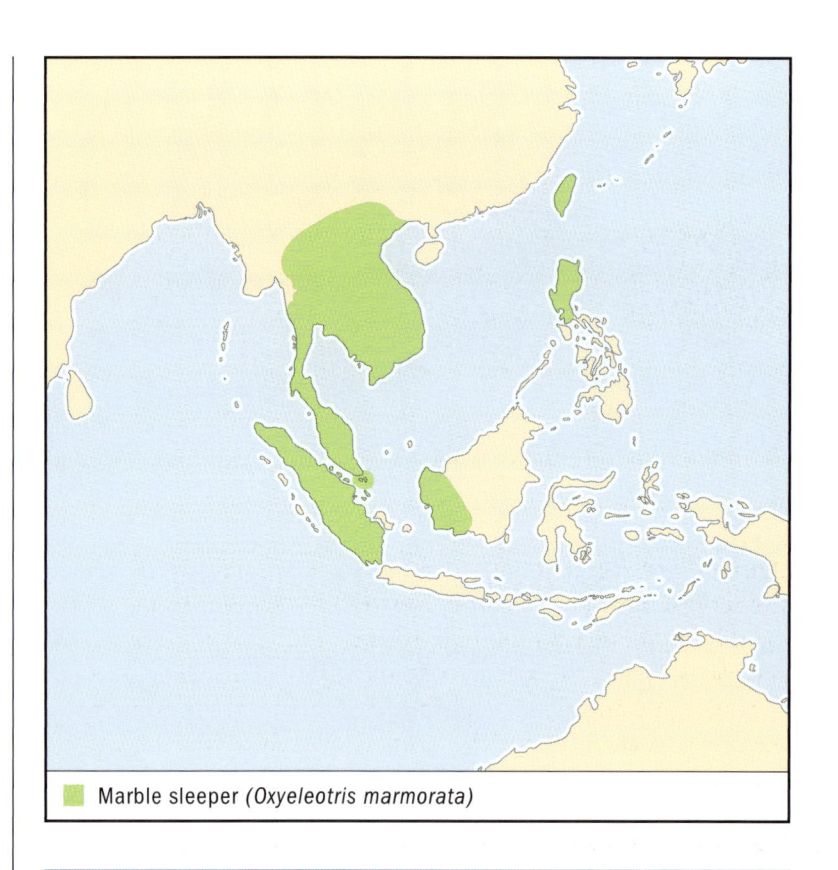

MARBLE SLEEPER
Oxyeleotris marmorata

Physical characteristics: Marble sleepers are the largest gobies, reaching a length of about 35 inches (90 centimeters). These gobies have a streamlined body, a flat head, two dorsal fins, and a rounded tail fin. The body is brown with dark blotches.

Geographic range: Marble sleepers live in Southeast Asia. They have been introduced into Taiwan for fish farming.

Habitat: Marble sleepers live in rivers, lakes, swamps, ditches, and ponds over muddy, sandy, or gravel bottoms. These fish also may be found in water with a low salt content around the mouths of rivers and canals.

Diet: Marble sleepers eat small fishes and invertebrates.

The marble sleeper is a highly prized food fish in Southeast Asia, where it is also raised in ponds. (Illustration by Amanda Humphrey. Reproduced by permission.)

Behavior and reproduction: Marble sleepers live alone and are active at night, prowling slow-moving streams, lakes, and swamps. During the day these fish rest at the bottom, taking cover among rocks and plants. Marble sleepers are able to reproduce when they are about 4 inches (10 centimeters) long. The males care for the eggs and guard the newly hatched young. The larvae drift freely at first but become bottom dwellers about twenty-five to thirty days after hatching.

Marble sleepers and people: Marble sleeper is a highly prized food fish in Southeast Asia, where it is also raised in ponds.

Conservation status: Marble sleepers are not threatened or endangered. ∎

FOR MORE INFORMATION

Books:

Ferrari, Andrea, and Antonella Ferrari. *Reef Life.* Buffalo, NY: Firefly, 2002.

Gilbert, Carter Rowell, and James D. Williams. *National Audubon Society Field Guide to Fishes: North America.* New York: Knopf, 2002.

Web sites:

Lee, H.J., and Jeffrey B. Graham. "Their Game Is Mud." *Natural History.* http://www.naturalhistorymag.com/0902/0902_feature.html (accessed on November 1, 2004).

"Stout Infantfish: *Schindleria brevipinguis*, Watson & Walker, 2004." Australian Museum Fish Site. http://www.amonline.net.au/fishes/fishfacts/fish/sbrevip.htm (accessed on November 1, 2004).

SURGEONFISHES AND RELATIVES
Acanthuroidei

Class: Actinopterygii
Order: Perciformes
Suborder: Acanthuroidei
Number of families: 6 families

suborder CHAPTER

PHYSICAL CHARACTERISTICS

Surgeonfishes and their relatives have small to medium-sized bodies that are narrow from side to side and may be disk-like, oval, or slightly long. Many of these fishes have sharp venomous spines or ridges. Many of these fishes are very colorful.

GEOGRAPHIC RANGE

Surgeonfishes and their relatives live in the Atlantic, Indian, and Pacific oceans.

HABITAT

Most surgeonfishes and their relatives live in shallow coral and rocky reefs. Some species live in estuaries (EHS-chew-air-eez), or the areas where rivers meet the sea, or even farther upstream into freshwater. One species lives in the open sea.

DIET

Most surgeonfishes and their relatives eat bottom-dwelling algae and invertebrates (in-VER-teh-brehts), or animals without backbones. Algae (AL-jee) are plantlike growths that live in water and have no true roots, stems, or leaves. Some species of these fishes can crush shells. One species eats mostly plants, and one species eats jellylike plankton, which is microscopic plants and animals drifting in water.

BEHAVIOR AND REPRODUCTION

Surgeonfishes and their relatives live alone, in pairs, in small groups, in schools of their own species, or in mixed-species schools. Many of these fishes defend their territories. Surgeonfishes and their relatives spawn, or release eggs, in pairs or in groups. Most of these fishes release free-floating eggs. One species deposits eggs on the bottom and takes care of them. The larvae of many surgeonfishes and their relatives live for a long time in the open sea. Larvae (LAR-vee) are animals in an early stage and must change form before becoming adults.

SURGEONFISHES AND THEIR RELATIVES AND PEOPLE

Many surgeonfishes and their relatives are used in aquariums. The larger species are caught and sold for food. Other fishes are caught and eaten by people who live near where the fish live.

CONSERVATION STATUS

Surgeonfishes and their relatives are not threatened or endangered.

Did You Know?
Yellow tangs are the number one aquarium fish export from the Hawaiian Islands.

What's in a Name?
Surgeonfish are called that because their venomous spines resemble scalpels, which are the knives surgeons use to cut into their patients.

Lined surgeonfish (*Acanthurus lineatus*)

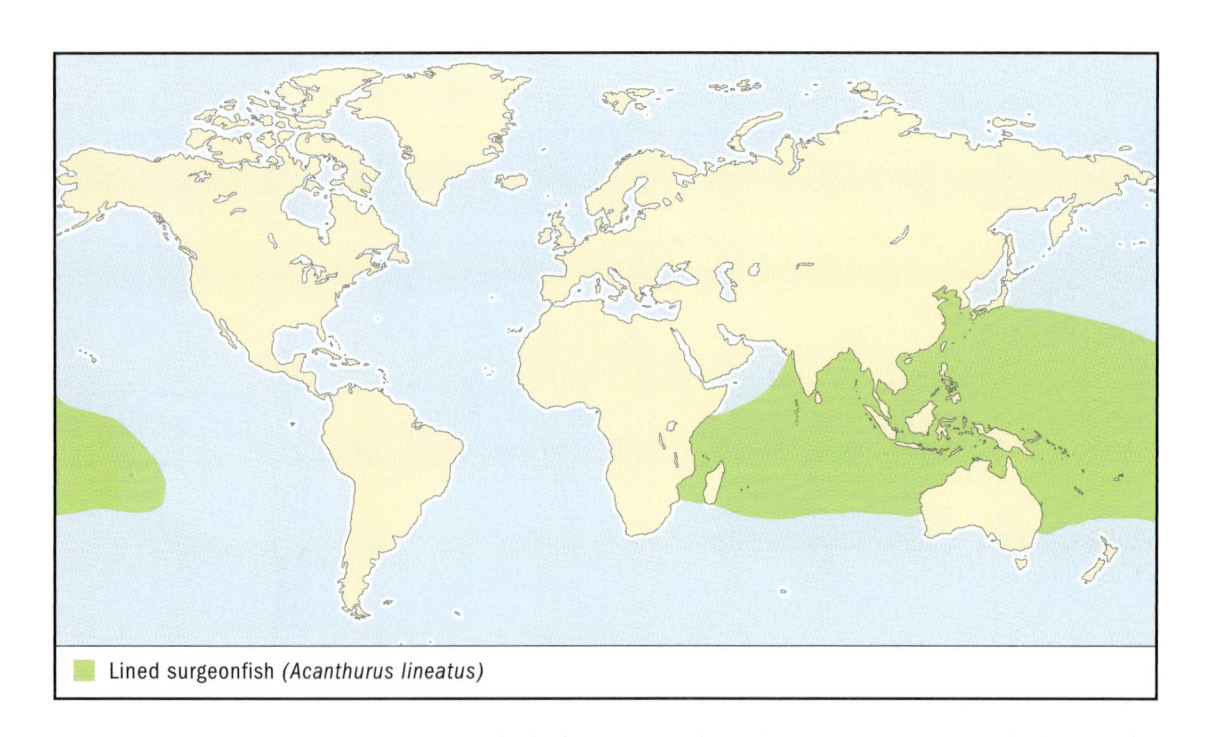

SPECIES ACCOUNTS

LINED SURGEONFISH
Acanthurus lineatus

Physical characteristics: Lined surgeonfish have a disk-like body that is narrow from side to side. There is a large, venomous spine on each side of the tail. The tail fin is shaped like a crescent moon. The body color is yellowish green with bright blue stripes that are edged with black on the sides of the fish but not on the head. The belly is bluish white. The tail fin has two up-and-down lines of dark blue against a background of purplish gray. The pelvic fins, the pair that corresponds to the rear legs of four-footed animals, are bright orange. The other fins are purplish gray at the edges and greenish yellow at the base. The dorsal and anal fins are long. The dorsal (DOOR-suhl) fin is the one along the midline of the back. The anal (AY-nuhl) fin is the one along the midline of the belly. Lined surgeonfish grow to a length of about 15 inches (38 centimeters).

Geographic range: Lined surgeonfish live in the Indian and Pacific oceans.

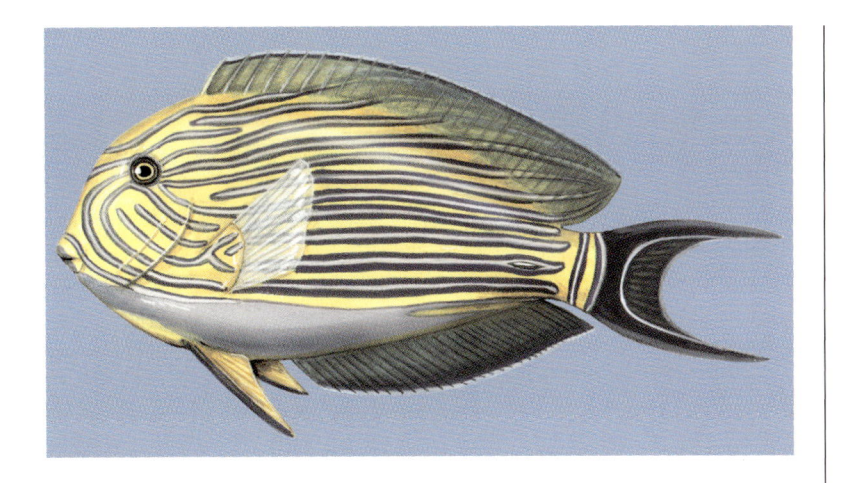

Lined surgeonfish patrol their territory on reefs and aggressively attack other fishes, using their tail spines as weapons. (Illustration by Joseph E. Trumpey. Reproduced by permission.)

Habitat: Lined surgeonfish live on reefs at a depth of 3 to 10 feet (1 to 3 meters).

Diet: Lined surgeonfish eat algae.

Behavior and reproduction: Lined surgeonfish patrol their territory on reefs and aggressively attack other fishes, using their tail spines as weapons. Their head becomes a darker color during these meetings. Lined surgeonfish travel to spawn in groups at specific sites, although they sometimes spawn in pairs. Eggs and larvae float in open water. Lined surgeonfish live as long as forty-five years.

Lined surgeonfish and people: Lined surgeonfish are collected for aquariums and are caught and eaten by people who live near where the fish live.

Conservation status: Lined surgeonfish are not threatened or endangered. ∎

Yellow tang (Zebrasoma flavescens)

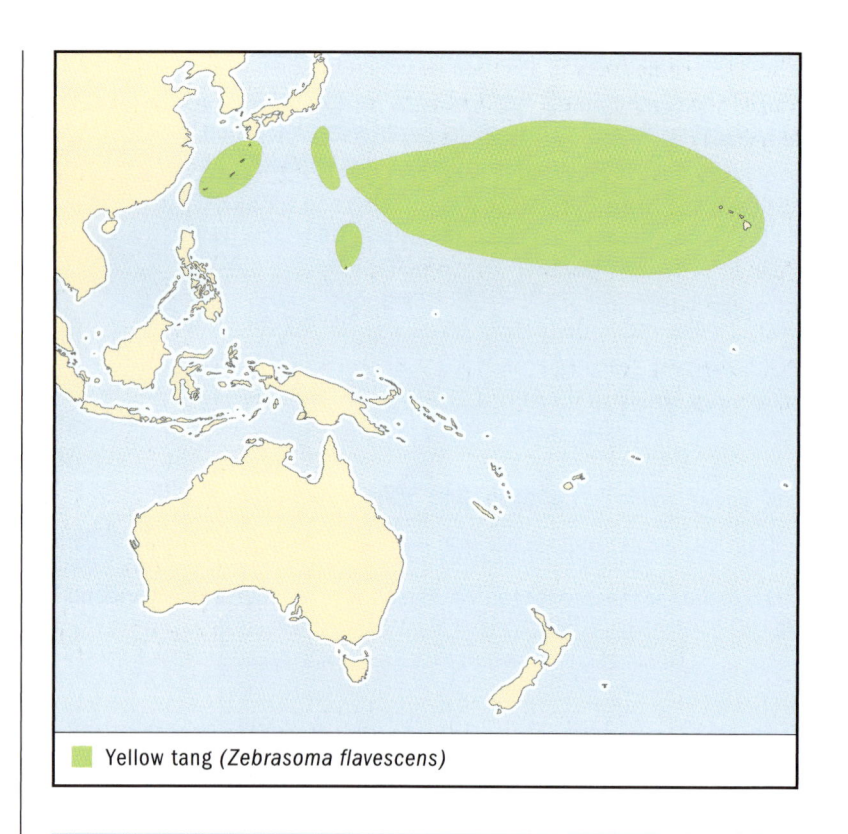

YELLOW TANG
Zebrasoma flavescens

Physical characteristics: Yellow tangs have a disk-like body that is narrow from side to side. The forehead curves in rather than out, and the snout is long. The dorsal fin sticks up high and has four to five spines. The anal fin has three spines. The body is bright yellow. Yellow tangs grow to a length of more than 8 inches (20 centimeters).

Geographic range: Yellow tangs live in the Pacific Ocean.

Habitat: Yellow tangs live in coral and rocky reefs and in bays and lagoons.

Diet: Yellow tangs eat algae.

Behavior and reproduction: Yellow tangs live in small groups or alone. The groups often move from point to point to browse on algae.

These fish sometimes live in mixed-species schools. Single males may defend territories, court passing females, and spawn with them in open water. Yellow tangs also sometimes spawn in groups. Eggs and larvae float in open water.

Yellow tangs and people: Yellow tangs are used in aquariums.

Conservation status: Yellow tangs are not threatened or endangered. ■

Yellow tangs sometimes live in mixed-species schools. (©Andrew G. Wood/Photo Researchers, Inc. Reproduced by permission.)

Moorish idol (*Zanclus cornutus*)

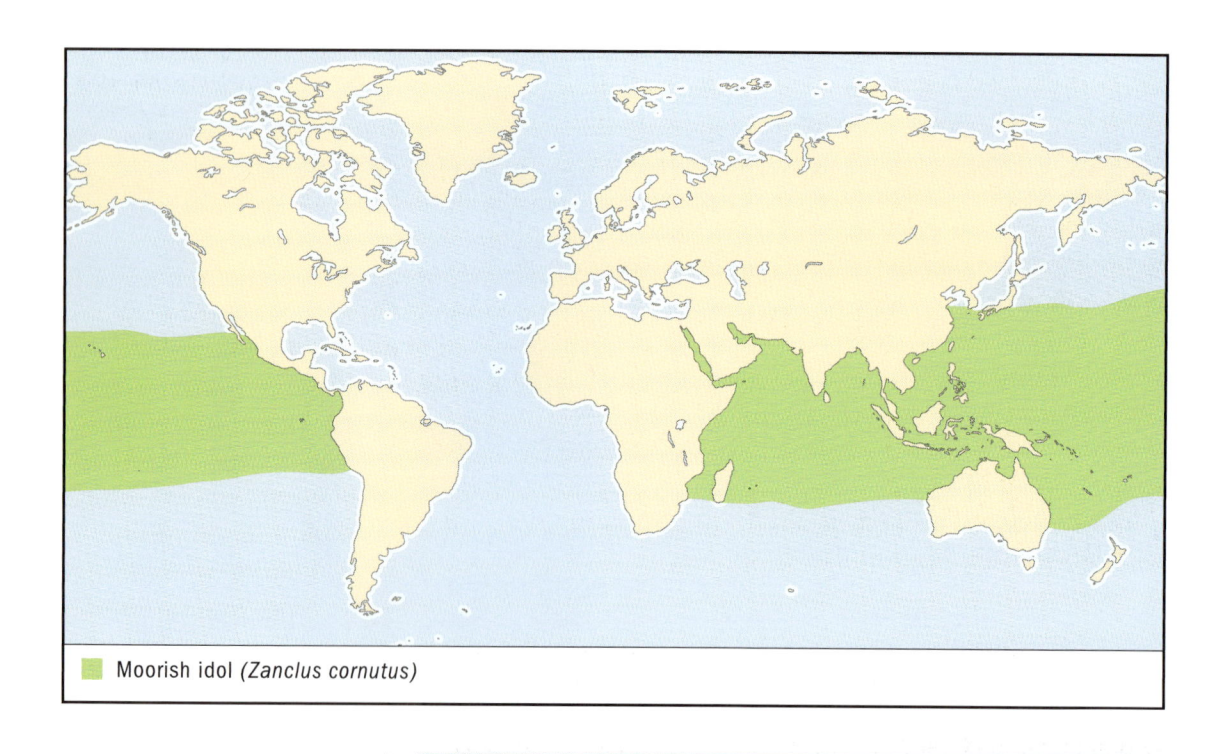

MOORISH IDOL
Zanclus cornutus

Physical characteristics: Moorish idols have a disk-like body that is narrow from side to side. The third spine in the dorsal fin is very long and whiplike. These fish have three up-and-down bands of white and yellow alternating with two bands of black. The tail fin is black and fringed with white or yellowish white. The snout has a small patch of yellow and a band of white. The snout is tubular. Adult Moorish idols grow to a length of at least 6 inches (15 centimeters).

Geographic range: Moorish idols live in the Indian and Pacific oceans.

Habitat: Moorish idols live in coral and rocky reefs and in lagoons.

Diet: Moorish idols eat bottom-dwelling invertebrates, especially sponges.

Behavior and reproduction: Moorish idols live alone, in pairs, or in small groups, but large groups may gather for spawning. Scientists

Moorish idols eat bottom-dwelling invertebrates, especially sponges. (Illustration by Joseph E. Trumpey. Reproduced by permission.)

know little about the reproduction of Moorish idols. These fish spawn in pairs in small or possibly large groups. Eggs and larvae float freely.

Moorish idols and people: Moorish idols are collected for aquariums but do not do well in captivity. They are eaten by people who live near where the fish live.

Conservation status: Moorish idols are not threatened or endangered. ∎

FOR MORE INFORMATION

Books:

Gilbert, Carter Rowell, and James D. Williams. *National Audubon Society Field Guide to Fishes: North America.* New York: Knopf, 2002.

Web sites:

"Marine Life Profile: Moorish Idol." Waikiki Aquarium Education Department. http://waquarium.mic.hawaii.edu/MLP/root/pdf/MarineLife/Vertebrates/MoorishIdol.pdf (accessed on November 4, 2004).

Wood, Lori. "The Yellow Tang." WhoZoo. http://www.whozoo.org/Anlife99/loriwood/tang3.htm (accessed on November 4, 2004).

BARRACUDAS, TUNAS, MARLINS, AND RELATIVES
Scombroidei

Class: Actinopterygeii
Order: Perciformes
Suborder: Scombroidei
Number of families: 6 families

suborder
CHAPTER

PHYSICAL CHARACTERISTICS

Barracudas, tunas, marlins, and their relatives have streamlined bodies. They are medium-sized (about 2 feet or 61 centimeters) to huge (16 feet or 5 meters) and are extremely fast swimmers. Some can leap high out of the water. Some of these fishes have nets of tiny blood vessels in their bodies that help them keep cool during their intense physical efforts.

GEOGRAPHIC RANGE

Barracudas, tunas, marlins, and their relatives live all over the world.

HABITAT

Most barracudas, tunas, marlins, and their relatives live in the open sea, usually near the surface. Some live in middle depths, and some live in estuaries (EHS-chew-air-eez), or the areas where rivers meet the sea. One species moves long distances upriver.

DIET

Most barracudas, tunas, marlins, and their relatives hunt for fish, squid, and crustaceans (krus-TAY-shuns), or water-dwelling animals that have jointed legs and a hard shell but no backbone. Some eat plankton, or microscopic plants and animals drifting in water.

BEHAVIOR AND REPRODUCTION

Some barracudas, tunas, marlins, and their relatives form large schools, but others live alone. They all spawn in groups. The eggs

> **A VALUABLE FISH**
>
> The belly meat of bluefin tuna reaches astronomical prices in the Japanese market for sashimi (sah-SHEE-mee), a dish of thinly sliced raw fish. A record price of $173,600 was reached for a 444-pound (201 kilograms) bluefin sold in Tokyo in January 2001.
>
> **MORE THAN A FISH STORY**
>
> A huge marlin is one of the main characters in *The Old Man and the Sea*, a famous story about respect and persistence by Ernest Hemingway, who won the Nobel Prize for Literature.

float freely and hatch into free-floating larvae (LAR-vee), which are an early stage that must change form before becoming adults.

BARRACUDAS, TUNAS, MARLINS, THEIR RELATIVES, AND PEOPLE

Barracudas, tunas, marlins, and their relatives are important food and sport fishes.

CONSERVATION STATUS

The World Conservation Union (IUCN) lists one species of barracudas, tunas, marlins, and their relatives as Critically Endangered, one as Endangered, and one as Vulnerable. Critically Endangered means facing an extremely high risk of extinction in the wild. Endangered means facing a very high risk of extinction in the wild. Vulnerable means facing a high risk of extinction in the wild.

Blue marlin (*Makaira nigricans*)

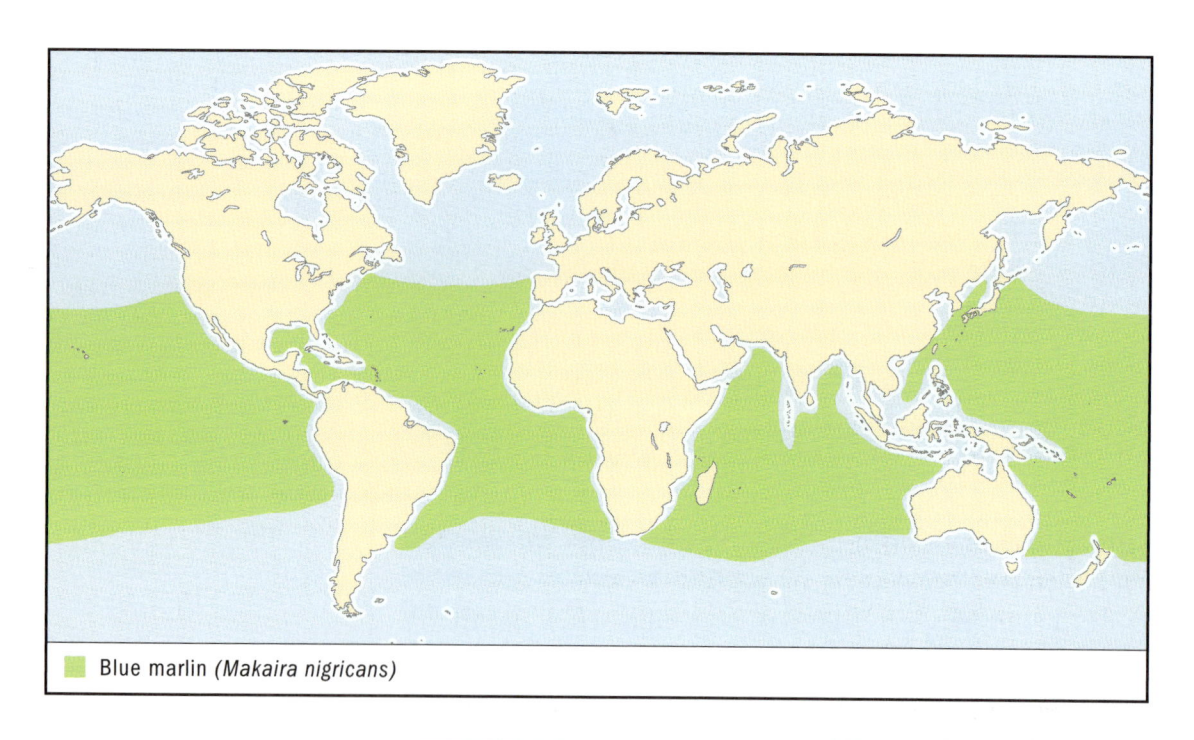

SPECIES ACCOUNTS

BLUE MARLIN
Makaira nigricans

Physical characteristics: Blue marlins have a long snout that forms a spear. These fish reach a length of approximately 16 feet (5 meters) and weigh more than 1,900 pounds (900 kilograms), almost one ton. The body is blue on the back and silvery white on the belly. There are about fifteen light-colored up-and-down bars on the sides. The forward part of the first dorsal fin is high and pointed. The first anal fin also is large and pointed. The dorsal (DOOR-suhl) fins are the ones along the midline of the back. The anal (AY-nuhl) fins are the ones along the midline of the belly. The tail fin is large and shaped like a crescent moon. The body is covered with scales that are deep in the skin. Each scale has one or two spines.

Geographic range: Blue marlin live in the Atlantic, Pacific, and Indian oceans.

Habitat: Blue marlin live near the surface in the ocean.

Diet: Blue marlin eat dolphinfishes, tuna-like fishes, and squid.

Marlins use their bills to stun their prey. (Illustration by Barbara Duperron. Reproduced by permission.)

Behavior and reproduction: Marlins use their bills to stun their prey, or animals hunted and caught for food. Scientists know little about the spawning grounds or seasons of blue marlin. The eggs are very small and hatch into free-floating larvae.

Blue marlin and people: Blue marlin is an important food and sport fish.

Conservation status: Blue marlin are not threatened or endangered. ∎

Atlantic bluefin tuna (*Thunnus thynnus*)

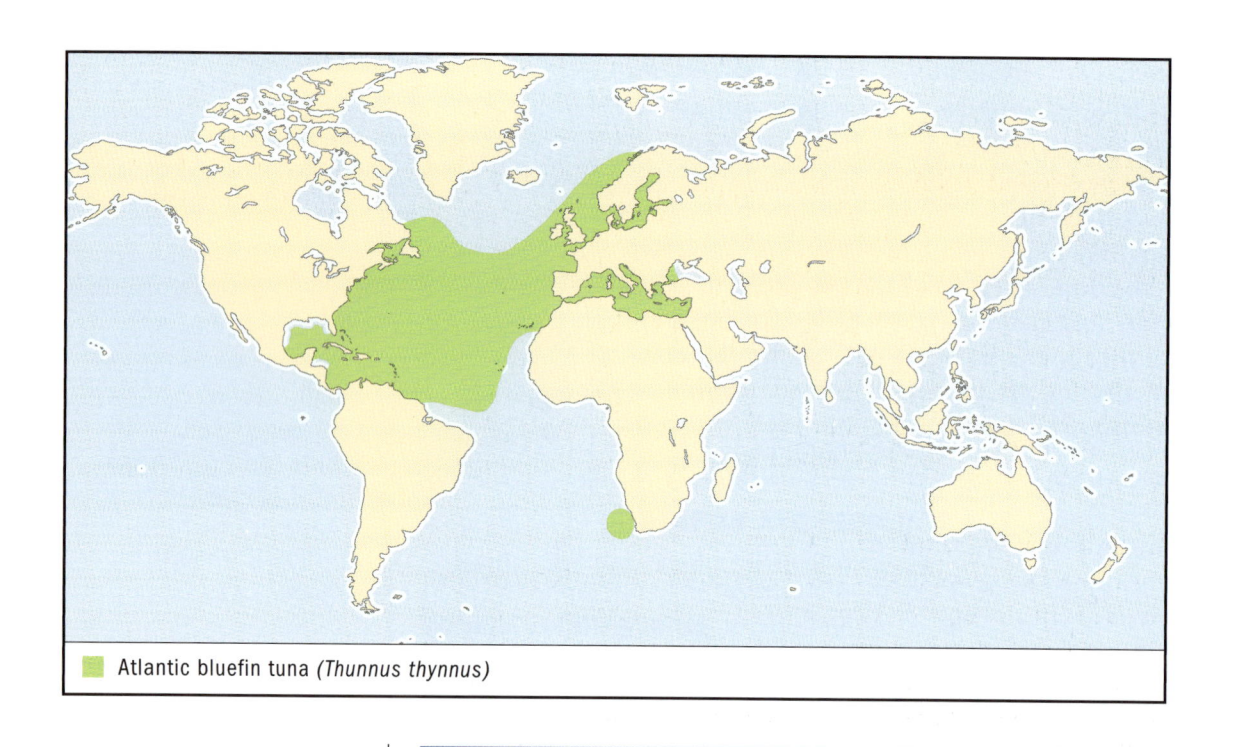

ATLANTIC BLUEFIN TUNA
Thunnus thynnus

Physical characteristics: Atlantic bluefin tuna reach a length of 10 feet (3 meters) but usually are about 6 feet (2 meters) long. The body is a symmetrical oval with pointed ends. The back is metallic dark blue, and the lower sides and belly are silvery white. The first dorsal fin is yellow or bluish, and the second is reddish brown. The second dorsal and anal fins are followed by seven to ten tiny fins. The second anal fin is silvery gray, and the small fins that follow it are dusky yellow edged with black. The front of the fish is wrapped in large scales, and the rest of the body is covered with small scales. Tunas have nets of tiny blood vessels that help them stay cool.

Geographic range: Atlantic bluefin tuna live in the Atlantic Ocean.

Habitat: Atlantic bluefin tuna live near the surface in open water.

Diet: Atlantic bluefin tuna eat fish, crustaceans, and squid.

Atlantic bluefin tuna reach a length of 10 feet (3 meters) but usually are about 6 feet (2 meters) long. (Illustration by Barbara Duperron. Reproduced by permission.)

Behavior and reproduction: Atlantic bluefin tuna travel far from their spawning grounds in the Gulf of Mexico and the Mediterranean Sea. Eastern and western Atlantic fish mix, but scientists are not sure how many fish travel all the way across the ocean. Atlantic bluefin tuna can reproduce when they are about four years old. Females weighing about 660 pounds (300 kilograms) produce as many as ten million eggs per spawning season.

Atlantic bluefin tuna and people: Atlantic bluefin tuna are important food and sport fish.

Conservation status: Atlantic bluefin tuna are not threatened or endangered. ∎

Great barracuda (*Sphyraena barracuda*)

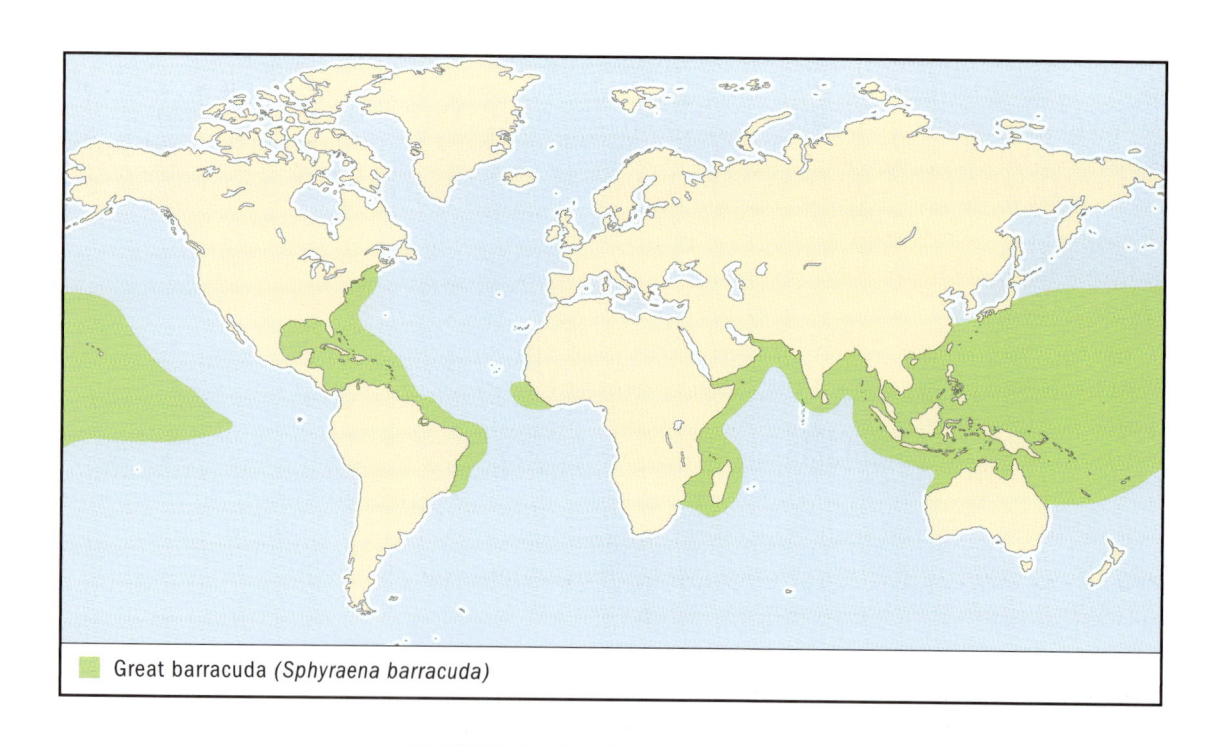

GREAT BARRACUDA
Sphyraena barracuda

Physical characteristics: Great barracudas reach a length of 79 inches (200 centimeters) but usually are about 51 inches (130 centimeters) long. The body is long and somewhat narrow from side to side. The head is large and has a long pointed snout. The mouth is large, and the lower jaw juts beyond the upper jaw. Great barracudas have strong pointed teeth of unequal sizes in both jaws and in the roof of the mouth. The two dorsal fins are far apart, and the first has five strong spines. The body is deep green to steel gray on the back, silver on the sides, and white on the belly. Adults have angled dark bars on the upper sides and usually have scattered inky blotches on the lower sides toward the rear.

Geographic range: Great barracudas live all over the world except the eastern part of the Pacific Ocean.

Habitat: Adult great barracudas usually live in reefs and offshore areas. The young live in shallow water over sandy and weedy bottoms.

Great barracudas are fierce hunters of small fish, squid, and crustaceans. (Illustration by Barbara Duperron. Reproduced by permission.)

Diet: Great barracudas are fierce hunters of small fish, squid, and crustaceans.

Behavior and reproduction: Adult great barracudas live alone, but the young form schools. Most male great barracudas can reproduce when they are two years old. Females can reproduce when they are four years old. Females spawn several times in one season.

Great barracudas and people: Great barracudas have attacked humans, but most attacks happened because the swimmer was carrying a silvery, bright object, which a barracuda mistakes for prey. Great barracudas are important game fish, but because it can cause a form of food poisoning, the meat is not eaten in most areas.

Conservation status: Great barracudas are not threatened or endangered. ∎

FOR MORE INFORMATION

Books:

Allen, Missy, and Michel Peissel. *Dangerous Water Creatures.* New York: Chelsea House, 1992.

Gilbert, Carter Rowell, and James D. Williams. *National Audubon Society Field Guide to Fishes: North America.* New York: Knopf, 2002.

Schultz, Ken. *Ken Schultz's Field Guide to Saltwater Fish.* New York: Wiley, 2004.

Web sites:

"Barracuda." Discoveryschool.com. http://school.discovery.com/schooladventures/planetocean/barracuda.html (accessed on November 5, 2004).

Empty Oceans, Empty Nets. PBS. http://www.pbs.org/emptyoceans/eden/tuna (accessed on November 5, 2004).

BUTTERFISHES AND RELATIVES
Stromateoidei

Class: Actinopterygii
Order: Perciformes
Suborder: Stromateoidei
Number of families: 6 families

suborder CHAPTER

PHYSICAL CHARACTERISTICS

Butterfishes and their relatives have large eyes, a small mouth, a forked tail fin, and a long dorsal fin. Between the gills and the esophagus, most of these fishes have a sac used for breaking down food. The inside of the sac is coated with tiny teeth. The body of butterfishes and their relatives is tapered at the ends and is either narrow from side to side or rounded in cross-section. These fishes reach a length of about 4 feet (1.2 meters). The scales usually are smooth. The color of adults varies from silver to dark brown, but young butterfishes usually have mottled colors. The dorsal and anal fins have spines. The pelvic fins are absent in some species, small in others, and large in others. The dorsal (DOOR-suhl) fin is the one along the midline of the back. The anal (AY-nuhl) fin is the one along the midline of the belly. The pelvic fins correspond to the rear legs of four-footed animals.

GEOGRAPHIC RANGE

Butterfishes and their relatives live in the Atlantic, Pacific, and Indian oceans.

HABITAT

Butterfishes and their relatives live in the ocean well offshore, close to the shore, or in large bays. Adults live in deeper waters, either on the bottom or in open water in middle depths. The young usually live near the surface, sometimes among jellyfishes.

phylum
class
subclass
order
monotypic order
○ suborder
family

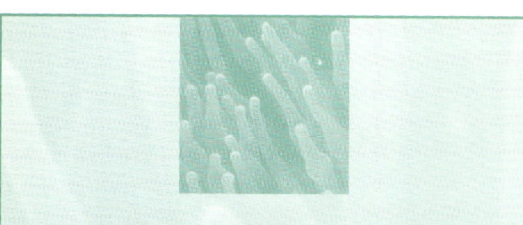

JELLY

Young butterfish are more resistant to jellyfish poison than are other fishes. The butterfish hovers under the bell of the jellyfish but may swim in and out of the tentacles to snatch food. The butterfish also sometimes feeds on the tentacles and sex organs of the jellyfish. Sometimes the jellyfish eats the butterfish.

Butter

Butterfish are named for their melt-in-your-mouth flavor.

DIET

Butterfishes and their relatives mostly eat invertebrates (in-VER-teh-brehts), or animals without a backbone. Some species eat small fish.

BEHAVIOR AND REPRODUCTION

Scientists know little about the behavior of butterfishes and their relatives other than that some of these fishes live among jellyfishes. Many species form schools. Some gather under floating wreckage and buoys and around boats. Butterfishes and their relatives release large numbers of eggs into open water. These fishes probably spawn once a year.

BUTTERFISHES AND THEIR RELATIVES AND PEOPLE

Butterfishes and their relatives are caught and sold for food in some areas, especially Japan and Southeast Asia.

CONSERVATION STATUS

Butterfishes and their relatives are not threatened or endangered.

Butterfish (Peprilus triacanthus)

BUTTERFISH
Peprilus triacanthus

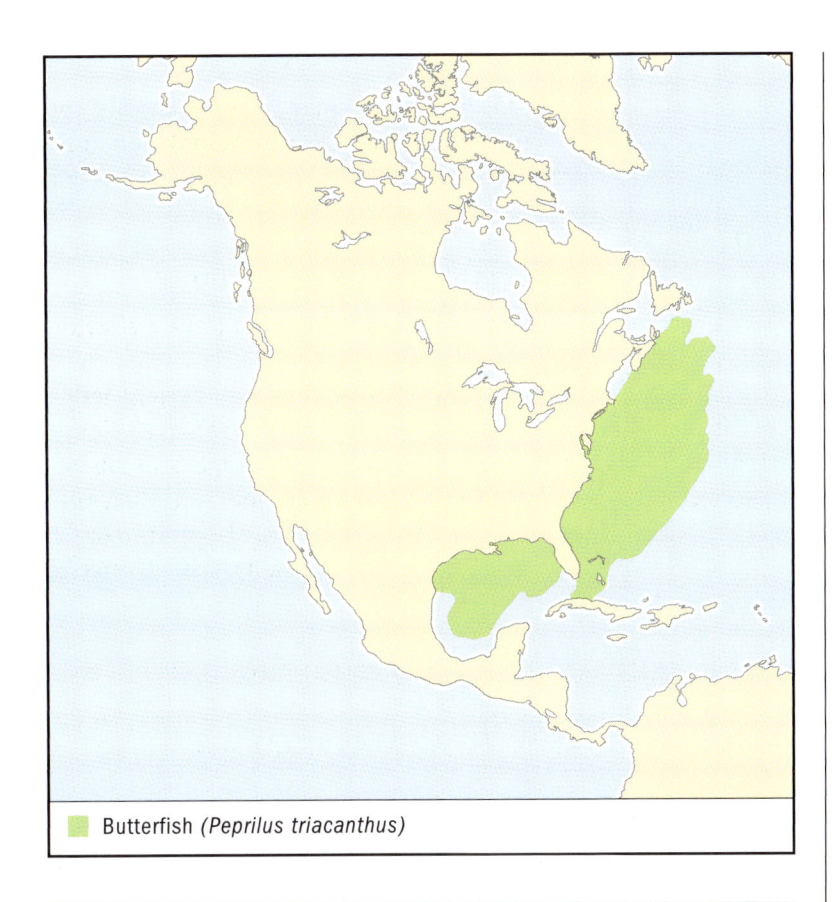

SPECIES ACCOUNT

Physical characteristics: Butterfish are about 12 inches (30 centimeters) long. The body is narrow from side to side and broad from back to belly. The single long dorsal and anal fins are tall and pointed near the front and taper toward the rear. The pectoral (PECK-ter-uhl) fins, the pair that corresponds to the front legs of four-footed animals, are long. The tail fin is deeply forked. There are no pelvic fins. The fish's back is grayish blue. The sides are silver with dark spots.

Geographic range: Butterfish live in the western part of the Atlantic Ocean and in the Gulf of Mexico.

Habitat: Butterfish live in open water or on the bottom, usually over sand. They may enter shallow bays and estuaries (EHS-chew-air-eez), or the areas where rivers meet the sea.

During their first year butterfish may live among jellyfishes or swim freely, but they form schools as adults. (Illustration by Dan Erickson. Reproduced by permission.)

Diet: Butterfish eat sea squirts, mollusks, and small crustaceans. Mollusks (MAH-lusks) are animals with a soft, unsegmented body that may or may not have a shell. Crustaceans (krus-TAY-shuns) are water-dwelling animals that have jointed legs and a hard shell but no backbone.

Behavior and reproduction: Butterfish are active day and night. During their first year these fish may live among jellyfishes or freely, but they form schools as adults. Butterfish can reproduce when they are one or two years old. They spawn once a year, scattering their eggs, which drift in open water.

Butterfish and people: Butterfish are important food fish.

Conservation status: Butterfish are not threatened or endangered. ∎

FOR MORE INFORMATION

Books:

Gilbert, Carter Rowell, and James D. Williams. *National Audubon Society Field Guide to Fishes: North America.* New York: Knopf, 2002.

Schultz, Ken. *Ken Schultz's Field Guide to Saltwater Fish.* New York: Wiley, 2004.

Web sites:

"Butterfish: *Poronotus triacanthus* (Peck) 1800." Fishes of the Gulf of Maine. http://gma.org/fogm/Poronotus_triacanthus.htm (accessed on February 11, 2005).

suborder CHAPTER

LABYRINTH FISHES
Anabantoidei

Class: Actinopterygii
Order: Perciformes
Suborder: Anabantoidei
Number of families: 5 families

PHYSICAL CHARACTERISTICS

Labyrinth fishes are about 1 to 24 inches (2.5 to 60 centimeters) long and have a special air-breathing organ called the labyrinth (LAB-uh-rinth). Most species have a space in their head bones that sharpens their hearing. The swim bladder, an internal sac that fishes use to control their position in the water, branches into two long pouches. Many species are beautifully colored.

GEOGRAPHIC RANGE

Labyrinth fishes live in Africa and Asia. Several species have been released accidentally to areas outside their natural range.

HABITAT

Many labyrinth fishes live in still bodies of water with thick plant life, but some live in cool, fast mountain streams. Most labyrinth fishes can live in water with a low oxygen level.

DIET

Most labyrinth fishes eat small invertebrates (in-VER-teh-brehts), or animals without backbones, and algae. Algae (AL-jee) are plantlike growths that live in water and have no true roots, stems, or leaves. Some species eat small fishes.

BEHAVIOR AND REPRODUCTION

Labyrinth fishes rise to the water surface to exchange the air in their air-breathing organ. Some leave the water and travel

phylum
class
subclass
order
monotypic order
○ **suborder**
family

over land to nearby bodies of water. Some labyrinth fishes release free-floating eggs and do not take care of them. Others build bubble nests and guard floating eggs and larvae (LAR-vee), or the early stage of the animal that must change form before becoming adults. Some bubble nests consist of only a few bubbles, but others are large. In some species of labyrinth fishes, the young develop in a parent's mouth. Some species release sticky eggs on the bottom of their habitat.

LABYRINTH FISHES AND PEOPLE

The larger species of labyrinth fishes are farmed for food. The smaller, colorful labyrinth fishes are used in aquariums.

CONSERVATION STATUS

The World Conservation Union (IUCN) lists three species of labyrinth fishes as Critically Endangered, three as Endangered, seven as Vulnerable, and the two as Conservation Dependent. Critically Endangered means facing an extremely high risk of extinction in the wild. Endangered means facing a very high risk of extinction in the wild. Vulnerable means facing a high risk of extinction in the wild. Conservation Dependent means if the conservation program were to end, the animal would be placed in one of the threatened categories.

Climbing perch (Anabas testudineus)

CLIMBING PERCH
Anabas testudineus

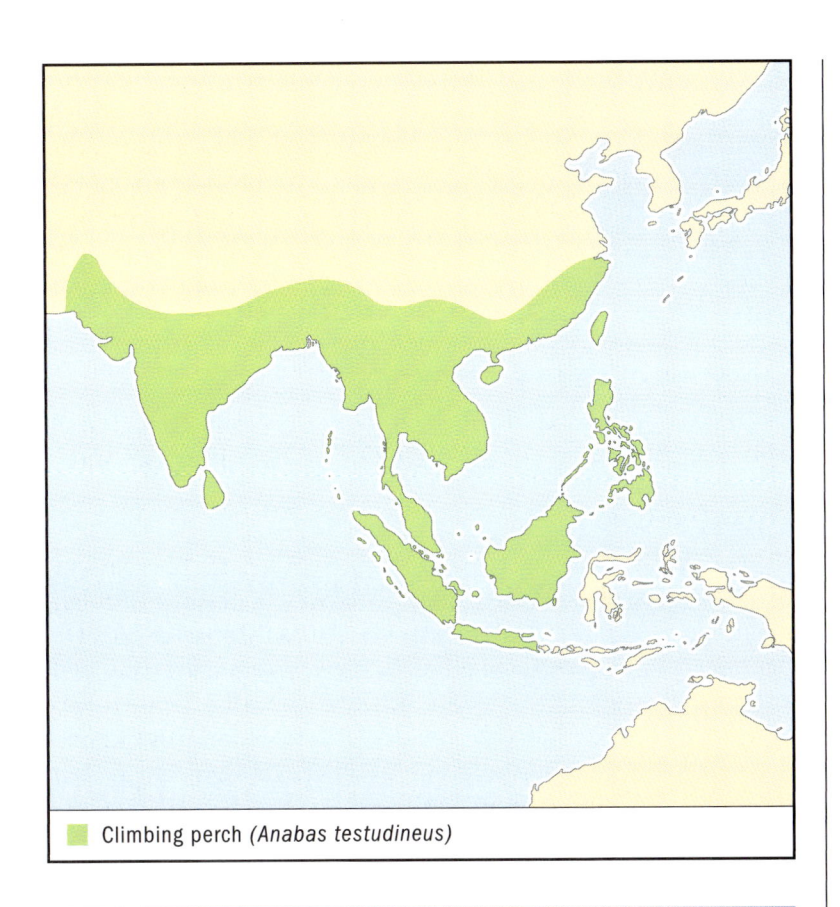

SPECIES ACCOUNTS

Physical characteristics: Climbing perch are about 10 inches (25 centimeters) long. The body shape ranges from oval in profile and narrow from side to side to long and slightly round in cross-section. The bones of the gill cover have strong spines. The dorsal and anal fins are long and have strong spines. The dorsal (DOOR-suhl) fin is the one along the midline of the back. The anal (AY-nuhl) fin is the one along the midline of the belly. The scales are rough. The air-breathing organ is very large. The body is light beige with darker spots. On each side of the fish there is a large black spot between the gill cover spines and another on the tail.

Geographic range: Climbing perch live in Asia. They have been accidentally released in the United States.

Labyrinth Fishes

Climbing perch can travel over land. They use the spiny bones on their gill covers and side-to-side wriggling of the body to move themselves forward. (Illustration by Michelle Meneghini. Reproduced by permission.)

Habitat: Climbing perch live in all types of fresh water.

Diet: Climbing perch eat plants, invertebrates, and small fish.

Behavior and reproduction: Climbing perch can travel over land. They use the spiny bones on their gill covers and side-to-side wriggling of the body to move themselves forward. These fish drown if they cannot rise to the surface to gulp air. To survive drought they bury themselves in the mud of drying-up water bodies. Climbing perch do not take care of their eggs or their young. Eggs hatch twenty-four hours after being released.

Climbing perch and people: Climbing perch is a popular food fish in Southeast Asia.

Conservation status: Climbing perch are not threatened or endangered. ∎

Siamese fighting fish (Betta splendens)

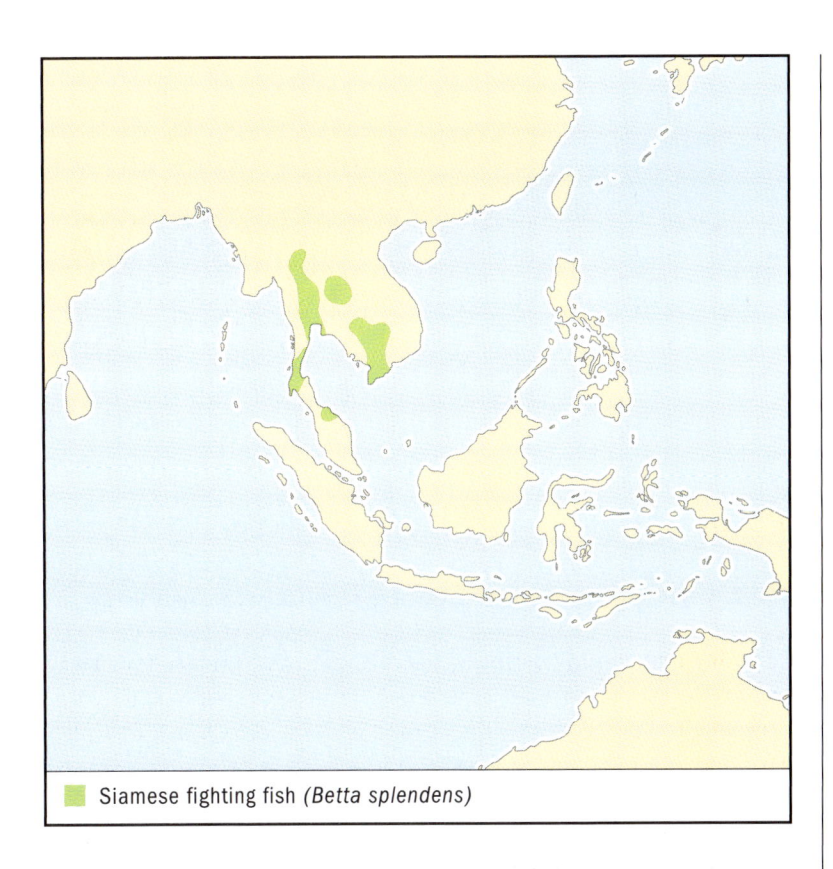

SIAMESE FIGHTING FISH
Betta splendens

Physical characteristics: Siamese fighting fish reach a length of about 2 inches (6 centimeters). They have a long tube-shaped body. Some species have large fanlike dorsal, anal, and tail fins. Wild Siamese fighting fish have a bluish body and blue and red fins. There are two shiny marks on the gill cover. Males have larger fins and are more brightly colored than females.

Geographic range: Siamese fighting fish live in Southeast Asia and in areas where they have been accidentally released, such as Florida, in the United States.

Habitat: Siamese fighting fish live in standing water with dense plant life, especially rice paddies and canals. They may dig into the

Siamese fighting fish are well known for their aggressive behavior, especially against males in their own species. (©A. N. T./Photo Researchers, Inc. Reproduced by permission.)

mud when the water level is low and can survive weeks in a small cocoon-like structure made of mud and probably mucus.

Diet: Siamese fighting fish eat invertebrates such as animal plankton and insect larvae.

Behavior and reproduction: Siamese fighting fish are well known for their aggressive behavior, especially against males in their own species. In small tanks, males fight until one of them dies. A male Siamese fighting fish builds a floating nest of bubbles and aggressively defends the territory around it. He mates with a female under the nest, placing sperm on the eggs as she lays them. The male then takes the eggs one at a time into his mouth and shoves them into the nest. The eggs hatch about thirty-six hours later, and the larvae swim free on the fourth day.

Siamese fighting fish and people: Siamese fighting fish are popular in aquariums.

Conservation status: Siamese fighting fish are not threatened or endangered. ■

FOR MORE INFORMATION

Books:

Ricciuti, Edward R. *Fish*. Woodbridge, CT: Blackbirch, 1993.

Web sites:

"The Fish That Climbs Trees." World Wildlife Fund. http://www.panda.org/news_facts/education/middle_school/species/perch.cfm (accessed on November 6, 2004).

"Labyrinth Fish: Anabantoidei." Mekong River Commission. http://www.mrcmekong.org/pdf/Anabantoids.pdf (accessed on November 6, 2004).

"Siamese Fighting Fish." All Science Fair Projects. http://www.all-science-fair-projects.com/science_fair_projects_encyclopedia/Siamese_fighting_fish (accessed on November 6, 2004).

> **SNAKEHEADS**
> **Channoidei**
>
> **Class:** Actinopterygii
> **Order:** Perciformes
> **Suborder:** Channoidei
> **Number of families:** 1 family

suborder CHAPTER

PHYSICAL CHARACTERISTICS

Snakeheads have a long tube-shaped body and flat head covered in large, shield-like scales. They have long soft dorsal and anal fins, a large mouth with large teeth on both upper and lower jaws, smooth or rough body scales, and an air-breathing organ in the head. The dorsal (DOOR-suhl) fin is the one along the midline of the back. The anal (AY-nuhl) fin is the one along the midline of the belly. Many snakeheads have large spots resembling eyes on the body and on the tail fin, up-and-down bands on the pectoral fins, and small spots on the body. The pectoral (PECK-ter-uhl) fins correspond to the front legs of four-footed animals.

GEOGRAPHIC RANGE

Snakeheads are native to Asia and Africa and have been introduced in the United States, Russia, and the islands of the South Pacific.

HABITAT

Most snakeheads live in still or slow-running waters, usually hiding under plants, rocks, and sunken trees. Some large species live in large rivers, swamps, ponds, and reservoirs. Most small species live in mountain streams. Many snakeheads can live in polluted water.

DIET

Adult snakeheads eat almost any animal smaller than their mouths, such as insects, fishes, frogs, tadpoles, lizards, geckos, mice, rats, and ducks.

phylum
class
subclass
order
monotypic order
○ **suborder**
family

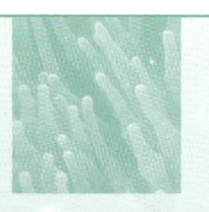

SNAKEHEAD INVASION

Scientists worry about a North American invasion of snakeheads because the fish eat up the food needed by other fishes and then eat the other fishes. Snakeheads have been a problem in Maryland, and on October 14, 2004, a snakehead was caught for the first time in Lake Michigan.

BEHAVIOR AND REPRODUCTION

All but one species of snakeheads are active during the day and hunt by ambush. Adults hunt alone, but young snakeheads hunt in schools. Snakeheads sometimes jump up from the water surface to grasp their prey. Snakeheads need to break the water surface once in a while to exchange the air in their breathing organ. These fishes drown if they cannot get to the surface to breathe. Some species of snakeheads can live out of water for several days if their bodies are wet. They can travel on land during the rainy season by using their bodies, pectoral fins, and tail fins.

Scientists know little about the reproduction of snakeheads. These fishes probably have only one mate and take care of their eggs and young. Many snakeheads clear plants and then build a simple circular nest at the water surface. The male encircles the female, squeezes out her eggs, and fertilizes, or places sperm on, them. The eggs float upward into the nest, which the parents guard. After hatching, the young are cared for by either parent, depending on species. In two species the male keeps the fertilized eggs and later the young in his mouth for a few days.

SNAKEHEADS AND PEOPLE

Most snakeheads are important food fishes in Southeast Asia and China, and the meat is considered delicious. Some medium-to-large species are farmed. Larger snakeheads are popular game fishes in Asia.

CONSERVATION STATUS

Snakeheads are not threatened or endangered.

Striped snakehead (Channa striata)

STRIPED SNAKEHEAD
Channa striata

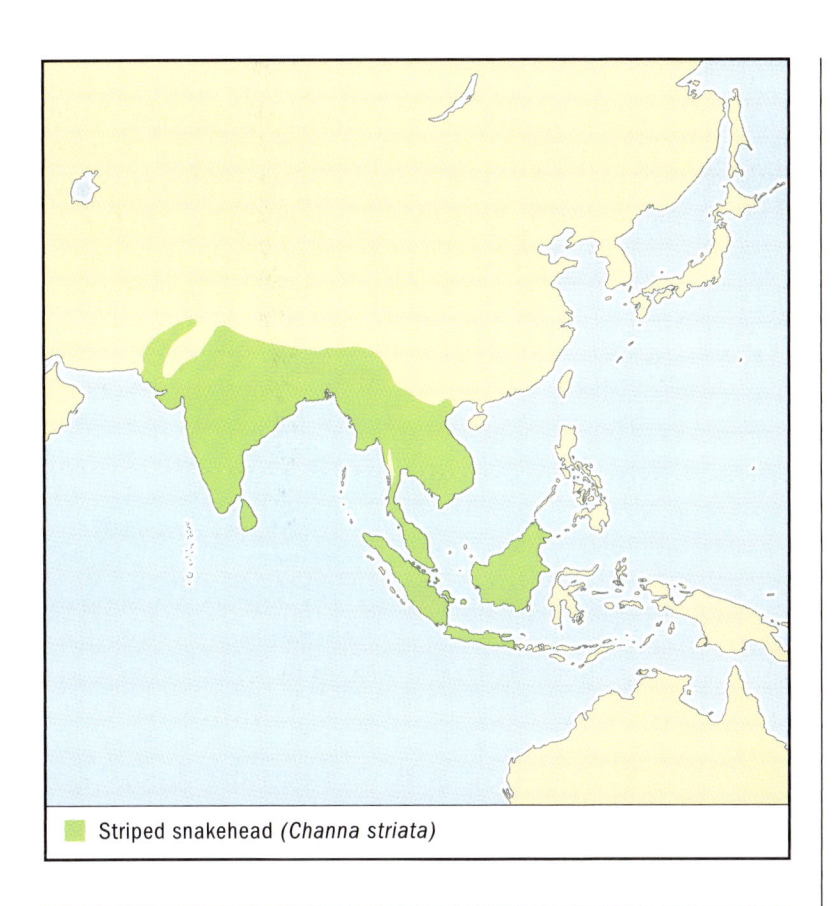

SPECIES ACCOUNT

Physical characteristics: Striped snakeheads are about 24 inches (60 centimeters) long. There are no scales on the underside of the jaw. The scales on the body are moderately large. The fish are dark brown on the back, but the color extends into irregular blackish bands on the sides. There are no bands or spots on the pectoral fins. Young striped snakeheads have a black spot at the end of the dorsal fin.

Geographic range: Striped snakeheads are native to Southeast Asia.

Habitat: Striped snakeheads live in still to slow-running waters with a muddy bottom, such as ponds, swamps, and ditches.

Diet: Striped snakeheads eat smaller fishes, frogs, prawns, and worms.

Striped snakeheads can survive in the bottom mud of lakes, swamps, and canals that have dried up. (Illustration by Michelle Meneghini. Reproduced by permission.)

Behavior and reproduction: Striped snakeheads can survive in the bottom mud of lakes, swamps, and canals that have dried up. They can move over land during the rainy season. Male and female striped snakeheads use their mouths and tails to clear away dense plants to make a doughnut-shaped floating nest about 12 inches (30 centimeters) in diameter, into which they place the eggs. The hatching period lasts about three days, during which the male guards the nest. After hatching, the young, still protected by the male, move in a dense school to look for food.

Striped snakeheads and people: Striped snakeheads are an important food fish.

Conservation status: Striped snakeheads are not threatened or endangered. ■

FOR MORE INFORMATION

Books:

Dolin, Eric Jay. *Snakehead: A Fish out of Water.* Washington, DC: Smithsonian Books, 2003.

Web sites:

Babin, Don. "Scientists Relieved They Don't Find Northern Snakehead in Chicago Harbor." *Great Lakes Directory.* http://www.greatlakesdirectory.org/il/101904_great_lakes.htm (accessed on November 8, 2004).

"Snakeheads: The Newest Aquatic Invader." U.S. Fish and Wildlife Service. http://contaminants.fws.gov/OtherDocuments/snakeheaddistill.pdf (accessed on November 8, 2004).

order CHAPTER

FLATFISHES
Pleuronectiformes

Class: Actinopterygii
Order: Pleuronectiformes
Number of families: 14 families

phylum
class
subclass
● order
monotypic order
suborder
family

PHYSICAL CHARACTERISTICS

Flatfishes have both eyes on the same side of the head. The body is disk-shaped or oval. These fishes are 1 inch (2.5 centimeters) to 6 feet, 6 inches (2 meters) long and weigh as much as 661 pounds (300 kilograms), but most are about 12 inches (30 centimeters) long. The eye side of most flatfishes is dark brown or black, sometimes with spots, bands, or wavy stripes. The other side is usually white or pale yellow. The dorsal (DOOR-suhl) fin, the one along the center of the back, extends from just above the eyes to the tail. The anal fin, the one along the midline of the belly, also is quite long. Adult flatfishes do not have a swim bladder, an internal sac that fishes use to control their position in the water.

GEOGRAPHIC RANGE

Flatfishes live all over the world.

HABITAT

Most flatfishes live in coastal waters over sand and mud bottoms.

DIET

Flatfishes eat invertebrates (in-VER-teh-brehts), or animals without backbones, and fishes.

BEHAVIOR AND REPRODUCTION

Except for halibuts, which chase other animals for food, flatfishes lie on the bottom and ambush their prey, or animals

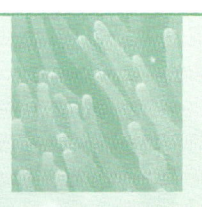

MOVING EYES

All flatfishes begin life with one eye on each side of the head. During the change from larvae to adults, one eye moves from one side of the head to the other, so that both eyes end up on the same side. Depending on the species, either the right or the left eye migrates. The eyes may be close together or far apart when the eye travel is completed.

killed for food. When flatfishes swim, they glide with wavy movements. Most flatfishes are active during the day, some around sunrise and sunset, and others at night. Flatfishes do not form schools.

Some flatfishes travel great distances to spawn once a year. Males of some species become aggressive toward one another during the mating season. Males and females probably pair up for spawning, or release of eggs. The eggs are fertilized (FUR-teh-lyzed), or joined with sperm, outside the female and drift in the water. When they hatch, flatfish larvae (LAR-vee), or the early stage that must change form before becoming adults, drift freely. After their eyes move to one side of their head, flatfishes live on the bottom.

FLATFISHES AND PEOPLE

Flatfishes are important food fishes.

CONSERVATION STATUS

The World Conservation Union (IUCN) lists one species of flatfishes as Endangered and one as Vulnerable. Endangered means facing a very high risk of extinction in the wild. Vulnerable means facing a high risk of extinction in the wild.

Peacock flounder (Bothus lunatus)

PEACOCK FLOUNDER
Bothus lunatus

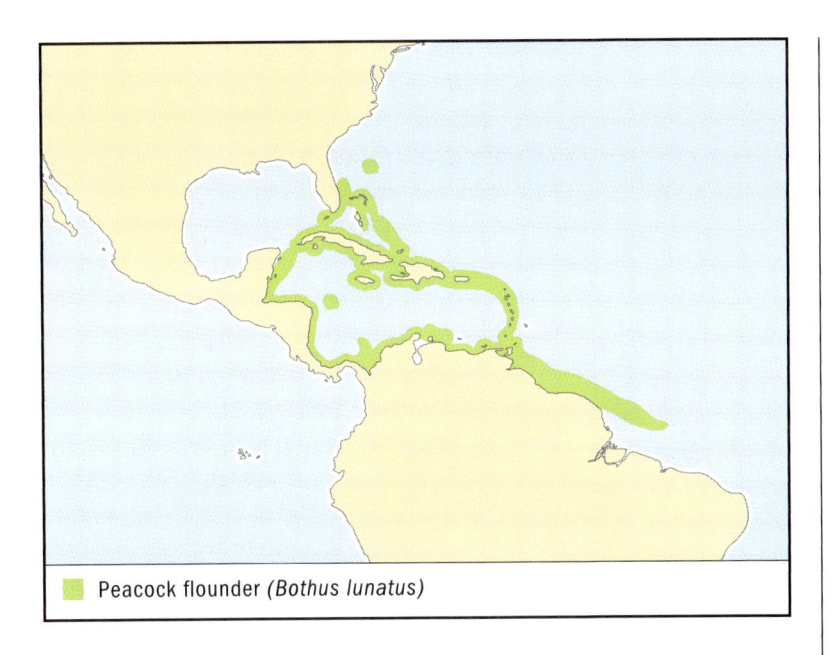

SPECIES ACCOUNTS

Physical characteristics: The eyes of peacock flounders are on the left side of the head. There is a wide space between the eyes, and the lower eye is farther forward than the upper eye. Males have a strong spine on their snout. The body is disk-shaped. The eye side of the body is grayish brown with many bright blue rings and two or three large black spots. Peacock flounders can grow to a length of about 18 inches (45 centimeters) but usually are about 14 inches (35 centimeters) long.

Geographic range: Peacock flounders live in the western part of the Atlantic Ocean from Bermuda to Brazil.

Habitat: Peacock flounders live in shallow water near the shore on sandy bottoms, on coral reefs, among sea grass, and in mangrove forests.

Diet: Peacock flounders eat small fishes, crustaceans, and octopuses. Crustaceans (krus-TAY-shuns) are water-dwelling animals that have jointed legs and a hard shell but no backbone.

The eyes of peacock flounders are on the left side of the head. (George Marler/Bruce Coleman Inc. Reproduced by permission.)

Behavior and reproduction: Peacock flounder are active during the day. They rest on the sandy bottom, waiting in ambush for their prey. When swimming, these fish glide just above the bottom using wavy movements. Peacock flounder can change colors rapidly to blend in with their background. To begin mating, male and female peacock flounders approach each other with pectoral fins held up. The pectoral (PECK-ter-uhl) fins correspond to the front legs of four-footed animals. The male then positions himself under the female, and the pair slowly rises off the bottom. The fish then release eggs and sperm at the same time and rapidly return to the bottom.

Peacock flounders and people: Peacock flounders are caught by accident by people trying to catch other fish.

Conservation status: Peacock flounders are not threatened or endangered. ∎

Pacific halibut (Hippoglossus stenolepis)

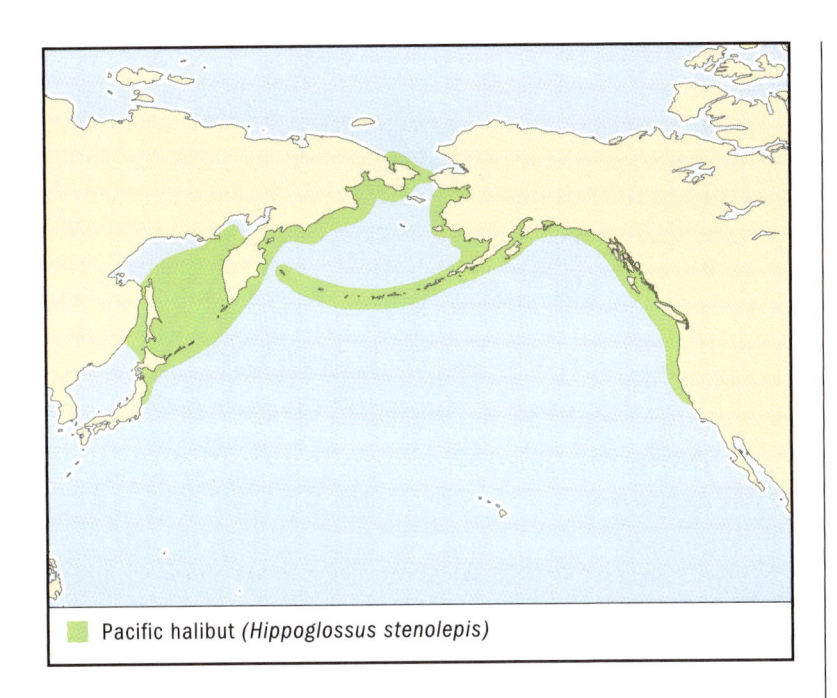

PACIFIC HALIBUT
Hippoglossus stenolepis

Physical characteristics: Female Pacific halibut reach a length of almost 9 feet (2.7 meters) and a weight of about 498 pounds (226 kilograms). Males are about half that size. The eyes of Pacific halibut are on the right side of the head, and the upper eye is farther forward than the bottom eye. The body is thick and diamond-shaped. The eye side is greenish brown to dark brown or black with lighter blotches. The other side usually is white, sometimes with blotches.

Geographic range: Pacific halibut live in the northern part of the Pacific Ocean.

Habitat: Pacific halibut live near the shore on a variety of bottom types.

Diet: Small Pacific halibut eat bottom-dwelling invertebrates and small fishes. Larger halibut eat almost anything they can catch.

Behavior and reproduction: Pacific halibut are active during the day. They often rise off the bottom and may come close to the surface when

Pacific halibut often rise off the bottom and may come close to the surface when chasing prey. (Illustration by Wendy Baker. Reproduced by permission.)

chasing prey. Pacific halibut spawn in deep water, move to shallower water for the summer, and then return to deep water. Females can reproduce when they are about twelve years old and males when they are about eight years old. The eggs are fertilized outside the female. Pacific halibut live about forty years.

Pacific halibut and people: Pacific halibut is an important food fish.

Conservation status: Pacific halibut are not threatened or endangered.

Common sole (*Solea solea*)

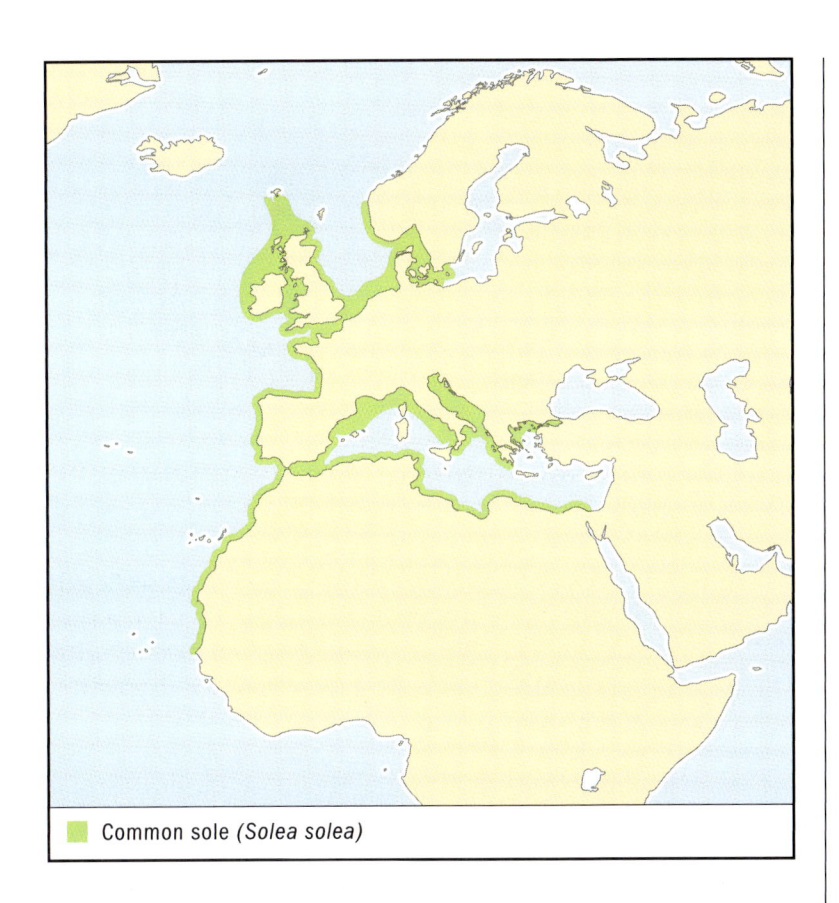

COMMON SOLE
Solea solea

Physical characteristics: The eyes of common sole are on the right side of the head. The body is long and thick. On the eyeless side, the head and snout are covered with white bumps. The eye side is dark brown or grayish brown with darker blotches. The eyeless side is creamy white. The dorsal and anal fins are edged in white, and the pectoral fin on the eye side has an oval black patch. These fish reach a length of about 28 inches (70 centimeters) and a weight of about 6 pounds (3 kilograms), but most are 12 to 16 inches (30 to 40 centimeters) long.

Geographic range: Common sole live in the Atlantic Ocean from Norway to Senegal.

Common sole spend the day partially buried or lying on the bottom. At night they sometimes move off the bottom. (Illustration by Wendy Baker. Reproduced by permission.)

Habitat: Common sole live on soft sandy or muddy bottoms.

Diet: Common sole eat small, bottom-dwelling invertebrates, but sometimes they eat small fishes.

Behavior and reproduction: Common sole are bottom dwellers that live alone. They spend the day partially buried or lying on the bottom. At night they sometimes move off the bottom. Common sole can reproduce when they are three to five years old. Spawning grounds are in both shallow and deep waters. The eggs float in open water. Common sole live seven to eight years.

Common sole and people: Common sole is an important food fish.

Conservation status: Common sole are not threatened or endangered. ∎

FOR MORE INFORMATION

Books:

Gilbert, Carter Rowell, and James D. Williams. *National Audubon Society Field Guide to Fishes: North America.* New York: Knopf, 2002.

Schultz, Ken. *Ken Schultz's Field Guide to Saltwater Fish.* New York: Wiley, 2004.

Web sites:

"The Flounders and Soles." Fishes of the Gulf of Maine. http://www.gma.org/fogm/flounders_soles.htm (accessed on November 9, 2004).

"Halibut." Seafood Choices Alliance. http://www.seafoodchoices.com/seasense/halibut.shtml (accessed on November 9, 2004).

Jamal, Rina Abdul. "Eye Travel." AnimalFact.com. http://www.animalfact.com/article1012.htm (accessed on November 8, 2004).

PUFFERFISHES, TRIGGERFISHES, AND RELATIVES
Tetraodontiformes

Class: Actinopterygii
Order: Tetraodontiformes
Number of families: 8 families

order
CHAPTER

phylum
class
subclass
● order
monotypic order
suborder
family

PHYSICAL CHARACTERISTICS

Pufferfishes, triggerfishes, and their relatives have teeth that are fused together. If present, the pelvic fins, the pair that corresponds to the rear legs of four-footed animals, are only spines on the belly. Other than that, these fishes are amazingly different from one another. The body shape ranges from long and thick to tall and narrow. The colors range from bright to dull and from solid to wild patterns. Some of these fishes have rounded foreheads and beaks, and others have a tubelike snout. Some of these fishes have body armor, some have spines covering their bodies, some produce poison, and some can blow themselves up like a balloon.

GEOGRAPHIC RANGE

Pufferfishes, triggerfishes, and their relatives live all over the world.

HABITAT

Most pufferfishes, triggerfishes, and their relatives live in the sea, but at least twenty species live in freshwater. Some of these fishes are bottom dwellers in deep and others in shallow water. Some of these fishes live in open water, and others enter estuaries (EHS-chew-air-eez), or the areas where rivers meet the sea. Some live on coral or rocky reefs. Most freshwater species are bottom dwellers.

DIET

Pufferfishes, triggerfishes, and their relatives eat plankton, algae, and invertebrates (in-VER-teh-brehts), or animals without backbones. Plankton is microscopic plants and animals drifting in water. Algae (AL-jee) are plantlike growths that live in water and have no true roots, stems, or leaves.

BEHAVIOR AND REPRODUCTION

To defend themselves, pufferfishes, triggerfishes, and their relatives use their body armor, ability to inflate, and ability to produce poison. The color patterns show attackers that these fishes are poisonous and help the fishes hide themselves in seaweed or coral. Some of these fishes live alone and are aggressive in defending their territory. Others gather in groups of hundreds in open water to look for food. Some species form mating pairs that patrol a home territory. Scientists know little about the reproduction of pufferfishes, triggerfishes, and their relatives. Some release eggs that sink to the bottom, and others release eggs that drift in open water. Some lay eggs in nests on the bottom and guard them. The eggs of most of these fishes hatch into free-floating larvae (LAR-vee), or the early stage that must change form before becoming adults.

PUFFERFISHES, TRIGGERFISHES, THEIR RELATIVES, AND PEOPLE

Many pufferfishes, triggerfishes, and their relatives are eaten by the people who live near where the fish live. Some of these fishes are caught for sport. Some are caught and sold for food but must be prepared very carefully because they are poisonous. Many species are collected for aquariums.

CONSERVATION STATUS

The World Conservation Union (IUCN) lists three species of pufferfishes, triggerfishes, and their relatives as Vulnerable, or facing a high risk of extinction in the wild.

Clown triggerfish (*Balistoides conspicillum*)

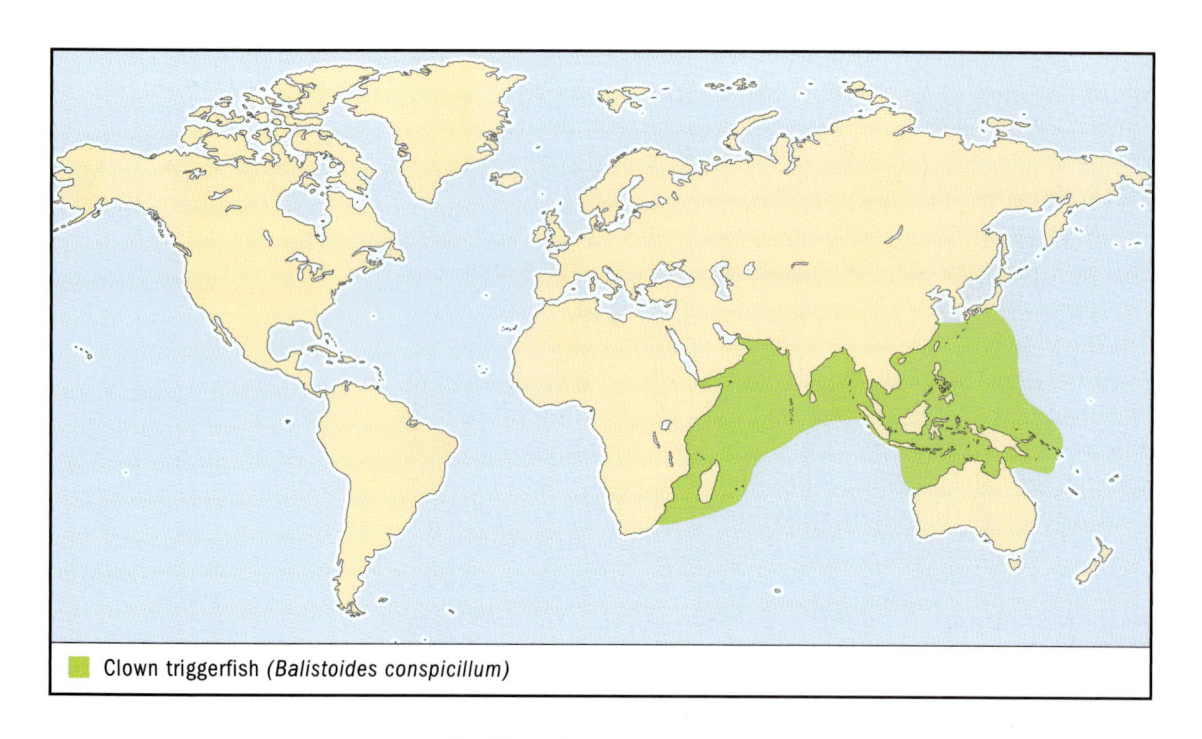

SPECIES ACCOUNTS

CLOWN TRIGGERFISH
Balistoides conspicillum

Physical characteristics: Clown triggerfish have an oval body that is narrow from side to side. The pelvic fins are fused into a single spine. There are three spines in the front dorsal fin. The second spine is the trigger for locking the first spine into an upright position. Clown triggerfish grow to a length of about 20 inches (50 centimeters). The bright color pattern of clown triggerfish gives the fish their name. The black background is covered by large white ovals on the bottom half and yellow rings on the upper half of the fish. The breast is white, and there is a white band below the eyes. The tail is white, and there is a pattern of black, white, black on the tail fin. Starting at the tip, the mouth colors are a wide band of yellow or orangish yellow, a narrow band of black, and a thin yellow stripe. The bases of the anal fin and the rear dorsal fin are light yellow. The anal (AY-nuhl) fin is the one along the midline of the belly. The dorsal (DOOR-suhl) fin is the one along the midline of the back. The pectoral (PECK-ter-uhl) fins correspond to the front legs and the pelvic fins to the rear legs of four-footed animals.

Clown triggerfish use their locking first dorsal spine as a defense against predators. (©Fred McConnaughey/Photo Researchers, Inc. Reproduced by permission.)

Geographic range: Clown triggerfish live in the Indian Ocean and the western part of the Pacific Ocean.

Habitat: Clown triggerfish live mainly on reefs.

Diet: Clown triggerfish eat bottom-dwelling invertebrates.

Behavior and reproduction: Clown triggerfish use their locking first dorsal spine as a defense against predators (PREH-duh-ters), or animals that hunt and kill other animals for food. These fish live alone and aggressively defend their territory. They spawn in pairs, laying eggs in a nest on the bottom and defending it. The larvae drift in the water.

Clown triggerfish and people: Clown triggerfish are used in aquariums.

Conservation status: Clown triggerfish are not threatened or endangered. ∎

White-spotted puffer (Arothron hispidus)

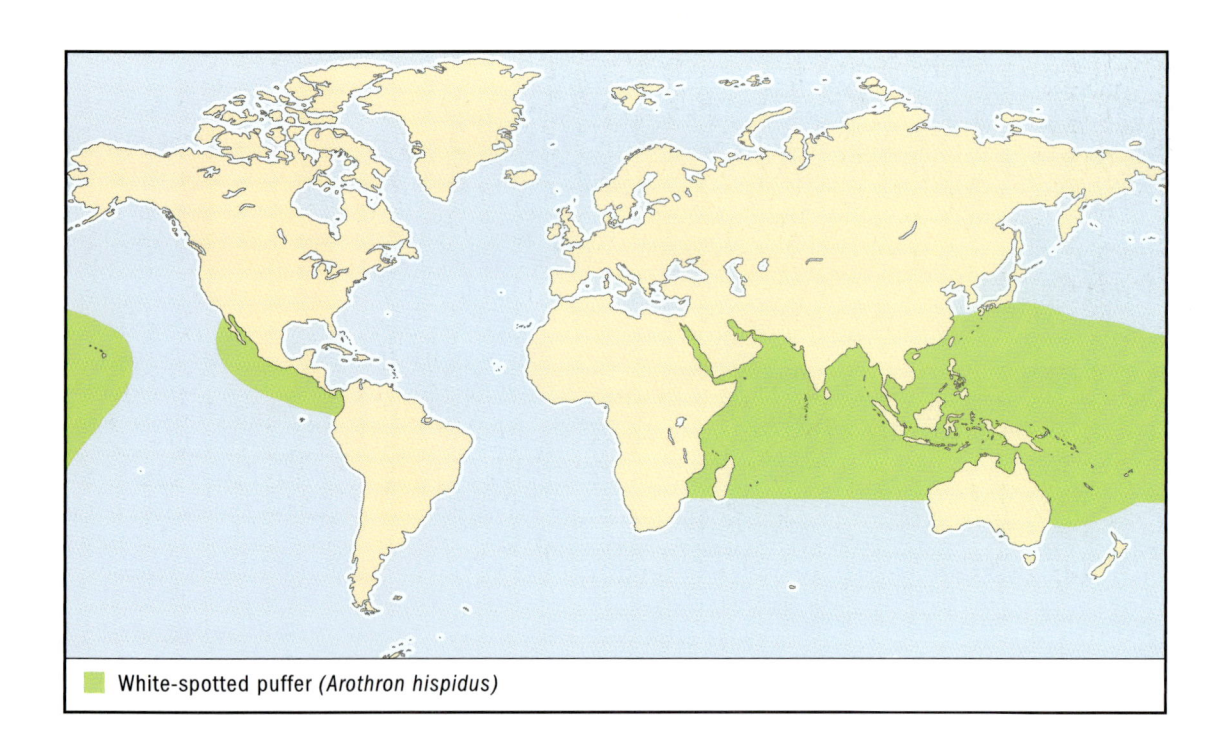

WHITE-SPOTTED PUFFER
Arothron hispidus

Physical characteristics: White-spotted puffers have a long thick body. Except for the snout and tail, the body is covered with small spines. The teeth are fused to one another. The dorsal and anal fins are short. The tail fin is rounded. Two fleshy tentacles emerge from each nostril. The color is greenish brown with small white spots on the back, sides, and tail fin. The belly has white bars. White-spotted puffers grow to a length of about 20 inches (50 centimeters).

Geographic range: White-spotted puffers live in the Indian Ocean and on both sides of the Pacific Ocean.

Habitat: White-spotted puffers live on reefs.

Diet: White-spotted puffers eat algae, waste material, and invertebrates.

Behavior and reproduction: To protect themselves from predators, white-spotted puffers rapidly fill themselves up like a water balloon. These fish live alone and are territorial. They may bury themselves

White-spotted puffers live alone and are territorial. They may bury themselves partially in the sand. (Carol Buchanan-V&W/ Bruce Coleman Inc. Reproduced by permission.)

partially in the sand. Scientists know little about how white-spotted puffers reproduce. The fish probably lay eggs on the bottom. The larvae drift in open water.

White-spotted puffers and people: White-spotted puffers are collected for aquariums.

Conservation status: White-spotted puffers are not threatened or endangered. ∎

Spotted toby (*Canthigaster solandri*)

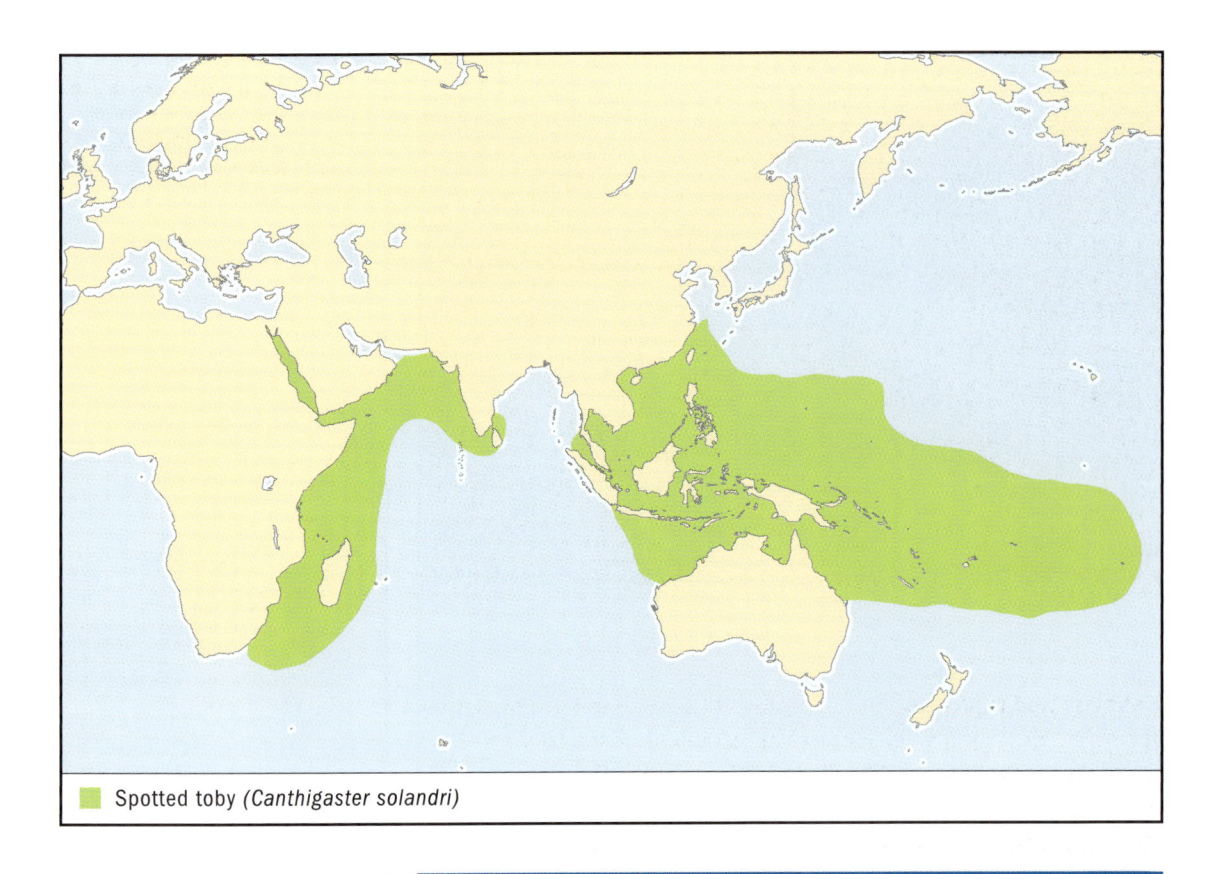

SPOTTED TOBY
Canthigaster solandri

Physical characteristics: Spotted tobies have a thick oval body, a long snout, prickles on the belly, and a rounded tail fin. They are orangish red with blue spots. The belly is white. There is a black spot ringed in pale blue directly below the base of the dorsal fin. The dorsal fin is short and white with a black base. The anal fin also is short. The skin contains a poison. Spotted tobies grow to a length of about 4 inches (10 centimeters).

Geographic range: Spotted tobies live in the western parts of the Indian and Pacific oceans.

Habitat: Spotted tobies live mainly in reefs.

Diet: Spotted tobies eat invertebrates and algae.

To protect themselves from predators, spotted tobies rapidly fill themselves up like a water balloon. (Kelvin Aitkin-V&W/ Bruce Coleman, Inc. Reproduced by permission.)

Behavior and reproduction: To protect themselves from predators, spotted tobies rapidly fill themselves up like a water balloon. They usually pair up but also live alone or in groups. They swim over a home range looking for food. They also swim up into open water. Pairs of spotted tobies lay eggs on algae growing on dead coral and rocks. The eggs are poisonous, and the fish do not take care of them. The larvae float in open water.

Spotted tobies and people: Spotted tobies are collected for aquariums.

Conservation status: Spotted tobies are not threatened or endangered.

FOR MORE INFORMATION

Books:

Allen, Missy, and Michel Peissel. *Dangerous Water Creatures*. New York: Chelsea House, 1992.

Gilbert, Carter Rowell, and James D. Williams. *National Audubon Society Field Guide to Fishes: North America*. New York: Knopf, 2002.

Niesen, Thomas M. *The Marine Biology Coloring Book*. 2nd ed. New York: HarperResource, 2000.

Ricciuti, Edward R. *Fish*. Woodbridge, CT: Blackbirch, 1993.

Web sites:

"Marine Life Profile: Clown Triggerfish." Waikiki Aquarium Education Department. http://waquarium.mic.hawaii.edu/MLP/root/pdf/MarineLife/Vertebrates/ClownTriggerfish.pdf (accessed on November 9, 2004).

"Pufferfish." All Science Fair Projects. http://www.all-science-fair-projects.com/science_fair_projects_encyclopedia/Pufferfish (accessed on November 9, 2004).

"Pufferfish Found to Contain Saxitoxin." *Neuroscience for Kids.* http://faculty.washington.edu/chudler/puffer.html (accessed on November 9, 2004).

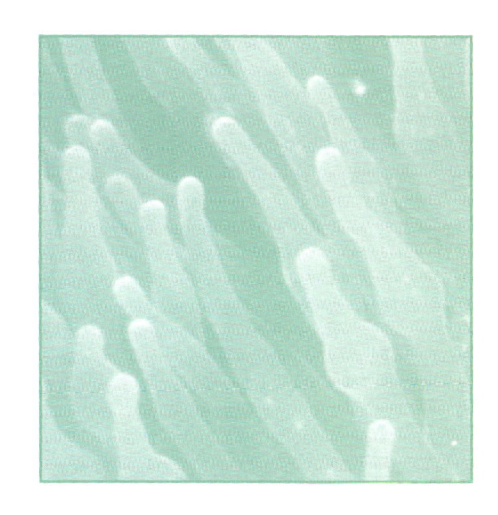

Species List by Biome

CONTINENTAL MARGIN
Atlantic cod
Atlantic manta
Atlantic mudskipper
Ayu
Bay anchovy
Blackbar soldierfish
Bluestreak cleaner wrasse
Butterfish
California flyingfish
California grunion
Californian needlefish
Clearnose skate
Clown triggerfish
Common dolphinfish
Common sole
Emerald notothen
Fire goby
Flathead mullet
Great barracuda
Green moray
Haddock
Inshore sand lance
Lancer dragonet
Largescale foureyes
Leafy seadragon
Lined seahorse
Lined surgeonfish
Lingcod
Miracle triplefin
Monkfish
Moorish idol
Nassau grouper
Northern stargazer
Ocean pout
Oriental helmet gurnard
Oyster toadfish
Pacific halibut
Peacock flounder
Pearlfish
Red boarfish
Red lionfish
Skinnycheek lanternfish
Slender giant moray
Sonora clingfish
Splitfin flashlightfish
Spotted ratfish
Spotted toby
Stout beardfish
Striped parrotfish
Striped poison-fang blenny
Threespine stickleback
Tiger shark
White shark
White-spotted puffer
Wolf-eel
Yellow tang

LAKE AND POND
Atlantic salmon
Australian smelt
Ayu
Bichir
Blackfin pearl killifish
Bowfin
Brook trout
Channel catfish
Chinook salmon
Climbing perch
Electric eel
Freshwater angelfish
Giant tigerfish
Green swordtail
Largemouth bass
Marble sleeper
Marbled swamp eel
Milkfish
Muskellunge
Pirate perch
Red-bellied piranha
Sea lamprey
Siamese fighting fish
Silver carp
Spotted gar
Squarehead catfish
Striped snakehead

OCEAN
American eel
Atlantic bluefin tuna

Atlantic hagfish
Atlantic manta
Atlantic salmon
Atlantic tarpon
Beluga sturgeon
Blue marlin
Bonefish
Chinook salmon
Coelacanth
Common dolphinfish
Great barracuda
Gulper eel
Hairyfish
Longnose lancetfish
Milkfish
Miracle triplefin
Oarfish
Oriental helmet gurnard
Rat-trap fish
Sargassumfish
Sea lamprey
Skinnycheek lanternfish
Threespine stickleback
Tripodfish

Viperfish
White shark

RIVER AND STREAM

American eel
Atlantic salmon
Atlantic tarpon
Australian smelt
Ayu
Banded archerfish
Beluga sturgeon
Bichir
Bowfin
Brook trout
Candiru
Channel catfish
Chinook salmon
Climbing perch
Clown loach
Electric eel
Flathead mullet
Freshwater angelfish
Freshwater butterflyfish
Giant tigerfish

Glass knifefish
Golden perch
Green swordtail
Largemouth bass
Largescale foureyes
Marble sleeper
Marbled swamp eel
Muskellunge
Red-bellied piranha
River hatchetfish
Sea lamprey
Silver carp
Slender giant moray
South American lungfish
Spotted gar
Squarehead catfish
Stoneroller
Threespine stickleback

SEASHORE

Bonefish
California grunion
Lined seahorse
Sea lamprey

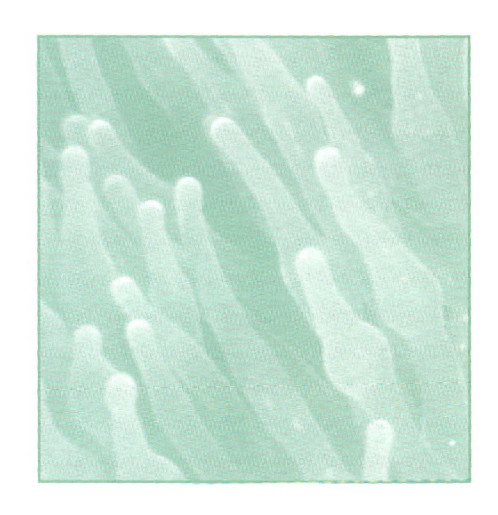

Species List by Geographic Range

ALBANIA
Beluga sturgeon
Common sole
Flathead mullet
Threespine stickleback

ALGERIA
Common sole
Flathead mullet
Threespine stickleback
White shark

ANGOLA
Atlantic mudskipper
Atlantic tarpon
Bichir
Flathead mullet
Freshwater butterflyfish
Giant tigerfish
White shark

ANTARCTICA
Emerald notothen

ANTIGUA AND BARBUDA
Atlantic manta
Atlantic tarpon
Bonefish
Flathead mullet
Lancer dragonet
Lined seahorse
Nassau grouper
Peacock flounder
Pearlfish
Striped parrotfish
Tiger shark

ARCTIC OCEAN
Atlantic hagfish
Chinook salmon

ARGENTINA
Atlantic tarpon
Blackfin pearl killifish
Flathead mullet
Glass knifefish
Marbled swamp eel
Red-bellied piranha
White shark

ARMENIA
Flathead mullet
Beluga sturgeon

ATLANTIC OCEAN
American eel
Atlantic bluefin tuna
Atlantic cod
Atlantic hagfish
Atlantic salmon
Blackbar soldierfish
Blue marlin
Bonefish
Butterfish
Common dolphinfish
Common sole
Great barracuda
Green moray
Gulper eel
Haddock
Hairyfish
Lancer dragonet
Lined seahorse
Longnose lancetfish
Monkfish
Nassau grouper
Oarfish
Peacock flounder
Pearlfish
Rat-trap fish
Sargassumfish
Sea lamprey
Stout beardfish
Striped parrotfish
Threespine stickleback
Tiger shark
Tripodfish
Viperfish

AUSTRALIA
Atlantic manta
Australian smelt
Banded archerfish
Bluestreak cleaner wrasse
Bonefish
Clown triggerfish
Flathead mullet
Golden perch
Leafy seadragon
Lined surgeonfish
Moorish idol
Miracle triplefin
Oriental helmet gurnard
Red boarfish
Red lionfish
Slender giant moray
Spotted toby
Striped poison-fang blenny
Tiger shark
White shark
White-spotted puffer

AZERBAIJAN
Beluga sturgeon
Flathead mullet

BAHAMAS
Atlantic tarpon
Bonefish
Butterfish
Flathead mullet
Lancer dragonet
Lined seahorse
Nassau grouper
Peacock flounder
Pearlfish
Striped parrotfish
Tiger shark

BAHRAIN
Atlantic manta
Bonefish
Flathead mullet
Moorish idol
Tiger shark
White-spotted puffer

BANGLADESH
Atlantic manta
Bonefish
Climbing perch
Clown triggerfish
Flathead mullet
Lined surgeonfish
Moorish idol
Oriental helmet gurnard
Squarehead catfish
Striped snakehead
Tiger shark
White-spotted puffer

BARBADOS
American eel
Atlantic manta
Atlantic tarpon
Bonefish
Flathead mullet
Green moray
Lancer dragonet
Lined seahorse
Nassau grouper
Peacock flounder
Pearlfish
Striped parrotfish
Tiger shark

BELARUS
Beluga sturgeon

BELGIUM
Atlantic cod
Atlantic salmon
Common sole
Haddock
Green swordtail
White shark

BELIZE
American eel
Atlantic tarpon
Bonefish
Flathead mullet
Lined seahorse
Marbled swamp eel
Nassau grouper
Peacock flounder
Striped parrotfish
Threespine stickleback
Tiger shark

BENIN
Atlantic mudskipper
Atlantic tarpon
Flathead mullet
Freshwater butterflyfish
Bonefish
Tiger shark

BOLIVIA
Electric eel
Glass knifefish
Marbled swamp eel
Red-bellied piranha
River hatchetfish
South American lungfish

BOSNIA AND HERZEGOVINA
Beluga sturgeon
Common sole
Flathead mullet
Threespine stickleback

BOTSWANA
Freshwater butterflyfish

BRAZIL
Atlantic manta
Atlantic tarpon
Blackbar soldierfish
Bonefish
Candiru
Electric eel
Flathead mullet

Freshwater angelfish
Glass knifefish
Green moray
Largescale foureyes
Lined seahorse
Marbled swamp eel
Nassau grouper
Peacock flounder
Pearlfish
Red-bellied piranha
River hatchetfish
South American lungfish
Striped parrotfish
Tiger shark
White shark

BRUNEI
Atlantic manta
Bluestreak cleaner wrasse
Bonefish
Climbing perch
Clown triggerfish
Flathead mullet
Lined surgeonfish
Moorish idol
Oriental helmet gurnard
Red lionfish
Spotted toby
Striped snakehead
Tiger shark
White-spotted puffer

BULGARIA
Beluga sturgeon
Flathead mullet
Threespine stickleback

BURUNDI
Bichir

CAMBODIA
Atlantic manta
Banded archerfish
Bluestreak cleaner wrasse
Bonefish
Climbing perch
Clown triggerfish
Flathead mullet
Lined surgeonfish
Marble sleeper
Moorish idol
Oriental helmet gurnard
Red lionfish
Siamese fighting fish
Spotted toby
Striped snakehead
Tiger shark
White-spotted puffer

CAMEROON
Atlantic mudskipper
Atlantic tarpon
Flathead mullet
Freshwater butterflyfish
Bonefish
Tiger shark

CANADA
American eel
Atlantic cod
Atlantic salmon
Atlantic tarpon
Bowfin
Brook trout
Butterfish
Channel catfish
Chinook salmon
Flathead mullet
Green moray
Haddock
Inshore sand lance
Largemouth bass
Lingcod
Monkfish
Muskellunge
Ocean pout
Pacific halibut
Sea lamprey
Spotted ratfish
Stoneroller
Threespine stickleback
White shark

CAPE VERDE
Atlantic manta
Bonefish
Green moray
Tiger shark

CHAD
Freshwater butterflyfish

CHILE
Flathead mullet
White shark

CHINA
Atlantic manta
Ayu
Banded archerfish
Bluestreak cleaner wrasse
Bonefish
Climbing perch
Clown triggerfish
Fire goby
Flathead mullet
Lined surgeonfish
Moorish idol
Oriental helmet gurnard
Red boarfish
Red lionfish
Silver carp
Slender giant moray
Spotted toby
Striped poison-fang blenny
Tiger shark
White shark
White-spotted puffer

COLOMBIA
Atlantic manta
Atlantic tarpon
Blackbar soldierfish

Species List by Geographic Range

Bonefish
Californian needlefish
Candiru
Electric eel
Flathead mullet
Freshwater angelfish
Glass knifefish
Green moray
Lined seahorse
Marbled swamp eel
Moorish idol
Nassau grouper
Peacock flounder
South American lungfish
Red-bellied piranha
River hatchetfish
Striped parrotfish
Tiger shark
White-spotted puffer

COMOROS
Bonefish
Fire goby
Flathead mullet
Lined surgeonfish
Moorish idol
Oriental helmet gurnard
Red lionfish
Spotted toby
Tiger shark
White-spotted puffer

COSTA RICA
American eel
Atlantic manta
Bonefish
Californian needlefish
Flathead mullet
Lined seahorse
Marbled swamp eel
Moorish idol
Nassau grouper
Peacock flounder
Striped parrotfish
Tiger shark
White-spotted puffer

CROATIA
Beluga sturgeon
Common sole
Flathead mullet
Threespine stickleback

CUBA
American eel
Atlantic manta
Atlantic tarpon
Blackbar soldierfish
Bonefish
Butterfish
Flathead mullet
Lancer dragonet
Lined seahorse
Nassau grouper
Peacock flounder
Pearlfish
Striped parrotfish
Tiger shark

CYPRUS
Common sole
Flathead mullet
Threespine stickleback

DEMOCRATIC REPUBLIC OF THE CONGO
Atlantic mudskipper
Atlantic tarpon
Bichir
Flathead mullet
Freshwater butterflyfish
Giant tigerfish

DENMARK
Atlantic salmon
Haddock
Threespine stickleback

DJIBOUTI
Atlantic manta
Bluestreak cleaner wrasse

Bonefish
Clown triggerfish
Flathead mullet
Moorish idol
Oriental helmet gurnard
Red lionfish
Spotted toby
Tiger shark
White-spotted puffer

DOMINICAN REPUBLIC
American eel
Atlantic manta
Atlantic tarpon
Blackbar soldierfish
Bonefish
Flathead mullet
Lancer dragonet
Lined seahorse
Nassau grouper
Peacock flounder
Pearlfish
Striped parrotfish
Tiger shark

ECUADOR
Atlantic manta
Bonefish
Californian needlefish
Electric eel
Flathead mullet
Glass knifefish
Green moray
Marbled swamp eel
Moorish idol
River hatchetfish
Tiger shark
White shark

EGYPT
Atlantic manta
Bluestreak cleaner wrasse
Bonefish
Flathead mullet
Moorish idol

Red lionfish
Spotted toby
Threespine stickleback
Tiger shark
White shark
White-spotted puffer

EL SALVADOR
Atlantic manta
Bonefish
Californian needlefish
Flathead mullet
Marbled swamp eel
Moorish idol
Tiger shark
White-spotted puffer

ERITREA
Atlantic manta
Bluestreak cleaner wrasse
Bonefish
Flathead mullet
Moorish idol
Oriental helmet gurnard
Red lionfish
Spotted toby
Tiger shark
White-spotted puffer

ESTONIA
Threespine stickleback

FIJI
Atlantic manta
Bluestreak cleaner wrasse
Bonefish
Fire goby
Flathead mullet
Lined surgeonfish
Moorish idol
Oriental helmet gurnard
Red lionfish
Slender giant moray
Spotted toby

Tiger shark
White-spotted puffer

FINLAND
Atlantic cod
Atlantic salmon
Threespine stickleback

FRANCE
Atlantic cod
Atlantic salmon
Common sole
Flathead mullet
Haddock
Sea lamprey
Threespine stickleback
White shark

FRENCH GUIANA
Atlantic manta
Atlantic tarpon
Blackbar soldierfish
Bonefish
Candiru
Electric eel
Flathead mullet
Freshwater angelfish
Glass knifefish
Green moray
Lancer dragonet
Largescale foureyes
Lined seahorse
Marbled swamp eel
Nassau grouper
Peacock flounder
Pearlfish
Red-bellied piranha
South American lungfish
Striped parrotfish
Tiger shark

GABON
Atlantic mudskipper
Bonefish

Flathead mullet
Tiger shark

GAMBIA
Atlantic mudskipper
Atlantic tarpon
Bonefish
Flathead mullet
Freshwater butterflyfish
Tiger shark

GEORGIA
Beluga sturgeon
Flathead mullet

GERMANY
Atlantic cod
Atlantic salmon
Common sole
Haddock
Threespine stickleback

GHANA
Atlantic mudskipper
Atlantic tarpon
Bonefish
Flathead mullet
Tiger shark

GREECE
Common sole
Flathead mullet
Threespine stickleback
White shark

GREENLAND
Atlantic cod
Sea lamprey

GRENADA
American eel
Atlantic manta
Atlantic tarpon

Bonefish
Flathead mullet
Green moray
Lancer dragonet
Lined seahorse
Nassau grouper
Peacock flounder
Pearlfish
Striped parrotfish
Tiger shark

GUAM
Bluestreak cleaner wrasse
Bonefish
Flathead mullet
Tiger shark

GUATEMALA
Atlantic manta
Bonefish
Californian needlefish
Flathead mullet
Green swordtail
Lined seahorse
Marbled swamp eel
Moorish idol
Peacock flounder
Striped parrotfish
Tiger shark
White-spotted puffer

GUINEA
Atlantic mudskipper
Atlantic tarpon
Bonefish
Flathead mullet
Tiger shark

GUINEA-BISSAU
Atlantic mudskipper
Atlantic tarpon
Bonefish
Flathead mullet
Tiger shark

GUYANA
Atlantic manta
Atlantic tarpon
Blackbar soldierfish
Bonefish
Candiru
Electric eel
Flathead mullet
Freshwater angelfish
Glass knifefish
Green moray
Lancer dragonet
Largescale foureyes
Lined seahorse
Marbled swamp eel
Nassau grouper
Peacock flounder
Pearlfish
Red-bellied piranha
River hatchetfish
Striped parrotfish
Tiger shark

HAITI
American eel
Atlantic manta
Atlantic tarpon
Blackbar soldierfish
Bonefish
Lancer dragonet
Lined seahorse
Nassau grouper
Peacock flounder
Pearlfish
Striped parrotfish
Tiger shark

HONDURAS
American eel
Atlantic manta
Atlantic tarpon
Bonefish
Californian needlefish
Flathead mullet
Green swordtail

Lined seahorse
Marbled swamp eel
Nassau grouper
Peacock flounder
Striped parrotfish
Tiger shark

ICELAND
Atlantic cod
Atlantic salmon
Bonefish
Haddock
Tiger shark

INDIA
Atlantic manta
Banded archerfish
Bluestreak cleaner wrasse
Bonefish
Climbing perch
Clown triggerfish
Flathead mullet
Lined surgeonfish
Moorish idol
Oriental helmet gurnard
Red lionfish
Slender giant moray
Spotted toby
Squarehead catfish
Striped snakehead
Tiger shark
White-spotted puffer

INDIAN OCEAN
Blue marlin
Bluestreak cleaner wrasse
Bonefish
Clown triggerfish
Coelacanth
Common dolphinfish
Fire goby
Great barracuda
Lined surgeonfish
Milkfish
Moorish idol
Oarfish

Oriental helmet gurnard
Rat-trap fish
Red lionfish
Sargassumfish
Skinnycheek lanternfish
Slender giant moray
Spotted toby
Tiger shark
Viperfish
White-spotted puffer

INDONESIA
Atlantic manta
Banded archerfish
Bluestreak cleaner wrasse
Bonefish
Climbing perch
Clown loach
Clown triggerfish
Fire goby
Flathead mullet
Lined surgeonfish
Marble sleeper
Moorish idol
Oriental helmet gurnard
Red lionfish
Splitfin flashlightfish
Spotted toby
Striped poison-fang blenny
Striped snakehead
Tiger shark
White-spotted puffer

IRAN
Atlantic manta
Beluga sturgeon
Bonefish
Clown triggerfish
Flathead mullet
Moorish idol
Tiger shark
White-spotted puffer

IRAQ
Bonefish
Flathead mullet

Moorish idol
Tiger shark
White-spotted puffer

IRELAND
Atlantic cod
Atlantic salmon
Bonefish
Common sole
Flathead mullet
Haddock
Sea lamprey
Threespine stickleback
Tiger shark

ISRAEL
Atlantic manta
Flathead mullet
Threespine stickleback

ITALY
Beluga sturgeon
Common sole
Flathead mullet
Sea lamprey
Threespine stickleback
White shark

IVORY COAST
Atlantic mudskipper
Atlantic tarpon
Bonefish
Flathead mullet
Tiger shark

JAMAICA
American eel
Atlantic manta
Blackbar soldierfish
Bonefish
Flathead mullet
Lancer dragonet
Lined seahorse

Nassau grouper
Peacock flounder
Pearlfish
Striped parrotfish
Tiger shark

JAPAN
Atlantic manta
Ayu
Bonefish
Chinook salmon
Fire goby
Flathead mullet
Lined surgeonfish
Moorish idol
Oriental helmet gurnard
Pacific halibut
Red lionfish
Splitfin flashlightfish
Threespine stickleback
Tiger shark
White shark
White-spotted puffer

JORDAN
Atlantic manta
Flathead mullet

KAZAKHSTAN
Flathead mullet
Beluga sturgeon

KENYA
Atlantic manta
Bonefish
Clown triggerfish
Flathead mullet
Lined surgeonfish
Moorish idol
Oriental helmet gurnard
Red lionfish
Spotted toby
Tiger shark
White-spotted puffer

KIRIBATI
Bluestreak cleaner wrasse
Bonefish
Fire goby
Flathead mullet
Lined surgeonfish
Moorish idol
Oriental helmet gurnard
Red lionfish
Spotted toby
Tiger shark
White-spotted puffer

KUWAIT
Atlantic manta
Bonefish
Flathead mullet
Moorish idol
Tiger shark
White-spotted puffer

LAOS
Marble sleeper

LATVIA
Threespine stickleback

LEBANON
Flathead mullet
Threespine stickleback

LESSER ANTILLES
American eel
Atlantic manta
Atlantic tarpon
Bonefish
Flathead mullet
Green moray
Lancer dragonet
Lined seahorse
Nassau grouper
Peacock flounder
Pearlfish

Striped parrotfish
Tiger shark

LIBERIA
Atlantic mudskipper
Atlantic tarpon
Bonefish
Flathead mullet
Tiger shark

LIBYA
Common sole
Flathead mullet
Threespine stickleback
White shark

LITHUANIA
Threespine stickleback

MACEDONIA
Common sole
Flathead mullet
Threespine stickleback

MADAGASCAR
Atlantic manta
Bonefish
Flathead mullet
Lined surgeonfish
Moorish idol
Oriental helmet gurnard
Red lionfish
Slender giant moray
Spotted toby
Tiger shark
White shark
White-spotted puffer

MALAYSIA
Atlantic manta
Banded archerfish
Bluestreak cleaner wrasse
Bonefish

Climbing perch
Clown triggerfish
Flathead mullet
Lined surgeonfish
Marble sleeper
Moorish idol
Oriental helmet gurnard
Red lionfish
Siamese fighting fish
Splitfin flashlightfish
Spotted toby
Striped snakehead
Tiger shark
White-spotted puffer

MALDIVES
Bluestreak cleaner wrasse
Bonefish
Tiger shark
White-spotted puffer

MALTA
Flathead mullet
Threespine stickleback

MARIANA ISLANDS
Bluestreak cleaner wrasse
Bonefish
Flathead mullet
Lined surgeonfish
Moorish idol
Spotted toby
Tiger shark
Yellow tang
White-spotted puffer

MARSHALL ISLANDS
Bluestreak cleaner wrasse
Bonefish
Fire goby
Flathead mullet
Lined surgeonfish
Moorish idol
Spotted toby

Tiger shark
Yellow tang
White-spotted puffer

MAURITANIA
Atlantic tarpon
Bonefish
Common sole
Flathead mullet
Tiger shark

MAURITIUS
Bonefish
Fire goby
Flathead mullet
Lined surgeonfish
Moorish idol
Tiger shark
White-spotted puffer

MEXICO
American eel
Atlantic manta
Atlantic tarpon
Bay anchovy
Bonefish
Butterfish
California grunion
Californian needlefish
Channel catfish
Clearnose skate
Flathead mullet
Green moray
Green swordtail
Lancer dragonet
Marbled swamp eel
Moorish idol
Nassau grouper
Peacock flounder
Sonora clingfish
Spotted gar
Spotted ratfish
Stoneroller
Striped parrotfish
Threespine stickleback

Tiger shark
White shark
White-spotted puffer

MICRONESIA
Atlantic manta
Bluestreak cleaner wrasse
Bonefish
Clown triggerfish
Flathead mullet
Lined surgeonfish
Moorish idol
Oriental helmet gurnard
Red lionfish
Spotted toby
Tiger shark
Yellow tang

MOLDOVA
Beluga sturgeon
Flathead mullet
Threespine stickleback

MONACO
Common sole
Flathead mullet
Sea lamprey
Threespine stickleback

MONGOLIA
Silver carp

MOROCCO
Atlantic tarpon
Bonefish
Common sole
Flathead mullet
Tiger shark
White shark

MOZAMBIQUE
Atlantic manta
Bonefish
Clown triggerfish

Fire goby
Flathead mullet
Lined surgeonfish
Moorish idol
Oriental helmet gurnard
Red lionfish
Slender giant moray
Spotted toby
Tiger shark
White shark
White-spotted puffer

MYANMAR
Atlantic manta
Banded archerfish
Bonefish
Climbing perch
Clown triggerfish
Flathead mullet
Lined surgeonfish
Moorish idol
Oriental helmet gurnard
Red lionfish
Striped snakehead
Tiger shark
White-spotted puffer

NAMIBIA
Atlantic tarpon
Flathead mullet
Freshwater butterflyfish
White shark

NAURU
Bluestreak cleaner wrasse
Bonefish
Clown triggerfish
Flathead mullet
Lined surgeonfish
Moorish idol
Oriental helmet gurnard
Red lionfish
Spotted toby
Tiger shark
White-spotted puffer

NEPAL
Squarehead catfish

NETHERLANDS
Atlantic cod
Atlantic salmon
Common sole
Haddock
Sea lamprey
Threespine stickleback
White shark

NEW ZEALAND
Bonefish
Flathead mullet
Tiger shark
White shark

NICARAGUA
American eel
Atlantic tarpon
Bonefish
Californian needlefish
Flathead mullet
Lined seahorse
Marbled swamp eel
Moorish idol
Nassau grouper
Peacock flounder
Striped parrotfish
Tiger shark
White-spotted puffer

NIGER
Freshwater butterflyfish

NIGERIA
Atlantic mudskipper
Atlantic tarpon
Bonefish
Flathead mullet
Freshwater butterflyfish
Tiger shark

NORTH KOREA
Atlantic manta
Ayu
Lined surgeonfish
Moorish idol
Red lionfish
Threespine stickleback
White shark

NORWAY
Atlantic cod
Atlantic salmon
Common sole
Haddock
Sea lamprey
Threespine stickleback

OMAN
Atlantic manta
Bonefish
Clown triggerfish
Flathead mullet
Moorish idol
Oriental helmet gurnard
Spotted toby
Tiger shark
White-spotted puffer

PACIFIC OCEAN
Blue marlin
Bluestreak cleaner wrasse
Bonefish
Chinook salmon
Clown triggerfish
Common dolphinfish
Fire goby
Great barracuda
Green moray
Lined surgeonfish
Longnose lancetfish
Milkfish
Miracle triplefin
Moorish idol
Oarfish
Oriental helmet gurnard
Pacific halibut

Ragfish
Rat-trap fish
Red boarfish
Red lionfish
Sargassumfish
Skinnycheek lanternfish
Slender giant moray
Splitfin flashlightfish
Spotted ratfish
Spotted toby
Striped poison-fang blenny
Threespine stickleback
Tiger shark
Viperfish
White shark
White-spotted puffer
Yellow tang

PAKISTAN
Atlantic manta
Bonefish
Climbing perch
Clown triggerfish
Flathead mullet
Moorish idol
Oriental helmet gurnard
Spotted toby
Striped snakehead
Tiger shark
White-spotted puffer

PALAU
Atlantic manta
Bluestreak cleaner wrasse
Bonefish
Clown triggerfish
Flathead mullet
Lined surgeonfish
Moorish idol
Red lionfish
Splitfin flashlightfish
Spotted toby
Tiger shark
Yellow tang
White-spotted puffer

PANAMA
American eel
Atlantic manta
Atlantic tarpon
Bonefish
Californian needlefish
Flathead mullet
Lined seahorse
Marbled swamp eel
Moorish idol
Nassau grouper
Peacock flounder
Striped parrotfish
Tiger shark
White-spotted puffer

PAPUA NEW GUINEA
Atlantic manta
Banded archerfish
Bluestreak cleaner wrasse
Bonefish
Clown triggerfish
Fire goby
Flathead mullet
Miracle triplefin
Oriental helmet gurnard
Red lionfish
Slender giant moray
Splitfin flashlightfish
Spotted toby
Striped poison-fang blenny
Tiger shark
White-spotted puffer

PARAGUAY
Glass knifefish
Marbled swamp eel
Red-bellied piranha
South American lungfish

PERU
Atlantic manta
Bonefish
Californian needlefish
Candiru
Electric eel
Flathead mullet
Freshwater angelfish
Glass knifefish
Green moray
Marbled swamp eel
Moorish idol
Red-bellied piranha
River hatchetfish
South American lungfish
Tiger shark
White shark

PHILIPPINES
Atlantic manta
Bluestreak cleaner wrasse
Bonefish
Climbing perch
Clown loach
Clown triggerfish
Fire goby
Flathead mullet
Lined surgeonfish
Marble sleeper
Moorish idol
Oriental helmet gurnard
Red boarfish
Red lionfish
Slender giant moray
Splitfin flashlightfish
Spotted toby
Striped poison-fang blenny
Tiger shark
White shark
White-spotted puffer

POLAND
Atlantic cod
Atlantic salmon
Common sole
Haddock
Threespine stickleback

PORTUGAL
Atlantic salmon
Flathead mullet
White shark

PUERTO RICO
American eel
Atlantic manta
Atlantic tarpon
Blackbar soldierfish
Bonefish
Flathead mullet
Green moray
Lancer dragonet
Nassau grouper
Peacock flounder
Pearlfish
Striped parrotfish
Tiger shark

QATAR
Atlantic manta
Bonefish
Flathead mullet
Moorish idol
Tiger shark
White-spotted puffer

REPUBLIC OF THE CONGO
Atlantic mudskipper
Atlantic tarpon
Bichir
Flathead mullet
Freshwater butterflyfish
Giant tigerfish

ROMANIA
Beluga sturgeon
Flathead mullet
Threespine stickleback

RUSSIA
Atlantic cod
Atlantic salmon
Beluga sturgeon
Chinook salmon
Flathead mullet
Haddock

Pacific halibut
Silver carp
Threespine stickleback
White shark

RWANDA
Bichir

ST. KITTS-NEVIS
American eel
Atlantic manta
Atlantic tarpon
Bonefish
Flathead mullet
Green moray
Lancer dragonet
Lined seahorse
Nassau grouper
Peacock flounder
Striped parrotfish
Tiger shark

ST. LUCIA
American eel
Atlantic manta
Atlantic tarpon
Bonefish
Flathead mullet
Green moray
Lancer dragonet
Lined seahorse
Nassau grouper
Peacock flounder
Striped parrotfish
Tiger shark

ST. VINCENT
American eel
Atlantic manta
Atlantic tarpon
Bonefish
Flathead mullet
Green moray
Lancer dragonet
Lined seahorse

Nassau grouper
Peacock flounder
Striped parrotfish
Tiger shark

SAMOA
Bluestreak cleaner wrasse
Bonefish
Flathead mullet
Lined surgeonfish
Moorish idol
Oriental helmet gurnard
Red lionfish
Spotted toby
Tiger shark
White-spotted puffer

SAN MARINO
Beluga sturgeon
Flathead mullet
Threespine stickleback

SÃO TOMÉ AND PRÍNCIPE
Atlantic mudskipper
Atlantic tarpon
Bonefish
Flathead mullet
Tiger shark

SAUDI ARABIA
Atlantic manta
Bluestreak cleaner wrasse
Bonefish
Flathead mullet
Moorish idol
Red lionfish
Spotted toby
Tiger shark
White-spotted puffer

SENEGAL
Atlantic mudskipper
Atlantic tarpon

Bonefish
Common sole
Flathead mullet
Tiger shark

SERBIA AND MONTENEGRO
Common sole
Flathead mullet
Threespine stickleback

SEYCHELLES
Bonefish
Fire goby
Flathead mullet
Oriental helmet gurnard
Spotted toby
Tiger shark
White shark
White-spotted puffer

SIERRA LEONE
Atlantic mudskipper
Atlantic tarpon
Bonefish
Flathead mullet
Tiger shark

SINGAPORE
Atlantic manta
Banded archerfish
Bluestreak cleaner wrasse
Bonefish
Climbing perch
Clown triggerfish
Flathead mullet
Lined surgeonfish
Moorish idol
Oriental helmet gurnard
Red lionfish
Spotted toby
Striped snakehead
Tiger shark
White-spotted puffer

SLOVENIA
Beluga sturgeon
Common sole
Flathead mullet
Threespine stickleback

SOLOMON ISLANDS
Atlantic manta
Banded archerfish
Bluestreak cleaner wrasse
Bonefish
Clown triggerfish
Fire goby
Lined surgeonfish
Moorish idol
Oriental helmet gurnard
Red lionfish
Splitfin flashlightfish
Spotted toby
Striped poison-fang blenny
Tiger shark
White-spotted puffer

SOMALIA
Atlantic manta
Bluestreak cleaner wrasse
Bonefish
Clown triggerfish
Flathead mullet
Lined surgeonfish
Moorish idol
Oriental helmet gurnard
Red lionfish
Spotted toby
Tiger shark
White-spotted puffer

SOUTH AFRICA
Atlantic manta
Bonefish
Clown triggerfish
Fire goby
Flathead mullet
Red lionfish

Slender giant moray
Spotted toby
Tiger shark
White shark

SOUTH KOREA
Atlantic manta
Ayu
Flathead mullet
Lined surgeonfish
Moorish idol
Red lionfish
Threespine stickleback
White shark

SPAIN
Atlantic salmon
Common sole
Flathead mullet
Sea lamprey
Threespine stickleback
White shark

SRI LANKA
Atlantic manta
Banded archerfish
Bluestreak cleaner wrasse
Bonefish
Clown triggerfish
Climbing perch
Flathead mullet
Lined surgeonfish
Moorish idol
Oriental helmet gurnard
Red lionfish
Slender giant moray
Spotted toby
Striped snakehead
Tiger shark
White-spotted puffer

SUDAN
Atlantic manta
Bonefish

Flathead mullet
Moorish idol
Red lionfish
Spotted toby
Tiger shark
White-spotted puffer

SURINAME
Atlantic manta
Atlantic tarpon
Blackbar soldierfish
Bonefish
Candiru
Electric eel
Flathead mullet
Glass knifefish
Green moray
Lancer dragonet
Largescale foureyes
Lined seahorse
Marbled swamp eel
Nassau grouper
Peacock flounder
Pearlfish
Red-bellied piranha
Striped parrotfish
Tiger shark

SWEDEN
Atlantic cod
Atlantic salmon
Common sole
Haddock
Sea lamprey
Threespine stickleback

SYRIA
Threespine stickleback

TAIWAN
Atlantic manta
Ayu
Banded archerfish
Bluestreak cleaner wrasse

Bonefish
Climbing perch
Clown triggerfish
Fire goby
Flathead mullet
Lined surgeonfish
Moorish idol
Oriental helmet gurnard
Red boarfish
Red lionfish
Silver carp
Slender giant moray
Spotted toby
Striped poison-fang blenny
Tiger shark
White shark
White-spotted puffer

TANZANIA
Atlantic manta
Bichir
Bonefish
Clown triggerfish
Flathead mullet
Lined surgeonfish
Moorish idol
Oriental helmet gurnard
Red lionfish
Spotted toby
Tiger shark
White-spotted puffer

THAILAND
Atlantic manta
Banded archerfish
Bluestreak cleaner wrasse
Bonefish
Climbing perch
Clown loach
Clown triggerfish
Flathead mullet
Lined surgeonfish
Marble sleeper
Moorish idol
Oriental helmet gurnard

Red lionfish
Siamese fighting fish
Spotted toby
Striped snakehead
Tiger shark
White-spotted puffer

TIMOR-LESTE
Atlantic manta
Bluestreak cleaner wrasse
Bonefish
Clown triggerfish
Flathead mullet
Lined surgeonfish
Moorish idol
Oriental helmet gurnard
Red lionfish
Spotted toby
Tiger shark
White-spotted puffer

TOGO
Atlantic mudskipper
Atlantic tarpon
Bonefish
Flathead mullet
Tiger shark

TONGA
Bluestreak cleaner wrasse
Bonefish
Flathead mullet
Lined surgeonfish
Moorish idol
Oriental helmet gurnard
Red lionfish
Spotted toby
Tiger shark
White-spotted puffer

TRINIDAD AND TOBAGO
American eel
Atlantic manta
Atlantic tarpon

Blackbar soldierfish
Bonefish
Flathead mullet
Green moray
Lancer dragonet
Largescale foureyes
Lined seahorse
Nassau grouper
Peacock flounder
Pearlfish
Striped parrotfish
Tiger shark

TUNISIA
Common sole
Flathead mullet
Threespine stickleback

TURKEY
Beluga sturgeon
Common sole
Flathead mullet
Threespine stickleback
White shark

TURKMENISTAN
Beluga sturgeon
Flathead mullet

TUVALU
Bluestreak cleaner wrasse
Bonefish
Fire goby
Flathead mullet
Lined surgeonfish
Moorish idol
Red lionfish
Oriental helmet gurnard
Spotted toby
Tiger shark
White-spotted puffer

UGANDA
Bichir

UKRAINE
Beluga sturgeon
Flathead mullet

UNITED ARAB EMIRATES
Atlantic manta
Bonefish
Flathead mullet
Moorish idol
Tiger shark
White-spotted puffer

UNITED KINGDOM
Atlantic cod
Atlantic salmon
Common sole
Flathead mullet
Haddock
Sea lamprey
Threespine stickleback
White shark

UNITED STATES
American eel
Atlantic cod
Atlantic manta
Atlantic salmon
Atlantic tarpon
Bay anchovy
Blackbar soldierfish
Bonefish
Bowfin
Brook trout
Butterfish
California flyingfish
California grunion
Californian needlefish
Channel catfish
Chinook salmon
Clearnose skate
Fire goby
Flathead mullet
Haddock
Inshore sand lance
Lancer dragonet
Largemouth bass
Lined seahorse
Lined surgeonfish
Lingcod
Monkfish
Moorish idol
Muskellunge
Nassau grouper
Northern stargazer
Ocean pout
Oriental helmet gurnard
Oyster toadfish
Pacific halibut
Peacock flounder
Pearlfish
Pirate perch
Red lionfish
Sea lamprey
Spotted gar
Spotted ratfish
Stoneroller
Striped parrotfish
Threespine stickleback
Tiger shark
White shark
White-spotted puffer
Wolf-eel
Yellow tang

URUGUAY
Atlantic tarpon
Blackfin pearl killifish
Bonefish
Flathead mullet
Glass knifefish
Lined seahorse
Marbled swamp eel
South American lungfish
Tiger shark
White shark

VANUATU
Atlantic manta
Banded archerfish
Bluestreak cleaner wrasse
Bonefish
Clown triggerfish
Fire goby
Flathead mullet
Lined surgeonfish
Miracle triplefin
Moorish idol
Oriental helmet gurnard
Red lionfish
Splitfin flashlightfish
Spotted toby
Tiger shark
White-spotted puffer

VENEZUELA
Atlantic manta
Atlantic tarpon
Blackbar soldierfish
Bonefish
Candiru
Electric eel
Flathead mullet
Glass knifefish
Green moray
Lancer dragonet
Largescale foureyes
Lined seahorse
Marbled swamp eel
Nassau grouper
Peacock flounder
Pearlfish
Red-bellied piranha
River hatchetfish
South American lungfish
Tiger shark

VIETNAM
Atlantic manta
Banded archerfish
Bluestreak cleaner wrasse
Bonefish
Climbing perch
Clown triggerfish
Flathead mullet
Lined surgeonfish

Species List by Geographic Range

Marble sleeper
Moorish idol
Oriental helmet gurnard
Siamese fighting fish
Spotted toby
Striped poison-fang blenny
Striped snakehead
Tiger shark
White shark
White-spotted puffer

YEMEN
Atlantic manta
Bluestreak cleaner wrasse
Bonefish
Clown triggerfish
Flathead mullet
Moorish idol
Oriental helmet gurnard
Red lionfish
Spotted toby

Tiger shark
White-spotted puffer

ZAMBIA
Freshwater butterflyfish
Giant tigerfish

ZIMBABWE
Freshwater butterflyfish

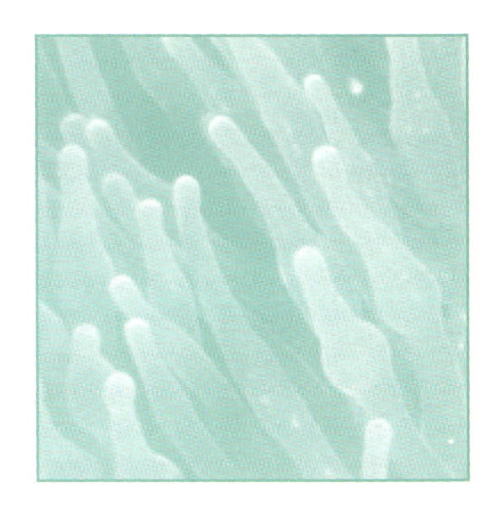

Index

Italic type indicates volume number; **boldface** type indicates entries and their pages; (ill.) indicates illustrations.

A

Acanthuroidei, 326–33
Acanthurus lineatus. See Lined surgeonfishes
Acipenseriformes. See Paddlefishes; Sturgeons
African mudfishes, 79, 80
Alabama sturgeons, 34
Albula vulpes. See Bonefishes
Albuliformes, 55–59
Alepisaurus ferox. See Longnose lancetfishes
Alligator gars, 38
American eels, 62–63, 62 (ill.), 63 (ill.)
Amia calva. See Bowfins
Amiiformes. See Bowfins
Ammodytes americanus. See Inshore sand lances
Anabantoidei. See Labyrinth fishes
Anabas testudineus. See Climbing perches
Anableps anableps. See Largescale foureyes
Anarrhichthys ocellatus. See Wolf-eels
Anchoa mitchilli. See Bay anchovies
Anchovies, 73, 74, 76–77, 76 (ill.), 77 (ill.)

Angelfishes, freshwater, 279–80, 279 (ill.), 280 (ill.)
Anglerfishes, 187–93
Angling, 188
Anguilla rostrata. See American eels
Anguilliformes. See Eels; Morays
Anomalops katoptron. See Splitfin flashlightfishes
Antifreeze, in southern codicefishes, 289
Antigonia rubescens. See Red boarfishes
Aphredoderus sayanus. See Pirate perches
Arapaimas, 47
Archerfishes, 260, 267–68, 267 (ill.), 268 (ill.)
Arkansas Department of Environmental Quality, 163
Arothron hispidus. See White-spotted puffers
Arowanas, 47
Asian arowanas, 47
Astroscopus guttatus. See Northern stargazers
Atheriniformes. See Rainbowfishes; Silversides
Atlantic bluefin tunas, 338–39, 338 (ill.), 339 (ill.)

Atlantic cods, 176–78, 176 (ill.), 177 (ill.)
Atlantic hagfishes, 3–4, 3 (ill.), 4 (ill.)
Atlantic mantas, 17–18, 17 (ill.), 18 (ill.)
Atlantic mudskippers, 322–23, 322 (ill.), 323 (ill.)
Atlantic salmons, 131–32, 131 (ill.), 132 (ill.)
Atlantic tarpons, 52–54, 52 (ill.), 53 (ill.)
Aulopiformes, 142–47
Australian smelts, 125–26, 125 (ill.), 126 (ill.)
Austrolebias nigripinnis. See Blackfin pearl killifishes
Ayu, 123–24, 123 (ill.), 124 (ill.)

B

Balistoides conspicillum. See Clown triggerfishes
Banded archerfishes, 267–68, 267 (ill.), 268 (ill.)
Barracudas, 334–42
Basses, 256–58, 261–62, 261 (ill.), 262 (ill.)
Bathypterois quadrifilis. See Tripodfishes

Batrachoidiformes. *See* Toadfishes
Bay anchovies, 76–77, 76 (ill.), 77 (ill.)
Beardfishes, 158–61
Beloniformes, 202–9
Beluga sturgeons, 35–36, 35 (ill.), 36 (ill.)
Beryciformes. *See* Flashlightfishes; Roughies; Squirrelfishes
Betta splendens. See Siamese fighting fishes
Bichirs, 28–31, 30 (ill.), 31 (ill.)
Blackbar soldierfishes, 227–28, 227 (ill.), 228 (ill.)
Blackfin pearl killifishes, 216–17, 216 (ill.), 217 (ill.)
Blackfishes. *See* Bowfins
Blennies, 299–304
Blennioidei. *See* Blennies
Blue marlins, 336–37, 336 (ill.), 337 (ill.)
Bluefin tunas, 335, 338–39, 338 (ill.), 339 (ill.)
Bluegills, 256
Bluestreak cleaner wrasses, 275–76, 275 (ill.), 276 (ill.)
Boarfishes, red, 231–32, 231 (ill.), 232 (ill.)
Bonefishes, 55–59, 57 (ill.), 58 (ill.)
Bony tongues, 46–49
Bothus lunatus. See Peacock flounders
Botia macraecanthus. See Clown loaches
Bottomfeeding fishes, 85
Bowfins, 41–45, 43 (ill.), 44 (ill.)
Brook trouts, 133–34, 133 (ill.), 134 (ill.)
Buckler dories, 230
Butterfishes, 343–46, 345 (ill.), 346 (ill.)
Butterflyfishes, freshwater, 48–49, 48 (ill.), 49 (ill.)

C

California flyingfishes, 205–6, 205 (ill.), 206 (ill.)
California grunions, 200–201, 200 (ill.), 201 (ill.)
Californian needlefishes, 207–8, 207 (ill.), 208 (ill.)
Callionymoidei, 313–16
Campostoma anomalum. See Stonerollers
Candirus, 102, 107–8, 107 (ill.), 108 (ill.)
Canthigaster solandri. See Spotted tobies
Cape dories, 229
Carapus bermudensis. See Pearlfishes
Carcharodon carcharias. See White sharks
Carps, 84–91
Catfishes, 101–8
Caviar, 33
Cephalaspidomorphi. *See* Lampreys
Chaca chaca. See Squarehead catfishes
Channa striata. See Striped snakeheads
Channel catfishes, 102, 103–4, 103 (ill.), 104 (ill.)
Channoidei. *See* Snakeheads
Chanos chanos. See Milkfishes
Characiformes. *See* Characins
Characins, 92–100
Chauliodus sloani. See Viperfishes
Cheilopogon pinnatibarbatus californicus. See California flyingfishes
Chimaeras, 9–20
Chinook salmons, 129–30, 129 (ill.), 130 (ill.)
Chondrichthyes. *See* Chimaeras; Rays; Sharks; Skates
Cichlids, 272–80
Ciguetera poison, 260

Class (Taxonomy), 257
Classification systems, 257
Cleaner gobies, 318
Cleaner wrasses, 273
Clearnose skates, 19–20, 19 (ill.), 20 (ill.)
Climbing perches, 349–50, 349 (ill.), 350 (ill.)
Clingfishes, 308–12
Clown knifefishes, 47
Clown loaches, 90–91, 90 (ill.), 91 (ill.)
Clown triggerfishes, 368–69, 368 (ill.), 369 (ill.)
Clupeiformes. *See* Herrings
Codicefishes, southern, 288–91
Cods, 173–80
Coelacanths, 21–27, 23 (ill.), 24 (ill.)
Common dolphinfishes, 263–64, 263 (ill.), 264 (ill.)
Common sole, 363–64, 363 (ill.), 364 (ill.)
Coryphaena hippurus. See Common dolphinfishes
Cottonfishes. *See* Bowfins
Cusk-eels, 167–72
Cypress trouts. *See* Bowfins
Cypriniformes, 84–91
Cyprinodontiformes. *See* Killifishes; Live-bearers

D

Dactyloptena orientalis. See Oriental helmet gurnards
Damselfishes, 272–74
Darters, 259–71
Dogfishes, freshwater. *See* Bowfins
Dolphinfishes, common, 263–64, 263 (ill.), 264 (ill.)
Dories, 229–32
Dragon fishes. *See* Asian arowanas
Dragonets, 313–16

Dragonfishes, 136–41
Dwarf gobies, 318

E

Eelpouts, 281–87
Eels, 1, 60–67
    cusk, 167–72
    electric, 109–15, 111 (ill.), 112 (ill.)
    gulper, 70–71, 70 (ill.), 71 (ill.)
    spiny, 55–56, 242–46
    swamp, 242–46
    wolf, 256, 281, 282, 283–84, 283 (ill.), 284 (ill.)
Eggs, sturgeon, 33
Eigenmannia lineata. See Glass knifefishes
Electric eels, 109–15, 111 (ill.), 112 (ill.)
Electrophorus electricus. See Electric eels
Elephantfishes, 47
Elephantnose fishes, 47
Elopiformes. *See* Ladyfishes; Tarpons
Emerald notothens, 290–91, 290 (ill.), 291 (ill.)
Enneapterygius mirabilis. See Miracle triplefins
Epinephelus striatus. See Nassau groupers
Erie Canal, 6
Esociformes. *See* Mudminnows; Pikes
Esox masquinongy. See Muskellunges
Eyes, moving flatfish, 358

F

Family (Taxonomy), 257
Fighting fishes, Siamese, 351–52, 351 (ill.), 352 (ill.)
Finding Nemo, 230
Fire gobies, 320–21, 320 (ill.), 321 (ill.)

Fish and Wildlife Service (U.S.)
    on carps, 85
    on catfishes, 102
    on Gasteristeiformes, 234, 236, 241
    on gobies, 319
    on killifishes, 211
    on livebearers, 211
    on loaches, 85
    on minnows, 85
    on Osmeriformes, 122
    on Perciformes, 258
    on Percoidei, 260
    on rainbowfishes, 199
    on salmons, 128
    on Scorpaeniformes, 249
    on silversides, 199
    on sturgeons, 34
    on threespine sticklebacks, 236
    on troutperches, 163
Fishing vs. angling, 188
Flashlightfishes, 223–28
Flatfishes, 357–65
Flathead mullets, 196–97, 196 (ill.), 197 (ill.)
Flatheads, 247–55
Florida gars, 38
Flounders, peacock, 359–60, 359 (ill.), 360 (ill.)
Flying gurnards, 247
Flyingfishes, 202–3, 205–6, 205 (ill.), 206 (ill.)
Foureyes, largescale, 212–13, 212 (ill.), 213 (ill.)
Freshwater angelfishes, 279–80, 279 (ill.), 280 (ill.)
Freshwater butterflyfishes, 48–49, 49 (ill.)
Freshwater dogfishes. *See* Bowfins

G

Gadiformes, 173–80
Gadus morhua. See Atlantic cods

Galaxiids, 121–26
Galeocerdo cuvier. See Tiger sharks
Gars, 37–40
Gasteropelecus sternicla. See River hatchetfishes
Gasterosteiformes, 233–41
Gasterosteus aculeatus. See Threespine sticklebacks
Genus (Taxonomy), 257
Giant morays, slender, 66–67, 66 (ill.), 67 (ill.)
Giant tigerfishes, 94–95, 94 (ill.), 95 (ill.)
Glass knifefishes, 114–15, 114 (ill.), 115 (ill.)
Glenn, John, 182
Gobies, 317–25
Gobiesocoidei. *See* Clingfishes; Singleslits
Gobioidei. *See* Gobies
Golden perches, 265–66, 265 (ill.), 266 (ill.)
Goldfishes, 85
Gonorynchiformes, 79–83
Graylings, 127
Great barracudas, 340–41, 340 (ill.), 341 (ill.)
Great Lakes, 6
Great Lakes Fishery Commission, 6
Green morays, 64–65, 64 (ill.), 65 (ill.)
Green swordtails, 214–15, 214 (ill.), 215 (ill.)
Greenlings, 247–49
Grenadiers, 173–80
Grindles. *See* Bowfins
Grinnells. *See* Bowfins
Groupers, Nassau, 269–70, 269 (ill.), 270 (ill.)
Gulf sturgeons, 34
Gulper eels, 70–71, 70 (ill.), 71 (ill.)
Gulpers, 68–69
Gurnards, 247–55

Gymnothorax funebris. See Green morays
Gymnotiformes. See Electric eels; South American knifefishes

H

Haddocks, 179–80, 179 (ill.), 180 (ill.)
Hagfishes, 1–4
Hairyfishes, 221–22, 221 (ill.), 222 (ill.)
Hakes, 173–80
Halfbeaks, 202–3
Halibuts, 357, 361–62, 361 (ill.), 362 (ill.)
Halosaurs, 55–56
Hatchetfishes, river, 98–99, 98 (ill.), 99 (ill.)
Hemingway, Ernest, 335
Herrings, 73–78
Hippocampus erectus. See Lined seahorses
Hippoglossus stenolepis. See Pacific halibuts
Histrio histrio. See Sargassumfishes
Huso huso. See Beluga sturgeons
Hydrocynus goliath. See Giant tigerfishes
Hydrolagus colliei. See Spotted ratfishes
Hypophthalmichthys molitrix. See Silver carps

I

Icefishes, cod. *See* Southern cod-icefishes
Icosteoidei. *See* Ragfishes
Icosteus aenigmaticus. See Ragfishes
Ictalurus punctatus. See Channel catfishes
Infantfishes, stout, 318
Inshore sand lances, 294–95, 294 (ill.), 295 (ill.)

Invasive species, snakeheads, 354
IUCN Red List of Threatened Species. *See* World Conservation Union (IUCN) Red List of Threatened Species

J

Jellyfishes, 344
John dories, 230

K

Killifishes, 210–18
Kingdom (Taxonomy), 257
Kneria wittei, 79
Knifefishes
 clown, 47
 South American, 109–15
Knots, eels in, 61

L

Labroidei, 272–80
Labroides dimidiatus. See Bluestreak cleaner wrasses
Labyrinth fishes, 347–52
Ladyfishes, 50–54
Lampreys, 5–8
Lampridiformes, 153–57
Lancer dragonets, 315–16, 315 (ill.), 316 (ill.)
Lancetfishes, longnose, 144–45, 144 (ill.), 145 (ill.)
Lanternfishes, 148–52
Largemouth basses, 261–62, 261 (ill.), 262 (ill.)
Largescale foureyes, 212–13, 212 (ill.), 213 (ill.)
Latimeria chalumnae. See Coelacanths
Leafy seadragons, 237–38, 237 (ill.), 238 (ill.)
Lepidosiren paradoxa. See South American lungfishes
Lepisosteiformes. *See* Gars

Lepisosteus oculatus. See Spotted gars
Leuresthes tenuis. See California grunions
Light production
 in dragonfishes, 136
 in flashlight, pineapple and pineconefishes, 224
 in rattrap fishes, 137, 141
Lined seahorses, 239–41, 239 (ill.), 240 (ill.)
Lined surgeonfishes, 328–29, 328 (ill.), 329 (ill.)
Lingcods, 254–55, 254 (ill.), 255 (ill.)
Lionfishes, red, 248, 252–53, 252 (ill.), 253 (ill.)
Live-bearers, 210–18
Lizardfishes, 142–47
Loaches, 84–85, 90–91, 90 (ill.), 91 (ill.)
Longnose lancetfishes, 144–45, 144 (ill.), 145 (ill.)
Lophiiformes. *See* Anglerfishes
Lophius americanus. See Monkfishes
Lungfishes, 21–27

M

Macquaria ambigua. See Golden perches
Makaira nigricans. See Blue marlins
Malacosteus niger. See Rat-trap fishes
Manta birostris. See Atlantic mantas
Mantas, Atlantic, 17–18, 17 (ill.), 18 (ill.)
Marble sleepers, 324–25, 324 (ill.), 325 (ill.)
Marbled swamp eels, 244–46, 244 (ill.), 245 (ill.)
Marlins, 334–42
Marshfishes. *See* Bowfins
Megalops atlanticus. See Atlantic tarpons

Meiacanthus grammistes. See Striped poison-fang blennies
Melanogrammus aeglefinus. See Haddocks
Menhadens, 73
Micropterus salmoides. See Largemouth basses
Milkfishes, 79–83, 81 (ill.), 82 (ill.)
Minnows, 84–91
    See also Mudminnows
Miracle triplefins, 303–4, 303 (ill.), 304 (ill.)
Mirapinna esau. See Hairyfishes
Monkfishes, 191–92, 191 (ill.), 192 (ill.)
Mooneyes, 47
Moorish idols, 332–33, 332 (ill.), 333 (ill.)
Morays, 60–67
Mudfishes, African, 79, 80
    See also Bowfins
Mudminnows, 116–20
Mudskippers, Atlantic, 322–23, 322 (ill.), 323 (ill.)
Mugil cephalus. See Flathead mullets
Mugiliformes. See Mullets
Mullets, 194–97
Muskellunges, 116, 118–19, 118 (ill.), 119 (ill.)
Myctophiformes. See Lanternfishes
Myripristis jacobus. See Blackbar soldierfishes
Myxine glutinosa. See Atlantic hagfishes
Myxini. See Hagfishes

N
Names, scientific, 257
Nassau groupers, 269–70, 269 (ill.), 270 (ill.)
Needlefishes, 202–9
Nemateleotris magnifica. See Fire gobies

Northern stargazers, 296–97, 296 (ill.), 297 (ill.)
Notothenioidei. See Southern cod-icefishes
Notothens, emerald, 290–91, 290 (ill.), 291 (ill.)

O
Oarfishes, 154, 155–56, 155 (ill.), 156 (ill.)
Ocean pouts, 285–86, 285 (ill.), 286 (ill.)
The Old Man and the Sea, 335
Oncorhynchus tshawytscha. See Chinook salmons
Opahs, 153–57
Ophidiiformes, 167–72
Ophiodon elongatus. See Lingcods
Opsanus tau. See Oyster toadfishes
Orange roughies, 223, 224
Order (Taxonomy), 257
Oriental helmet gurnards, 250–51, 250 (ill.), 251 (ill.)
Osmeriformes, 121–26
Osteoglossiformes, 46–49
Overfishing cod, 175
Oxyeleotris marmorata. See Marble sleepers
Oyster toadfishes, 182, 184–85, 184 (ill.), 185 (ill.)

P
Pacific halibuts, 361–62, 361 (ill.), 362 (ill.)
Paddlefishes, 32–36
Pallid sturgeons, 34
Pantodon buchholzi. See Freshwater butterflyfishes
Paradiplogrammus bairdi. See Lancer dragonets
Parrotfishes, 272–74, 277–78, 277 (ill.), 278 (ill.)
Peacock flounders, 359–60, 359 (ill.), 360 (ill.)

Pearl essence, 74
Pearlfishes, 168, 170–72, 170 (ill.), 171 (ill.)
Peprilus triacanthus. See Butterfishes
Perches, 256–58, 259–71
    climbing, 349–50, 349 (ill.), 350 (ill.)
    pirate, 163, 164–65, 164 (ill.), 165 (ill.)
    See also Surfperches; Troutperches
Perciformes, 256–58
Percoidei, 259–71
Percopsiformes, 162–66
Periophthalmus barabarus. See Atlantic mudskippers
Petromyzon marinus. See Sea lampreys
Phycodurus eques. See Leafy seadragons
Phylum (Taxonomy), 257
Pikes, 116–20
Pilchards, 73
Pineapplefishes, 223, 224
Pineconefishes, 223, 224
Pipefishes, 233, 234
Piranhas, 93, 96–97, 96 (ill.), 97 (ill.)
Pirate perches, 163, 164–65, 164 (ill.), 165 (ill.)
Plecoglossus altivelis. See Ayu
Pleuronectiformes. See Flatfishes
Poison
    ciguetera, 260
    jellyfish, 344
Poison-fang blennies, striped, 301–2, 301 (ill.), 302 (ill.)
Polymixia nobilis. See Stout beardfishes
Polymixiiformes. See Beardfishes
Polypteriformes. See Bichirs
Polypterus ornatipinnis. See Bichirs
Postage stamps, fish on, 211

Pterois volitans. See Red lionfishes
Pterophyllum scalare. See Freshwater angelfishes
Pufferfishes, 366–74
Puffers, whitespotted, 370–71, 370 (ill.), 371 (ill.)
Pygmy herrings, Sanaga, 73
Pygocentrus nattereri. See Red-bellied piranhas

R

Ragfishes, 305–7, 306 (ill.), 307 (ill.)
Rainbowfishes, 198–201
Raja eglanteria. See Clearnose skates
Rat-trap fishes, 137, 140–41, 140 (ill.), 141 (ill.)
Rays, 9–20
Red boarfishes, 231–32, 231 (ill.), 232 (ill.)
Red light production, in rat-trap fishes, 137, 141
Red lionfishes, 248, 252–53, 252 (ill.), 253 (ill.)
Red List of Threatened Species. See World Conservation Union (IUCN) Red List of Threatened Species
Red-bellied piranhas, 96–97, 96 (ill.), 97 (ill.)
Regal tangs, 230
Regalecus glesne. See Oarfishes
Retropinna semoni. See Australian smelts
Rice fishes, 202–3
River hatchetfishes, 98–99, 98 (ill.), 99 (ill.)
Rock whitings, 272–74
Roughies, 223–28

S

Saccopharyngiformes. See Gulpers; Swallowers

Saccopharynx ampullaceus. See Gulper eels
Salmo salar. See Atlantic salmons
Salmoniformes. See Salmons
Salmons, 127–35
Salvelinus fontinalis. See Brook trouts
Sanaga pygmy herrings, 73
Sand lances, inshore, 294–95, 294 (ill.), 295 (ill.)
Sandfishes, 79, 80
Sarcopterygii. See Coelacanths; Lungfishes
Sardines, 73
Sargasso Sea, 188
Sargassumfishes, 189–90, 189 (ill.), 190 (ill.)
Sashimi, 335
Sauries, 202–3
Scaled lings. See Bowfins
Scales, herring, 74
Scarus iseri. See Striped parrotfishes
Scientific names, taxonomy and, 257
Scombroidei, 334–42
Scorpaeniformes, 247–55
Scorpionfishes, 247–55
Sculpins, 247–49
Sea catfishes, 102
Sea cucumbers, 168
Sea lampreys, 7–8, 7 (ill.), 8 (ill.)
Sea urchins, 318
Seadragons, leafy, 237–38, 237 (ill.), 238 (ill.)
Seahorses, 233–41
Shads, 73
Sharks, 9–20
Shortnose sturgeons, 34
Siamese fighting fishes, 351–52, 351 (ill.), 352 (ill.)
Siluriformes. See Catfishes
Silver carps, 88–89, 88 (ill.), 89 (ill.)
Silversides, 198–201

Singleslits, 308–12
Skates, 9–20
Skinnycheek lanternfishes, 151–52, 151 (ill.), 152 (ill.)
Slender giant morays, 66–67, 66 (ill.), 67 (ill.)
Slime and hagfishes, 2
Smelts, 121–26
Snakeheads, 353–56
Soldierfishes, 223, 224, 227–28, 227 (ill.), 228 (ill.)
Sole, common, 363–64, 363 (ill.), 364 (ill.)
Solea solea. See Common sole
Sonora clingfishes, 310–11, 310 (ill.), 311 (ill.)
South American knifefishes, 109–15
South American lungfishes, 25–26, 25 (ill.), 26 (ill.)
Southern cod-icefishes, 288–91
Space Shuttle, oyster toadfishes on, 182
Species
    invasive, 354
    taxonomy and, 257
    See also specific species
Speckled cats. See Bowfins
Sphyraena barracuda. See Great barracudas
Spiny eels, 55–56, 242–46
Splitfin flashlightfishes, 225–26, 225 (ill.), 226 (ill.)
Spotted gars, 39–40, 39 (ill.), 40 (ill.)
Spotted ratfishes, 11–12, 11 (ill.), 12 (ill.)
Spotted tobies, 372–73, 372 (ill.), 373 (ill.)
Sprats, 73
Squarehead catfishes, 105–6, 105 (ill.), 106 (ill.)
Squirrelfishes, 223–28
Stamps, postage, 211
Stargazers, northern, 296–97, 296 (ill.), 297 (ill.)
Stephanoberyciformes, 219–22

Sticklebacks, 233–41
Stomiiformes, 136–41
Stonerollers, 86–87, 86 (ill.), 87 (ill.)
Stout beardfishes, 160–61, 160 (ill.), 161 (ill.)
Stout infantfishes, 318
Striped parrotfishes, 277–78, 277 (ill.), 278 (ill.)
Striped poison-fang blennies, 301–2, 301 (ill.), 302 (ill.)
Striped snakeheads, 355–56, 355 (ill.), 356 (ill.)
Stromateoidei, 343–46
Strongylura exilis. See Californian needlefishes
Strophidon sathete. See Slender giant morays
Sturgeons, 32–36
Surfperches, 272–80
Surgeonfishes, 326–33
Swallowers, 68–69
Swamp eels, 242–46
Swordtails, green, 214–15, 214 (ill.), 215 (ill.)
Synbranchiformes. *See* Spiny eels; Swamp eels
Synbranchus marmoratus. See Marbled swamp eels

T

Tangs
    regal, 230
    yellow, 327, 330–31, 330 (ill.), 331 (ill.)
Tarpons, 50–54
Taxonomy, 257
Tetraodontiformes, 366–74
Threespine sticklebacks, 235–36, 235 (ill.), 236 (ill.)
Thunnus thynnus. See Atlantic bluefin tunas
Tiger sharks, 13–13, 13 (ill.), 14 (ill.)
Tigerfishes, giant, 94–95, 94 (ill.), 95 (ill.)
Tineselfishes, 230

Toadfishes, 181–86
Tobies, spotted, 372–73, 372 (ill.), 373 (ill.)
Tomicodon humeralis. See Sonora clingfishes
Toxotes jaculatrix. See Banded archerfishes
Trachinoidei, 292–98
Trematomus bernacchii. See Emerald notothens
Triggerfishes, 366–74
Triplefins, miracle, 303–4, 303 (ill.), 304 (ill.)
Tripodfishes, 146–47, 146 (ill.), 147 (ill.)
Troutperches, 162–66
Trouts, 127, 133–34, 133 (ill.), 134 (ill.)
Tunas, 256, 334–42

U

Urinary tract, candirus in, 102
U.S. Fish and Wildlife Service. *See* Fish and Wildlife Service (U.S.)

V

Vandellia cirrhosa. See Candirus
Venom
    scorpionfish, 248
    weeverfish, 293
Viperfishes, 138–39, 138 (ill.), 139 (ill.)

W

Water quality and pirate perches, 163
Weeverfishes, 292–98
Whale sharks, 10
Whalefishes, 219–22
White sharks, 15–16, 15 (ill.), 16 (ill.)
White sturgeons, 34
Whitefishes, 127

White-spotted puffers, 370–71, 370 (ill.), 371 (ill.)
Wolf herrings, 73
Wolf-eels, 256, 281, 282, 283–84, 283 (ill.), 284 (ill.)
World Conservation Union (IUCN) Red List of Threatened Species
    on anglerfishes, 188
    on Atlantic cods, 178
    on blennies, 300
    on bony tongues, 47–48
    on carps, 85
    on catfishes, 102
    on characins, 93
    on coelacanths, 22, 24
    on cuskeels, 169
    on dragonets, 314
    on flatfishes, 358
    on Gadiformes, 175
    on Gasteristeiformes, 234
    on gobies, 318
    on haddocks, 180
    on herrings, 75
    on killifishes, 211
    on Labroidei, 273–74
    on labyrinth fishes, 348
    on lined seahorses, 241
    on livebearers, 211
    on loaches, 85
    on lungfishes, 22
    on minnows, 85
    on mudminnows, 117
    on Nassau groupers, 270
    on needlefishes, 203–4
    on Osmeriformes, 122
    on Perciformes, 257–58
    on Percoidei, 260, 270
    on pikes, 117
    on pufferfishes, 367
    on rainbowfishes, 199
    on rays, 10
    on salmons, 128
    on Scombroidei, 335
    on Scorpaeniformes, 248–49

on sharks, 10, 16
on silversides, 199
on skates, 10
on sturgeons, 33–34
on swamp and spiny eels, 243
on toadfishes, 183
on triggerfishes, 367
on troutperches, 163
on weeverfishes, 293
on white sharks, 16

Wrasses, 272–74, 275–76, 275 (ill.), 276 (ill.)

X

Xiphophorus hellerii. See Green swordtails

Y

Yellow tangs, 327, 330–31, 330 (ill.), 331 (ill.)

Z

Zanclus cornutus. See Moorish idols
Zebrafishes, 85
Zebrasoma flavescens. See Yellow tangs
Zeiformes. *See* Dories
Zoarces americanus. See Ocean pouts
Zoarcoidei, 281–87